Mrs Horace Hall
Ann Arbor
Mich

PETERSON'S

FAMILIAR SCIENCE;

OR, THE

SCIENTIFIC EXPLANATION OF COMMON THINGS.

EDITED BY

R. E. PETERSON,
MEMBER OF THE ACADEMY OF NATURAL SCIENCES, PHILADELPHIA.

TO WHICH IS ADDED

Scientific Amusements for Young People,

BY

JOHN HENRY PEPPER,
F.C.S., A. INST. C.E., LATE PROFESSOR OF CHEMISTRY AT THE ROYAL POLYTECHNIC

REVISED EDITION.

PHILADELPHIA:
SOWER, POTTS & CO.
530 MARKET STREET & 523 MINOR STREET.

OFFICE OF THE CONTROLLERS OF PUBLIC SCHOOLS,
First School District of Pennsylvania,

PHILAD'A, Sept. 11, 1851

At a Meeting of the Controllers of Public Schools, First District of Pennsylvania, held at the Controllers' Office, Tuesday, Sept. 9, 1851, the following resolution was adopted:—

Resolved, That the work entitled "Familiar Science" be introduced into the Grammar Schools of this District.

ROBERT J. HEMPHILL, *Secretary.*

At a meeting of the Board of Education of the Brooklyn Public Schools, held Dec. 2, 1851, the following resolution was adopted:—

Resolved, That "Peterson's Familiar Science" be adopted as a text-book for use in the Public Schools.

W. S. DILLINGHAM,
Chairman of Com. on School Books.

Attest, S. L. HOLMES, *Sec'y.*

ELECTROTYPED BY L. JOHNSON & CO.
PHILADELPHIA.

PREFACE TO REVISED EDITION.

TWELVE years have elapsed since the American edition of "Familiar Science" was first presented to the public. The advancement of every branch of knowledge during this period has rendered a revised edition a necessity.

The editor has, however, retained all the old text, except some portions which might be deemed superfluous. A large amount of additional matter—the results of recent investigations and discoveries—has been introduced in the present edition. This work has been liberally patronized, both by teachers and heads of families,—more than one hundred and twenty thousand copies having been sold. The editor entertains the hope that the present edition will be received with equal favor.

The valuable little work of Professor PEPPER, entitled "Scientific Amusements," has been added as an Appendix to the work.

PREFACE.

A PART of the following work is from the pen of the Rev. Dr. Brewer, of Trinity Hall, Cambridge, also Head Master of King's College School, Norwich, in union with King's College, London. It contains much useful as well as practical scientific knowledge in a very popular and entertaining form.

The work, however, as it emanated from the English press was not only in many points unsuited to the American pupil, but was exceedingly deficient in its arrangement. The editor has endeavored to remedy these defects by making many additions, as well as by altering those parts which were purely applicable to Great Britain, and adapting the whole to our own country. As to the *arrangement*, he feels confident it will be the means of facilitating the acquirement of the great amount of useful information embodied in the work, and also of classifying in the mind of the pupil the different branches of which it treats.

"No science is more generally interesting than that which explains the common phenomena of life. We see that salt and snow are both white, a rose red, leaves green, and the violet a deep purple; but how few persons ever ask the reason why! We know that a flute produces a musical sound, and a cracked bell a discordant one,—that fire is hot, ice cold, and a candle luminous,—that water boils when subjected to heat, and freezes from cold; but when a child looks up into our face and asks us 'why?' how many times is it silenced with a frown, or called 'very foolish for asking such silly questions'!"*

This book, intended for the use of families and schools, explains about two thousand of these questions, and is written in language so plain as to be understood by all. Care has been taken, however, in the endeavor to render it intelligible to the young, to avoid that childish simplicity which might be unacceptable to those of riper years.

A *very full* index is appended to the work, to facilitate the pupil's researches.

In the Preface to the English edition, already mentioned, there is an anecdote related which is so appropriate that it is here given in full:—

"A remarkable instance came before the author a few months since of the statement made in the early part of this Preface. The conversation was about smoke,—why it was black, and not white like the fine dust of lime. A little child who was present asked, 'Why is the kettle so black with smoke?' Her papa answered, 'Because it has been on the fire.' 'But,' urged the child, 'what is the good of its being black?' The gentleman replied, 'Silly child, you ask very foolish questions: sit down, and hold your tongue.'"

Information of that description is just what children

* Dr. Brewer's Preface.

love to gain, and what many older persons, who are even tolerably well informed, are not competent to give.

The editor trusts his book may prove an interesting and useful companion to both old and young, either in the family circle or in the school-room.

Twenty-five thousand copies of the English edition of the above work were sold in London in less than two years.

PHILADELPHIA, April, 1851.

The following is extracted from a letter received by the Editor from the Rev. Dr. Brewer.

"ROBERT E. PETERSON, ESQ.

"DEAR SIR:—I have received the American edition of my *Guide to Familiar Science*, and think it very handsomely printed and *skilfully rearranged*. I shall esteem it an honor to give my full consent to your expressing my approbation of your edition of my Familiar Science, and I thank you for the kindness in having sent me a copy.

"Dear sir,
"Yours truly,
"E. C. BREWER.

"ST. HELEN, ISLE OF JERSEY,
"31 Dec. 1851.

CONTENTS.

PART I.—HEAT.

PART II.—NON-METALLIC ELEMENTS.

PART III.—METALS.

PART IV.—ORGANIC CHEMISTRY.

PART V.—METEOROLOGY.

CONTENTS.

PART I.—HEAT.

PART II.—NON-METALLIC ELEMENTS.

PART III.—METALS.

PART IV.—ORGANIC CHEMISTRY.

PART V.—METEOROLOGY.

PART VI.—OPTICS.

PART VII.—SOUND, AND ATTRACTION.

PART VIII.—MISCELLANEOUS.

SCIENTIFIC AMUSEMENTS.

PART I.

HEAT.

CHAPTER I.—THE SUN.

SECTION I.—THE SUN THE PRIMARY SOURCE OF HEAT.

1. WHAT is heat?

A. That invisible agent which produces the sensation of warmth.

2. Is that invisible agent known by any other name than heat?

A. Yes: it is called Caloric.

3. What is the principal source of heat?

A. The SUN is an inexhaustible source of heat.

4. Does the heat of the Sun possess any properties different from those of artificial heat?

A. The heat of the Sun passes readily through glass, whereas this property is possessed by artificial heat in a small degree

SECTION II.—CALORIC.

5. How is the sensation of heat produced?

A. When we touch a substance hotter than ourselves, a subtle invisible stream flows from the hotter substance, and produces on our nerves the sensation of warmth.

6. What is that "subtle invisible stream" called, which flows from the hotter substance?

A. CALORIC. Caloric, therefore, is the agent which produces the sensation of warmth; but the sensation itself is called Heat.

7. Is caloric equally distributed over the globe?

A. No: at the equator the average temperature is 82½°, while at the poles it is believed to be about 13° below zero.

"*Average Temperature*," the mean or medium temperature.

"ZERO," the point from which a thermometer is graduated.

CHAPTER II.—ELECTRICITY A SOURCE OF HEAT.

SECTION I.—ELECTRICITY PRODUCED BY FRICTION.

8. WAS electricity known to the ancients?

A. Yes: they knew that when amber (the Greek word for which is ηλεκτρον—electron) is rubbed, it acquires the property of attracting other bodies.

9. Do all bodies, when rubbed, acquire this kind of attraction?

A. They do not. Glass, silk, wax, dry paper, hair, wool, and many other substances called non-conductors, possess this property.

10. Why are glass, silk, wax, &c. called non-conductors?

A. Because electricity does not pass through them freely.

11. Through what bodies does electricity pass readily?

A. Through metals, plants, animals, liquids, and many other substances, called conductors.

12. Why are these substances called conductors?

A. Because they conduct the electricity from one body to another.

13. Why is electricity excited by friction?

A. Electricity, like heat, exists in all matter; but it is often in a latent state: friction disturbs it, and brings it into active operation.

"*Latent*," hidden, concealed.

14. How may large quantities of electricity be developed by friction?

A. By the rapid escape of steam through a small orifice. The friction of the condensed particles of water driven out by the steam is a powerful source of electricity.

It is on this principle that Sir Charles Armstrong constructed the Hydro-Electric machine, which develops electricity in enormous quantities.

15. When you rub a piece of paper with Indian rubber, why does it often adhere to the table?

A. Because the friction of the Indian rubber against the surface of the paper develops electricity, to which this adhesiveness is mainly to be attributed.

16. If you dry a piece of common brown paper by the fire, and draw it once or twice across a piece of woollen cloth, why will it stick fast to the wall?

A. Because the friction develops electricity on the paper, which manifests itself by this property of adhesion.

17. When a glazier is mending a window and cleans the pane with his brush, why do the loose pieces of putty on the opposite side of the window-pane frequently dance up and down?

A. Electricity is excited on both sides of the glass by the friction of the brush; and as soon as the fragments of putty touch the excited part of the glass they become charged with electricity and fall on the wooden ledge, which, being a conductor, deprives them of their electricity; then they fly up again to receive a fresh charge, which process being often repeated causes the commotion in the pieces of putty referred to in the question.

18. Why does brushing the hair for a long time frequently make the head itch?

A. 1st. Because the friction of the hair-brush excites electricity in the hair, which thus becomes overcharged and irritates the skin; and,

2d. The hair-brush excites increased action in the vessels and nerves of the scalp, producing a slight degree of inflammation, which is indicated by a sensation of itching.

19. Does electricity present any appearance by which it can be known?

A. No: electricity, like heat, is in itself invisible; though often accompanied by both light and heat.

20. Is electricity accompanied by any odor?

A. Yes: near a large electrical machine in good action there is always a peculiar odor, resembling that of sulphur and phosphorus. This odor is called "OZONE," generated by the action of lightning on the oxygen of the air.

21. Has this peculiar odor called "Ozone" been observed in thunder-storms?

A. Yes: sometimes the sulphurous odor prevails, and sometimes the phosphoric.

22. Why are there different colors in the Aurora Borealis, such as white, yellow, red, and purple?

A. Because the electric fluid passes through air of different densities. The most rarefied air produces a white light; the most dry air, red; and the most damp produces yellow streaks.

SECTION II.—LIGHTNING.

23. What is lightning?

A. Lightning is accumulated electricity discharged from the clouds.

24. What produces electricity in the clouds?

A. 1st. The evaporation from the earth's surface;

2d. The chemical changes which take place on the earth's surface; and,

3d. Currents of air of unequal tempera ture, which excite electricity by friction, as they come in contact with each other.

25. What causes the discharge of an electric cloud?

A. When a cloud overcharged with electric fluid approaches another which is undercharged, the fluid rushes from the former into the latter, till both contain the same quantity.

There are two kinds of Electricity,—one Vitreous, the other Resinous: more frequently called Positive and Negative Electricity.

26. Is there any other cause of lightning besides the one just mentioned?

A. Yes: sometimes mountains, trees, and steeples will discharge the lightning from a cloud floating near; and sometimes electric fluid rushes out of the earth into the clouds.

27. How high are the lightning-clouds from the earth?

A. Sometimes they are four or five miles high; and sometimes they actually touch the earth with one of their edges; but they are rarely discharged in a thunder-storm when they are more than seven hundred yards above the surface of the earth.

28. How high are the clouds, generally?

A. In a fine day, the clouds are often four or five miles above our heads; but the average height of the clouds is from one and a half to two miles.

29. Why is lightning sometimes forked?

A. Because the lightning-cloud is at a great distance; and the resistance of the air is so great that the electrical current is diverted into a zigzag course.

30. How does the resistance of the air make the lightning zigzag?

A. As the lightning condenses the air in the immediate advance of its path, it flies from side to side, in order to pass where there is the least resistance.

31. Why are there sometimes two flashes of forked lightning at the same moment?

A. Because (in very severe storms) the flash divides into two or more parts, each of which assumes the zigzag form.

32. Why is the flash sometimes quite straight?

A. Because the lightning-cloud is near the earth; and, as the flash meets with very little resistance, it is not diverted: in other words, the flash is straight.

33. What is sheet-lightning?

A. Either the reflection of distant flashes not distinctly visible, or beneath the horizon; or else several flashes intermingled.

34. What other form does lightning occasionally assume?

A. Sometimes the flash is globular; which is the most dangerous form of lightning.

35. Why is a flash of lightning generally followed by pouring rain?

A. The flash produces a change in the physical condition of the air, rendering it unable to hold as much water in solution as it could before; in consequence of which, a part is given off in heavy rain.

36. Why is a flash of lightning generally followed by a gust of wind?

A. Because the physical condition of the air is disturbed by the passage of the lightning, and wind is the result of this disturbance.

37. Why is there no thunder to what is called summer-lightning?

A. Because the lightning-clouds are so far distant that the sound of the thunder is lost before it reaches the ear.

38. When lightning flashes from the earth to the clouds, what is the flash called?

A. It is popularly called the "returning stroke," because the earth, being overcharged with electric fluid, returns the surplus quantity to the clouds.

39. Why is lightning more common in summer and autumn than in spring and winter?

A. Because the heat of summer and autumn produces great evaporation, and the conversion of water into vapor always develops electricity.

40. Why is a tree sometimes scorched by lightning, as if it had been set on fire?

A. The electric fluid scorches by its own positive heat.

41. When does lightning pass from the earth to the clouds?

A. When the clouds are in a "negative' state of electricity.

42. When does lightning pass from the clouds to the earth?

A. When the clouds are in a "positive" state of electricity.

43. What is meant by the clouds being in a "positive state of electricity"?

A. When the clouds contain more electric fluid than they generally do, they are said to be in a "positive state of electricity."

44. What is meant by the clouds being in a "negative state of electricity"?

A. When the clouds contain less electric fluid than they generally do, they are said to be in a "negative state of electricity."

45. Does the flash proceed from a negative or a positive body?

A. Always from a positive body; that is, from one overcharged with electric fluid.

§ I.—DANGER FROM LIGHTNING.

46. Why does lightning sometimes kill men and beasts?

A. Because, when the electric current passes through a man or beast, it produces so violent an action upon the nerves that it destroys life.

47. When is a person struck dead by lightning?

A. Only when his body forms a part of the lightning's path; that is, when the electric fluid (in its way to the earth) actually passes through his body.

48. Why are persons sometimes maimed by lightning?

A. Because the electric fluid produces an action upon the nerves sufficient to injure them, but not to destroy life.

49. Lightning sometimes assumes the appearance of balls of fire which fall to the earth: what are they?

A. Masses of explosive gas formed in the air: they generally move more slowly than the ordinary lightning.

50. Why are these balls of fire very dangerous?

A. Because, when they fall, they explode like a cannon, and occasion much mischief.

51. Do these balls of fire ever run along the ground?

A. Yes: sometimes they run a considerable distance along the ground, and explode in a mass.

At other times they split into numerous smaller balls, each of which explodes in a similar manner.

52. What mischief do these balls of fire produce?

A. They set fire to houses and barns, and kill all cattle and human beings that happen to be in their course.

53. What places are most dangerous during a thunder-storm?

A. It is very dangerous to be near a tree or lofty building, and also to be near a river or any running water.

54. Why is it dangerous to be near a tree or lofty building during a thunder-storm?

A. Because a tall pointed object (like a tree or spire) will frequently discharge a lightning-cloud; and, if any one were standing near, the lightning might diverge from the tree and pass through the fluids of the human body.

55. How can a tree or spire discharge a lightning-cloud?

A. A lightning-cloud floating over a plain may be too far off to be discharged, but, as a tree or spire would shorten this distance, it might no longer be too far off to be discharged.

For example: if a lightning-cloud were seven hundred yards above the earth, it would be too far off to be discharged; but a spire fifty yards high would make the cloud only six hundred and fifty yards from a conductor; in consequence of which the cloud might be instantly discharged.

56. What parts of a dwelling are most dangerous during a thunder-storm?

A. The fireplace, (especially if the fire be lighted,) the attics, and the cellar. It is also imprudent to sit close by the walls, to ring the bell, or to bar the shutters during a thunder-storm.

57. Why is it dangerous to sit before a fire during a thunder-storm?

A. Because the heated air and soot are conductors of lightning, especially when connected with such excellent conductors as the stove or grate.

58. Why are attics and cellars more dangerous in a thunder-storm than the middle story of a house?

A. Because lightning sometimes passes from the clouds to the earth, and sometimes from the earth to the clouds: in either case the middle story would be the safest place.

59. Why is it dangerous to lean against a wall during a thunder-storm?

A. Because the electric fluid will sometimes run down a wall, and (as a man is a better conductor than a wall) would leave the wall and run down the man.

60. Why is it dangerous to ring a bell during a thunder-storm?

A. Bell-wire is an excellent conductor; and if a person were to touch the bell-handle, the electric fluid, passing down the wire, might run through his hand and injure it.

61. Why is it dangerous to be in a crowd during a thunder-storm?

A. For two reasons:—1st. Because a mass of people forms a better conductor than an individual; and,

2d. Because the vapor arising from a crowd increases its conducting power.

62. Why is the danger increased by the vapor which rises from a crowd?

A. Because vapor is a conductor; and the more conductors there are the greater the danger will be.

63. Why is a theatre dangerous during a thunder-storm?

A. Because the vapor arising from so many living bodies is an excellent conductor of lightning.

64. If a person be abroad in a thunder-storm, what place is the safest?

A. Any place about twenty or thirty feet from a tall tree, building, or stream of water.

65. Why would it be safe to stand twenty or thirty feet from a tall tree during a thunder-storm?

A. Because the tall tree is a conductor; and we should not be sufficiently near the tree for the lightning to diverge from it to us.

66. If a person be in a carriage in a thunder-storm, in what way can he travel most safely?

A. He should not lean against the carriage, but should sit upright.

67. Why should not a person lean against the carriage in a storm?

A. Because the electric fluid might run down the sides of the carriage, and, if a person were leaning against them, would make a choice of him for a conductor, and perhaps destroy life.

68. Why is a mattress, bed, or hearth-rug a good security against injury from lightning?

A. Because they are all non-conductors; and lightning always makes choice of the best conductors.

69. Is it better to be wet or dry during a thunder-storm?

A. To be wet. If a person be in the open field, the best thing he can do is to stand about twenty feet from some tree and get completely drenched to the skin.

70. Why is it better to be wet than dry?

A. Because wet clothes form a better conductor than the fluids of our body; and therefore lightning would more readily pass down our wet clothes.

§ II.—LIGHTNING-CONDUCTORS.

71. What is a lightning-conductor?

A. A metal rod fixed in the earth, running up the whole height of a building and rising in a point above it.

72. What metals are the best conductors of electricity?

A. Pure silver and copper are the best conductors of electricity; but all the metals are good conductors.

73. What is the use of a lightning-conductor?

A. As metal is a most excellent conductor, lightning (which makes choice of the best conductors) will run down a metal rod rather than the walls of the building.

74. Why should lightning-conductors be pointed?

A. Because points conduct electricity away silently and imperceptibly, but knobs produce an explosion which would endanger the building.

Points empty the clouds of electricity, acting at a much greater distance than knobs: thus, a Leyden-jar of considerable size may be safely and silently discharged by holding the point of a needle an inch or two off.

Blades of grass, ears of wheat, and other pointed objects serve to empty the clouds of their electricity.

75. How can lightning-conductors be productive of harm?

A. If the rod be broken, the electric fluid (being obstructed in its path) will damage the building.

76. Is there any other evil to be apprehended from a lightning-rod?

A. Yes: if the rod be not large enough to conduct the whole current to the earth, the lightning will fuse the metal and injure the building.

77. Why are boughs of trees broken off by lightning?

A. Because the mechanical force of the lightning is very great; and, as the boughs of a tree often impede the passage of the electric fluid, they will be broken off by this force.

78. Why is an electric shock felt most at the elbow-joint?

A. Because the path of the fluid is obstructed by the joint; and the shock felt at the elbow is caused by the fluid leaping from one bone to another.

79. Is not air a conductor of lightning?

A. No: dry air is not a conductor of lightning.

80. Why does lightning part the air through which it passes? It does not part a rod of iron.

A. As iron is a conductor, it allows the fluid to pass freely through it; but air (being a non-conductor) resists its passage.

81. Does lightning go through the inside or down the outside of a tree?

A. It runs down the outside of a tree, but

passes through the inside of a man, as it always chooses the best conductors.

82. What effects are produced when electricity strikes solid imperfect conductors?

A. It rends them to pieces or shatters them into fragments.

83. Give an example of these effects of electricity.

A. Lightning separates the air with great force, producing the crashing noise known as thunder; it breaks glass into fragments and rends trees into splinters when it passes through any of these bodies on its way to the earth.

84. What effect is produced when electricity passes through good conductors?

A. It flows along gently and quietly, and would not even ruffle a feather resting upon them.

85. Give an example of electricity passing through a conductor.

A. It will pass quietly down a lightning-rod and enter the earth unperceived, because the metallic rod is a good conductor.

§ III.—EFFECTS OF LIGHTNING.

86. What are fulgurites?

A. Hollow tubes produced in sandy soils by the action of lightning.

87. How does lightning produce fulgurites?

A. When it enters the earth it fuses (that is, melts) the flinty matter of the soil into a vitreous (or glassy) substance, called a fulgurite.

88. Why is the bark of a tree often ripped quite off by a flash of lightning?

A. Because the latent heat of the tree (being very rapidly developed by the electric fluid) forces away the bark in its impetuosity to escape.

Some part of this is probably due to the simple mechanical force of the lightning.

89. How does lightning sometimes knock down houses and churches?

A. The steeple or chimney is first struck: the lightning then darts to the iron bars and clamps employed in the building, and (as it darts from bar to bar) shatters to atoms the bricks and stones which oppose its progress.

90. Why does the lightning fly about from place to place?

A. Because it always takes in its course the best conductors.

91. Why does lightning turn milk sour?

A. Lightning causes the gases of the air through which it passes to combine, and thus produces a poison, called nitric acid, some small portion of which, mixing with the milk, turns it sour.*

Sometimes the mere heat of the air during the storm turns milk sour.

92. What is the difference between combining and mixing?

A. When different ingredients are mingled together without undergoing any chemical change, they are said to be mixed; but when the natural properties of each are altered by the union, then those ingredients are said to be combined.

93. Give an example.

A. Different-colored sands (shaken together in a bottle) will mix, but not combine; but water poured on quicklime will combine with the lime, and not mix with it.

94. Why are different grains of sand said to be mixed when they are shaken together?

A. Because (though mingled together) the property of each grain remains the same as it was before.

95. Why is water, poured on lime, said to combine with it?

A. Because the properties of each are altered by the mixture: the lime alters the

* The air is composed of two gases, called oxygen and nitrogen, mixed together, but not combined. Oxygen, combined with nitrogen, produces five deadly poisons, viz.: nitrous oxide, nitric oxide, hyponitrous acid, nitrous acid, and nitric acid, according to the proportion of each gas in the combination.

character of the water, and the water that of the lime.

96. Do oxygen and nitrogen combine, or only mix together, in atmospheric air?

A. They only mix together, as grains of sand would do when shaken in a bottle. When oxygen and nitrogen combine, they do not constitute air, but acid poisons.

97. Why does lightning turn beer sour, although contained in a close cask?

A. Because, if beer be new and the process of fermentation incomplete, lightning will so accelerate the process as to turn the sugar into acetic acid at once, without its passing through the intermediate state of alcohol.

98. Why are not old beer and strong porter made sour by lightning?

A. Because the fermentation is more complete, and, therefore, is less affected by electrical influence.

99. Why is metal sometimes fused by lightning?

A. Because the dimension of the metal is too small to afford a path for the electric current.

100. Why does lightning purify the air?

A. For two reasons:—

1st. Because the electric fluid produces "nitric acid" in its passage through the air; and,

2d. Because the agitation of the storm stirs up the air.

The "nitric acid" is produced by the combination of some portions of the oxygen and nitrogen of the air.

101. How does the production of nitric acid purify the air?

A. Nitric acid acts very powerfully in destroying the exhalations which arise from putrid vegetable and animal matters.

102. Does not lightning sometimes affect the character of iron and steel?

A. Yes: bars of iron and steel are sometimes rendered magnetic by lightning.

103. Give me an instance of the magnetic effects of lightning.

A. Sometimes it will reverse the needle of the magnet, and sometimes destroy its magnetism altogether.

104. What is meant by the magnetic needle being reversed?

A. That part of the needle which ought to point toward the north is made to point toward the south; and that part which ought to point south is made to point toward the north.

SECTION III.—THUNDER.

105. What is thunder?

A. The noise made by the concussion of

the air when it closes again, after it has been separated by the lightning-flash.

A part of the noise is owing to certain physical and chemical changes produced in the air by the electric fluid.

106. Why is thunder sometimes one vast crash?

A. Because the lightning-cloud is near the earth; and as all the vibrations of the air (on which sound depends) reach the ear at the same moment, they seem like one vast crash.

107. Why is the peal sometimes an irregular, broken roar?

A. Because the lightning-cloud is at a great distance; and as some of the vibrations of the air have much farther to travel than others, they reach the ear at different times, and produce a continuous sound.

108. Which vibrations will be soonest heard?

A. Those produced in the lowest portions of the air.

109. Why will those vibrations be heard first which are made last?

A. Because the flash (which produces the sound) is almost instantaneous, but sound takes a whole second of time to travel three hundred and eighty yards.

110. If a thunder-cloud were one thousand nine hundred yards off, how long would the peal last?

A. Five seconds: we should first hear the vibrations produced in those portions of the air contiguous to the earth; then those more remote; and it would be five seconds before those vibrations could reach us which were made in the immediate vicinity of the cloud.

380 × 5 = 1900.

A popular method of telling how far off a storm is, is this. The moment you see the flash, put your hand upon your pulse, and count how many times it beats before you hear the thunder: if it beats six pulsations, the storm is one mile off; if twelve pulsations, it is two miles off; and so on.

111. Why is thunder sometimes like a deep growl?

A. Because the storm is far distant, and the sound of the thunder indistinct.

112. Is not the sound of thunder affected by local circumstances?

A. Yes: the flatter the country the more unbroken is the peal. Mountains break the peal and make it harsh and irregular.

113. What is the cause of rolling thunder?

A. The vibrations of air (having different lengths to travel) reach the ear at successive intervals.

The reverberation (or echo) among the massive clouds contributes in some measure to this effect.

114. Do thunderbolts ever drop from the clouds?

A. No: the notion of thunderbolts arises either from the globular form which lightning sometimes assumes, or else from the gaseous fire-balls which sometimes fall from the clouds.

See Question 49.

115. Why is the thunder often several moments after the flash?

A. Because it has a long distance to travel. Lightning travels nearly a million times faster than thunder: if, therefore, the thunder is very distant, the sound will not reach the earth till a considerable time after the flash.

116. Why does a thunder-storm generally follow very dry weather?

A. Because dry air (being a non-conductor) will not relieve the clouds of their electricity: therefore the fluid accumulates, till the clouds are discharged in a storm.

117. Why does a thunder-storm rarely succeed wet weather?

A. Because moist air or falling rain (being a conductor) carries down the electric fluid gradually and silently to the earth.

118. What kind of weather generally precedes a thunder-storm?

A. It is generally preceded by hot weather.

119. Give an example of heat produced by chemical action.

A. The chemical action between the oxygen of the air and any combustible substance, as wood, coal, &c., will produce heat.

CHAPTER III.—CHEMICAL ACTION A SOURCE OF HEAT.

120. WHAT is meant by chemical action being the source of heat?

A. Many things, when their chemical constitution is changed, (either by the abstraction of some of their gases, or by the combination of others not before united,) evolve heat while the change is going on.

SECTION I.—EXPANSION.

121. What effect has heat upon substances generally?

A. It expands them, or enlarges their dimensions.

122. Do liquids expand by heat?

A. They do: the particles of which they are formed are not so firmly held together by cohesion as the particles of solid bodies; they therefore more readily expand by heat.

123. What liquid expands most on the application of heat?

A. Water. A cubic inch of boiling water when changed into steam expands to nearly a cubic foot. That is, it expands to about seventeen hundred times its original bulk.

124. What is the difference between a gas and a liquid?

A. Gases are very elastic, but liquids are not.

125. Illustrate what is meant by the elasticity of gas.

A. If from a vessel full of gas half were taken out, the other half would immediately spread itself out and fill the same space as was occupied by the whole.

126. Prove that a liquid is not very elastic.

A. If from a gallon of water you take half, the remaining four pints will take up only half the room that the whole gallon previously did: a liquid, therefore, is not elastic like gas.

Strictly speaking, a liquid is slightly elastic; inasmuch as it may be compressed, and will afterwards recover its former dimensions.

§ I.—EXPANSION OF LIQUIDS AND GASES.

127. Does heat expand air?

A. Yes: if a bladder nearly filled with air be tied up at the neck and laid before the fire, the air will expand till the bladder bursts.

128. Why will the air expand if the bladder be laid before the fire?

A. Because the heat of the fire will drive the particles of air apart from each other, and cause them to occupy more room than they did before.

129. Why will a ball of lead fall to the bottom of a pail of water, while a ball of cork of the same size will swim?

A. Because the lead is heavier and the

cork is lighter than the same bulk of water.

130. Why will a ball of cork fall through the air, while a soap-bubble of the same size ascends?

A. Because the ball of cork is heavier than the air, and the soap-bubble is lighter than its own bulk of air.

131. But the soap-bubble is filled with air: therefore why is it lighter than the air around it?

A. Because the soap-bubble is filled by the breath, which is warm air; and, as heat expands all bodies, the air in the soap-bubble is made to occupy a larger space than the same quantity of air outside of the bubble, and for this reason it is rendered lighter.

132. But suppose cold air were forced into the soapy water: would the bubbles ascend?

A. No: if the air forced through the pipe were of the temperature of the surrounding atmosphere, the bubbles would not rise.

133. Why would they not rise?

A. Because, the air inside of the bubbles being of the temperature of the surrounding atmosphere, the air contained in them would weigh as much as the same bulk of air outside of the bubbles.

134. Why do balloons ascend?

A. Because they are filled with air lighter than the same bulk of air surrounding the balloon.

135. Does heat expand every thing else besides air and water?

A. Yes: every thing that man is acquainted with is expanded by heat.

136. What is meant by COLD?

A. It is merely the absence of Heat.

All bodies contain heat; but inferior degrees of heat are designated by the term "cold."

137. Most bodies contract by cold: is there an exception to this rule?

A. Yes: water when cooling from about seven degrees above its freezing-point undergoes a regular expansion; and in becoming solid a still further expansion takes place.

138. How great is the expansion of freezing water?

A. It amounts to about one-seventh of its bulk. That is, a two-gallon measure containing seven quarts of water would be quite full when perfectly frozen.

139. Mention some of the effects of the expansion of freezing water.

A. Rocks are often rent asunder by it; lead and iron pipes are burst; and a brass globe filled with water and closed by a screw was burst, by the freezing of the water, with a force of not less than twenty-eight thousand pounds.

140. Why do unslit chestnuts crack with a loud noise when roasted?

A. Because they contain a great deal of air, which is expanded by the heat of the fire; and the air, not being able to escape, bursts violently through the thick rind, slitting it, and making a great noise.

141. What occasions the loud crack or report which we hear?

A. 1st. The sudden bursting of the shell makes a report, in the same way as a piece of wood or glass would do if snapped in two; and,

2d. The escape of hot air from the chestnut makes a report similar to that of gunpowder when it escapes from a gun.

142. Why does the sudden bursting of the shell, or snapping of a piece of wood, make a report?

A. Because a violent stroke is given to the air when the attraction of cohesion is thus suddenly overcome. This stroke produces rapid undulations in the air, which, striking upon the ear, give the sensation of sound.

143. Why does the escape of air from the chestnut, or the explosion of gunpowder, produce a report?

A. Because the sudden expansion of the imprisoned air produces a partial vacuum; the report is caused by the rushing of fresh air to fill up this vacuum.

144. If a chestnut be slit before it is roasted, it will not crack: why is this?

A. Because the heated air of the chestnut

can then escape freely through the slit in the rind.

145. Why does an apple split and spurt about when roasted?

A. Because it contains a quantity of air, which, being expanded by the heat of the fire, bursts through the peel, carrying the juice of the apple along with it.

146. Does an apple contain more air in proportion than a chestnut?

A. Yes, much more. There is as much condensed air in a common apple as would fill a space forty-eight times as large as the apple itself.

147. How can all this air be stowed in an apple?

A. The inside of an apple consists of little cells, each of which contains a portion of air.

148. When an apple is roasted, why is one part made soft, while all the rest remains hard?

A. Because the air in the cells next the fire is expanded, and escapes; the cells are broken, and their juices mixed together: so the apple collapses, (from loss of air and juice,) and feels soft in those parts.

149. What is meant by the apple collapsing?

A. It means that the plumpness gives way, and the apple becomes soft and shrivelled.

150. Why do sparks of fire start with a crackling noise from pieces of wood laid upon a fire?

A. Because the air (expanded by the heat) forces its way through the pores of the wood, and carries along with it the covering of the pores which resisted its passage.

151. What is meant by the "pores of the wood"?

A. Very small holes in the wood, through which the sap circulates.

152. What are the sparks of fire which burst from the wood?

A. Very small pieces of wood made red-hot, and separated from the log by the force of the air when it bursts from its confinement.

153. Why does light, porous wood make more snapping than any other kind?

A. Because the pores are very large, and contain more air than those of wood of a closer grain.

154. Why does green wood make less snapping than dry?

A. Because the pores, being filled with sap, contain very little air.

155. Why does dry wood burn more easily than green or wet wood?

A. Because the pores of dry wood are filled with air, which supports combustion; but the pores of green or wet wood are filled with moisture, which extinguishes flame.

156. Why does moisture extinguish flame?

A. 1st. Because it prevents the carbon of the fuel from mixing with the oxygen of the air, to form carbonic acid gas; and,

2d. Because heat is perpetually carried off by the formation of the sap or moisture into steam.

157. Why do stones snap and fly about when heated in a fire?

A. Because the close texture of the stones prevents the hot air enclosed in them from escaping; in consequence of which, it bursts forth with great violence, tearing the stones to atoms, and scattering the fragments.

Probably some part of this effect is due to the setting free of the water of crystallization.

158. When bottled ale or porter is set before a fire, why is the cork sometimes forced out?

A. Because the carbonic acid gas of the liquor expands by the heat, and drives out the cork.

Carbonic acid gas is a compound of carbon and oxygen.

159. Why does ale or porter froth more after it has been set before the fire?

A. Because the heat of the fire expands the carbonic acid gas of the liquor, and produces bubbles or froth.

160. When a boy makes a paper balloon, and sets fire to the cotton or sponge, (which has been previously steeped in spirits of wine,) why is the balloon inflated?

A. Because the air of the balloon is expanded by the flame.

161. Why does the balloon rise after it has been inflated by the expanded air?

A. Because the same quantity of air is expanded to three or four times its original volume, and made so much lighter that even when all the paper, wire, and cotton are added, it is still lighter than the same bulk of common air..

162. Why does smoke rush up a chimney?

A. Because the heat of the fire expands the air in the chimney; which, being thus made lighter than the air around, rises up the chimney, and carries the smoke in its current.

163. Why will a long chimney smoke, unless the fire be pretty fierce?

A. Because the heat of the fire will not be sufficient to rarefy all the air in the chimney.

164. Why will the chimney smoke, unless the fire be strong enough to heat all the air in the chimney-flue?

A. Because the cold air (condensed in the upper part of the flue) will sink from its own weight, and sweep the ascending smoke back into the room.

165. What is the use of a cowl upon a chimney-pot?

A. It acts as a screen, to prevent the wind from blowing into the chimney.

166. What harm would the wind do if it were to blow into a chimney?

A. 1st. It would prevent the smoke from issuing out of the top of the chimney; and,

2d. The cold air (introduced into the chimney by the wind) would fall down the flue, and drive the smoke with it into the room.

167. How are houses and other buildings heated with hot air?

A. The fire is kindled in a grate or stove which is erected in the cellar. This fire heats the air in contact with it in the air-chamber, as it is called, and, as heated air always ascends, it is forced up through pipes into the different apartments of the building

168. What is an air-chamber?

A. It is an enclosure around the furnace or stove, with openings below to admit the cold air from the cellar to rush in to supply the place of the heated air which ascends into the rooms above.

169. Why is cold air introduced into the air-chamber?

A. Because the air in the chamber when heated expands and becomes lighter than the same bulk of cold air; and, as this heated air ascends through the pipes, the cold air rushes in to supply its place, and becomes heated in its turn.

170. Why are the bricks and flagstones of pavements frequently loosened after a frost?

A. Because the moisture beneath them expanded during the frost, and raised the bricks and flagstones from their beds; but afterward the moisture thawed and condensed again, leaving the bricks and stones loose.

171. Why do doors swell in rainy weather?

A. Because the air is filled with vapor, which, penetrating into the pores of the wood, forces its particles farther apart, and swells the door.

172. Why do doors shrink in dry weather?

A. Because the moisture is absorbed from the wood; and, as the particles are brought closer together, the size of the door is lessened: in other words, the wood shrinks.

§ II.—EXPANSION OF METALS.

173. What metal is distinguished from all others by its fluidity at ordinary temperatures?

A. Mercury, or quicksilver.

174. Does mercury, like other metals, expand by heat?

A. It readily expands or contracts with every variation of temperature.

Though fluid at all common temperatures, mercury solidifies at 40° below zero. In the Polar regions thermometers filled with mercury are often useless. Mercury when frozen is malleable.

175. For what philosophical instruments is mercury generally used?

A. Its regular expansion and contraction by every increase or diminution of temperature renders it preferable to all other liquids for filling the tubes of barometers and thermometers.

176. Why does the mercury of a thermometer rise in hot weather?

A. Because heat expands the metal, which (being increased in bulk) occupies a larger space, and consequently rises higher in the tube.

177. Why is a glass broken when hot water is poured into it?

A. Because the inside of the glass is suddenly expanded by the hot water before the outside: so the glass snaps, in consequence of this unequal expansion.

178. Why is not the outside of the glass expanded by the hot water, as well as the inside?

A. Because glass is a bad conductor of heat, and breaks before the heat of the inner surface is conducted to the outside.

179. Why does a glass snap because the inner surface is hotter than the outer?

A. Because the inner surface is expanded, and not the outer; in consequence of which an opposing force is created, which breaks the glass.

180. If a bar of metal be accurately measured when cold, and afterward heated very hot, will its dimensions be found to have increased?

A. Yes: all metals expand by heat; and a bar of iron when hot will measure more than when it is cold.

181. Will the iron contract in size on cooling, after it has been heated?

A. Yes: it will return to its former dimensions on getting cold.

182. Why do most persons dip their razor in hot water before shaving with it?

A. Because the heat of the water expands the edge, by that means rendering it more fine and sharp.

183. Why does a wheelwright make the tire red-hot which he fixes on a wheel?

A. 1st. That, by its expansion, it may fit on more easily; and,

2d. That it may gird the wheel more tightly by contracting when it cools.

184. Why does a stove make a crackling noise when a fire is very hot?

A. Because it expands from the heat, and the particles of iron, in expanding, produce a crackling noise.

185. Why does a stove make a similar crackling noise when a large fire is put out?

A. Because it contracts when the fire is

removed; and the particles of iron, in contracting, produce a crackling sound.

186. Why does the plaster around a grate or furnace crack and fall away?

A. Because, when the fire is lighted, the iron-work expands more than the brick-work and plaster, and separates from them; but when the fire is put out the metal shrinks again, and leaves the "setting" behind.

The "setting" is a technical word for the plaster, &c. in immediate contact with the grate or furnace.

187. Why does the plaster fall away?

A. As a chink is left between the "setting" and the grate, the plaster will frequently fall away from its own weight.

188. What other cause contributes to bring the plaster down?

A. As the heat of the fire varies, the size of the iron grate or furnace varies also; and this swelling and contracting keep up such a constant disturbance about the plaster that it cracks and falls off.

189. If the boiler or kettle attached to a kitchen-range be filled with cold water some time after the fire has been lighted, it will be very likely to crack or burst. Why is this?

A. Because the heat of the fire has caused the metal of which the boiler is composed to expand; but the cold water very suddenly contracts those parts with which it comes in contact, and, as one part is larger than the other, the boiler cracks or bursts.

190. When the stopper of a decanter or smelling-bottle sticks, why will a cloth wrung out of hot water and wrapped around the neck of the bottle loosen the stopper?

A. Because the hot cloth heats the neck of the bottle, causing it to expand, and consequently loosens the stopper.

191. Why does the stopper of a decanter stick fast if it be put in damp?

A. If the stopper be damp, it fits the decanter air-tight; and, if the decanter was last used in a heated room, as soon as the hot air enclosed in the inside has been condensed by the cold, the weight of the external air will be sufficient to press the stopper down and make it stick fast.

192. Why does a damp stopper fit a decanter air-tight?

A. Because the moisture fills up all the inequalities (that is, roughness) in the ground-glass stopper and neck of the decanter, and thus prevents the escape of the air.

193. Why does the stopper of a smelling-bottle very often stick fast?

A. Because the contents of a smelling-bottle are very volatile, and leave the neck of the bottle and the stopper damp.

§ III.—VENTILATION.

194. What is ventilation?

A. The renewal of fresh air,—a continual change of air.

From the Latin *ventilo,* to blow or fan.

195. Is the air in a room in the same perpetual motion as the air out-of-doors?

A. Yes: there are always two currents of air in the room we occupy,—one of hot air, flowing out of the room, and another of cold air, flowing into the room.

196. How do you know that there are these two currents of air in every occupied room?

A. If a lighted candle be held near the crevice at the top of the door, the flame will be blown outward, (toward the hall;) but if the candle be held at the bottom of the door, the flame will be blown inward, (into the room.)

This is not the case if a fire be in an open fireplace in the room. When a fire is lighted, an inward current is drawn through all the crevices.

197. Why would the flame be blown outward (toward the hall) if a candle were held at the top of the door?

A. Because the air of the room, being heated and consequently rarefied, ascends; and (floating about the upper part of the room) some of it escapes through the crevice at the top of the door, producing a current of air outward, (into the hall.)

198. Why would the flame be blown inward (into the room) if the candle were held at the bottom of the door?

A. Because a partial vacuum is made at the bottom of the room as soon as the warm air of the room has ascended to the ceiling or made its escape from the room, and cold air from the hall rushes under the door to supply the void.

199. What is meant by a "partial vacuum being made at the bottom of the room"?

A. A vacuum means a place from which the air has been taken; and a "partial vacuum" means a place from which a part of the air has been taken. Thus, when the air near the floor ascends to the ceiling, a partial vacuum is made near the floor.

200. How is the vacuum filled up again?

A. It is filled up by colder air, which rushes (under the door and through the window-crevices) into the room.

201. Give an illustration.

A. If a pail be dipped into a pond and filled with water, a hole (or vacuum) is made in the pond as large as the pail; but the moment the pail is drawn out, the vacuum is filled up by the water around.

202. Show how this illustration applies.

A. The heated air which ascends from the bottom of a room is removed like the water in the pail; and, as the void was instantly supplied by other water in the pond, so the void of air is supplied by the air around.

203. Why is a room (even without a fire) generally warmer than the open air?

A. Because the air in a room is not subject to much change, and soon becomes of the same temperature as our skin, when it no longer feels cold.

204. Why do we generally feel colder out-of-doors than in-doors?

A. Because the air which surrounds us out-of-doors is always changing; and, as fast as one portion of air has become warmer by contact with our body, another colder portion surrounds us, to absorb more heat.

205. Why is there a strong draught through the key-hole of a door?

A. Because the air in the room we occupy is warmer than the air out-of-doors: therefore the air from out-of-doors rushes through the keyhole into the room, and causes a draught.

206. Why is there a strong draught under the door and through the crevice on each side?

A. Because cold air rushes from the hall to supply the void in the room caused by the escape of warm air up the chimney and through the crevices in the upper parts of the doors.

207. If you open the lower sash of a window, there is

more draught than if you open the upper sash: explain the reason of this.

A. If the lower sash be open, cold external air will rush freely into the room, and cause a great draught inward; but, if the upper sash be open, the heated air of the room will rush out, and of course there will be less draught inward.

208. By which means is a room better ventilated,—by opening the upper or the lower sash?

A. A room is better ventilated by opening the upper sash, because the hot, vitiated air (which always ascends toward the ceiling) can escape more easily.

209. By which means is a hot room more quickly cooled,—by opening the upper or the lower sash?

A. A hot room is cooled more quickly by opening the lower sash, because the cold air can enter more freely at the lower part of the room than at the upper.

210. Which is the hottest place in a church or theatre?

A. The gallery.

211. Why is the gallery of all public buildings hotter than the lower parts?

A. Because the heated air of the building ascends, and all the cold air (which can enter through the doors and windows) keeps near the floor till it has become heated.

212. How are mines ventilated?

A. The mine is furnished with two shafts or flues. These flues are so arranged that air forced down one shall traverse the whole extent of the mine before it escapes by the other. By keeping up a fire in one of these shafts, the air is rarefied or expanded within, causing an ascending current, carrying with it all the noxious gases and rendering the air pure.

213. What effect is produced upon air by rarefaction?

A. It is made lighter and ascends through colder strata, as a cork put at the bottom of a basin of water rises to the surface.

214. Why should stoves be fixed as near the floor of a room as possible?

A. In order that the air in the lower part of the room may be heated by the fire.

215. Would not the air in the lower part of a room be heated equally well if the stove were more elevated?

A. No: the heat of a fire has very little effect upon the air below the level of the grate; and therefore every grate should be as near the floor as possible.

216. Our feet are very frequently cold when we sit close by a good fire: explain the reason of this.

A. As the fire consumes the air which passes over it, cold air rushes through the crevices of the doors and windows, along the floor of the room, to supply the deficiency; and these currents of cold air, rushing constantly over our feet, deprive them of their warmth.

217. What is smoke?

A. Small particles of carbon separated by combustion from the fuel, but not consumed.

218. Why do smoke and steam curl as they ascend?

A. Because they are forced round and round by the ascending and descending currents of air.

219. Why do some chimneys smoke?

A. Because fresh air is not admitted into a room as fast as it is consumed by the fire; in consequence of which a current of air rushes down the chimney to supply the deficiency, driving the smoke along with it.

220. Why cannot air be supplied as fast as it is consumed by the fire?

A. Curtains around the windows, sand-bags at the thresholds of the doors, and all such contrivances, keep out the draught.

221. Why will the air come down the chimney?

A. Because it can get into the room in no other way, if the doors and windows are all made air-tight.

222. What is the best remedy in such a case?

A. The speediest remedy is to open the door or window; but by far the best remedy is to carry a small tube from the hearth into the external air.

223. Why is that the best remedy?

A. Because the fire will be plentifully supplied with air by the tube: the doors and windows may all remain air-tight, and we may enjoy a warm fireside without the inconvenience of draughts of air and cold feet.

224. Why is a chimney raised so high above the roof?

A. That it may not smoke, as all flues do which are too short.

225. What is meant by the flue of a chimney?

A. That part of a chimney through which the smoke passes.

226. Why does a chimney smoke if the flue be very short?

A. Because the draught of a short flue is too slack to carry the smoke up the chimney.

227. Why is the draught of a short flue more slack than that of a long one?

A. Because the air contained in a short flue does not become sufficiently rarefied to cause a strong draught.

228. Why is the fire always dull and sluggish if the chimney-flue be very short?

A. Because the draught is bad; and, as the rarefied air passes very tardily up the chimney, fresh air flows as tardily toward the fire to supply it with oxygen.

229. Why does not smoke acquire its full velocity in a short flue?

A. Because the higher smoke ascends, provided the fire be clear and hot and the flue unobstructed, the faster it moves: if, therefore, a flue be very short, the smoke never acquires its full velocity.

230. Does the draught of a chimney depend on the speed of the smoke through the flue?

A. Yes: the more quickly hot air flies up the chimney, the more quickly cold air will rush toward the fire to supply the place; and, therefore, the higher the flue the greater the draught.

231. Why are the chimneys of manufactories made so very high?

A. To increase the intensity of the fire.

232. Why is the intensity of a fire increased by lengthening the flue?

A. Because, the draught being greater, more fuel is consumed in the same time, and, of course, the intensity of the heat is proportionally greater.

233. If a short chimney cannot be lengthened, what is the best way to prevent smoking?

A. To contract the opening of the chimney contiguous to the fire.

234. Why will a smaller opening in that part of the chimney near the fire prevent smoking?

A. Because the air will be compelled to pass nearer the fire, and, being more heated, will rise through the chimney more rapidly:

this increase of heat will, therefore, compen sate for the shortness of the flue.

235. Why will a room be full of smoke if there be two fires in it?

A. Because the fiercer fire will exhaust the most air, and draw from the smaller one to supply its demand.

236. Why will a chimney smoke if there be a fire in two rooms communicating with each other?

A. Because, whenever the door between the two rooms is opened, air will rush from the chimney of the inferior fire to supply the other, and both rooms will be filled with smoke.

237. What is the best remedy in this case?

A. Let a tube be carried from the hearth of each fire into the external air; and then each fire will be so well supplied that neither will need to borrow from the other.

238. Why does a house in a valley very often smoke?

A. Because the wind, striking against the surrounding hills, bounds back again upon the chimney, and destroys its draught.

239. What is the common remedy in this case?

A. To fix a cowl on the chimney-top, which will turn like a weathercock and present its back to the wind.

240. Why will not a cowl always prevent a chimney smoking?

A. Because, if the wind be strong, and

there were a steeple or hill near the chimney, it would keep the opening of the cowl toward the hill; and then the reflected wind would blow into the cowl and down the chimney.

241. As a cowl is not a perfect remedy, can any other be suggested?

A. Yes: if the chimney-flue be carried higher than the hill, no wind can enter the flue.

242. If a chimney-flue be carried higher than the hill, why cannot the wind enter it?

A. Because the reflected wind would strike against the sides of the chimney-flue, and not pass over the opening at all.

243. In what other cases will a chimney smoke?

A. If the door and fireplace be both on the same side of the room, the chimney will very often smoke.

244. Why will a chimney smoke if the door and fireplace be both on the same side?

A. Because, whenever the door is opened, a current of air will blow obliquely into the chimney-place, and drive the smoke into the room.

245. What remedy can be applied to this evil?

A. The door must be set opposite to the chimney-place, or nearly so; and then the draught from the door will blow the smoke up the chimney, and not into the room.

246. Why will a chimney smoke if it need sweeping?

A. Because loose soot obstructs the free passage of the smoke, delays its current, and prevents the draught.

247. Why will a chimney smoke if it be out of repair?

A. 1st. Because the loose mortar and bricks obstruct the smoke; and,

2d. Cold air, oozing through the chinks, chills the air in the chimney and prevents its ascent.

248. Why does an old-fashioned farm-house chimney often smoke?

A. Because the opening of the chimney-place is so very large that much of the air which goes up the chimney has never passed near enough to the fire to become heated; and this cold air (mixing with the hot) so reduces the temperature of the air in the chimney that it ascends very slowly, and the draught is destroyed.

249. Why does a chimney smoke if the draught be slack?

A. Because the current of air up the chimney is not powerful enough to buoy up the smoke through the flue.

250. Why do almost all chimneys smoke in gusty weather?

A. Because the column of smoke is suddenly

chilled by the wind, and, being unable to ascend, rushes back into the room.

251. What is the use of a chimney-pot?

A. It serves to increase the draught when the opening of a chimney is too large.

252. How does a chimney-pot increase the draught of a chimney?

A. As the same quantity of hot air has to escape through a smaller opening, it must pass through more quickly.

253. Why do blowers, when placed before a grate, tend to kindle the fire?

A. Because the air (by passing through the fire) is made much hotter, and ascends the chimney more rapidly.

254. Why is a fire better supplied with oxygen while the blower is before it?

A. Because the blower increases the draught; and the faster the hot air flies up the chimney, the faster will cold air rush toward the fire to supply it with oxygen.

255. Why does a parlor often smell disagreeably of soot in summer-time?

A. Because the air in the chimney (being colder than the air in the parlor) descends from the chimney into the room, impregnated with the disagreeable smell of the soot.

256. Why does smoke sometimes descend before it rains?

A. Because the air is less dense, and cannot buoy up the air: in other words, the damp air is lighter than the smoke.

257. Why does a downward current of cold air bring rain?

A. Because it condenses the warm vapor, which then descends in the form of rain.

258. Why does a poker laid across a dull fire revive it?

A. For two reasons: 1st. Because the poker concentrates the heat, and therefore increases it; and,

2d. Air is arrested in the narrow aperture between the poker and the coals, and a draught created.

259. Why are fires placed on the floor of a room, and not toward the ceiling?

A. Because heated air always ascends: if, therefore, the fire were not near the floor, the air of the lower part of the room would never be heated by the fire.

260. If you take a poker out of the fire and hold the hot end downward, why is the handle intensely hot?

A. Because the hot end of the poker heats the air around it, and this hot air in its ascent heats the poker and the hand which holds it.

261. How should a red-hot poker be carried so as not to burn the fingers?

A. With the hot end upward; for then the

air heated by the poker would not pass over the hand and scorch it.

SECTION II.—CONDUCTION OF HEAT.

262. What is meant by conduction of heat?

A. The passage of heat from one body or particle of a body to another by actual contact.

§ I.—CONDUCTORS OF HEAT.

263. Why do some things feel colder than others?

A. Principally because they are better conductors, and draw off heat from the body much faster.

264. What are the best conductors of heat?

A. Dense, solid bodies, such as metal and stone.

265. Which metals are the most rapid conductors of heat?

A. The best conductors of heat are silver, gold, copper, and iron. Lead is not so good a conductor of heat as the other metals.

266. Which is the better conductor of heat,—copper or glass?

A. Copper. If the extremities of a rod of copper and one of glass be placed in the fire, and the other ends be held in the hand, the heat will be found to ascend rapidly through the copper wire, while the end of the glass rod will be comparatively cool.

267. What are the worst conductors of heat?

A. All light and porous bodies, such as hair, fur, wool, charcoal, and so on.

Two of the worst conductors known are hare's fur and eider-down: the two next worst are beaver's fur and raw silk; then wood and lamp-black; then cotton and fine lint; then charcoal, wood-ashes, &c.

268. Why does a piece of wood blazing at one end not feel hot at the other?

A. Because wood is so bad a conductor that heat does not traverse freely through it: hence, though one end of a stick be blazing, the other end may be quite cold.

269. Why does hot metal feel more intensely warm than hot wool?

A. Because metal gives out a much greater quantity of heat in the same space of time, and the influx of heat is, consequently, more perceptible.

270. Why does money in our pocket feel very hot when we stand before a fire?

A. Because metal is an excellent conductor, and rapidly becomes heated. For the same reason, it rapidly becomes cold whenever it comes in contact with a body colder than itself.

271. Why does a poker, resting on a fender, feel colder than the hearth-rug, which is farther off the fire?

A. Because the poker is an excellent conductor, and draws heat from the hand much more rapidly than the woollen hearth-rug, which is a very bad conductor. Though both, therefore, are equally warm, the poker seems to be the colder.

272. Why does an iron pump-handle feel intensely cold in winter?

A. Because it is an excellent conductor, and draws off the heat of our hand so rapidly that the sudden loss produces a sensation of intense coldness.

273. Is the iron handle of the pump really colder than the wooden pump itself?

A. No: every inanimate substance exposed to the same temperature possesses in reality the same degree of heat.

274. Why does the iron handle seem so much colder than the wooden pump?

A. Merely because the iron is a better conductor, and therefore draws off the heat from our hand more rapidly than wood does.

275. Why does a stone or marble hearth feel colder to the feet than a carpet or hearth-rug?

A. Because stone and marble are good conductors, but woollen carpets and hearth-rugs are very bad conductors.

276. How does the stone hearth make our feet cold?

A. As soon as the hearth-stone has absorbed a portion of heat from our foot, it instantly disposes of it and calls for a fresh supply, till the hearth-stone has become of the same temperature as the foot placed upon it.

277. Do not also the woollen carpet and hearth-rug conduct heat from the human body?

A. Yes; but, being very bad conductors, they convey the heat away so slowly that the loss is scarcely perceptible.

278. Is the cold hearth-stone in reality of the same temperature as the warm carpet?

A. Yes: every thing in the room is really of one temperature, but some things feel colder than others, because they are better conductors.

279. How long will the hearth-stone feel cold to the feet resting on it?

A. Till the feet and the hearth-stone are of the same temperature; and then the sensation of cold in the hearth-stone will subside.

280. Why would not the hearth-stone feel cold when it is of the same temperature as our feet?

A. Because the heat would no longer rush out of our feet into the hearth-stone, in order to produce equilibrium.

281. Why does the hearth-stone (when the fire is lighted) feel hotter than the hearth-rug?

A. Because the hearth-stone is an excellent conductor, and parts with its heat very readily; but the woollen hearth-rug (being a bad conductor) parts with its heat very slowly.

282. Why does parting with heat rapidly make the hearth-stone feel warm?

A. Because the rapid influx of heat raises

the temperature of our body so suddenly that we cannot help perceiving the increase.

283. Why does the non-conducting power of the hearth-rug prevent its feeling so hot as it really is?

A. Because it parts with its heat so slowly and gradually that we scarcely perceive its transmission into our feet.

284. Why are cooking-vessels often furnished with wooden handles?

A. Because wood is not a good conductor, like metal; and therefore wooden handles prevent the heat of the vessel from rushing into our hands to burn them.

285. Why is the handle of a metal teapot made of wood?

A. Because wood is a bad conductor: therefore the heat of the boiling water is not so quickly conveyed to our hand by a wooden handle as by one made of metal.

286. Why would a metal handle burn the hand of the tea-maker?

A. Because metal is an excellent conductor: therefore the heat of boiling water would rush so quickly into the metal handle that it would burn the hand.

287. Prove that a metal handle would be hotter than a wooden one.

A. If we touch that portion of the metal into which the wooden handle is fixed, we shall find that the wooden handle feels cold, but the metal intensely hot.

288. When we plunge our hands into a basin of water, why does it produce a sensation of cold?

A. Because water is a better conductor than air, and, as it draws off the heat from our hands more rapidly, it feels colder.

289. Why does the conducting power of water make it feel colder than air?

A. Because it abstracts heat from our hands so rapidly that we feel its loss; but the air abstracts heat so very slowly that its gradual loss is hardly perceptible.

290. Is water a good conductor of heat?

A. No: no liquid is a good conductor of heat; but water is a much better conductor than air.

291. Why is water a better conductor of heat than air?

A. Because it is more dense than air; and the conducting power of any substance depends upon its solidity, or the closeness of its particles.

292. How do you know that water is not a good conductor of heat?

A. Because it may be made to boil at its surface, without imparting sufficient heat to melt ice a quarter of an inch below the surface.

293. Why are not liquids good conductors of heat?

A. Because the heat which should be transmitted produces evaporation, and flies off in the vapor.

294. Why are hot bricks wrapped in cloth employed in cold weather to keep the feet warm?

A. Because bricks are bad conductors of heat, and cloth or flannel still worse; in consequence of which, a hot brick wrapped in flannel will retain its heat a very long time.

295. How is a room warmed by a stove?

A. The air nearest the fire is made hot first, and rises; cold air then descends, is heated, and ascends in like manner; and this interchange goes on till all the air of the room is warmed.

296. If air be a bad conductor of heat, why should we not feel as warm without clothing as when we are wrapped in wool and fur?

A. Because the air (which is cooler than our body) is never at rest; and every fresh particle of air draws off a fresh portion of heat.

297. Why are woollens and furs used for clothing in cold weather?

A. Because they are very bad conductors of heat, and therefore prevent the warmth of the body from being drawn off by the cold air.

298. Do not woollens and furs actually impart heat to the body?

A. No: they merely prevent the heat of the body from escaping.

299. Where would the heat escape to if the body were not wrapped in wool or fur?

A. The heat of the body would fly off into the air; for the cold air (coming in contact with the body) would gradually draw away its heat till it was as cold as the air itself.

300. What, then, is the principal use of clothing in winter-time?

A. 1st. To prevent the animal heat from escaping too freely; and,

2d. To protect the body from the external air, (or wind,) which would carry away its heat too rapidly.

301. Why are beasts covered with fur, hair, or wool, and birds with feathers?

A. Because fur, hair, wool, and feathers are very slow conductors of heat; and, as dumb animals cannot be clad like human beings, God has given them a robe of hair or wool to keep them warm.

302. Why are wool, fur, hair, and feathers such slow conductors of heat?

A. Because a great quantity of air lurks between the fibres; and air is a very bad conductor of heat.

303. Why is moderately loose clothing warmer than that which fits tightly?

A. Because air is a bad conductor; and the quantity of air confined between our bodies and clothing prevents—

1st. The heat of our bodies from escaping; and,

2d. The external air from coming into contact with our bodies.

But if our clothing is sufficiently loose to admit of a free circulation of air, we shall feel cold; and, on the contrary, if it fits very tightly, it impedes the free circulation of the blood, and we feel cold.

304. Does not the bad conducting power of air enable persons to judge whether an egg be new or stale?

A. Yes. Touch the larger end of the shell with your tongue: if it feels warm, the egg is stale; if not, it is new-laid.

305. Why will the shell of a stale egg feel warm to the tongue?

A. Because the thick end of an egg contains a small quantity of air between the shell and the white: when the egg is stale, the white shrinks, and the confined air accordingly expands, breaks the membrane which surrounds the contents of the egg, and permits them to come in contact with the shell.

306. Why do we feel colder in windy weather than on a calm day?

A. Because the particles of air pass over us more rapidly, and every fresh particle takes from us some portion of heat.

307. Why do the inhabitants of the Polar regions wear skins with the fur inward?

A. Because the dry skin prevents the wind from penetrating to their body, and the air between the hairs of the fur soon becomes heated by the body; in consequence of which the Laplander in his fur is clad in a case of hot air, impervious to the cold and wind.

308. Show the wisdom of God in making the air a bad conductor.

A. If air were a good conductor, (like iron and stone,) heat would be drawn so rapidly from our body that we should be chilled to death. Similar evils would be felt by all the animal and vegetable world.

309. Why are rooms much warmer for being furnished with double doors and windows?

A. Because air is a bad conductor; and the air confined between the double doors and windows opposes both the escape of warm air out of the room and of cold air into the room.

310. Why is a room warmer when the window-curtains are drawn or the shutters shut?

A. Because air is a bad conductor; and the air confined between the curtains or shutters and the window opposes both the escape of warm air out of the room and of cold air into it.

311. Why does a linen shirt feel colder than a cotton one?

A. Because linen is a much better conductor than cotton, and therefore (as soon as it touches the body) it draws away the heat more rapidly, and produces a greater sensation of cold.

312. Why is the face cooled by wiping the temples with a fine linen handkerchief?

A. Because the fine fibres of the linen have a strong capillary attraction for moisture, and are excellent conductors of heat; in consequence of which, the moisture and heat are abstracted from the face by the linen, and a sensation of coolness is produced.

"Capillary attraction," *i.e.* the attraction of a thread or hair. The wick of a candle is wet with grease, because the melted tallow runs up the cotton from capillary attraction.

313. Why would not a cotton handkerchief do as well?

A. Because the coarse fibres of cotton have very little capillary attraction and are very bad conductors; in consequence of which, the heat of the face would be increased, rather than diminished, by the use of a cotton handkerchief.

314. Is the earth a good conductor of heat?

A. No: the earth is a very bad conductor of heat.

315. Why is the earth a bad conductor of heat?

A. Because its particles are not continuous; and the power of conducting heat depends upon the continuity of matter.

316. Why is the earth below the surface warmer in winter than the surface itself?

A. Because the earth is a bad conductor of heat; and therefore, although the ground be frozen, the frost never penetrates, in our latitude, more than a few inches below the surface.

In high latitudes, the earth is frozen to the depth of several feet.

317. Why is the earth below the surface cooler in summer than the surface itself?

A. Because the earth is a bad conductor of heat; and therefore, although the surface be scorched by the burning sun, the intense heat cannot penetrate to the roots of large plants and trees.

318. Show the wisdom of God in making the earth a bad conductor.

A. If the heat and cold could penetrate the earth as freely as the heat of a fire penetrates iron, the springs would be dried up in summer and frozen in winter, and all vegetation would perish.

319. Why does the Bible say that God "giveth snow like wool"?

A. Because snow (being a very bad conductor of heat) protects vegetables and seeds from the frost and cold.

320. How does the non-conducting power of snow protect vegetables from the frost and cold?

A. It prevents the heat of the earth from being drawn off by the cold air which rests upon it.

321. Why is water from a spring always cool, even in summer?

A. Because the earth is so bad a conductor that the burning rays of the sun can penetrate only a few inches below the surface; in consequence of which, the springs of water are not affected by the heat of summer.

322. Why is it cool under a shady tree on a hot summer's day?

A. 1st. Because the overhanging foliage screens off the rays of the sun;

2d. As the rays of the sun are warded off, the air beneath the tree is not heated by the reflection of the earth; and,

3d. The leaves of the trees, being non-conductors, allow no heat to penetrate them.

323. Why do persons use paper or woollen kettle-holders?

A. Because paper and woollen are both very bad conductors of heat; in consequence of which, the heat of the kettle does not readily pass through them to the hand.

324. Does the heat of the boiling kettle never get through the woollen or paper kettle-holder?

A. Yes; but, though the kettle-holder became as hot as the kettle itself, it would never feel so hot.

325. Why would not the kettle-holder feel so hot as the kettle, when both are of the same temperature?

A. Because it is a very bad conductor, and disposes of its heat too slowly to be perceptible; but metal, being an excellent conductor, disposes of its heat so quickly that the sudden influx is painful.

326. Why is the lid of a kettle intensely hot when the water boils?

A. Because the bright metal lid is an admirable conductor; and therefore the heat from the boiling water rushes into the hand the moment we touch it.

327. Why are ice-houses lined with straw, and generally whitewashed on the outside?

A. 1st. Because straw is a very bad conductor of heat, and therefore prevents the external heat from getting to the ice; and,

2d. The whitewashed roof and walls prevent the absorption of heat.

328. Why will a little oil on the surface of water prevent its freezing?

A. Because oil is a bad conductor, and prevents heat from leaving the water.

329. A silver teaspoon becomes more heated by hot tea than one of inferior metal, (as German silver, pewter, &c.:) why is this?

A. Because silver is a better conductor than German silver or pewter.

German silver is composed of 31½ parts of nickel, 25½ of zinc, 40½ of copper, and 2½ of iron.

Pewter is, generally speaking, an alloy of tin and lead,—sometimes with a little antimony or copper combined in different proportions, according to the purposes for which it is designed.

330. Why does a metal spoon left in a saucepan retard the process of boiling?

A. Because the metal spoon (being an excellent conductor) carries off the heat from the water; and, as heat is carried off by the spoon, the water takes a longer time to boil.

331. Why does paint preserve wood?

A. 1st. Because it covers the surface of the wood, and prevents both air and damp from penetrating into the pores;

2d. Because paint, (especially white paint,) being a bad conductor, keeps the wood at a more uniform temperature; and,

3d. Because it fills up the pores of the wood, and prevents insects and vermin from harboring in it and eating up the fibre.

332. Why are the poker and tongs intensely hot when they rest against the stove which contains a good fire?

A. Because they are excellent conductors of heat, and draw it rapidly from the stove with which they are in contact.

333. Why are furnaces and stoves built of bricks?

A. Because bricks are bad conductors, and prevent the escape of heat; in consequence of which, they are employed where great heat is required.

334. If a stove be placed in the middle of a room, should it be made of bricks or iron?

A. A stove in the middle of a room should be made of iron, because iron is an excellent conductor and rapidly communicates heat to the air around.

§ II.—CONVECTION.

335. What is meant by the convection of heat?

A. Heat communicated by being carried to another thing or place; as the hot water resting on the bottom of a kettle carries heat to the water through which it ascends.

336. Are liquids good conductors of heat?

A. No: liquids are bad conductors, and are, therefore, made hot by convection.

337. Why are liquids bad conductors of heat?

A. Because heat converts a liquid into steam, and flies off with the vapor instead of being conducted through the liquid.

338. Explain how water is made hot.

A. The water nearest the fire is first heated, and rises to the top; while its place is supplied by colder portions, which are heated, in turn, till all the water is boiling hot.

Fig. 1.

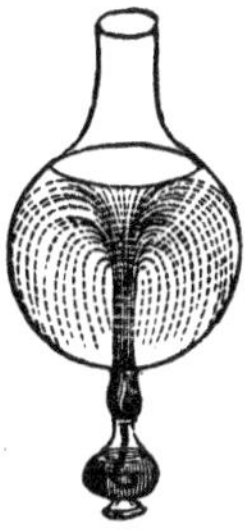

The movements of the particles of water in boiling will be understood by reference to Fig. 1.

339. Why is water in continual motion when it is boiling?

A. This commotion is mainly produced by the ascending and descending currents of hot and cold water, and by the escape of steam.

340. How do these two currents pass each other?

A. The hot ascending current rises through the centre of the mass of water, while the cold descending currents pass down by the metal sides of the kettle.

341. Why is heat applied to the bottom, and not to the top, of the kettle?

A. Because the heated water always ascends to the surface, heating the water through which it passes: if, therefore, heat were applied to the top of a vessel, the water below the surface would not be heated.

342. As the lower part of a grate is made red-hot by the fire above, why would not the water boil if fire were applied to the top of a kettle?

A. The iron of a grate is an excellent conductor: if, therefore, one part be heated, the heat is conducted to every other part. But water is a very bad conductor, and will not diffuse heat in a similar way.

343. Prove that water is a bad conductor of heat.

A. When a blacksmith immerses red-hot iron in a tank of water, the water which surrounds the iron is made boiling hot, while that below the surface remains quite cold.

344. If you wish to cool liquids, where should the cold be applied?

A. To the surface of the liquid; because the cold portions will always descend, and allow the warmer parts to come in contact with the cooling substance.

345. Does boiling water get hotter by being kept on the fire?

A. No; not if the steam be suffered to escape.

346. Why does not boiling water get hotter if the steam be suffered to escape?

A. Because the water is converted into steam as fast as it boils; and the steam carries away the additional heat.

347. Why does soup keep hot longer than boiling water?

A. Because the grease and various ingredients floating in the soup oppose the ascending motion of the hot particles, and prevent their rising freely to the surface.

348. If you wanted to keep water hot for a long time, how could it be done?

A. By adding a little starch or flour to the water.

349. Why would a little starch added to boiling water serve to keep it hot?

A. Because it would oppose the ascending motion of the hot particles of water, and prevent their rising freely to the surface.

350. Why do chocolate, Indian-mush, &c. remain hot longer than water?

A. Because the ascending motion of the hot particles is opposed by the mush or chocolate, and cannot so quickly reach the surface.

351. How is air heated?

A. By "convective currents."

352. Explain what is meant by "convective currents."

A. When a portion of air is heated, it rises in a current, carrying the heat with it; other colder air succeeds, and, being heated in a similar way, ascends also: these are called "convective currents."

"Convective currents;" so called from the Latin words *cum-vectus*, (carried with;) because the heat is "carried with" the current.

353. Is air heated by the rays of the sun?

A. No: air is not heated, in any sensible degree, by the action of the sun's rays passing through it.

354. Why, then, is the air hotter on a sunny day than on a cloudy one?

A. Because the sun heats the surface of the earth, and the air resting on the earth is heated by contact: as soon as it is heated it ascends; while its place is supplied by colder portions, which are heated in turn also.

355. If air be a bad conductor, why does hot iron become cold by exposure to the air?

A. Because it is made cold—

1st. By "convection;" and,

2d. By "radiation."

356. How is hot iron made cold by convection?

A. The air resting on the hot iron (being intensely heated) rapidly ascends with the heat it has absorbed; colder air succeeding absorbs more heat and ascends also; and this process is repeated till the hot iron is completely cooled.

357. How is broth cooled by being left exposed to the air?

A. It throws off some heat by radiation; but it is mainly cooled by convection.

358. How is hot broth cooled by convection?

A. The air resting on the hot broth (being heated) ascends; colder air succeeding absorbs more heat, and ascends also; and this process is repeated till the broth is made cool.

The particles on the surface of the broth sink as they are cooled, and warmer particles rise to the surface, which gradually assists the cooling-process.

359. Why are hot tea and broth cooled faster by being stirred?

A. 1st. Because the agitation assists in bringing its hottest particles to the surface;

2d. The action of stirring agitates the air, and brings it more quickly to the broth or tea; and,

3d. As the hotter particles are more rapidly brought into contact with the air, therefore convection is more rapid.

Blowing tea or broth cools it on the same principle.

360. If a shutter be closed during the day, the stream of light piercing through the crevice seems in constant agitation: why is this?

A. Because little motes and particles of dust, thrown into agitation by the violence of the convective currents, are made visible by the strong beam of light thrown into the room through the crevice of the shutter.

361. When potatoes are boiled, why are those at the top of the boiler cooked sooner than those nearer the fire?

A. 1st. Because the hottest particles of the water rise to the top of the boiler, and the coldest particles sink to the bottom; and,

2d. Because the top of the boiler is always enveloped with very hot escaping steam; in consequence of which, the potatoes at the top are subjected to more intense heat than those at the bottom of the boiler.

362. Why does milk boil more quickly than water?

A. Milk is a thicker liquid than water,

and consequently less steam escapes through the milk than through the water: therefore the heat of the whole mass of the milk rises more quickly.

363. Can any other reason be assigned why milk boils sooner than water?

A. As soon as the milk becomes heated, a thin skin forms over the surface of the milk, which prevents the escape of the steam, and therefore heats the mass of the milk more quickly.

SECTION III.—CHANGE OF STATE.

364. What does change of state mean?

A. The change which a substance undergoes on exposure to heat: thus, cold water may be made to boil, or, if the temperature be reduced, to freeze. Some solid substances, such as wax, or metals, change their state and liquefy by heat.

365. Why does melted wax become hard when cold?

A. Because the particles collapse, and, being packed more closely together, form a solid.

366. What is the difference between a liquid and a solid?

A. In a solid the particles adhere more closely than in a liquid. The tendency of heat is to drive particles of matter asunder:

it thus liquefies solids by separating the particles of which they are composed.

367. Why will hot iron bend more easily than cold?

A. Because it is not so solid. The particles are driven farther apart by heat, and the attraction of cohesion is thereby weakened: therefore the particles can be made to move on each other more readily.

368. What would be the effect of the application of a greater amount of heat?

A. The particles would be driven so far asunder as to cause the iron to liquefy, in which state the particles move among each other with but little resistance.

369. Why are some substances solid, others liquid, and others gaseous?

A. Because the particles which compose some substances are nearer together than they are in others. Those in which the particles are closest are solid; those in which they are farthest apart are gaseous; and the rest are liquid.

370. Why does heat change a solid, like ice, first into a liquid, and then into a gas?

A. Because heat drives the component particles farther asunder: hence a certain quantity of heat changes solid ice into a liquid, and a further addition of heat changes the liquid into steam.

371. Is steam visible or invisible?

A. Steam is invisible; but when it comes in contact with the air, being condensed into small drops, its vapor instantly becomes visible.

372. How do you know that steam is invisible?

A. If you look at the spout of a boiling kettle, you will find that the steam which issues from the spout is invisible for about half an inch; after which its vapor becomes visible.

373. Why is the steam invisible for half an inch?

A. Because it is not condensed by the air as it issues from the spout; but when it spreads and comes in contact with a larger volume of air, the invisible steam is readily condensed into visible drops.

374. Why do steam-engines sometimes burst, or blow up?

A. Because steam is very elastic; and this elasticity increases in a greater proportion than the heat which produces it: unless, therefore, some vent be freely allowed, steam will burst the vessel which confines it.

§ I.—LATENT HEAT.

375. Why does steam burn so much more severely than boiling water?

A. Steam condenses as soon as it is exposed to the cold, and gives out all the heat by which it was produced: therefore, as one thousand degrees of heat become latent in steam, it gives out that amount when condensed, which is much greater than the heat of boiling water.

376. Is there heat even in ice?

A. Yes; but it is latent,—that is, not perceptible to our senses.

"Latent," from the Latin word *lateo*, to lie hid.

377. How do you know there is heat, if you cannot perceive it?

A. The temperature of ice is 32° by the thermometer; but if ice be melted over a fire, (although 140° of heat are absorbed by the process,) it will feel no hotter than before.

378. What becomes of the 140° of heat which went into the ice to melt it?

A. It is hidden in the water; or, to speak more scientifically, it is stored up in a latent state.

379. How much heat may be thus secreted or made latent?

A. All things contain a vast quantity of latent heat; but as much as 1140° of heat may remain latent in water.

380. How can 1140° of heat be added to water without being perceptible to our feelings?

A. 1st. 140° of heat are hidden in water when ice is melted by the sun or fire;

2d. 1000° more of heat are secreted when water is converted into steam. Thus, before ice is converted into steam, 1140° of heat become latent.

One pint of boiling water (212° according to the thermometer) will make eighteen hundred pints of steam; but the steam is no hotter to the touch than boiling water; both are 212°: therefore, when water is converted into steam, 1000° of heat become latent. Hence, before ice is converted into steam, it must contain 1140° of latent heat.

381. Why does cold water poured on lime make it intensely hot?

A. Because heat is evolved by the chemical action which takes place when the cold water combines with the lime.

Heat is always evolved when a fluid is converted into a solid form. Heat is always absorbed when a solid is changed into a liquid state. As the water is changed from its liquid form when it is taken up by the lime, therefore heat is given off.

382. Where does the heat come from?

A. It was in the water and lime before, but was in a latent state.

383. Was there heat in the cold water and lime before they were mixed together?

A. Yes: all bodies contain heat,—the coldest ice as well as the hottest fire.

384. Explain by illustration what you mean.

A. Water is cold, and sulphuric acid is cold; but if these two cold liquids be mixed together they will produce intense heat.

§ II.—EBULLITION.

385. What is ebullition?

A. Ebullition, or boiling, is occasioned by the formation of bubbles of vapor within the body of the evaporating liquid, which, by reason of their lightness, rise to the surface and then break.

386. Do all liquids boil at the same temperature?

A. No: the boiling-point occurs in different liquids at very different temperatures.

387. What is meant by the boiling-point?

A. The temperature at which liquids become gaseous.

388. Why does milk boil over more readily than water?

A. Because the steam is retained in the boiling milk by a thin skin, or scum, which forms on the surface. The accumulation of steam finally bursts this scum, and in its escape carries with it the boiling milk.

389. Why does water simmer before it boils?

A. Because the particles of water near the bottom of the kettle, being formed into steam sooner than the rest, shoot upward, but are condensed again, as they rise, by the cold water, and produce what is called "simmering."

390. What is meant by simmering?

A. A gentle tremor or undulation on the

surface of the water. When water simmers, the bubbles collapse beneath the surface, and the steam is condensed to water again; but when water boils, the bubbles rise to the surface, and the steam is thrown off.

Collapse,—that is, burst.

391. Why does a kettle sing when the water simmers?

A. Because the air contained in the water escapes by fits and starts through the spout of the kettle, which makes a noise like the sound of a wind-instrument.

392. Why does not a kettle sing when the water boils?

A. Because all the water is boiling hot; so the steam escapes in a continuous stream, and not by fits and starts.

393. When does a kettle sing most?

A. When it is set on the side of the fire to boil.

394. Why does a kettle sing more when it is set on the side of a fire than when it is set in the midst of the fire?

A. Because the heat is applied so unequally that one side is made hotter than the other; in consequence of which, the steam is more diffused.

395. Why does a kettle sing when the boiling water begins to cool again?

A. Because the upper surface cools first,

and the steam which rises from the lower part of the kettle escapes by fits and starts.

396. Why does the water boil sooner when the kettle is placed over the fire?

A. Because the particles of water which are heated rise through the whole body of colder water; whereas when the side of the kettle is placed against the fire the heated particles rise only up the side of the kettle.

397. Why does boiling water swell?

A. Because it is expanded by the heat; that is, the heat of the fire drives the particles of water farther apart from each other; and therefore they take up more room: in other words, the water swells.

398. What is meant when it is said that "heat drives the particles of water farther apart from each other"?

A. Water is composed of little globules, like very small grains of sand: the heat drives these particles away from each other, and, as they then require more room, the water swells.

399. Why does boiling water bubble?

A. Because the vapor (rising through the water) is diffused, and forces up bubbles in its effort to escape.

All the air of water is expelled at the commencement of its boiling.

400. Why does a kettle sometimes boil over?

A. Because the water is expanded by

heat: if, therefore, a kettle is filled with cold water, some of it must run over as soon as it is made hot.

401. But a kettle will boil over, although it has not been filled full of water: how do you account for that?

A. If a fire be very brisk, the air and vapor are expelled so rapidly that the bubbles are very numerous, and, towering one above another, reach the top of the kettle, and fall over.

402. Why is a pot which was full to overflowing while the water was boiling hot, not full a short time after it has been taken off the fire?

A. Because while the water is boiling it is expanded by the heat, and fills the pot even to overflowing; but when it becomes cool it contracts again, and occupies a much less space.

403. Why does the water of a kettle run out of the spout when it boils?

A. Because the lid fits so tightly that the steam cannot lift it up and escape; being confined, therefore, in the kettle, it presses on the water with great power, and forces it out of the spout.

404. What causes the rattling noise so often made by the lid of a saucepan or boiler?

A. The steam as it escapes forces up the lid of the boiler, and the weight of the lid carries it back again; this, being done frequently, produces a rattling noise.

405. If the steam could not lift up the lid of the boiler, how would it escape?

A. If the lid fitted so tightly that the steam could not raise it up, the boiler would burst into fragments.

406. When steam pours out from the spout of a kettle, the stream begins apparently half an inch off the spout: why does it not begin close to the spout?

A. Steam is really invisible; and the half-inch between the spout and the stream of mist is the real steam, before it has been condensed by air.

407. Why is not all the steam invisible as well as that half-inch?

A. Because the invisible particles are condensed by the cold air, and, rolling one into another, look like a thick mist.

408. What becomes of the steam? for it soon vanishes.

A. After it has been condensed into mist, it mingles with the air and is dispersed abroad as invisible vapor.

409. And what becomes of the invisible vapor?

A. Being lighter than air, it ascends to the upper regions of the atmosphere, where (being again condensed) it contributes to form clouds.

410. Why will a pot filled with water never boil, when immersed in another vessel full of water?

A. Because water can never be heated

above the boiling-point: all the heat absorbed by water after it boils is employed in generating steam.

411. How does the conversion of water into steam prevent the inner pot from boiling?

A. As soon as the water in the larger pot is boiling hot, (or 212°,) steam is formed and carries off some of its heat: therefore 212° of heat can never pass through it, to raise the water in the inner vessel to boiling-heat.

412. Why do sugar, salt, &c. retard the process of boiling?

A. Because they increase the density of water; and whatever increases the density of a fluid retards its boiling.

413. If you want water to boil without the vessel containing it coming in contact with the fire, what plan must you adopt?

A. The vessel containing the water to be boiled must be immersed in a vessel containing a denser fluid, as boiling brine or syrup.

414. Why would the inner vessel boil if the outer vessel contained boiling brine?

A. Because brine will not boil till it is raised to 218° or 220°. Therefore 212° of heat may easily pass through it, to raise the vessel immersed in it to 212°, which is the boiling-point of water.

415. Why will brine impart to another vessel more than 212° of heat, and water not so much?

A. Because no liquid can impart so high a degree of heat as its own boiling-temperature: as water boils at 212°, it cannot impart 212° of heat; but as brine will not boil without 218° of heat, it can impart enough to make water boil.

416. Why can liquids impart no extra heat after they boil?

A. Because all extra heat is spent in making steam. Hence water will not boil a vessel of water immersed in it, because it cannot impart to it 212° of heat; but brine will, because it can impart more than 212° of heat before it is itself converted into steam.

Ether	boils at...... 96°	Syrup	boils at....221°
Alcohol	" ......176°	Oil of turpentine	" ....316°
Water	" ......212°	Sulphuric acid	" ....620°
Water with one-fifth salt	" ......219°	Mercury	" ....662°

Any liquid which boils at a lower degree can be made to boil, if immersed in a liquid which boils at a higher degree. Thus, a cup of ether can be made to boil in a saucepan of water; a cup of water, in a saucepan of brine or syrup. But a cup of water will not boil if immersed in ether; nor a cup of syrup in water.

§ III.—EVAPORATION.

417. What is meant by evaporation?

A. The transformation of liquid and, in some cases, of solid substances, into a gaseous state by the action of heat.

418. Has the state of the atmosphere any effect on evaporation?

A. Yes: the evaporation is greatest when the weather is dry and warm.

419. Do all liquids evaporate with the same rapidity?

A. No: ether evaporates more rapidly than alcohol, and alcohol more rapidly than water.

420. In what way may the evaporation of any liquid be increased?

A. By increasing the surface. Water will evaporate more rapidly if poured into a saucer than if put into a bottle, because a larger surface is exposed to the action of the air when in the saucer.

421. What effects are produced by evaporation?

A. The liquid vaporized absorbs heat from the body whence it issues; and the body deprived of the liquid by evaporation loses heat.

422. How may a glass bottle containing water be cooled?

A. By wrapping it in a wet cloth.

423. Why would the wet cloth cool the water?

A. The evaporation of the moisture of the cloth would absorb the heat from the water in the bottle.

If the cloth were dipped in alcohol instead of water, the water in the bottle would be rendered colder; because alcohol evaporates more readily than water. Ether, which is more volatile than alcohol, would produce a still greater degree of cold.

424. If you wet your finger and hold it up in the air, why does it feel cold?

A. Because the moisture on the finger quickly evaporates, and, as it evaporates, absorbs heat from the finger, making it feel cold.

425. If you bathe your temples with ether, why does it allay inflammation and feverish heat?

A. Because ether evaporates very rapidly, and, as it evaporates, absorbs heat from the burning head, producing a sensation of cold.

426. Why is ether better for this purpose than water?

A. Because ether requires less heat to convert it into vapor; in consequence of which, it evaporates more quickly.

Ether is converted into vapor by 100° of heat; but water requires 212° of heat to convert it into steam.

427. Why does ether very greatly relieve a scald or burn?

A. Because it evaporates very rapidly, and, as it evaporates, carries off the heat of the burn.

428. Why do we feel cold when we have wet feet or clothes?

A. Because the moisture of our shoes or clothes rapidly evaporates, and, as it evaporates, absorbs heat from our body, which makes us feel cold.

429. Why do wet feet or clothes give us "cold"?

A. Because the evaporation of the moisture absorbs heat so abundantly from the surface of our body that its temperature is lowered below its natural standard; in consequence of which, health is injured.

430. Why is it dangerous to sleep in a damp bed?

A. Because the heat is continually absorbed from the surface of our body to convert the damp of the sheets into vapor; in consequence of which, our animal heat is reduced below the healthy standard.

431. Why is health injured when the temperature of the body is reduced below its natural standard?

A. Because the balance of the circulation is destroyed: blood is driven away from the external surface by the chill and thrown upon the internal organs, which are oppressed by this increased load of blood.

432. Why do we not feel the same sensation of cold if we throw a thick covering over our wet clothes?

A. Because the thick covering, being air-tight, prevents evaporation, and, as the moisture cannot evaporate, no heat is absorbed from our bodies.

433. Why do not sailors get cold, who are frequently wet all day with sea-water?

A. 1st. Because the salt of the sea retards evaporation, and, as the heat of their body is drawn off gradually, the sensation of cold is prevented; and,

2d. The salt of the sea acts as a stimulant, and keeps the blood circulating near the surface of the body.

434. Why does sprinkling a hot room with water cool it?

A. Because the heat of the room causes a rapid evaporation of the sprinkled water; and, as the water evaporates, it absorbs heat from the room, which cools it.

435. Why is it customary, in very hot countries, to sit in rooms separated by curtains instead of walls or doors, and to keep these curtains constantly sprinkled with water?

A. Because curtains are bad conductors of heat, and the rapid evaporation of water reduces the temperature of the room ten or fifteen degrees.

436. Why does watering the streets and roads cool them?

A. Because they part with their heat to promote the evaporation of the water sprinkled on them.

437. Why does a shower of rain cool the air in summer-time?

A. Because the wet earth parts with its heat to promote evaporation; and when the earth is cooled, it cools the air also.

438. Why is linen dried by being exposed to the wind?

A. Because the wind or currents of air accelerate evaporation, by removing the vapor from the surface of the wet linen as fast as it is formed.

439. Why is linen dried sooner in the open air than in a confined room?

A. Because the currents of air cause the particles of vapor to be more rapidly removed from the surface of the linen by evaporation.

440. Why are wet summers generally succeeded by cold winters?

A. Because the great evaporation carried on through the wet summer reduces the temperature of the earth lower than usual, and produces cold.

441. Why are our Eastern and many of our Western States warmer and the winters less severe than formerly?

A. Because they are better drained and better cultivated, and consequently there is less evaporation now than formerly.

442. Why does draining land promote warmth?

A. Because it diminishes evaporation; in consequence of which, less heat is abstracted from the earth.

443. Why does cultivation increase the warmth of a country?

A. 1st. Because hedges and belts of trees are multiplied;

2d. The land is better drained; and,

3d. The vast forests are cut down.

444. Why do hedges and belts of trees promote warmth?

A. Because they retard evaporation, by keeping off the wind.

445. If belts of trees promote warmth, why do forests produce cold?

A. 1st. Because they detain and condense the passing clouds;

2d. They prevent the access of both wind and sun;

3d. The soil of forests is always covered with long damp grass, rotting leaves, and thick brushwood; and,

4th. In every forest there are always many hollows full of stagnant water, which cause evaporation.

446. Why do long grass and rotting leaves promote cold?

A. Because they are always damp; and evaporation, which they promote, is constantly absorbing heat from the earth beneath.

447. Why are France and Germany warmer now than when the vine would not ripen there?

A. Chiefly because their vast forests have been cut down, and the soil is better drained and cultivated.

448. What becomes of the water of ponds in summer-time?

A. Ponds are often left dry in summer-time because their water is evaporated by the air.

449. How is this evaporation produced and carried on?

A. The heat of the air changes the surface

of the water into vapor, which, blending with the air, is soon wafted away; and similar evaporation is repeatedly produced, till the pond is left quite dry.

450. Why are the wheels of some machines kept constantly wet with water?

A. To carry off (by evaporation) the heat which arises from the rapid motion of the wheels.

451. Why is the surface of the ground hardened by the sun?

A. Because the moisture of the ground is exhaled by evaporation; and as the earthy particles are brought closer together, the mass becomes more solid.

452. Show the wisdom of God in this arrangement.

A. If the soil did not become crusty and hard in dry weather, the heat and drought would penetrate the soil and kill both seeds and roots.

453. Why does bread become hard after it has been kept a few days?

A. Because the vapor and gases escape, leaving the solid particles dry, so that they collapse and become more firm and hard.

454. Why are glue, gum, starch, and paste adhesive?

A. Because the water used with them rapidly evaporates, and leaves them solid; and they insinuate themselves so intimately into the pores of the substances with which they come in contact that when the water evaporates the whole is one solid mass.

They lose their adhesiveness when dissolved in water, and therefore must always be suffered to become dry before they will hold with tenacity.

455. Why is tea cooled faster in a saucer than in a cup?

A. Because evaporation is increased by increasing the surface; and as tea in a saucer presents a larger surface to the air, its heat is more rapidly carried off by evaporation.

It is also cooled by convection.

456. Why is not the vapor of the sea salt?

A. Because the salt is always left behind in the process of evaporation.

457. What is that white crust which appears in hot weather upon clothes wetted with sea-water?

A. The salt of the water, left on the clothes by evaporation.

458. Why does this white crust always disappear in wet weather?

A. Because the moisture of the air dissolves the salt; in consequence of which, it is no longer visible.

459. Why should not persons who take violent exercise wear very thick clothing?

A. Because it prevents the perspiration from evaporating. When the heat of the body is increased by exercise, perspiration reduces the heat, by evaporation, to a healthy standard:

as thick clothing prevents this evaporation, it is injurious to health.

460. Why do day-laborers usually wear flannel next their body, even in hot weather?

A. Because exercise promotes perspiration; and as flannel is a bad conductor of heat, it prevents the evaporation of the moisture from chilling the body and reducing its heat below the healthy standard.

461. Why will not lucifer-matches ignite if they are damp?

A. 1st. Because the cold produced by the evaporation of the water neutralizes the heat produced by the friction of the match across the bottom of the lucifer-box; and,

2d. Because the damp prevents the free accession of oxygen to the match, without which it cannot burn.

462. Why does water in a very exposed place freeze more rapidly than that which is under cover or in a place less exposed?

A. 1st. Because evaporation goes on more rapidly when water is exposed, and carries away heat from the general mass; and,

2d. Any covering will radiate heat into the water below, and prevent the mass from cooling down to the requisite temperature to cause congelation.

463. Why does paint often blister from heat?

A. Because the heat, penetrating through

paint, extracts some little moisture from the wood and turns it into vapor, or steam: as this vapor requires room, it throws up blisters in the paint to make room for its expanded bulk.

464. Why are flowers more fragrant in damp weather?

A. Because the volatile particles which constitute the perfume of the flowers are prevented, by the vapor of the air, from circulating freely through the surrounding atmosphere.

Many of the essential oils, and other volatile substances which produce odors in plants, require the presence of much moisture for their perfect development.

§ IV.—VAPORIZATION.

465. What is meant by vaporization?

A. The conversion of a liquid into vapor by boiling.

466. Explain the difference between evaporation and vaporization.

A. Evaporation is effected by exposure to the air without boiling, whilst vaporization requires the air of sufficient heat to produce ebullition.

"Ebullition," from the Latin *ebullio*, to boil.

467. Why does hot iron make a hissing noise when plunged into water?

A. Because the hot iron converts into steam the particles of water which come in immediate contact with it; and, as the steam flies upward, it passes by other particles of water not yet vaporized: the collision produces very rapid vibrations in the air, and a hissing noise is the result.

468. Why does water make a hissing noise when it is poured on fire?

A. Because the part which comes in contact with the fire is immediately converted into steam, and, as it flies upward, meets other particles of water not yet vaporized: the collision produces very rapid vibrations in the air, and a hissing noise is the result.

469. Why is water converted into steam by the heat of the fire?

A. Because, when the heat of the fire enters the water, it separates its globules into very minute particles, which, being lighter than air, fly off from the surface in the form of steam.

470. Why does a drop of water sometimes roll along a piece of hot iron without leaving the least trace?

A. Because the bottom of the drop is turned into vapor, which buoys the drop up, without allowing it to touch the iron.

471. Why does it roll?

A. Because the current of air which is always passing over a heated surface drives it along.

472. Why does a laundress put a little saliva on a flat-iron to know if it be hot enough?

A. Because, when the saliva sticks to the

iron and is evaporated, she knows it is not sufficiently hot; but when it runs along the iron, it is.

473. Why is the flat-iron hotter if the saliva runs along it than if it adheres till it is evaporated?

A. Because, when the saliva runs along the iron, the heat is sufficient to convert the bottom of the drop into vapor; but if the saliva will not roll, the iron is not sufficiently hot to convert the bottom of the drop into vapor.

474. By wetting the hand, it may be safely thrust through a stream of molten (that is, red-hot) iron: explain this.

A. The moisture of the hand is converted into steam by the heat of the iron: this envelop of steam completely shields the hand from the injurious effect of the molten metal, by preventing the iron from coming in contact with the skin.

§ V.—LIQUEFACTION.

475. What is meant by liquefaction?

A. The state of being melted, as ice is melted by the heat of the sun.

When metals are melted, they are said to be fused.

476. Why is ice melted by the heat of the sun?

A. Because, when the heat of the sun enters the solid ice, it forces its particles asunder, till their attraction of cohesion is sufficiently overcome to convert the solid ice into a liquid.

477. The temperature of ice is 32°: if you pour just enough boiling water over the ice to melt it, will the temperature of the water be increased?

A. No: the heat of the boiling water is consumed in melting the ice; but pour boiling water on ice-cold water, and the temperature is immediately increased.

478. Why does wax become soft before it turns liquid?

A. Because it absorbs heat sufficient to loosen the contact of its particles before it has absorbed sufficient to liquefy the mass.

479. Why are metals melted by the heat of fire?

A. Because, when the heat of the fire enters the solid metal, it forces its particles asunder, till their attraction of cohesion is sufficiently overcome to convert the solid metal into a liquid.

480. Why does not wood melt, like metal?

A. Because the heat of the fire decomposes the wood into gas, smoke, and ashes, and the different parts separate from each other.

481. Why does salt crackle when thrown into the fire?

A. Salt contains water; and the crackling of the salt is owing to the sudden conversion of this water into steam.

SECTION IV.—RADIATION.

482. What is meant by radiation?

A. Radiation means the emission of rays. Thus, the sun radiates both light and heat; that is, it emits rays of light and heat in all directions.

483. When is heat radiated from one body to another?

A. When the two bodies are separated by a non-conducting medium: thus, the sun radiates heat toward the earth, because the air (which is a very bad conductor) comes between.

484. On what does radiation depend?

A. On the roughness of the radiating surface: thus, if metal be scratched, its radiating power is increased, because the heat has more points to escape from.

485. Does a fire radiate heat?

A. Yes; and because burning fuel emits rays of heat, therefore we feel warm when we stand before a fire.

486. Why does our face feel uncomfortably hot when we approach a fire?

A. Because the fire radiates heat upon the face, which, not being covered, feels the effect immediately.

487. Why does the fire heat the face more than it does the rest of the body?

A. Because the rest of the body is covered

with clothing, which, being a bad conductor of heat, prevents the same sudden and rapid transmission of heat to the skin.

488. Do those substances which radiate heat absorb heat also?

A. Yes: those substances which radiate most also absorb most heat, and those which radiate least also absorb least heat.

489. Does any thing else radiate heat besides the sun and fire?

A. Yes: all things radiate heat in some measure, but not equally well.

490. What things radiate heat the next best to the sun and fire?

A. All dull and dark substances are good radiators of heat, but all light and polished substances are bad radiators.

491. What is meant by being a "bad radiator of heat"?

A. To radiate heat is to throw off heat by rays, as the sun: a polished tin pan does not throw off the heat of boiling water from its surface, but retains it.

492. Why is a tin pan filled with hot water employed as a foot-warmer?

A. Because polished tin (being a bad radiator of heat) keeps hot a very long time, and warms the feet resting upon it.

493. Why would the tin foot-warmer get cold sooner if the polish were injured?

A. Because polished tin throws off its heat very slowly; but dull, scratched, painted, or dirty tin throws off its heat very quickly.

494. Why does snow at the foot of a hedge or wall melt sooner than that in an open field?

A. Because the hedge or wall radiates heat into the snow beneath, which melts it.

495. How is hot iron cooled by radiation?

A. While its heat is being carried off by "convection," the hot iron throws off heat on all sides by radiation also.

496. Why should the flues connected with stoves, &c. be always blackened with black-lead?

A. In order that the heat of the flue may be more readily diffused throughout the room. Black-lead radiates heat more freely than any other known substance.

In heating a room with steam, black pipes tend to cool the hot vapor.

497. Why does a polished metal teapot make better tea than a black earthen one?

A. Because polished metal (being a very bad radiator of heat) keeps the water hot much longer; and the hotter the water is, the better it "draws" the tea.

498. Why will not a dull black teapot make good tea?

A. Because the heat of the water flies off so quickly through the dull black surface of the teapot that the water is very rapidly cooled, and cannot "draw" the tea.

499. Do not the poorer classes generally prefer the little black earthen teapot to the bright metal one?

A. Yes; because they set it near the fire "to draw;" in which case the little black teapot will make the best tea.

500. Why will a black teapot make better tea than a bright metal one if it be set near the fire to draw?

A. Because the black teapot will absorb heat plentifully from the fire, and keep the water hot; whereas a bright metal teapot set near the fire would throw off the heat by reflection.

501. Then sometimes a black earthen teapot is the best, and sometimes a bright metal one?

A. Yes. When a teapot is set on the stove "to draw," black earthen is the best, because it absorbs heat; but when a teapot is not set on the stove, bright metal is the best, because it radiates heat very slowly, and therefore keeps the water hot.

502. Would a metal pot serve to keep water hot if it were dull and dirty?

A. No. It is the bright polish of the metal which makes it a bad radiator: if it were dull, scratched, or dirty, the heat would escape very rapidly.

Water in hot weather is also kept cooler in bright metal than in dull or earthen vessels.

503. Why are dinner-covers made of bright tin or silver?

A. Because light-colored and highly-polished metal is a very bad radiator of heat; and therefore bright tin or silver will not allow the heat of the cooked food to escape through the cover by radiation.

504. Why should a meat-cover be very brightly polished?

A. To prevent the heat of the food from escaping by radiation. If a meat-cover be dull or scratched, it will absorb heat from the food beneath, and, instead of keeping it hot, make it cold.

505. Why is meat very subject to taint on a moonlight night?

A. Because it radiates heat very freely on a bright moonlight night; in consequence of which, it is soon covered with dew, which produces rapid decomposition.

506. How do moonlight nights conduce to the rapid growth of plants?

A. Radiation is carried on very rapidly on bright moonlight nights; in consequence of which, dew is very plentifully deposited on young plants, which conduces much to their growth and vigor.

507. Why is the air resting on the surface of the earth colder than that in the higher regions?

A. Because the earth radiates more heat

than the leaves of lofty trees, and therefore more rapidly condenses and freezes the vapor of the air.

508. Why are shrubs more liable to be frost-bitten than trees?

A. Because they do not rise far above the surface of the earth; and, as the air contiguous to the earth is made colder by radiation than that in the higher regions, the low shrub is often frost-bitten when the lofty tree is uninjured.

SECTION V.—REFLECTION.

509. What is meant by reflecting heat?

A. To reflect heat is to throw it back in rays from the surface of the reflecting body toward the place whence it came.

510. What are the best reflectors of heat?

A. All bright surfaces and light colors.

511. Are good absorbers of heat good reflectors also?

A. No: those things which absorb heat best reflect heat worst, and those which reflect heat worst absorb it best.

512. Why are those things which absorb heat unable to reflect it?

A. Because if a substance sucks in heat like a sponge, it cannot throw it off from its surface; and if a substance throws off heat from its surface, it cannot drink it in.

513. Why do not plate-warmers blister and scorch the wood behind?

A. Because the bright tin front throws the heat of the fire back again, and will not allow it to penetrate to the wood behind.

514. If metal be so excellent a conductor of heat, how can it reflect heat, or throw it off?

A. Polished metal is a conductor of heat only when that heat is communicated by actual contact; but whenever heat falls upon bright metal in rays, it is reflected back again, and the metal remains cool.

515. What is meant by "heat falling upon metal in rays," and not "by contact"?

A. If a piece of metal were thrust into a fire, it would be in actual contact with the fire; but if it were held before a fire, the heat of the fire would fall upon it in rays.

516. What is the use of the tin screen or reflector used in roasting?

A. It throws the heat of the fire back upon the meat, and therefore both assists the process of roasting and helps to keep the kitchen cool.

517. How does a tin reflector tend to keep the kitchen cool?

A. By confining the heat of the fire to the hearth, and preventing its dispersion throughout the kitchen.

518. Why would not the tin reflector do as well if it were painted?

A. Because it would then absorb heat, and

not reflect it at all. A plate-warmer should never be painted, but should be kept very clean, bright, and free from scratches.

519. Why will not a polished tin pan bake bread so well as an iron one?

A. Because the bright metal reflects the heat, and therefore will not brown the crust which surrounds the bottom and sides of the pan; consequently, the top of the bread would be burnt before the bottom and sides of the loaf were brown.

520. How may a new tin pan be made to bake bread as well as an iron one?

A. By holding it for a time over the flame of a candle, until the outside is thoroughly blackened: it would then absorb heat and brown the bread.

521. Why should the top of a kettle be clean and well polished?

A. Because polished metal will not radiate heat; and if the top of the kettle is well polished, the heat is retained and not suffered to escape by radiation.

522. Why will a kettle be slower in boiling if the bottom and sides are clean and bright?

A. Because bright metal does not absorb heat, but reflects it; and, as the heat is thrown off from the surface of bright metal by reflection, a new kettle takes a longer time to boil.

523. Why is light-colored clothing preferable for summer-wear?

A. Because light colors throw off the heat of the sun by reflection, and are very bad absorbents of heat; in consequence of which, they never become so hot from the scorching sun as dark colors do.

524. Why is not light-colored clothing worn in winter?

A. Because light colors will not absorb heat, like black and other dark colors; and therefore white or light-colored dresses are not so warm as dark ones.

525. Why are shoes hotter for being dusty?

A. Because dull, dusty shoes absorb heat from the sun, earth, and air; but shoes brightly polished throw off the heat of the sun by reflection.

SECTION VI.—ABSORPTION.

526. What is the difference between conducting heat and absorbing heat?

A. To conduct heat is to transmit it from one body to another through a conducting medium: to absorb heat is to draw it up, as a sponge sucks up water.

527. Give an example.

A. Black cloth absorbs, but does not conduct, heat: thus, if black cloth be laid in the sun, it will absorb the rays very rapidly;

but, if one end of the black cloth were made hot, it would not conduct the heat to the other end.

528. Are good conductors of heat good absorbers also?

A. No: every good conductor of heat is a bad absorber of it; and no good absorber of heat can be a good conductor.

529. Is iron a good absorber of heat?

A. No: iron is a good conductor, but a very bad absorber, of heat.

530. Why do the fire-irons (which lie upon a fender) remain cold, although they are before a good fire?

A. Because they are bad absorbers of heat; in consequence of which, they remain cold, unless they come in contact with the stove or fire.

531. If a piece of brown paper be submitted to the action of a burning-glass, it will catch fire much sooner than a piece of white paper would: explain the reason.

A. Because white paper reflects the rays of the sun, or throws them back; in consequence of which, it appears more luminous, but is not so much heated as dark brown paper, which absorbs the rays and readily becomes heated to ignition.

Besides, brown paper is of a looser and more combustible fabric than white paper.

532. Why is the temperature of islands more equable than that of continents?

A. Because the water around the island

absorbs the extreme heat of summer, and gives out heat to mitigate the extreme cold of winter.

533. Islands are warmer in winter than continents: explain the reason of this.

A. Unless the sea be frozen, (which is rarely the case,) it is warmer than the frozen land; and the warmth of the sea-air helps to mitigate the intense cold of the land-air.

534. How does the ceaseless change of air tend to decrease the warmth of a naked body?

A. The air which surrounds the body absorbs as much heat from it as it can while it remains in contact: being then blown away, it makes room for a fresh coat of air, which absorbs more heat.

535. Does the air which surrounds a naked body become by contact as warm as the body itself?

A. It would do so if it remained motionless; but, as it is continually changing, it absorbs as much heat as it can in the time, and passes on.

536. Why does fanning the face in summer make it cool?

A. Because the fan puts the air in motion, and makes it pass more rapidly over the face; and, as the temperature of the air is always lower than that of the human face, each puff of air carries off some portion of its heat.

537. Does a fan cool the air?

A. No: it makes the air hotter, by imparting to it the heat out of our face; but it cools our face, by transferring its heat to the air.

538. Does fanning make the air itself cooler?

A. No: fanning makes the air hotter and hotter.

539. How does fanning the face increase the heat of the air?

A. The air absorbs more heat by being driven rapidly over the body: each current becomes heated, and flies off to make way for another cooler current.

540. If fanning makes the air hotter, why can it make a person feel cooler?

A. Because the air absorbs the heat of the face.

541. Why is broth cooled by blowing it?

A. Because the breath causes a rapid current of air to pass over the broth; and, as the air is colder than the broth, it continually absorbs heat from it, and makes it cooler and cooler.

542. Would not the air absorb heat from the broth just as well without blowing?

A. No. Air is a very bad conductor: unless, therefore, the current be rapid, the air nearest the surface of the broth would soon become as hot as the broth itself.

543. Would not hot air part with its heat instantly to the circumjacent air?

A. No, not instantly. Air is so bad a conductor that it parts with its heat very slowly: unless, therefore, the air be kept in continual motion, it will cool the broth very slowly.

544. Why does wind generally feel cool?

A. Because it drives the air more rapidly over our body; and this rapid current of air draws off a large quantity of heat.

545. Why does air absorb heat more quickly by being set in motion?

A. Because air is a bad conductor, and, if at rest, would soon become of the same temperature as our bodies; but every fresh gust of air absorbs a fresh portion of heat; and the more rapid the succession of gusts, the greater will be the quantity of heat absorbed.

546. If the air were hotter than our body, would the wind feel cool?

A. No: the air would feel insufferably hot if it were hotter than our body.

547. Why would the air feel intensely hot if it were warmer than our body?

A. Because it would add to the heat of our body, instead of diminishing it.

548. Is the air ever as hot as the human body?

A. In some climates it is; and, when that is the case, the heat is almost insupportable.

549. Why does a kettle boil faster when the bottom and sides are covered with soot?

A. Because the black soot absorbs heat very quickly from the fire, and the metal conducts it to the water.

550. Why do we wear white linen and a black outer dress if we want to be warm?

A. Because the black outer dress quickly absorbs heat from the sun, and the white linen, being a bad absorbent, abstracts no heat from the warm body.

551. What colors are warmest for dresses?

A. For outside garments, black is the warmest, and then such colors as approach nearest to black, (as dark blue and green.) White is the coldest color for external clothing.

552. How can you prove that dark colors are warmer than light ones?

A. If a piece of black and a piece of white cloth be laid upon snow, in a few hours the black cloth will have melted the snow beneath; whereas the white cloth will have produced little or no effect upon it.

The darker any color is, the warmer it is, because it is a better absorbent of heat. The order may be thus arranged:—1. Black, (warmest of all;) 2. Violet; 3. Indigo; 4. Blue; 5. Green; 6. Red; 7. Yellow; and, 8. White, (coldest of all.)

553. Why are black kid gloves unpleasantly hot for summer-wear?

A. 1st. Because black absorbs the solar heat; and,

2d. Kid will not allow the heat of our hand to escape readily through the glove.

554. Why are Lisle-thread gloves agreeably cool for summer-wear?

A. 1st. Because thread absorbs perspiration; and,

2d. It conducts away the heat of our hot hands.

555. Are Lisle-thread gloves absorbents of heat?

A. No: Lisle-thread gloves are generally of a gray or lilac color, and therefore do not absorb solar heat.

556. Why does hoar-frost remain on tombstones long after it has melted from the grass and gravel-walks of a churchyard?

A. Because tombstones, being white, will not absorb heat, like the darker grass and gravel; in consequence of which, they remain too cold to thaw the frost congealed upon their surface.

557. If black absorbs heat, why have negroes black skins, and not white skins, which would not absorb heat at all?

A. Because black will not blister from the heat of the sun. Although, therefore, the black skin of the negro absorbs heat more plentifully than the white skin of a European, yet the blackness prevents the sun from blistering or scorching it.

558. How is it known that the black color prevents the sun from either blistering or scorching the skin?

A. If you put a white glove on one hand and a black glove on the other when the sun is burning hot, the hand with the white glove will be scorched, but not the other.

559. Which hand will feel the hotter?

A. The hand with the black glove will feel the hotter, but will not be scorched by the sun; whereas the hand with the white glove, though much cooler, will be severely scorched.

560. Why is the skin of a negro never scorched or blistered by the hot sun?

A. Because the black color absorbs the heat, conveys it below the surface of the skin, and converts it into sensible heat and perspiration.

561. Why does the white European skin blister and scorch when exposed to the hot sun?

A. Because white will not absorb heat, and therefore the hot sun rests on the surface of the skin and scorches it.

562. Why is water in hot weather kept cooler in a bright tin vessel than in an earthen one?

A. Because bright metal will not absorb heat from the hot air like an earthen vessel; in consequence of which, the water is kept cooler.

563. In what state should a saucepan be in order that it may boil quickly?

A. All those parts which come in contact with the fire should be covered with soot, or be black, in order to absorb heat; but all the rest of the saucepan should be as bright as possible, to prevent the escape of heat by radiation.

CHAPTER IV.—MECHANICAL ACTION.

SECTION I.—PERCUSSION.

564. How is heat produced by mechanical action?

A. 1. By Percussion; 2. By Friction; and, 3. By Condensation, or Compression.

565. What is meant by percussion?

A. The act of striking; as when a blacksmith strikes a piece of iron on his anvil with his hammer.

566. Why does striking iron make it red-hot?

A. Because it condenses the particles of the metal, and makes the latent heat sensible.

567. Does cold iron contain heat?

A. Yes: every thing contains heat; but when a thing feels cold, its heat is latent.

568. What is meant by latent heat?

A. Heat not perceptible to our feelings. When any thing contains heat without feeling the hotter for it, that heat is called "latent heat."

569. Does cold iron contain latent heat?

A. Yes; and when a blacksmith compresses the particles of iron by his hammer, he brings out latent heat, and this makes the iron red-hot.

570. How did blacksmiths light their matches before the general use of lucifers?

A. They used to place a soft iron nail upon their anvil, strike it two or three times with a hammer, and the point became sufficiently hot to light a brimstone match.

571. How can a nail beaten by a hammer ignite a brimstone match?

A. The particles of the nail, being compressed by the hammer, can no longer contain so much heat in a latent state as they did before: some of it, therefore, becomes sensible, and increases the temperature of the iron.

572. Why does striking a flint against a piece of steel produce a spark?

A. Because it compresses those parts of the flint and steel which strike together; in consequence of which, some of their latent heat is disturbed, and exhibits itself in a spark.

573. How does this development of heat produce a spark and set tinder on fire?

A. A very small fragment either of the

steel or flint is knocked off red-hot, and sets fire to the tinder on which it falls.

574. Why is it needful to keep blowing the tinder with the breath?

A. In order that the increased supply of air may furnish the tinder with more oxygen to assist combustion.

575. Why do horses sometimes strike fire with their feet?

A. Because, when their iron shoes strike against the flint-stones of the road, very small fragments either of the shoes or stones are knocked off red-hot.

576. What makes these fragments red-hot?

A. The percussion condenses the part struck; in consequence of which, some of its latent heat is rendered sensible, and exhibits itself in these red-hot fragments.

SECTION II.—FRICTION.

577. What is meant by friction?

A. The act of rubbing two things together; as the Indians rub two pieces of wood together to produce fire.

578. How do the Indians produce fire by merely rubbing two pieces of wood together?

A. They take a piece of dry hard wood sharpened to a point, which they rub quickly up and down a flat piece of soft wood till a groove is made; and the dust collected in this groove catches fire.

579. Why does the dust of the wood catch fire by rubbing?

A. Because latent heat is developed from the wood by friction.

The best woods for this purpose are boxwood against mulberry, or laurel against poplar or ivy.

580. Do not carriage-wheels sometimes catch fire?

A. Yes; when the wheels are dry, or fit too tightly, or revolve very rapidly.

581. Why do wheels catch fire in such cases?

A. Because the friction of the wheels against the axle-tree disturbs their latent heat, and produces ignition.

582. What is the use of greasing cart-wheels?

A. Grease lessens the friction; and because there is less friction the latent heat of the wheels is less disturbed.

583. Why does rubbing our hands and faces make them feel warm?

A. 1st. Because friction excites the latent heat of our hands and faces, and makes it sensible to our feeling; and,

2d. The blood is made to circulate more quickly; in consequence of which, the quantity of heat left in its passage is increased.

584. When a man has been almost drowned, why is suspended animation restored by rubbing?

A. 1st. Because friction excites the latent heat of the half-inanimate body; and,

2d. It makes the blood circulate more quickly, which increases the animal heat.

585. Why do two pieces of ice rubbed together melt?

A. Ice contains 140° of latent heat; and when two pieces are rubbed together some of this latent heat is made sensible, and melts the ice.

586. Why do carpenters' tools (such as gimlets, saws, files, &c.) become hot when used?

A. Because the friction of the tools against the wood disturbs its latent heat, and makes it sensible.

587. Give an illustration of this.

A. When a cannon is bored, the borers become so intensely hot from friction that they would blister the hands if touched.

588. Why do these borers become intensely hot?

A. Because the friction of the borers against the metal is so great that it sets free a large quantity of latent heat.

589. Why does a wet sponge clean a slate?

A. Because the water holds in solution the pencil-marks made on the slate, and the mechanical friction employed in wiping the slate detaches the particles of pencil-dust.

SECTION III.—CONDENSATION OR COMPRESSION.

590. What is meant by compression?

A. The act of bringing parts nearer together, as a sponge is compressed by being squeezed in the hand.

The reduction of matter into a smaller compass by an external or mechanical force is called Compression.

The reduction of matter into a smaller compass by some internal action (as by the escape of caloric) is called Condensation.

591. Cannot heat be evolved from common air merely by compression?

A. Yes: if a piece of tinder be placed at the bottom of a glass tube, and the air in the tube compressed by a piston, the tinder will catch fire.

In a common syringe or squirt, the rod (which holds the sucker and is forced up and down) is called "the piston."

592. Why will the tinder catch fire?

A. Because the air is compressed; and its latent heat, being liberated, sets fire to the tinder at the bottom of the tube.

593. When an air-gun is discharged in the dark, why is the discharge accompanied with a slight flash?

A. Because the air is very rapidly condensed, and its latent heat developed in a flash of light.

If a glass lens be fixed in the copper ball where the air of the gun is condensed, a flash of light may be distinctly discerned at the stroke of the piston.

594. Why does the hole made by a shot or cannon-ball in a wall or timber look as if it were burnt?

A. Because the shot or cannon-ball was so

heated by the discharge as actually to scorch the material into which it penetrated.

595. Why are shot and cannon-balls heated by being discharged from a gun or cannon?

A. Because the air is so rapidly condensed when the discharge is made that sufficient latent heat is developed to make the shot or balls hot.

PART II.

NON-METALLIC ELEMENTS.

596. WHAT is meant by non-metallic elements?

A. Those elementary bodies which do not belong to the class of metals.

Elementary bodies are those which have never been decomposed; that is, do not appear to be composed of any compounds, but are pure substances in themselves. At present there are reckoned fifteen non-metallic elementary substances and forty-seven which belong to the class of metals.

CHAPTER I.—OXYGEN AND OXIDES.

597. WHAT is the difference between oxygen and an oxide?

A. Oxygen is a gas, and an oxide is a compound formed by the union of oxygen with other bodies.

SECTION I.—OXYGEN.

598. What is oxygen?

A. A gaseous body, which is found largely diffused throughout all nature, being an important element of air and water, rocks, earths, minerals, &c.

The name *gas* is given to any fluid capable of existing in an aeriform state under ordinary atmospheric pressure and temperature.

599. When, and by whom, was oxygen discovered?

A. It was discovered in 1774, by Scheele, in Sweden, and Dr. Priestley, in England, independent of each other. They described it under different names.

600. Who gave it the name of oxygen? and what is the signification of the word?

A. Lavoisier gave it the name, which is derived from two Greek words: *οξυς*, (oxus,) *an acid*, and *γεννaω*, (gennao,) *I produce*.

This name was given to it because it was then thought to be the sole acidifying principle. Modern discoveries have rectified this error, by proving the existence of acids in the composition of which there is no oxygen.

601. Is oxygen ever found in a liquid or solid state?

A. No: when pure, it is known only in the gaseous state: all efforts to reduce it to a liquid or solid condition by cold or pressure have completely failed.

602. Has oxygen any taste or smell?

A. It is, when pure, colorless, tasteless, and inodorous.

603. Of what use is oxygen in the atmosphere?

A. It sustains animal life and supports combustion.

Oxygen gas forms one-fifth of the bulk of our atmosphere.

604. Why do we feel braced and light-hearted on a fine spring or frosty morning?

A. 1st. Because there is more oxygen in the air on a fine spring or frosty morning than there is on a wet day; and,

2d. A brisk and frosty air has a tendency to brace the nervous system.

605. Is oxygen necessary to the growth of plants?

A. It is: in the process of germination oxygen is consumed. The larger the quantity of oxygen that surrounds a germinating seed, the quicker will be its growth.

606. What is meant when it is said that the oxygen of the air "supports combustion"?

A. It means that the oxygen of the air makes fuel burn.

607. How does the oxygen of the air make fuel burn?

A. The fuel is decomposed by heat into hydrogen and carbon; and these elements, combining with the oxygen of the air, produce combustion.

608. What are the uses of the oxygen of the air?

A. To support combustion and sustain animal and vegetable life.

609. What is meant when it is said that oxygen "sustains life"?

A. It means, if a person could not inhale oxygen, he would die.

610. What good does this inspiration of oxygen do?

A. 1st. It gives vitality to the blood; and,

2d. It is the cause of animal heat.

Whenever oxygen combines very rapidly with other elementary bodies, light and heat are evolved.

SECTION II.—OXIDES.

611. What are oxides?

A. The compounds formed by the union of oxygen with other bodies bear the general name of oxides.

612. What is rust?

A. The oxidation of iron in moist air.

"Oxidation," impregnation with oxygen.

613. Why does iron rust?

A. Because water is decomposed when it comes in contact with the surface of iron: and the oxygen of the water, combining with iron, produces an oxide, which is generally called rust.

Water is composed of oxygen and hydrogen in the following proportions: 8 pounds of oxygen and 1 pound of hydrogen = 9 pounds of water.

614. Why does air rust iron?

A. Because the oxygen of the air combines with the surface of the metal and produces oxide of iron, which is generally called "rust."

An oxide of iron, copper, &c. is oxygen in combination with iron, copper, &c.

615. Does iron rust in dry air?

A. No: iron undergoes no change in dry air.

616. Why does hot iron scale and peel off when struck with a hammer?

A. Because the oxygen of the air very

readily unites with the surface of the hot iron, and forms a metallic oxide, (or rust,) which scales off when struck with a hammer.

617. Why do stoves and fire-irons become rusty in rooms which are not occupied?

A. Because the air is damp; and moist air oxidizes iron and steel.

"Oxidizes;" that is, rusts.

618. In what part of the year is it most difficult to keep stoves and fire-irons bright?

A. In autumn and winter, because in those seasons the air contains more moisture.

619. Why is it more difficult to keep stoves and fire-irons bright in autumn and winter than in spring and summer?

A. Because the capacity of the air for holding water is constantly on the decrease after the summer is over; in consequence of which, vapor is deposited on every thing with which the air comes in contact.

620. Why does greasing iron prevent its becoming rusty?

A. Because grease prevents the humidity of the air from coming in contact with the surface of the iron.

621. Why does painting iron prevent it from rusting?

A. Because paint prevents the moist air from coming in contact with the iron.

622. Why will bright iron lose its polish by being put into a fire?

A. Because the oxygen of the air very readily unites with the surface of hot iron, and forms a metallic oxide, which displays itself, in this case, by a dull leaden color, instead of a red rust.

623. Why do not stoves rust so frequently as pokers and tongs?

A. Because stoves are generally covered with plumbago, or black-lead.

624. What is plumbago, or black-lead?

A. A mixture of charcoal and iron.

Plumbago, strictly speaking, is a chemical union of carbon and iron, in the following proportions:—91 parts carbon and 9 iron. But the black-lead sold in shops is a mixture of charcoal and iron-filings.

A most excellent varnish to prevent rust is made of one pint of fat-oil varnish, mixed with five pints of highly-rectified spirits of turpentine, rubbed on the iron or steel with a piece of sponge. This varnish may be applied to bright stoves, and even mathematical instruments, without injuring their delicate polish.

625. Why does ornamental steel of a purple or lilac color rust more readily than polished white steel?

A. Because the lilac tinge is produced by partial oxidation; and the process which forms rust has, therefore, already commenced.

626. How can lilac steel be kept free from rust?

A. By keeping it in a very dry place.

627. If dry air contains oxygen, why does it not rust iron as well as moist air?

A. Because moisture is always needed in order to bring into action the affinity of oxygen for steel.

628. When a black subsoil is dug or ploughed up, it turns of a reddish-brown color after a short time: why is this?

A. Because the soil contained a certain compound of iron, called the "protoxide," which is black: this protoxide of iron, absorbing more oxygen from the moist air, is converted into another compound, called the "peroxide of iron," which is of a reddish, rusty color.

There are two oxides of iron,—one containing more oxygen than the other. The protoxide, which contains the least oxygen, is black; the peroxide, which contains the most oxygen, is red.

629. Do any other metals besides iron combine rapidly with oxygen?

A. Yes; copper, lead, mercury, and even silver to some extent.

630. Why does copper tarnish?

A. The tarnish of copper is caused by its oxidation; that is, the oxygen of the air combines with the surface of the copper and covers it with a dark tarnish.

631. Why does lead become darker by being exposed to the air?

A. Because the vapor of the air combines with the lead, and oxidizes its surface; but, instead of becoming rusty, the surface assumes a darker hue.

632. Why does lead lose its brightness and become dull by being exposed to the air?

A. The dulness of the lead is caused by the presence of a carbonate of the oxide. When the oxide is formed, it attracts carbonic acid from the air, and, combining with it, produces a carbonate, which gives the dull tint to old lead.

633. Why is it difficult to keep silver bright?

A. Because the vapor of the air oxidizes its surface, and tarnishes it.

634. Why does salt turn silver black?

A. Because it precipitates an oxide of silver on the surface of the spoon, the color of which is black.

"Marking-ink" is made of soda and the nitrate of silver,—the black mark being due to the oxide precipitated on the cloth.

635. How can the black stain of silver made by salt be removed?

A. By washing the silver in hartshorn or common ammonia: by this means the oxide will be re-dissolved, and the blackness entirely disappear.

636. Why do silver teapots and spoons tarnish more quickly than pure silver?

A. Because alloy of some baser metal is used, to make them more hard and lasting; and this alloy oxidizes more quickly than silver itself.

637. Why does German silver turn a dingy yellow in a few hours?

A. Because German silver has a great affinity for oxygen, and shows its oxidation by a sickly yellow tarnish, instead of rust.

638. If quicksilver (or mercury) will tarnish like copper and lead, why does it preserve its brilliancy in barometers and thermometers?

A. Because the air is excluded; and no moisture can come in contact with it to oxidize (or tarnish) it.

639. Is gold affected by the atmosphere?

A. Not readily: gold will never combine with oxygen of itself, (that is, without aid.)

640. Which of the metals is capable of resisting oxidation altogether?

A. Plat'inum; in consequence of which, the graduated arcs of delicate "instruments for observation" are made of platinum in preference to any other metal, and because it never rusts it is used for points to lightning-rods.

641. Why is platinum used for the graduated arcs of delicate mathematical instruments, rather than any other metal?

A. Because it will never oxidize, but retains its bright surface in all weathers, free from rust and tarnish.

642. For what other scientific purpose is platinum now used?

A. For crucibles in which acids are employed, and for galvanic batteries.

643. Why are crucibles in which acids are employed made of platinum?

A. Because the acid would act upon other

metals, or upon glass, and prevent the experimenter's success.

644. Before platinum was discovered, which of the metals was employed for the same purpose?

A. Gold.

Platinum, (a white metal,) so called from "plata," the Spanish word for silver. It was introduced from South America into England by Mr. Wood, A.D. 1749.

645. Which of the metals have the greatest affinity for oxygen?

A. Those called potassium and sodium.

Potas'sium and so'dium derive their names from potash and soda. Potas'sa is the oxide of potassium: soda is the oxide of sodium.

646. How is the affinity of potassium and sodium for oxygen shown?

A. They decompose water as soon as they are brought into contact with it.

647. What effect has potassium on water?

A. It catches fire the moment it is thrown into water, and burns with a vivid flame which is still further increased by the combustion of hydrogen, separated from the water.

Water is composed of oxygen and hydrogen; and potassium separates the two gases.

648. What effect has sodium on water?

A. It does not take fire as potassium does, but undergoes very rapid oxidation.

CHAPTER II.—HYDROGEN AND WATER.

649. WHAT is the distinction between hydrogen and water?

A. Hydrogen is an inflammable gas; and water is composed of hydrogen and oxygen.

SECTION I.—HYDROGEN.

650. What is hydrogen?

A. An inflammable gas. The gas used in our streets is hydrogen driven out of coal by heat. Hydrogen is the principal ingredient of water.

Coal-gas (properly speaking) is carburetted hydrogen; that is, carbon and hydrogen.
Hydrogen derives its name from two Greek words, ὑδωρ, (udor,) *water*, and γεννάω, (gennao,) *I produce.*

651. When was hydrogen gas discovered?

A. It was discovered in the sixteenth century, by Paracelsus, a Swiss philosopher, but was first investigated by Henry Cavendish in the year 1781.

652. Has hydrogen any taste or color?

A. It has, when pure, neither taste, color, nor smell. When it has any odor, it arises from impurities.

653. Does hydrogen support life?

A. No: it destroys it, rather by excluding oxygen than by its own injurious effects.

654. Does hydrogen gas, like oxygen, support combustion?

A. No: it is highly combustible, but does not support combustion. Uniting with oxygen it forms water.

655. What are the peculiar characteristics of hydrogen gas?

A. 1st. It is the lightest of all known substances;

2d. It will burn with a very pale flame, forming water by uniting with the oxygen of the air;

3d. A lighted candle immersed in this gas will be instantly extinguished.*

656. For what uses is hydrogen gas employed?

A. 1st. Owing to its lightness, it is used to inflate balloons; and,

2d. Burned with oxygen it is used in the hydrogen blowpipe.

657. What is a blowpipe?

A. A tube, usually bent near the end, terminated with a finely-pointed nozzle, for

---

* Hydrogen gas may be made thus:—Put some pieces of zinc or iron filings into a glass; pour over them a little sulphuric acid (vitriol) diluted with twice the quantity of water; then cover the glass over for a few minutes, and hydrogen gas will be given off.

EXPERIMENTS.—If a flame be put into the glass, an explosion will take place.

If the experiment be tried in a phial which has a piece of tobacco-pipe run through the cork, and a light be held a few moments to the top of the pipe, a flame will be made.

If a balloon be held over the phial, so that the gas can inflate it, the balloon will ascend in a very few minutes.

blowing through the flame of a lamp or gas-jet, and producing thereby a small conical flame possessing very intense heat.

658. Describe the hydrogen blowpipe.

A. A mixture of oxygen and hydrogen, when ignited, produces an intense heat, and constitutes the hydrogen blowpipe.

659. Who invented the hydrogen blowpipe?

A. Dr. Hare, of Philadelphia.

660. Describe the Drummond light.

A. It is the ignited flame of a mixture of oxygen and hydrogen, projected against lime; the lime becomes intensely luminous, and forms the well-known Drummond light.

SECTION II.—WATER.

661. What is water?

A. Water is a fluid, composed of oxygen and hydrogen, in the proportion of eight parts of oxygen to one part of hydrogen.

662. Why is water fluid?

A. Because its particles are kept separate by latent heat: when a certain quantity of this latent heat is driven out, water becomes solid, and is called ice.

By increasing its latent heat the particles of water are again subdivided into invisible steam.

663. Is water generally diffused throughout organic bodies?

A. It is. The sea covers nearly three-fourths of the earth's surface; the air is impregnated with water in the form of vapor; and water enters into the composition of all plants, animals, and even of some minerals.

664. Has pure water any taste or smell?

A. It has neither; and when viewed in small quantities it is colorless, but in a large mass it has a bluish tint.

665. What peculiar properties belong to water?

A. It is a conductor of electricity, and possesses the power of dissolving many substances.

666. Is water ever found in a state of perfect purity?

A. No: even rain and snow contain the various gases of the atmosphere.

667. What is meant by hard water?

A. Water in which the salts of lime and other substances have been dissolved.

668. Why is pump-water called hard water?

A. Because it is laden with foreign matters, and will not readily dissolve substances immersed in it.

669. What makes pump-water hard?

A. When it filters through the earth, it becomes impregnated with sulphate of lime, and many other impurities from the earths and minerals with which it comes in contact.

670. What is the cause of mineral springs?

A. When water trickles through the ground, it dissolves some of the substances with which it comes in contact: if these substances are metallic, the water will partake of their mineral character.

Some water is imbued with lime, some with salt, &c. &c.

671. Why is it difficult to wash the hands clean with hard water?

A. Because the soda of the soap combines with the sulphuric acid of the hard water,—and the oil of the soap with the lime,—and floats in flakes on the top of the water.

Sulphate of lime consists of sulphuric acid and lime.

672. Why is it difficult to wash in salt water?

A. Because it contains muriatic acid; and the soda of soap combines with the muriatic acid of the salt water, and produces a cloudiness.

673. Does the clearness of water imply purity?

A. It does not: water may be very clear and yet very impure and unwholesome. For example, the well-water in cities, though apparently pure, is unfit for drinking.

674. Cannot the purity of water be restored by filtering it?

A. It cannot: no ordinary filtration can remove dissolved impurities.

675. What are the qualifications of good drinking-water?

A. It should be clear, and when poured into a tumbler it should sparkle with the gases rising through it.

676. What gases rise through pure water?

A. Oxygen and carbonic acid gas give to water its refreshing and thirst-quenching properties.

677. Why is water which has stood long in a warm room disagreeable to the taste?

A. Because the gases have escaped from it, which renders it flat and stale. Sunlight will have the same effect as a warm room.

678. What is another test of good water?

A. Water which cattle drink most readily is clear, soft, and soap forms with it a lather freely.

679. Why is soft water preferable to hard water for drinking?

A. If we drink hard water, it not only lies heavily on the stomach, but has to be freed from its impurities by distillation through the capillaries, before the blood can receive it.

680. What is the cause of petrifactions?

A. While water runs under ground, its impurities are held in solution by the presence of carbonic acid; but when the stream reaches the open air its carbonic acid escapes, and these impurities are precipitated on various substances lying in the course of the stream.

These impurities are especially carbonate of lime and iron.

681. Why does water clean dirty linen?

A. Because it dissolves the stains, as it would dissolve salt.

682. Why does soap greatly increase the cleansing power of water?

A. Because many stains are of a greasy nature; and soap has the power of uniting with greasy matters and rendering them soluble in water.

683. Why is rain-water soft?

A. Because it is not impregnated with earths and minerals.

684. Why is it more easy to wash with soft water than with hard?

A. Because soft water unites freely with soap, and dissolves it, instead of decomposing it, as hard water does.

685. Why do wood-ashes make hard water soft?

A. 1st. Because the carbonic acid of wood-ashes combines with the sulphate of lime in the hard water, and converts it into chalk; and,

2d. Wood-ashes convert some of the soluble salts of water into insoluble, and throw them down as a sediment; in consequence of which, the water remains more pure.

686. Why has rain-water an unpleasant smell when it is collected in a tub or tank?

A. Because it is impregnated with decomposed organic matters washed from roofs, trees, or the casks in which it is collected.

687. Why does melted sugar or salt give a flavor to water?

A. Because the sugar or salt, being disunited into very minute particles, floats about the water, and mixes with every part.

688. Why does hot water melt sugar and salt quicker than cold water?

A. Because the heat, entering the pores of the sugar or salt, opens a passage for the water.

689. Why is sea-water brackish?

A. 1st. Because the sea contains mines of salt at the bottom of its bed;

2d. It is impregnated with bituminous matter, which is brackish; and,

3d. It contains many putrid substances of a brackish nature.

690. The water at the equator contains more salt than sea-water in higher latitudes. Explain this.

A. Owing to the greater heat of the sun near the equator, the evaporation is greater; and when sea-water is evaporated the salt is left behind.

691. Why is not rain-water salt, although most of it is evaporated from the sea?

A. Because salt will not evaporate; and, therefore, when sea-water is turned into vapor its salt is left behind.

692. Why does running water oscillate and whirl in its current?

A. 1st. Because it impinges against its banks, and is perpetually diverted from its forward motion; and,

2d. Because a river at its centre flows faster than at its sides.

693. Why does a river flow more tardily at its sides than at its centre?

A. Because it rubs or impinges against its banks, and is delayed in its current by this friction.

CHAPTER III.—NITROGEN AND AIR.

SECTION I.—NITROGEN.

694. WHAT is nitrogen?

A. An invisible gas which abounds in animal and vegetable substances. The following are its peculiar characteristics:—

1st. It will not burn;

2d. An animal cannot live in it;

3d. It is the principal ingredient in common air.*

Nearly four gallons out of every five of air are nitrogen gas.

"Nitrogen," that is, generator of nitre; also called *azote*, from the Greek words *a*, (a,) *privative*, or *to deprive of*, and ζωη, (zoe,) *life*.

695. When, and by whom, was nitrogen discovered?

A. In the year 1772, by Rutherford.

696. Is nitrogen capable of sustaining combustion?

A. No: nitrogen, like hydrogen, is incapable of sustaining combustion or animal existence, although it has no positive poisonous properties.

697. Has nitrogen any color?

A. No: nitrogen has neither color, taste, nor smell.

698. What is supposed to be one of the uses of nitrogen?

A. We are doubtless unacquainted with many of its uses; but its presence in the atmosphere counteracts the evil effects of pure oxygen upon the human system.

699. What evil effect would ensue if oxygen were inhaled by a human being or animal for any length of time?

A. It would cause inflammation, and finally death.

---

* Nitrogen gas may easily be obtained thus:—Put a piece of burning phosphorus on a little stand in a plate of water, and cover a bell-glass over it. (Be sure the edge of the glass stands in the water.) In a few minutes the oxygen of the air will be taken up by the burning phosphorus, and nitrogen alone will be left in the bell-glass.

The white fume which will arise and be absorbed by the water in this experiment is phosphoric acid,—that is, phosphorus combined with the oxygen of the air.

SECTION II.—AIR.

700. What are the elements of atmospheric air?

A. Oxygen and nitrogen mixed together in the following proportions: about four gallons of nitrogen and one of oxygen will make five gallons of common air.

701. Is not the air we breathe almost wholly composed of nitrogen?

A. It is: nearly four-fifths of the air is nitrogen, and the other one-fifth is oxygen.

But nitrogen is a gas which cannot support animal life; whereas the air or atmosphere which we breathe is a thin, transparent fluid which surrounds the earth, and supports animal life by respiration.

702. Why is there so much nitrogen in the air?

A. In order to dilute the oxygen. If the oxygen were not thus diluted, fires would burn out too quickly, and life would be too rapidly exhausted.

703. What is meant by diffusion?

A. That process by which gases and liquids, when in contact, pass through each other and intermingle.

704. What part does this law of diffusion perform in nature?

A. The accumulation of gases unfit for animal and vegetable life is, by diffusion, silently dispersed, and the air is kept comparatively pure.

705. If it were not for the law of diffusion, what would occur on lighting the first fire?

A. The oxygen of the air would separate from the nitrogen, and a universal conflagration would ensue.

706. What effect has the law of the diffusion of gases upon vegetation?

A. Carbonic acid, which is necessary to vegetable life, is by this provision diffused throughout all the particles of air.

707. What effect has the diffusion of gases upon respiration?

A. The minute cells of the lungs would not be freed from the carbonic acid which they contain, and death must ensue.

708. Is air material? that is, is it composed of matter?

A. It is. We do not see the air in the room, because it is transparent; but we feel it when we run or fan ourselves, and we hear through the medium of the air: therefore it is material, or composed of matter; for matter is that which is perceived by our senses.

709. Is air invisible?

A. No: for, although we cannot perceive it immediately around us, when we look up into the firmament illuminated by the sun, the air appears of a beautiful azure. This is the mass of the atmosphere. Distant mountains appear of a blue color, owing to our viewing them through the atmosphere.

710. Why can we not see the air immediately around us of the same beautiful azure?

A. So small a portion of air reflects little or no color, while a mass would be capable of reflecting a beautiful tint. So it is with a small quantity of sea-water dipped up in a glass: it would appear perfectly colorless: yet the deepest part of the ocean appears of a dark green, approaching to a black.

Sir David Brewster has shown that the blue color of the atmosphere is due to reflected light. It absorbs the yellow and red rays and reflects the blue.

CHAPTER IV.—CARBON.

711. What is carbon?

A. A solid substance generally of a dark or black color, well known under the forms of charcoal, lamp-black, soot, &c.

712. Carbon occurs in nature crystallized in two forms: what are they?

A. The Diamond and Graphite.

Graphite, from the Greek γραφειν, (graphein,) *to write.* It is also known by the name of plumbago, or black-lead, and is used for making pencils for drawing and writing.

713. Why does Indian-rubber erase pencil-marks from paper?

A. Because Indian-rubber contains a very large quantity of carbon. Black-lead is carbon and iron.

Now, the carbon of the Indian-rubber has so great an attraction for the black-lead that it takes up the loose traces of it left on paper by the pencil.

Caoutchouc, or Indian-rubber, is a compound of carbon and hydrogen. Graphite, plumbago, or black-lead, is a mineral substance, composed chiefly of carbon with a very small proportion of iron.

714. Where is the diamond chiefly found?

A. In India, the island of Borneo, Brazil, and Australia. It has also been found in North Carolina and Georgia in the United States.

715. Where is graphite found?

A. In Ceylon, Germany, England, and other places; but the purest graphite comes from Ceylon.

716. What is a crystal?

A. The geometrical form possessed by a vast number of mineral and saline substances, whose particles combine with one another by the attraction of cohesion, according to certain laws, the investigation of which belongs more properly to the science of crystallography.

717. What peculiar properties does the diamond possess?

A. It possesses a degree of hardness superior to that of any other mineral: it scratches all other bodies, but is scratched by none.

It acquires positive electricity by friction,

but does not retain it for more than half an hour.

It possesses either single or double refraction according to its crystalline form.

When exposed to the sun's rays for a certain time, or to the blue rays of the prismatic spectrum, it becomes phosphorescent.

"Phosphorescence," that property possessed by certain substances of emitting a light of their own.

718. Can the diamond be burnt?

A. Yes; but it requires a very strong heat. When burnt in oxygen it forms carbonic acid.

719. Can you give an example of carbon in its uncrystallized state?

A. Lamp-black—the soot produced by the imperfect combustion of oil or resin—is pure carbon in its uncrystallized or amorphous state.

"*Amorphous*," shapeless, without form.

720. What is charcoal?

A. Wood which has been exposed to a red heat till it has been deprived of all its gases and volatile parts.

721. Why does charcoal remove the taint of meat?

A. Because it absorbs all putrescent effluvia, whether they arise from animal or vegetable matter.

722. What other kinds of charcoal are there?

A. Coke, the charcoal of bituminous coal, and anthracite, which is a mineral charcoal.

Anthracite differs from bituminous coal in containing no bitumen, and, therefore, burning without flame or smoke.

723. Why is a charcoal fire hotter than a wood fire?

A. Because charcoal is very pure carbon; and, as it is the carbon of fuel which produces the glowing heat of combustion, therefore the purer the carbon the more intense will the heat of the fire be.

724. What is coal?

A. A fossil fuel of vegetable origin, found under the surface of the earth. The largest coal-fields in the world are in North America.

Coal is also found in great abundance in Great Britain, France, Germany, India, China, and Australia.

725. What is jet?

A. A species of bituminous coal, found in Saxony and Prussia. The coarser kinds are used for fuel, and the finer sorts for the manufacture of breastpins, ear-rings, and other trinkets.

726. Why does coal make such excellent fuel?

A. Because it contains a large amount of carbon and hydrogen gas in a very compact and convenient form.

727. Why will not stones do for fuel as well as coal?

A. Because they contain no hydrogen and little or no carbon.

728. Why will not iron cinders burn?

A. Because they contain impurities, which are not so ready to combine with oxygen as carbon and hydrogen are.

729. Of what are oil, tallow, and wax composed?

A. Principally of carbon and hydrogen gas. The solid part is carbon, the volatile part is hydrogen gas.

730. Why are timbers which are to be exposed to damp first charred?

A. Because charcoal undergoes no change by exposure to air and water; in consequence of which, timber will resist weather much longer after it has been charred.

731. Why should sick persons eat dry toast rather than bread and butter?

A. Because the charcoal surface of the toast helps to absorb the acids and impurities of a sick stomach.

Other reasons might be given which belong to the science of medicine.

732. Why does a piece of burnt bread make impure water fit to drink?

A. Because the surface of the bread (which has been reduced to charcoal by being burnt) absorbs the impurities of the water and makes it palatable.

733. Why are water and wine casks charred inside?

A. Because charring the inside of a cask reduces it to a kind of charcoal; and charcoal (by absorbing animal and vegetable impurities) keeps the liquor sweet and good.

734. Why is water purified by being filtered through charcoal?

A. Because charcoal absorbs the impurities of the water, and removes all disagreeable tastes and smells, whether they arise from animal or vegetable matter.

SECTION I.—CARBONIC ACID.

735. What is carbonic acid gas?

A. A gas formed by the union of carbon and oxygen: it used to be called fixed air.

Three pounds of carbon and eight pounds of oxygen will form eleven pounds of carbonic acid.

736. Where is carbonic acid found?

A. In the air we breathe, in mines and cellars, in water, in effervescing wines, and in many minerals.

At Brohl, near Lake Laach, which occupies the crater of an extinct volcano in Rhenish Prussia, six hundred thousand pounds' weight of carbonic acid gas is discharged from the ground every twenty-four hours.

737. What gas is generated by a lighted candle or lamp?

A. Carbonic acid gas,—formed by the union of the carbon of the oil or tallow with the oxygen of the air.

738. Under what circumstances does carbon most readily unite with oxygen?

A. 1st. When its temperature is raised:

thus, if carbon be red-hot, oxygen will most readily unite with it; and,

2d. When it forms part of the fluid blood.

739. Why do oxygen and carbon so readily unite in the blood?

A. Because the atoms of carbon are so loosely attracted by the other materials of the blood that they unite very readily with the oxygen of the air inhaled.

740. Is carbonic acid wholesome?

A. No: it is fatal to animal life, and, whenever it is inhaled, acts like a narcotic poison,—producing drowsiness, which sometimes ends in death.

In the island of Java is a valley about three-quarters of a mile in circumference, in which the carbonic acid gas rises to eighteen feet above the surface: from this cause the whole of the valley is devoid of animal and vegetable life. A dog thrown down into it dies in fourteen seconds, and birds attempting to fly across the valley drop down dead. It is called the poison, or Upas valley, and is the terror of the neighboring inhabitants. This valley is the crater of an extinct volcano.

741. How can any one know if a place be infested with carbonic acid gas?

A. If a pit or well contain carbonic acid, a candle let down into it will be instantly extinguished. The rule, therefore, is this:—where a candle will burn, a man can live; but what will extinguish a candle will also destroy life.

742. Why does a miner lower a lighted candle into a mine before he descends?

A. Because the candle will be extinguished

if the mine contain carbonic acid gas; but if the candle be not extinguished, the mine is safe, and the man may fearlessly descend.

743. Why does a crowded room produce headache?

A. Because we breathe air vitiated by the crowd.

744. Why is the air of a room vitiated by a crowd?

A. Because it is deprived of its due proportion of oxygen and laden with carbonic acid.

745. How is the air of a room affected thus by a crowd?

A. The elements of the air inhaled are separated in the lungs: the oxygen is converted in the blood into carbonic acid, and the carbonic acid, together with the nitrogen, is thrown back again by the breath into the room.

746. Is all the nitrogen rejected by the lungs?

A. Yes: all the nitrogen of the air is always expired.

747. Why is a crowded room unwholesome?

A. Because the oxygen of the air is absorbed by the lungs; and carbonic acid gas (which is a noxious poison) is substituted for it.

748. Mention the historical circumstances so well known in connection with the "Black Hole of Calcutta."

A. In the reign of George II. the Raja

(or Prince) of Bengal* marched suddenly to Calcutta, to drive the English from the country. As the attack was unexpected, the English were obliged to submit, and one hundred and forty-six persons were taken prisoners.

749. What became of those prisoners?

A. They were driven into a place about eighteen feet square, and fifteen or sixteen feet in height, with only two small grated windows. One hundred and twenty-three of the prisoners died in one night; and of the twenty-three who survived the larger portion died of putrid fevers after they were liberated.

750. Why were they suffocated in a few hours from confinement in this close, hot prison-hole?

A. Because the oxygen of the air was soon consumed by so many lungs, and its place supplied by carbonic acid, exhaled by the hot breath.

751. Why did the captives in the Black Hole die sleeping?

A. 1st. Because the absence of oxygen quickly affects the vital functions, depresses the nervous energies, and produces a lassitude which ends in death; and,

2d. Carbonic acid gas, being a narcotic

* The Sur Raja, at Dowlat,—a young man of violent passions, who had just succeeded to the throne, A.D. 1756.

poison, produces drowsiness and death in those who inhale it.

752. Why are the jungles of Java and Hindostan so fatal to life?

A. Because vast quantities of carbonic acid are thrown off by decaying vegetables in these jungles; and, as the wind cannot penetrate the thick brushwood to blow the pernicious gas away, it settles there, and destroys animal life.

753. Why do persons in a crowded church feel drowsy?

A. 1st. Because the crowded congregation inhale a large portion of the oxygen of the air, which alone can sustain vitality and healthy action; and,

2d. The air of the church is impregnated with carbonic acid gas, which, being a strong narcotic, produces drowsiness in those who inhale it.

754. Why do persons who are much in the open air enjoy the best health?

A. Because the air they inhale is much more pure.

755. Why is country air more pure than the air in cities?

A. 1st. Because there are fewer inhabitants to vitiate the air;

2d. There are more trees to restore the equilibrium of the vitiated air; and,

3d. The free circulation of air keeps it pure and wholesome,—in the same way as running streams are pure and wholesome, while stagnant waters are the contrary.

756. Why does the scantiness of a country population render the country air more pure?

A. Because the fewer the inhabitants the less carbonic acid will be exhaled; and thus country-people inhale pure oxygen, instead of air impregnated with the narcotic poison called carbonic acid gas.

757. Why do trees and flowers help to make country air wholesome?

A. 1st. Because trees and flowers absorb the carbonic acid generated by the lungs of animals, putrid substances, and other noxious exhalations; and,

2d. Trees and flowers restore to the air the oxygen which man and other animals inhale.

758. Why is the air of cities less wholesome than country air?

A. 1st. Because there are more inhabitants to vitiate the air;

2d. The sewers, drains, and filth of a city very greatly vitiate the air;

3d. The streets and alleys prevent a free circulation; and,

4th. There are fewer trees to absorb the

excess of carbonic acid gas and restore the equilibrium.

759. Why are persons who live in close rooms and crowded cities generally sickly?

A. Because the air they breathe is not pure, but is, in the first place, defective in oxygen, and, in the second, is impregnated with carbonic acid gas.

760. Where does the carbonic acid gas of close rooms and cities come from?

A. From the lungs of the inhabitants, the sewers, drains, and other like places, in which organic substances are undergoing decomposition.

761. What becomes of the carbonic acid gas of crowded cities?

A. Some of it is absorbed by vegetables: the rest is blown away by the wind, and diffused through the whole volume of the air.

762. Does not this constant diffusion of carbonic acid gas affect the purity of the whole air?

A. No; because it is wafted by the wind from place to place, and absorbed in its passage by the vegetable world.

763. What is choke-damp?

A. Carbonic acid gas accumulated at the bottom of wells, mines, and pits, which renders them noxious, and often fatal to life.

764. Why is not this carbonic acid gas taken up by the air and diffused, as it is in cities?

A. Because, being heavier than common air, it cannot rise from the well or pit; and no wind can get to it, to blow it away.

765. Why are persons sometimes killed by leaning over beer-vats?

A. Because vats where beer has been made contain a large quantity of carbonic acid gas, produced by the "vinous fermentation" of the beer; and when a man incautiously leans over a beer-vat and inhales the carbonic acid, he is immediately killed thereby.

766. Why are persons often killed who enter beer-vats to clean them?

A. Because carbonic acid gas, being heavier than atmospheric air, often rests upon the bottom of a vat: when, therefore, a person enters the vat and stoops to clean the bottom, he inhales the pernicious gas, which kills him.

767. Why are persons sometimes killed by having a charcoal fire in their bedrooms?

A. Because the carbon of the burning charcoal unites with the oxygen of the air, and forms carbonic acid gas, which is a narcotic poison.

768. If carbonic acid gas settles at the bottom of a room, how can it injure a person lying on a bed raised considerably above the floor?

A. Because all gases diffuse themselves

through each other, as a drop of ink would diffuse itself through a cup of water. If, therefore, a person slept for six or eight hours in a room containing carbonic acid, enough of the gas would be diffused throughout the room to produce death.

The heat of the fire assists the process of diffusion.

769. What are the chief sources of carbonic acid?

A. 1st. The breath of animals;

2d. The decomposition of vegetable and animal matter; and,

3d. Limestone, chalk, and all calcareous stones, in which it exists in a solid form.

770. From which of these sources is carbonic acid most likely to accumulate to a noxious extent?

A. From the fermentation and putrefaction of decaying vegetable and animal matters.

771. How can this accumulation of carbonic acid be prevented?

A. By throwing quicklime into places where such fermentation and putrefaction are going on.

772. How will quicklime prevent the accumulation of carbonic acid?

A. Quicklime will absorb the carbonic acid, and produce a combination called "carbonate of lime."

773. Does not heavy rain, as well as quicklime, prevent the accumulation of carbonic acid?

A. Yes: an abundant supply of water will

prevent the accumulation of carbonic acid, by dissolving it.

Red-heat (as a pan of red-hot coals or a piece of red-hot iron) will soon absorb the carbonic acid gas accumulated in a pit or well.

774. What effect has carbonic acid on the water in which it is dissolved?

A. It renders it slightly acid to the taste.

775. Why does gunpowder explode?

A. Because of the instantaneous production and expansion of carbonic acid, sulphurous acid, and nitrogen.

Gunpowder consists of seventy-six parts of saltpetre, fourteen of charcoal, and ten of sulphur.

776. Why is boiled water flat and insipid?

A. Because the whole of the carbonic acid is expelled by boiling, and escapes into the air.

777. Why does fresh spring-water sparkle when poured from one vessel to another?

A. Because fresh spring or pump water contains carbonic acid; and it is the presence of this gas which makes the water sparkle.

Much of the froth and bubbling of ale, beer, water, &c., when they are "poured high," is due to simple mechanical action.

778. Why is beer flat if the cask be left open too long?

A. Because too much of the carbonic acid gas produced by fermentation is suffered to escape.

779. Why are beer and porter made stale by being exposed to the air?

A. Because too much of the carbonic acid gas produced by fermentation is suffered to escape.

780. Why does beer turn flat if the vent-peg be left out of the tub?

A. Because the carbonic acid gas escapes through the vent-hole.

781. Why does sal-æratus make cakes light, particularly if they be mixed with sour milk?

A. Because the acid of the milk disengages the carbonic acid contained in the sal-æratus.

782. Why does wood decay?

A. Because the oxygen of the air unites with the carbon and hydrogen of the wood, and forms carbonic acid and water.

783. Why do persons throw lime into sinks and sewers to prevent their offensive smell in summer-time?

A. Because they contain large quantities of carbonic acid gas, which readily combines with lime, and, producing "carbonate of lime," neutralizes the offensive gases.

784. Why is quicklime formed by burning limestone in a kiln?

A. Because the carbonic acid (which rendered it mild) is driven off by the heat of the kiln; and the lime becomes quick, or caustic.

785. What is mortar?

A. Quicklime mixed with sand and water.

786. Why does mortar become hard after a few days?

A. Because the lime re-imbibes from the air the carbonic acid which had been expelled by fire; and the loose powder again becomes as hard as the original limestone.

787. Explain in what way mortar is adhesive.

A. When the carbonic acid is expelled, the hard limestone is converted into quicklime, which, being mixed with sand and water, becomes a soft and sticky plaster; but as soon as it is placed between bricks, it imbibes carbonic acid again, and hardens into limestone.

788. Wherein does limestone differ in appearance from quicklime?

A. Limestone is a hard, rocky substance, but quicklime is friable.

789. Why is water fresh from the pump more sparkling than after it has been drawn some time?

A. Because water fresh from the pump contains carbonic acid, which soon escapes into the air and leaves the water flat and stale.

790. Why should hard water used for washing be exposed to the air?

A. Because it is made more soft by exposure to the air.

Most spring-water holds lime in solution as a bicarbonate, in consequence of the presence of abundant carbonic acid. Carbonic acid escapes by exposure to air, and the lime is consequently deposited as a carbonate.

791. Why is hard water made more soft by exposure to the air?

A. 1st. Because the mineral salts which cause its hardness subside; and,

2d. Because the carbonic acid of the water makes its escape into the air.

792. What is choke-damp?

A. Carbonic acid gas accumulated at the bottom of wells and pits. It is called choke-damp because it chokes, or suffocates, every animal that attempts to inhale it.

It suffocates without getting into the lungs, by closing the outer orifice spasmodically.

793. Why are rotting leaves hot?

A. Because the fermentation of rotting leaves produces carbonic acid gas, which production is always attended with heat: in fact, rotting is a species of slow combustion.

The carbon of the leaves unites with the oxygen of the air to produce carbonic acid gas, and the new combinations disturb latent heat and make it sensible.

§ —EFFERVESCENCE.

794. From what is the word effervescence derived?

A. From the Latin word *effervesco*, to boil.

795. Can the capacity of water for dissolving carbonic acid be increased?

A. Yes. Carbonic acid may be forced into water by pressure to a considerable extent.

796. To what practical uses has this capacity of water for dissolving carbonic acid been applied?

A. Effervescing draughts are made upon this principle.

797. Explain the cause of effervescence in these beverages.

A. The carbonic acid of the beverage, being prevented by the cork from escaping, is forced into the liquor by pressure, and absorbed by it; but when the cork or pressure is removed, some of the carbonic acid flies off in bubbles, or effervescence.

798. Why does aerated water effervesce when the cork is removed?

A. While the bottle remains corked, carbonic acid is forced into the water by pressure, and absorbed by it; but when the cork or pressure is removed, some of the carbonic acid flies off in effervescence.

799. Why does soda or mineral water effervesce?

A. Into soda or mineral water is forced many times its own bulk of carbonic acid gas, which makes its escape in effervescence as soon as the cork is removed.

800. Why does ginger-pop fly about in froth when the string of the cork is cut?

A. Because it contains carbonic acid gas. While the cork is fast, the carbonic acid is forced into the liquor; but when the pressure is removed, the gas is given off in effervescence.

All vinous fermentation produces carbonic acid.

801. Why does bottled ale froth more than draught ale?

A. Because the pressure is greater in a bottle than in a tub which is continually tapped; and effervescence is always increased by pressure.

802. What produces the froth of bottled ale?

A. Carbonic acid generated by the vinous fermentation of the liquor. This gas is absorbed by the ale so long as the bottle is well corked, but is given off in froth when the pressure of the cork is removed.

803. What gives the pleasant acid taste to soda or mineral water, ginger-beer, champagne, and cider?

A. The presence of carbonic acid, generated by fermentation, and liberated by effervescence when the pressure of the cork is removed.

804. Why does the effervescence of soda or mineral water and ginger-beer so soon go off?

A. Because the carbonic acid which produced the effervescence very rapidly escapes into the air.

805. Why does the cork of a champagne-bottle fly off the instant it has been loosened from the neck of the bottle?

A. Because the great quantity of carbonic

acid gas contained in the liquor can no longer be confined, and, seeking to escape, drives out the cork with great violence.

806. When the cork of a champagne or mineral-water bottle is drawn, why is a loud report made?

A. Because champagne and mineral-water contain a great amount of carbonic acid gas, which, being suddenly liberated, strikes against the air and produces the report.

807. Why does hartshorn take out the red spot in cloth produced by any acid?

A. Because hartshorn is an alkali; and the peculiar property of every alkali is to neutralize acids.

Soda, potash, magnesia, &c. are alkalies.

Upon this principle, effervescing drinks are made of carbonate of soda (an alkali) and citric or tartaric acid. Effervescence is produced by the giving off of carbonic acid during the process of neutralization.

The carbonic acid is formed by the carbon of the carbonate of soda combining with the oxygen of the acid.

808. What is an alkali?

A. The converse of an acid, as bitter is the converse of sweet, or insipid the converse of pungent.

SECTION II.—CARBURETTED HYDROGEN.

809. What is marsh-gas, or fire-damp?

A. Carburetted hydrogen gas accumulated on marshes, in stagnant waters, and in coal-pits: it is frequently called "inflammable air."

810. What kind of gas is used in lighting the streets and buildings of cities?

A. Carburetted hydrogen.

811. What is carburetted hydrogen gas?

A. Carbon combined with hydrogen.

812. How may carburetted hydrogen gas be procured on marshes?

A. By stirring the mud at the bottom of any stagnant pool, and collecting the gas, as it escapes upward, in an inverted glass vessel.

813. What is coal-gas?

A. Carburetted hydrogen extracted from coals by the heat of fire.

814. Why is carburetted hydrogen gas called fire-damp, or inflammable air?

A. Because it very readily catches fire and explodes when a light is introduced to it, provided atmospheric air be present.

815. Why is carburetted hydrogen gas frequently called marsh-gas?

A. Because it is generated in meadows and marshes from putrefying vegetable substances.

816. What gas is evolved by the wick of a burning candle?

A. Carburetted hydrogen gas. The carbon and hydrogen of the tallow combine into a gas from the heat of the flame; and this gas is called carburetted hydrogen, or inflammable air.

817. Why do coal-mines frequently explode?

A. Because the carburetted hydrogen gas generated in those mines explodes when a light is incautiously introduced.

818. How can miners see in the coal-pits if they may never introduce a light?

A. Sir Humphry Davy invented a lantern for the use of miners, called "the Safety-Lamp," which may be used without danger.

The safety-lamp was invented in the year 1815.

819. Who was Sir Humphry Davy?

A. A very ingenious chemist, born in Cornwall, 1788, and died at Geneva in 1829.

820. What is the safety-lamp?

A. A kind of lantern, covered with a fine gauze wire instead of glass or horn.

821. How does this fine gauze wire prevent an explosion in the coal-mine?

A. By preventing the flame of the lamp from communicating with the inflammable gas of the mine.

The interstices of the gauze wire must not exceed one-twentieth of an inch in diameter, and there should not be fewer than six hundred and twenty-five apertures to the square inch.

822. Why will not flame pass through very fine wire gauze?

A. Because the metal wire is a very rapid conductor of heat; and when the flame of gas burning in the lamp reaches the wire gauze, so much heat is conducted away by the wire that the flame is extinguished.

823. Does the gas of the coal-pit get through the wire gauze into the lantern?

A. Yes; and the inflammable gas ignites and burns inside the lamp. When this is the case, the miner is in danger, and should withdraw.

When the carburetted hydrogen gas takes fire from the miner's candle, the miner sometimes perishes in the blast of the flame, and sometimes is suffocated by the carbonic acid which is thus produced.

CHAPTER V.—PHOSPHORUS AND PHOSPHURETTED HYDROGEN.

SECTION I.—PHOSPHORUS.

824. What is phosphorus?

A. A pale, amber-colored substance, resembling wax in appearance. The word is derived from two Greek words, which mean, *to produce* or *carry light*, φος φερειν, (phospherein.)

825. How is phosphorus obtained?

A. By heating bones to a white heat: by this means the animal matter and charcoal are consumed, and a substance called "phosphate of lime" is left behind.

826. What is the phosphate of lime?

A. Phosphorus united to oxygen and lime:

when sulphuric acid is added and the mixture heated, the lime is attracted to the acid, and pure phosphorus remains.

If powdered charcoal be added, phosphorus may be procured by distillation.

827. When, and by whom, was phosphorus discovered?

A. This element was discovered in 1669, by Brandt, of Hamburg.

828. Is phosphorus inflammable?

A. It is so exceedingly inflammable that it sometimes takes fire by the heat of the hand: great care, therefore, is required in its management, as a blow or hard rub will very often kindle it.

829. Of what is the ignitable part of lucifer or friction matches made?

A. Of phosphorus. Above two hundred and fifty thousand pounds are used every year in London alone for the manufacture of lucifer or friction matches.

830. Why will lucifer or friction matches ignite when drawn across any rough surface?

A. Because they are tipped with phosphorus, which has an affinity for oxygen at the lowest temperature; so that the little additional heat caused by the friction of the match across the bottom of the lucifer-box is sufficient to ignite it, and at the same time to ignite the sulphur with which the match is tipped.

831. What peculiar property has phosphorus?

A. It is luminous in the dark; and even in daylight it appears to be surrounded by a light cloud.

It should always be kept under water, and great care used in handling it, as the burns made by it are very difficult to heal.

832. Why are putrefying fish luminous?

A. Because the carbon of the fish, uniting with oxygen, forms carbonic acid; and the phosphoric acid of the fish, being thus deprived of oxygen, is converted into phosphorus. As soon as this is the case, the phosphorus begins to unite with the oxygen of the air, and becomes luminous.

Carbonic acid is a compound of carbon and oxygen.

Phosphoric acid is a compound of phosphorus and oxygen. If the oxygen be taken from phosphoric acid, the residue, of course, is phosphorus.

The luminousness spoken of is due to the slow combustion of the phosphorus while it is uniting with the oxygen of the air.

833. Why is the sea often luminous in summer-time?

A. "The waters of the ocean," says Silliman, "especially in warm latitudes, are often covered with little animalcules which become luminous at night when the water is agitated. The cause of phosphorescence is not known."

SECTION II.—PHOSPHURETTED HYDROGEN.

834. From what do the very offensive effluvia of churchyards arise?

A. From a gas called phosphuretted hydrogen, which is phosphorus combined with hydrogen gas.

835. Who was the discoverer of phosphuretted hydrogen?

A. Sir Humphry Davy, in the year 1812.

836. Why does a putrefying dead body smell so offensively?

A. Because phosphuretted hydrogen gas always rises from putrefying animal substances.

The escape of ammonia and sulphuretted hydrogen contributes also to this offensive smell.

837. What is the cause of the ignis-fatuus, jack-o'-lantern, or will-o'-the-wisp?

A. This luminous appearance, which haunts meadows, bogs, and marshes, arises from the gas of putrefying animal and vegetable substances,—especially from decaying fish.

838. What gases arise from these putrefying substances?

A. Phosphuretted hydrogen, from putrefying animal substances; and

Carburetted hydrogen, from decaying vegetable matters.

839. How is the gas of ignis-fatui ignited on bogs and meadows?

A. Impure phosphuretted hydrogen bursts spontaneously into flame whenever it mixes with air or pure oxygen gas.

Pure phosphuretted hydrogen will not ignite spontaneously: this spontaneous ignition is due to the presence of a small quantity of the vapor of an exceedingly volatile liquid compound of phosphorus with hydrogen, which is occasionally produced with the gas itself.

If phosphorus be boiled with milk of lime, and the beak of the retort be placed under water, bubbles of phosphuretted hydrogen will rise successively through the water, and, on reaching the surface, burst into flame.

840. Why does an ignis-fatuus, or will-o'-the-wisp, fly from us when we run to meet it?

A. Because we produce a current of air in front of ourselves when we run toward the ignis-fatuus, which drives the light gas forward.

841. Why does an ignis-fatuus follow us when we run from it?

A. Because we produce a current of air in the way we run, which attracts the light gas in the same course, drawing it after us as we run away from it.

842. May not many ghost-stories have arisen from some ignis-fatuus lurking about churchyards?

A. Perhaps all the ghost-stories which deserve any credit at all have arisen from the ignited gas of churchyards, lurking about tombs,—to which fear has added its own creations.

CHAPTER VI.—COMBUSTION.

843. How is heat evolved by combustion?

A. By chemical action. As latent heat is liberated, when water is poured upon lime, by chemical action, so latent heat is liberated in combustion by chemical action also.

844. What chemical action takes place in combustion?

A. The elements of the fuel combine with the oxygen of the air.

845. What three elements are necessary to produce combustion?

A. Hydrogen gas, carbon, and oxygen gas, —the two former in the fuel, the last in the air which surrounds the fuel.

846. Is combustion always accompanied by light and heat?

A. Combustion is always accompanied by heat, and frequently, but not always, by light.

847. Give an example of great heat without light.

A. The air which issues from the top of the chimney of a lamp will make a piece of fine iron wire red-hot when held several inches above the flame.

848. What are the elements of fuel?

A. As bread is a compound of flour, yeast, and salt, so fuel is a compound of hydrogen and carbon.

849. What causes the combustion of the fuel?

A. The hydrogen gas of the fuel, being set free, and ignited by a match, unites with the oxygen of the air and makes a yellow flame: this flame heats the carbon of the fuel, which, also uniting with the oxygen of the air, produces carbonic acid gas.

850. What is the difference between combustion and ignition?

A. Some substances, when heated to a certain point, emit light without wasting away: this is called incandescence, or ignition; but when they waste away it is called combustion.

A metal wire can be heated red-hot and suffered to cool without changing its state; but a piece of charcoal when heated to redness will waste away. The metal is in a state of ignition, and the charcoal in a state of combustion.

851. What is fire?

A. Heat and light, produced by the combustion of inflammable substances.

852. Why does fire produce heat?

A. Because it liberates latent heat from the air and fuel.

853. What chemical changes in air and fuel are produced by combustion?

A. 1st. Some of the oxygen of the air, combining with the hydrogen of the fuel, condenses into water; and,

2d. Some of the oxygen of the air, combining with the carbon of the fuel, forms carbonic acid gas.

854. When we burn a candle or a lump of coal, is the matter of which it is composed destroyed?

A. It is not: the component parts of the candle and coal enter into new forms,—namely, of gas and smoke, which are dissipated in the air, and of soot and ashes which are not consumed.

855. Why is a fire, after it has been long burning, red-hot?

A. Because the whole surface of the fuel is so thoroughly heated that every part of it is undergoing a rapid union with the oxygen of the air.

856. In a blazing fire, why is the upper surface of the coal black and the lower surface red?

A. Because carbon, being solid, requires a great degree of heat to make it unite with the oxygen of the air; in consequence of which, the hot under surface of coal is frequently red, from its union with oxygen, while the cold upper surface remains black.

857. Which burns the more quickly, a blazing fire or a red-hot one?

A. Fuel burns most quickly in a blazing fire.

858. Why does blazing wood burn more quickly than red-hot coal?

A. Because the inflammable gases of the fuel (which are then escaping) greatly assist the process of combustion.

859. Why do the coals of a clear, bright fire burn out more slowly than blazing coals?

A. Because most of the inflammable gases and much of the solid fuel have been consumed already, so that there is less food for combustion.

860. What is smoke?

A. Unconsumed parts of fuel (principally carbon) separated from the solid mass, and carried up the chimney by currents of hot air.

861. Why is there more smoke when fresh fuel is added than when the fuel is red-hot?

A. Because carbon, being solid, requires a great degree of heat to make it unite with oxygen, or, in other words, to bring it into a state of perfect combustion: when fresh fuel is laid on, more carbon is separated than can be reduced to combustion, and the surplus flies off in smoke.

862. Why is there so little smoke with a red-hot fire?

A. Because the entire surface of the fuel is in a state of combustion; and, as very little carbon remains unconsumed, there is but little smoke.

863. Why are there bright and dark spots in a clear cinder fire?

A. Because the intensity of the combustion is greater in some parts of the fire than it is in others.

864. Why is the intensity of the combustion so unequal?

A. Because the air flies to the fire in various and unequal currents.

865. Why do we see all sorts of grotesque figures in hot coals?

A. Because the intensity of combustion is unequal, owing to the unequal manner in which the air flies to the fuel; and the various shades of yellow, red, and white heat, mingling with the black of the unburnt coal, produce strange and fantastic figures.

866. Why does paper burn more readily than wood?

A. Because it is of a more fragile texture, and therefore its component parts are more easily heated.

867. Why does wood burn more readily than coal?

A. Because it is not so solid, and therefore its elemental parts are more easily separated and made hot.

868. When a coal-fire is lighted, why is charcoal laid at the bottom, against the grate?

A. Because charcoal, in consequence of its fragile texture, very readily catches fire.

869. Why is wood laid on the top of the paper?

A. Because wood, being more substantial, burns longer than paper, and therefore affords a longer contact of flame to heat the coal.

870. Why would not paper kindle a fire as well as charcoal?

A. Because paper burns out so rapidly that it would not afford sufficient contact of flame to heat the coal to combustion.

871. Why will not a log of solid wood kindle without shavings, straw, or paper?

A. Because wood is too substantial to be heated into combustion by the feeble flame issuing from a match.

872. Why would not paper do as well if placed on the top of the wood?

A. Because the blaze tends upward: if, therefore, the paper were placed on the top, its blaze would afford no contact of flame to the fuel lying below.

873. Why should coal be placed above the wood?

A. Because otherwise the flame of the fuel would not rise through the coal to heat it.

874. Why is a fire kindled at the lowest bar of the grate?

A. That the flame may ascend through the fuel to heat it. If the fire were kindled from the top, the flame would not come in contact with the fuel placed below.

875. Why will cinders become red-hot more quickly than coal?

A. Because they are sooner reduced to a state of combustion, as they are more porous and less solid.

876. Why are cinders lighter than coal?

A. Because they are full of little holes, from which vapor, gases, and other volatile parts have been driven off by previous combustion.

877. Why will not wet kindling-wood light a fire?

A. 1st. Because the moisture of the wet kindling-wood prevents the oxygen of the air from getting to the fuel; and,

2d. The heat of the fire is perpetually drawn off by the conversion of water into steam.

878. Why does dry wood burn better than green?

A. 1st. Because none of its heat is carried away by the conversion of water into steam; and,

2d. The pores of dry wood, being filled with air, supply the fire with oxygen.

879. Why do two pieces of wood burn better than one?

A. 1st. Because they help to retain the heat of the passing smoke and throw it on the fuel; and,

2d. The air, impinging against the pieces of wood, is thrown upon the fire in a kind of eddy or draught.

880. Why will not wood or paper burn if steeped in a solution of potash, phosphate of lime, or ammonia (hartshorn)?

A. Because any "alkali" (such as potash) will arrest the hydrogen which escapes from the fuel, and prevent its combination with the oxygen of the air.

881. Why does a jet of flame sometimes burst into the room through the bars of a stove?

A. Because the iron bars conduct heat to

the interior of the fuel, and the volatile gas which escapes from it is kindled by the glowing coals over which it passes.

882. Why is this jet sometimes of a greenish-yellow color?

A. Either because some lumps of coal lie over the hot bars, or because the coal below is not red-hot; in consequence of which, some of the gas, which is of a greenish color, escapes unburnt.

883. Why does the gas escape unburnt?

A. Because neither the bars nor the coal over which it passes are red-hot.

884. Why does a bluish flame sometimes flicker on the surface of hot cinders?

A. Because the gas from the hot coal at the bottom of the grate, mixing with the carbon of the coal above, produces an inflammable gas, called carbonic oxide, which burns with a blue flame.

885. Why is the light of a fire more intense sometimes than it is at others?

A. The intensity of fire-light depends upon the whiteness to which the carbon is reduced by combustion. If carbon be white-hot, its combustion is perfect and the light intense: if not, the light is obscured by smoke.

886. Why will not cinders blaze as well as fresh coal?

A. The flame of coal is made chiefly by hydrogen gas: as soon as this gas has been consumed, the hot cinders produce only a gas, called carbonic acid, which is neither luminous nor visible.

887. Where does the hydrogen gas of a fire come from?

A. All fuel is composed of carbon and hydrogen gas, which are separated from each other by the process of combustion.

888. Why does a fire burn clearest on a frosty night?

A. Because the volatile gases are more quickly consumed, and the solid carbon is plentifully supplied with oxygen from the air to make it burn brightly and intensely.

889. Why does a fire burn more intensely in winter than in summer?

A. Because the air is colder in winter than it is in summer.

890. Why does the coldness of the air increase the heat of a fire?

A. 1st. Because air condensed by the cold supplies more oxygen than a similar volume of warmer air; and,

2d. Condensed air, being heavy, falls more rapidly into the place of the hot ascending air, to supply the fire with nourishment.

891. Ashes or cinders are put over the fire at night to prevent its burning away: can you tell the reason for thus covering the fire?

A. The ashes or cinders prevent the oxygen of the air from gaining free access to the fire; and, as fire will not burn without a supply of oxygen, it keeps alive for several hours without being wasted.

892. Why does the air flow to the fire more tardily for being rarefied?

A. Because the greater the contrast between the external air and that which has been heated by the fire, the more rapid will be the current of air toward that fire.

893. Why does rarefied air afford less nourishment to fire than cold air?

A. Because rarefied air contains less oxygen than the same quantity of condensed air, inasmuch as the same quantity of oxygen is diffused over a larger volume of air.

894. Why does a fire burn more fiercely in the open air?

A. 1st. Because the air out-of-doors is more dense than the air in-doors; and,

2d. It has freer access to the fire.

895. Why is the air out-of-doors more dense than that in-doors?

A. Because it has freer circulation; and as soon as any portion has been rarefied it instantly rises, and is supplied by colder currents.

896. Why does a fire not burn so fiercely in a thaw as in a frost?

A. Because the air is laden with vapor; in consequence of which, it moves more slowly, and is too much rarefied to afford plentiful nourishment to the fire.

897. Why does a fire burn so fiercely in windy weather?

A. Because the air is rapidly changed, and affords plentiful nourishment to the fire.

898. Why does a pair of bellows get a fire up?

A. Because it drives the air more rapidly to the fire; and the plentiful supply of oxygen soon makes the fire burn intensely.

899. What gas is generated in a common fire by combustion?

A. Carbonic acid gas, formed by the union of the carbon of the fuel with the oxygen of the air.

900. What is carbonic acid gas?

A. Carbon (or charcoal) combined with oxygen gas.

901. If a piece of paper be laid flat on a clear fire, it will not blaze, but char: explain this.

A. The carbon of a clear fire, being sufficiently hot to unite with the oxygen of the air, produces carbonic acid gas, which soon envelops the paper laid flat upon the cinders; but carbonic acid gas will not blaze.

902. If you blow the paper, it will blaze immediately: explain this.

A. By blowing the paper or opening a door suddenly, the carbonic acid is dissipated, and the paper fanned into flame.

903. Why does water extinguish a fire?

A. 1st. Because the water forms an envelope over the fuel, which keeps it from the air; and,

2d. The conversion of water into steam draws off the heat of the burning fuel.

904. A little water makes a fire fiercer, while a larger quantity of water puts it out: explain this.

A. Water is composed of oxygen and hydrogen: when, therefore, the fire is sufficiently intense to decompose the water into its simple elements, it serves as fuel to the flame.

905. How can water serve as fuel to fire?

A. Because the hydrogen of the water burns with a flame; and the oxygen of the water increases the intensity of that flame.

906. When a house is on fire, is too little water worse than none?

A. Certainly. Unless water be supplied so plentifully as to extinguish the fire, it will increase its intensity, like fuel.

907. When will water extinguish fire?

A. When the supply is so rapid and abundant that the fire cannot decompose it.

908. Cannot wood be made to blaze without actual contact with fire?

A. Yes: if a piece of wood be held near the fire for a little time, it will blaze, even though it does not touch the fire.

909. Why will wood blaze, even if it does not touch the fire?

A. Because the heat of the fire drives out the hydrogen gas of the wood; which gas is inflamed by contact with the red-hot coals.

910. Why will an adjoining house sometimes catch fire, though no flame of the burning house touches it?

A. Because the heat of the burning house sets at liberty the hydrogen gas of the wood-work of the adjoining house; and this gas is ignited by the flames or red-hot bricks of the house on fire.

911. On what does the intensity of fire depend?

A. The intensity of fire is always in proportion to the quantity of oxygen with which it is supplied.

912. Why is a dull fire revived by sweeping the hearth and bars of the grate?

A. Because the air, which was arrested by the loose dust and cinders, finds its way freely to the fire as soon as these obstacles are swept away.

The brightness of a fire depends on its supply of oxygen derived from the air.

913. Why does stirring a dull fire serve to quicken it?

A. Because it breaks up the clotted cinders and coals, making a passage for the air into the very heart of the fire.

914. Why will powdered sulphur quench fire more readily than water?

A. 1st. Because powdered sulphur has a very strong affinity for oxygen, and converts it into sulphurous acid: the fire is thus deprived of its essential food, (oxygen,) and is, in fact, starved out; and,

2d. Because sulphurous acid throws off dense white fumes, and surrounds the fire with an incombustible atmosphere.

When we burn sulphur in air, it throws off suffocating white fumes, called sulphurous acid: the ignition of a common sulphur-match is an example.

915. When is a substance said to be incombustible?

A. When it is incapable of entering into combination with oxygen.

916. Why do lamps smoke?

A. Either because the wick is cut unevenly, or else because it is raised up too high.

917. Why does a lamp smoke when the wick is cut unevenly?

A. 1st. Because the points of the jagged edge, being very easily separated from the wick, load the flame with more carbon than it can consume; and,

2d. As the heat of the flame is greatly diminished by these bits of wick, it is unable to consume even the usual quantity of smoke.

918. Why does a lamp smoke when the wick is turned up too high?

A. Because more carbon is separated

from the wick than can be consumed by the flame.

919. Why does a lamp-glass diminish the smoke of a lamp?

A. 1st. Because it increases the supply of oxygen to the flame, by producing a draught; and,

2d. It concentrates and reflects the heat of the flame; in consequence of which, the combustion of the carbon is more perfect, and very little escapes unconsumed.

SECTION I.—SPONTANEOUS COMBUSTION.

920. What is meant by spontaneous combustion?

A. Combustion produced without the application of flame.

921. Give an example of spontaneous combustion.

A. Goods packed in a warehouse will often catch fire of themselves, especially such goods as cotton, flax, hemp, rags, &c.

922. Why do such goods sometimes catch fire of themselves?

A. Because they are piled together in very large masses in a damp state or place.

923. What is generally the cause of spontaneous combustion?

A. The piled-up goods ferment from heat and damp, and during fermentation carbonic acid gas is formed, which is attended with combustion.

924. Why does this produce spontaneous combustion?

A. The damp produces decay, or the decomposition of the goods; and the great heat of the piled-up mass makes the decaying goods ferment.

925. How does this fermentation produce combustion?

A. During fermentation, carbonic acid gas is given off by the goods, and a slow combustion ensues, till at length the whole pile bursts into flame.

926. Why is the heat of a large mass of goods greater than that of a smaller quantity?

A. Because the carbonic acid cannot escape through the massive pile; and the products of decomposition, being confined, hasten further changes.

927. Why do hay-stacks sometimes catch fire of themselves?

A. Either because the hay was put up damp, or else because rain has penetrated the stack.

928. Does heat always produce light?

A. No: the heat of a stack of hay, though very great, is not sufficient to produce light.

929. Why will a hay-stack catch fire if the hay be damp?

A. Because damp hay soon decays, and undergoes a state of fermentation, during which carbonic acid gas is given off, and the stack catches fire.

930. Why do greasy rags sometimes catch fire?

A. Because they very readily ferment, and during fermentation throw off exceedingly inflammable gases.

Lamp-black mixed with linseed oil is very liable to spontaneous combustion.

SECTION II.—FLAME.

931. What is flame?

A. The rapid combustion of volatile matter.

932. Why is the flame of a good fire yellow?

A. Because both the hydrogen and carbon of the fuel are in a state of perfect combustion. It is the white heat of the carbon which renders flame luminous.

933. Why is a yellow flame brighter than a red-hot coal?

A. Because yellow rays produce the greatest amount of light. Red rays produce the greatest amount of heat.

934. Why is the flame of a candle extinguished when blown by the breath, and not made more intense like a fire?

A. Because the flame of a candle is confined to a very small wick, from which it is severed by the breath, and, being unsupported, must go out.

935. Why is a smouldering wick sometimes rekindled by blowing it?

A. Because air is carried to it by the breath

with great rapidity; and the oxygen of the air kindles the red-hot wick, as it would kindle charred wood.

936. Why is not the red-hot wick kindled by the air around it without blowing?

A. Because oxygen is not supplied with sufficient freedom unless air be blown to the wick.

937. When is this experiment most likely to succeed?

A. In frosty weather; because the air contains more oxygen when it is condensed by the cold.

938. Why does the wick of a candle when the flame has been blown out very readily catch fire?

A. Because the wick is already hot, and a very little extra heat will throw it into flame.

939. Why does the extra heat revive the flame?

A. Because it again liberates the hydrogen of the tallow, and ignites it.

940. Explain how a candle burns when lighted.

A. 1st. The heat of the lighted wick decomposes the tallow into its elementary parts of carbon and hydrogen, and the hydrogen of the tallow, combining with the oxygen of the air, produces flame; and,

2d. The substance in the wick, having its temperature raised by the application of heat, combines with the oxygen of the atmosphere, and this combination, attended with the evolution of heat, sustains the process of combustion.

941. Where is the tallow or wax of a candle decomposed?

A. In the wick. The melted tallow or wax rises up the wick by capillary attraction, and is rapidly decomposed by the heat of the flame.

"Capillary attraction," from *capillus*, a hair.
Fluids rise in tubes of very narrow bore much above the level of the liquid in which the tubes are placed.

942. Why is the flame of a candle hot?

A. Because the flame liberates latent heat from the air and tallow.

943. How is latent heat liberated by the flame of a candle?

A. When the elements of the tallow combine with the oxygen of the air, latent heat is liberated by the chemical changes.

944. Why does the flame of a candle produce light?

Fig. 2.

A. Because the chemical changes made by combustion excite undulations of ether, which, striking the eye, produce light.

945. Why is the flame of a candle yellow?

A. It is not entirely so. Only the outer coat of the flame is yellow: the lower part is violet, and the inside of the flame hollow.

946. Describe the different parts of the flame of a common candle.

A. The flame consists of three cones. The innermost cone is hollow, the outside cone is yellow, and the intermediate one is of a dingy purple hue. (See Fig. 2.)

947. Why is the outside of the flame yellow?

A. Because the carbon of the tallow, being in a state of perfect combustion, is made white-hot.

948. Why is the lower part of the flame purple?

A. Because it is overloaded with hydrogen, raised from the tallow by the burning wick; and this gas (which burns with a blue flame) gives the dark tinge to the lower part of the candle-flame.

949. Why is the inside of the flame hollow?

A. Because it is filled with vapor raised from the candle by the heat of the wick and not yet reduced to a state of combustion.

950. Why is the intermediate cone of a flame purple as well as the bottom of the flame?

A. Because the gases are not in a state of perfect combustion, but contain an excess of hydrogen, which gives the flame a purple tinge.

951. Why is not the middle cone in a state of perfect combustion, as well as the outer one?

A. Because the outer cone prevents the oxygen of the air from getting to the middle of the flame; and without the free access of oxygen gas there is no such thing as complete combustion.

952. Why does the flame of a candle point upward?

A. Because it heats the surrounding air, which, therefore, rapidly ascends, driving the flame upward at the same time.

953. Why is the flame of a candle pointed at the top like a cone?

A. Because the supply of hot vapor diminishes as it ascends, and, as it affords less resistance to the air, is reduced to a mere point.

954. Why are the lower parts of a flame less volatile than the upper?

A. Because they are laden with unconsumed gas and watery vapor, which present considerable resistance to the air.

955. Why does the flame of a candle make a glass which is held over it damp?

A. Because a "watery vapor" is made by the combination of the hydrogen of tallow with the oxygen of the air; and this "vapor" is condensed by the cold glass held above the flame.

956. Why does the hand held above a candle suffer more from heat than when it is placed below the flame or on one side of it?

A. Because the hot gases and air, in their ascent, come in contact with the hand placed above the flame; but when the hand is placed below the flame or on one side, it only feels heat from radiation.

"Radiation," emission of rays. The candle-flame throws out rays of light and heat in all directions; but when the hand is held above the flame, it feels not only the heat of the rays, but also that of the ascending current of hot air, &c.

957. Why is a rush-light extinguished more readily than a cotton-wick candle?

A. Because a hard rush imbibes the melted fat or wax much more slowly than porous cotton; as it imbibes less fat, it supplies a smaller volume of combustible gases, and of course the light is more easily extinguished.

958. Why is a gas-flame more easily extinguished when the jet is very slightly turned on than when it is in full stream?

A. Because there is less volume of combustible gases in the small flame than in the full blaze.

959. Why does an extinguisher put a candle out?

A. Because the air in the extinguisher is soon exhausted of its oxygen by the flame; and when there is no oxygen flame goes out.

960. Why does not a candle set fire to a piece of paper twisted into an extinguisher and used as such?

A. 1st. Because the flame very soon exhausts the oxygen contained in the paper extinguisher; and,

2d. The flame invests the inside of the paper extinguisher with carbonic acid gas, which prevents it from blazing.

961. A long wick is covered with an efflorescence at the top: what does this arise from?

A. The knotty or flowery appearance of the top of a wick arises from an accumulation of particles partly separated, but still loosely hanging to the wick.

962. Why do common candles require snuffing?

A. Because the heat of the flame is not sufficient to consume the wick; and the longer the wick grows the less heat the flame produces.

963. Why do wax candles never need snuffing?

A. Because the wick of wax candles is made of very fine thread, which the heat of the flame is sufficient to consume: the wick of tallow candles, on the other hand, is made of coarse cotton, which is too substantial to be consumed by the heat of the flame, and must be cut off by snuffers.

964. Why does a pin stuck in a rush-light extinguish it?

A. Because a pin, being a good conductor, carries away the heat of the flame from the wick, and prevents the combustion of the tallow.

965. What is the smoke of a candle?

A. Solid particles of carbon separated from the wick and tallow, but not consumed.

966. Why are not all the particles consumed?

A. The combustion of the carbon depends

upon its combining with the oxygen of the air: as the outer surface of the flame prevents the access of air to the interior parts, much of the carbon of those parts passes off in smoke.

967. Why does a candle flicker, especially just previous to its being burnt out?

A. Because it is unequally supplied with combustible gases. When a candle is nearly burnt out, there is not sufficient tallow or wax to keep up the regular supply of combustible gas; in consequence of which, the flame flickers (that is, blazes) when it is supplied with gas, and goes out for a moment when the supply is defective.

PART III.

METALS.

CHAPTER I.—METALS AND ALLOYS.

SECTION I.—METALS.

968. WHAT are some of the properties of metals?

A. They are brilliant when polished; are, with few exceptions, the heaviest of all known substances; and are malleable, ductile, fusible, and opaque. They are also good conductors of heat and electricity.

969. What is meant by malleable?

A. A metal is said to be malleable when it spreads out when beaten. A piece of glass would fly to pieces if struck with a hammer; while a piece of metal would spread out into a thin plate.

"Malleable," from the Latin *malleus*, a hammer.

970. What is understood by ductile?

A. When a metal possesses the property of being drawn out into a wire without breaking, it is said to be ductile.

971. What is the meaning of fusible?

A. Capable of being fused, or melted.

972. Are all metals solid?

A. Yes; with one exception,—mercury, or quicksilver; which is fluid under ordinary temperatures.

973. Name the principal useful metals.

A. Gold, silver, iron, copper, mercury, tin, lead, and zinc.

There are many other metals; but the above-named are the most useful.

974. What peculiar properties belong to gold?

A. It is more malleable than any other metal. It does not tarnish by exposure to air or water.

A single grain of gold may be beaten out to cover a surface of nearly thirty square yards.

975. What peculiar properties belong to pure silver?

A. It is supposed to be the best conductor of heat and electricity.

976. What are the peculiar properties of iron?

A. It is more ductile than any other known metal, and is strongly attracted by the magnet.

An iron wire one-thirty-sixth of an inch in diameter will support a weight of sixty pounds.

The loadstone, or natural magnet, is an oxide of iron.

977. What are the peculiar properties of copper?

A. It is very malleable and ductile. It is hard, elastic, and sonorous.

Copper was first wrought by the Greeks in the island of Cyprus, —whence it derives its name.

Copper plates when corroded by an acid form a rust called verdigris. Verdigris is manufactured largely in France.

978. What are the peculiar properties of mercury?

A. It is a fluid; it is of a silvery white color; it possesses a high degree of lustre, and readily expands and contracts with changes of temperature.

The property of expanding and contracting in any alteration of temperature renders it a suitable fluid for the tubes of thermometers. The color known as vermilion, and the medicine called calomel, are prepared from quicksilver.

979. What is the peculiar property of tin?

A. It has a silvery whiteness and brilliancy, and is very malleable. Plates of tin called tin-foil are so thin that one thousand of them are only one inch in thickness.

980. What is block tin?

A. Tin purified by heat, and run into moulds, which form blocks of great size.

981. What is sheet tin, such as is used in the manufacture of pans and other utensils?

A. It is sheet iron dipped into melted tin, a portion of which adheres to the surface as tin, and another enters into the iron and alloys with it.

The ancients are supposed to have made use of tin; and there is good reason for believing that it was obtained by the Phœnicians, from Cornwall and Spain, at least one thousand years before Christ.

982. What are the peculiar properties of lead?

A. It is a very soft metal, being easily scratched by the finger-nail. It is very malleable, and may be rolled into very thin plates.

983. Why are leaden water-pipes sometimes injurious?

A. Because lead is easily acted on by soft water containing oxygen and carbonic acid; and, as lead is poisonous, the particles contained in the water render it unwholesome.

984. Has spring-water the same effect on lead?

A. No: most spring-waters contain salts of various kinds, which prevent the decomposition of the lead.

985. Is lead useful in the arts?

A. Yes: the white lead and red lead used by painters are made from lead. Litharge is also a preparation of lead.

A worker in lead is called a plumber,—from the Latin *plumbum*, lead.

Shot are made of an alloy, or compound of lead and arsenic. The arsenic serves to render the lead more hard and brittle.

986. What is the peculiar property of zinc?

A. It is not readily acted on by the air or water. For this reason it is used for roofing, lining of refrigerators, gutters, &c., and is also employed for coating iron to prevent rusting.

987. What is iron thus coated with zinc called?

A. Galvanized iron.

988. To what other important use is zinc applied?

A. Zinc is used in the construction of voltaic or galvanic batteries.

In commerce zinc is known by the name of spelter. Large quantities are obtained from the mines of Silesia.

989. Of all the metals, which is the most important and useful?

A. Iron.

990. What constitutes the great difference between iron and other metals?

A. Its hardness. By a peculiar process it may be converted into steel, which is so hard that it will cut any known substance except the diamond.

991. What is cast iron?

A. Iron-ore melted in a furnace and, while in the liquid state, suffered to run into moulds of sand.

992. What is wrought iron?

A. It is made from cast iron, which, after being powerfully heated in a furnace, is made into lumps, which are hammered and drawn while hot, between rollers, into bars.

993. What is steel?

A. Wrought or bar iron surrounded with charcoal, and placed during six or eight days in a furnace intensely heated: the carbon unites with the iron, and forms what is called "carburet of iron," (or steel.)

When the bars are taken out of the furnace they are covered with blisters,—whence the name of blistered steel.

994. What is cast steel?

A. The blistered bars of steel are broken up and heated in a furnace until complete fusion or melting takes place. This is cast steel.

Shear steel is made by breaking the blistered bars into pieces about eighteen inches in length; four of these bars and one about double the length are bound together, heated, hammered, heated again, and then drawn out into bars of any required dimensions.

Shear steel derives its name from its being used for making shears for dressing woollen cloth.

995. What remarkable property belongs to steel?

A. That of becoming hard when suddenly cooled.

SECTION II.—ALLOYS.

996. What is an alloy?

A. The combination of one or more metals is called an alloy. All compound metals are alloys.

997. What is an amalgam?

A. The combination of quicksilver with a metal.

998. Name some of the principal alloys.

A. Bronze, bell-metal, brass, pewter, German silver, Britannia metal, solders, &c.

999. What are the component parts of the gold coins of the United States?

A. They are made of gold, silver, and copper.

90 parts of gold, 2½ of silver, and 7½ of copper.

1000. What are the component parts of the silver coins of the United States?

A. Silver and copper.

90 parts of silver, 10 of copper.

1001. What is jeweller's gold?

A. An alloy of gold and copper with silver: this gold is liable to tarnish; but its brilliancy can easily be restored by immersing the metal in ammonia.

1002. What is Dutch gold?

A. It is properly an alloy of copper and zinc; but the name is generally applied to the bronze and copper leaf which is made in Germany and sold, like gold-leaf, in books.

1003. What is German silver?

A. German silver, or white copper, (sometimes called argentan,) is an alloy of copper, zinc, and nickel.

1004. What is brass?

A. It is an alloy composed of copper and zinc.

1005. What is bronze?

A. An alloy of copper and tin. It is used for statues and other works of art. Guns and cannon for field-service are made of bronze.

1006. Why would not iron answer as well as bronze for field-pieces?

A. As it has neither so much strength nor tenacity as bronze, the pieces must necessarily be made heavier.

1007. In what respect is iron preferable to bronze for field-pieces?

A. Iron is less expensive than bronze, and is more capable of sustaining long-continued firing with larger charges. Iron cannon are better calculated for the heavy firing of sieges.

A charge is the powder with which a gun or cannon is loaded.

1008. What is pewter?

A. An alloy of tin and lead.

1009. What is bell-metal?

A. It is a mixture of copper and tin, but contains more tin than bronze does.

1010. What is Britannia metal, such as coffee-pots, teapots, &c., are made of?

A. It is an alloy of tin with lead, copper, zinc, antimony, &c., according to its quality.

1011. What is type-metal?

A. The metal of which printing-types are formed is an alloy of lead, tin, and antimony.

1012. How is iron galvanized?

A. By plunging it into melted zinc,—when an alloy is formed on the surface, which prevents oxidation, or rust.

1013. How are looking-glasses silvered?

A. An amalgam, or compound of quicksilver and tin, is spread over the surface of a plate of glass.

1014. What is common solder?

A. Solder is a mixture of lead and tin.

Plumber's solder, 1 part tin, and 1 lead. Tinner's solder, 1 part tin, and 2 lead. Fusible solder, 2 parts tin, 2 parts lead, and 5 parts bismuth; melts at 197°.

CHAPTER II.—GLASS, PORCELAIN, EARTHENWARE.

1015. WHAT is glass?

A. Glass is a mixture of silex and an alkali (usually the carbonate of potash or soda) with lime or oxide of lead, according to the quality of glass to be manufactured. These substances are melted together at a high temperature, which expels the carbonic acid. The mass is left to cool, until it is in a proper state for working.

1016. How is glass worked?

A. Articles of blown glass, such as bottles, &c., are made thus. The workman has an iron tube, five or six feet long, with a mouth-piece of wood, to prevent the heat of the tube from injuring his mouth: this tube he inserts into the pasty glass, and collects a lump large enough to form a bottle; he then rolls it on a marble slab into a pear-shaped ball; this is inserted into a metal mould which opens and shuts on hinges: he then blows through the tube so as to expand the cooling glass into the shape of the mould; the mould is then opened, and the bottle is taken out at the end of the tube; it is then touched with a rod of cold iron, which cracks off the bottle at its mouth-piece.

1017. How is plate-glass made?

A. It is cast on a flat metal table, and, after careful annealing, is ground and polished by machinery.

"Annealing," a process which renders glass less brittle or liable to break. This extreme brittleness is prevented by placing the glass in an oven, where it will cool very slowly. It requires some hours, or even days, to cool.

1018. How is plate-glass ground?

A. One plate of glass is attached to a table, and a smaller one is firmly fixed in a wooden frame. The smaller one is made to move over the lower plate by means of machinery. At first, moistened sand is thrown between the plates; as they become smoother, wet emery of different degrees of fineness is used, instead of the sand; lastly, it is polished with putty of tin.

"Putty of tin" is made thus. Tin is heated above its melting-point, it then oxidizes rapidly, and is converted into a whitish powder used in the arts for polishing, under the name of putty powder, or putty of tin.

1019. For what purpose is plate-glass used?

A. For mirrors and large window-panes.

1020. How are mirrors made?

A. They are made of plate-glass covered with an alloy of mercury and tin.

The alloy is formed of 30 parts mercury, 70 tin.

1021. What is porcelain?

A. All kinds of china-ware, such as are used for dishes, cups, &c., are denominated porcelain: some kinds are much finer and more beautiful than others.

The first royal table-service of English manufacture was made for Queen Charlotte, wife of George III., by Josiah Wedgwood, who was forthwith appointed her royal potter. This kind of ware was afterwards called Queensware.

1022. Of what is porcelain composed?

A. The chief materials used in its manufacture are a certain clay derived from decomposed feldspar, calcined flints finely ground, together with a portion of feldspar reduced to powder.

"Feldspar," a kind of mineral. "Calcined," heated intensely so as to crumble.

1023. How are these materials mixed together?

A. They are put into a kind of mill, which is a large cylindrical vessel or tub, into which a small stream of water is constantly suffered to trickle. The mass is now ground or mixed into a kind of pap or dough. This dough is kneaded or worked with the hands until the mass is quite smooth and of a uniform color. It is now ready for moulding.

1024. What is moulding?

A. Forming the dough or paste into the shape required, such as bowls, plates, cups, &c.

1025. How are these articles moulded?

A. The operation is performed on a machine called a potter's lathe. A small piece of the clay or dough is placed upon this lathe, and, owing to the rapid rotary motion of the machine, the workman is able to shape a vessel by keeping his hands constantly wet; he moulds it to a proper size by means of pegs and gauges. It is suffered to dry partially, and is then placed upon another lathe, when it is shaped more evenly and accurately and smoothed and burnished with a polished steel surface. The vessels are then put into a kiln and baked.

1026. How long is porcelain usually baked?

A. It requires forty hours or more.

1027. How is the gloss given to china plates?

A. This is called glazing. Glaze is made in various ways, according to the quality of the articles to be glazed.

Gypsum, silica, and a little porcelain clay are ground together and diffused through water. Sometimes a little lead is added. Each article is dipped for a moment in this mixture and withdrawn. The water sinks into the substance, leaving the powder evenly spread on its surface. They are once more dried, and put into a kiln which is fired at an extremely high temperature. The ware is then finished, unless it is to be gilded or otherwise ornamented.

1028. How is stoneware, such as is used for jugs, jars, &c., made?

A. This is a very coarse kind of porcelain, made from clay containing oxide of iron and a little lime.

1029. How is stoneware glazed?

A. By throwing common salt into the heated furnace: this is volatilized by the vapor of water which is always present, and the silica of the clay of which the ware is composed. This fuses over the surface of the ware and gives a thin but excellent glaze.

"Volatilize," to fly off. "Fuses," melts or liquefies by heat.

1030. What is earthenware?

A. This is composed of a species of clay mixed with silica. It is moulded in the same manner as porcelain, dried and baked in a kiln: it is then glazed with a mixture which contains the oxides of lead and tin, after which it is reheated.

Articles glazed with this mixture are very improper for culinary vessels, as the lead in the glaze is affected by acids.

PART IV.

ORGANIC CHEMISTRY.

1031. What is organic chemistry?

A. The chemistry of compounds obtained either directly or indirectly from organic substances, vegetable or animal.

1032. What are the elements which compose organic substances generally?

A. All organic substances, with comparatively few exceptions, are composed of carbon, hydrogen, oxygen, and nitrogen.

Sulphur and phosphorus are occasionally associated with these, and also certain compounds containing chlorine, iodine, &c.

CHAPTER I.—SUGAR.

1033. Of what is sugar composed?

A. Of carbon, hydrogen, and oxygen.

1034. Is sugar a vegetable substance?

A. Yes: it is found in the juice of many plants and in the sap of several trees; but it is extracted in the greatest abundance from the juice of the sugar-cane, which is cultivated for that purpose in the Southern States.

1035. From what other sources is sugar obtained?

A. From the sugar-maple, which grows abundantly in the United States, and from beet-root.

The sugar-maple is a species of maple, the botanical name of which is *Acer saccharinum.*

1036. How is sugar made from the sugar-cane?

A. The cane is crushed, and the expressed juice mixed with a small quantity of slacked lime and heated to near the boiling-point: the clear liquid thus produced is rapidly evaporated in an open pan, after which it is transferred to a shallow vessel and left to crystallize, during which time it is frequently agitated, in order to hinder the formation of large crystals: it is then drained from the syrup, or molasses. This is what is called raw or Muscovado sugar; after which it is refined.

1037. How is sugar refined?

A. By re-dissolving it in water, and adding a certain quantity of albumen in the shape of blood or white of egg, and sometimes a little lime-water, and heating the whole to the boiling-point.

1038. What effect has the albumen on the sugar?

A. It coagulates, and forms a kind of network of fibres, which enclose and separate from the liquid all the impurities suspended in it.

1039. What is the next process toward making sugar?

A. It is then filtrated through charcoal, evaporated, and put into conical earthen moulds, where it solidifies. It is then drained and dried, and the product is the ordinary loaf-sugar.

1040. What is grape-sugar?

A. It is the sugar of fruits, and is abundantly diffused throughout the vegetable kingdom. It is called grape-sugar because it may be extracted in large quantities from the juice of sweet grapes. Grape-sugar forms the solid crystalline portion of honey.

CHAPTER II.—FERMENTATION AND PUTREFACTION.

SECTION I.—FERMENTATION.

1041. WHAT is fermentation?

A. Fermentation is a change effected in the elements of a body composed of carbon, hydrogen, and oxygen.

1042. What new compounds are produced by the change called fermentation?

A. Alcohol and carbonic acid. The alcohol is still further changed, unless the process be checked, into acetic acid, or vinegar.

1043. What are the elements of grape-sugar?

A. Carbon, oxygen, and hydrogen, in equal proportions.

1044. What changes does sugar undergo by fermentation?

A. It is first decomposed, and then its elements reunite in different proportions, producing alcohol, carbonic acid, and water.

Of sugar, one portion is alcohol and another carbonic acid,—as may be seen by the following table:—

	Carb.	Oxy.	Hyd.
Every atom of anhydrous sugar contains	12	12	12
Two atoms of alcohol contain	8	4	12
Four atoms of carbonic acid contain...............	4	8	0
	12	12	12

"Anhydrous sugar" is sugar dried at 300°.

1045. How does sugar form alcohol by fermentation?

A. Two-thirds of its carbon and one-third

of its oxygen reunite with the hydrogen and generate alcohol.

1046. How does sugar form carbonic acid by fermentation?

A. The remaining one-third of its carbon and two-thirds of its oxygen reunite and generate carbonic acid.

1047. What becomes of the alcohol which is thus generated by fermentation?

A. It mixes with the water, and forms the intoxicating part of beer and wine.

1048. What becomes of the carbonic acid which is generated by fermentation?

A. It escapes into the air.

1049. Why is barley malted?

A. Because germination is produced by the artificial heat, and in germination the starch of the grain is converted into sugar.

1050. What is alcohol?

A. The spirit of beer and wine, obtained by fermentation.

1051. Of what elements is alcohol composed?

A. Of carbon, oxygen, and hydrogen.

Of alcohol, 4 parts are carbon, 2 oxygen, and 6 hydrogen.

1052. What is meant by spirit above and below proof?

A. If we say that spirit is ten over proof, we mean that one hundred gallons of it will require ten gallons of water to reduce the spirit to proof strength. So, on the converse, if we say that spirit is ten under proof, we mean that ten gallons of water must be taken from the spirit to raise it to proof strength.

The strength of spirit is now tested by an instrument called the hydrometer.

1053. Why is it not needful to put yeast into grape-juice in order to produce fermentation?

A. Because grape-juice contains a sufficient quantity of a nitrogenized substance (like yeast) to produce fermentation.

"Nitrogenized," that is, containing nitrogen.

1054. Of what does the juice of grapes consist?

A. Mainly of water, holding in solution albumen, sugar, cream of tartar, &c.

1055. How is wine made?

A. The albumen contained in the juice of the grapes undergoes a change, and acquires the power of exciting fermentation in any liquid containing sugar.

1056. What is the albumen called when it possesses this property?

A. It is called lees of wine.

1057. How are champagne and sparkling hock made?

A. The fermentation of the grape-juice is checked before it is complete: the wine is bottled, and the process of fermentation is continued in the bottles.

1058. Why do these wines sparkle?

A. Because the carbonic acid, being disengaged under considerable pressure, is retained in the wine.

1059. Why do not grapes ferment while they hang on the vine?

A. Because the water of the juice evaporates through the skin, and allows the grapes to shrivel and dry up after they are ripe.

Fermentation cannot occur unless the sugar be dissolved in a sufficient quantity of water.

1060. What is gluten?

A. A tough, elastic substance, composed of carbon, oxygen, hydrogen, and nitrogen.

1061. Does malt contain gluten?

A. Yes. The infusion of malt called "sweet-wort" contains an abundance of gluten; and the yeast, which converts its sugar into alcohol, converts this gluten into yeast.

1062. How is barley malted?

A. It is moistened with water, and heaped up; by which means great heat is produced, which makes the barley sprout.

1063. Why is not the barley suffered to grow as well as sprout?

A. Because plants in the germ contain more sugar than in any other state: as soon as the germ puts forth shoots, the sugar of the plant is consumed to support the shoot.

1064. How is barley prevented from shooting in the process of malting?

A. It is put into a kiln as soon as it

sprouts, and the heat of the kiln checks or destroys the young shoot.

1065. What is yeast?

A. The foam of beer, or of some similar liquor, produced by fermentation.

1066. Why is yeast used in brewing?

A. Because it consists of a substance called gluten, undergoing putrefaction; in which state it possesses the peculiar property of exciting fermentation.

If the gluten were not in a putrefying state, it could not produce fermentation.

1067. Why is yeast needful in order to make malt into beer?

A. Because the presence of a putrefying body containing nitrogen is essential in order to convert sugar into alcohol.

1068. What effect has yeast upon the sweet-wort?

A. It causes the sugar to be converted into alcohol and carbonic acid.

1069. Why is porter much darker than ale or beer?

A. Because the malt of which porter is made is dried at a higher temperature, and slightly charred.

Small beer is a weak wort fermented, and contains 1½ per cent. of alcohol.

Ale is a stronger wort, and contains 7 per cent. of alcohol.

Porter contains 4½ per cent. of alcohol.

Brown Stout contains 6¾ per cent. of alcohol.

Burton Ale contains 8½ per cent. of alcohol.

"Wort" is the fermentable infusion of malt or grain.

1070. What is the froth or scum of fermented liquors?

A. Putrefying glutinous substances, of a nature similar to yeast, which rise to the surface from their lightness.

1071. Why is beer flat if the cask be left open too long?

A. Because too much of the carbonic acid gas produced by fermentation is suffered to escape.

1072. Why does milk turn sour?

A. Because it undergoes fermentation, during which "lactic acid" is formed, and the milk becomes sour.

The lactic acid is formed from the sugar of milk by fermentation.

1073. Why does milk turn sour in hot weather much sooner than in cold?

A. Because heat very greatly accelerates the process of fermentation, during which lactic acid is formed.

1074. Why cannot stale milk be boiled without curdling it?

A. Because stale milk is in an incipient state of fermentation, which the heat of the fire greatly accelerates; and the lactic acid which is formed during fermentation, mixing with the casein of the milk, coagulates it.

1075. Why does a small portion of corrosive sublimate keep paste from turning sour?

A. Corrosive sublimate, being a powerful

antiseptic, prevents fermentation, which is the cause of the paste turning sour.

1076. What is bread?

A. It is a kind of food prepared generally from the flour of wheat mixed with water to a dough, and submitted to the action of heat to bake. This kind of bread is called unfermented or unleavened bread.

1077. What is leavened bread?

A. It is flour mixed to a dough with water, to which is added a little leaven (or dough which has been fermented) or yeast.

1078. What effect has the yeast on the dough?

A. It assists in the fermentation of the dough, by which means carbonic acid is generated in the mass and makes the bread porous and light: it is then placed in the oven, and this gas, expanding by heat, raises the dough still more, and puts a stop to any further fermentation.

1079. How does fermentation make the dough rise?

A. During fermentation, carbonic acid gas is evolved; but the sticky texture of the dough will not allow it to escape; so it forces up little bubbles all over the dough.

1080. Why is new bread indigestible?

A. Because the change called "panary fermentation" is not completed.

"Panary," from the Latin word *panis*, bread. "Panary fermentation" means the fermentation that dough undergoes in order to become bread.

The sugar of the dough is converted into alcohol and carbonic acid by fermentation: the dough, being adhesive, prevents the escape of these products till the mass is baked, —when the gas expands and bursts through the mass, leaving a number of holes or bladders, showing where it was confined.

So long as the bread is warm, the process of fermentation is going on: therefore bread should never be eaten till it is twenty-four hours old.

1081. Why does baking dough convert it into bread?

A. When dough formed of flour is baked, a portion of its starch is changed into a gum called dextrin.

A similar change is produced upon the farinaceous portion of the dough. The yeast added to the dough converts part of the starch and sugar into alcohol and carbonic acid: of these the alcohol evaporates in the oven, and the carbonic acid forces the dough into bubbles in its effort to escape, rendering the bread light and full of holes.

In 100 pounds of bread and 100 pounds of dough there are—

	Starch.	Sugar.	Dextrin.
In dough.........	68 pounds..........	5 pounds.........	0 × 100
In bread.........	53½ "	3½ "	18 × 100

Whence it will be seen that 16½ pounds of starch have been converted into the gum called dextrin by baking.

Dextrin is a gummy matter similar to that which composes the cells of wood, (called cellulin,) except that it is soluble in cold water.

Diastase is a peculiar vegetable principle of malt, extracted by water, which converts starch into dextrin or sugar.

1082. Why is dough placed before the fire?

A. 1st. Because the heat of the fire increases the fermentation; and,

2d. It expands the gas confined in the little bubbles; in consequence of which, the bubbles are enlarged, and the dough becomes lighter and more porous.

1083. Why will dough not rise in cold weather unless it be placed near the fire?

A. Because it gets cold; and then the air in the little bubbles condenses, the paste falls, and the bread becomes close and heavy.

1084. Why is well-made bread full of holes or bubbles?

A. Because the fermentation of the dough throws up little bubbles filled with carbonic acid gas; and when the dough is baked, these bubbles are made permanent in the bread.

SECTION II.—PUTREFACTION.

1085. What is the difference between fermentation and putrefaction?

A. Fermentation is a change effected in the elements of a body composed of carbon, oxygen, and hydrogen, without nitrogen: putrefaction is a change effected in the elements of a body composed of carbon, oxygen, hydrogen, and nitrogen.

1086. What new compounds are produced by the change called putrefaction?

A. The carbon, oxygen, hydrogen, and nitrogen of the original substance, being separated by decomposition, reunite in the following manner:—1. Carbon and oxygen unite to form carbonic acid; 2. Oxygen and hydrogen unite to form water; 3. Hydrogen and nitrogen unite to form ammonia.

Hartshorn is a solution of ammonia in water.

When bodies containing sulphur and phosphorus putrefy, the sulphur and phosphorus unite with hydrogen, and form sulphuretted and phosphuretted hydrogen gases.

1087. What becomes of these several products of putrefaction?

A. They are all elastic bodies, and escape into the air.

Water is elastic and gaseous when in the condition of vapor.

1088. What is the cause of the offensive smell which issues from putrefying bodies?

A. The evolution of ammonia, or of sulphuretted and phosphuretted hydrogen gases, —all of which have pungent and offensive odors.

1089. What change is produced in gluten by putrefaction?

A. Its elements are loosened from their former conditions of combination, and rearranged, with the addition of oxygen from the air, into a new series.

1090. Why do boiled eggs discolor a silver spoon?

A. Because they contain a small portion of sulphur, which unites with the silver (for which it has a great affinity) and tarnishes it.

Both the white and yolk contain sulphur,—the latter more abundantly.

1091. What causes the offensive smell of stale hard-boiled eggs?

A. The hydrogen of the egg combining with the sulphur and phosphorus form sulphuretted and phosphuretted hydrogen,—both of which gases have an offensive odor.

Of an egg, 55 parts are carbon, 16 nitrogen, 7 hydrogen, and the remaining 22 are oxygen, phosphorus, and sulphur.

1092. Decaying vegetables are first of a brownish tint: why do they afterward turn of a blackish color?

A. Because the hydrogen of the decaying vegetables is separated from the mass by the process of decay, and leaves a larger proportion of carbon behind.

Vegetable fibre contains 52½ per cent. of carbon; when partially decayed, 54 per cent.; when black with decay, 56 per cent.

1093. Why are decaying vegetables always moist?

A. Because the hydrogen and oxygen of the vegetables are given up by decay, and unite to form water.

Decaying vegetables combine into the following new forms:—1st. The oxygen and hydrogen form into water; 2d. The carbon unites with the oxygen of the air, and produces carbonic acid gas.

1094. Why does meat putrefy sooner in hot, damp weather than in cold?

A. 1st. Because the carbon of the meat unites with the oxygen of the air more readily when hot than cold; and,

2d. Because the damp deposited on the surface of the meat is of itself one of the compounds of putrefaction, and leaves an excess of hydrogen in the meat.

Thus the original proportions and combinations of the meat are altered and decomposed.

Putrefaction is simply the decomposition of the original elements, and their reunion in a new order. The new order is as follows:—

1st. Carbon and oxygen unite to form carbonic acid; 2d. Hydrogen and oxygen unite to form water; 3d. Hydrogen and nitrogen unite to form ammonia.

Carbon unites with oxygen with a readiness proportioned to its heat: when red-hot, the combination is most easily effected.

The chief reason why salt preserves meat is that it absorbs the water from it and deprives it of hydrogen.

1095. Why does meat putrefy most rapidly in very changeable weather?

A. Because moisture is more freely deposited on the meat in very changeable weather; and this moisture is a chief compound of putrefaction.

1096. How can the taint of meat be removed?

A. Either by washing it with pyroligneous acid, or by covering it for a few hours with common charcoal, or by putting a few lumps of charcoal into the water in which it is boiled.

1097. Why do these things destroy the taint of meat?

A. Because they combine with the putrescent particles, and neutralize their offensive taste and smell.

1098. Why does stagnant water putrefy?

A. Because leaves, plants, insects, &c., are decomposed in it.

1099. Why is stagnant water full of worms, &c.?

A. Because numberless insects lay their eggs in the leaves and plants floating on the surface: these eggs are soon hatched, and produce swarms of worms and insects.

1100. Why is flowing water free from these impurities?

A. 1st. Because the motion of running water prevents fermentation;

2d. It dissolves the putrid substances which happen to fall into it; and,

3d. It casts on the bank, by its current, such substances as it cannot dissolve.

1101. Birds, after they are killed, keep longer in their feathers than when they are plucked. Why is this?

A. Because the feathers prevent the air or damp from getting so readily to the bird, to produce decay.

1102. Why does unseasoned wood decay much more rapidly than wood well seasoned?

A. Because the albumen which the sap contains produces a species of fermentation, during which the cellulin and ligneous matter of the wood are turned into carbonic acid and water.

"Albumen," a substance resembling the white of an egg.

"Cellulin," the substance which composes the cells of wood, as wax composes the cells of a honey-comb.

"Ligneous matter," or vegetable fibre, is the hard or woody part of wood.

1103. Why is wood placed in a stream of running water to season it?

A. Because the running water washes away the sap, and thus prevents fermentation and decay.

1104. Why will solutions of salts prevent the decay of wood steeped therein?

A. Because the salts unite with the albumen of the sap, coagulate it, and prevent fermentation.

CHAPTER III.—COMPONENTS OF THE ANIMAL BODY.

1105. WHAT is albumen?

A. The serum, or fluid portion of the blood, (which, after exposure to the air, is separated from the more solid part,) the vitreous and crystalline humors of the eye, the brain, spinal marrow, and nerves, all contain albumen.

It exists most abundantly, and in its purest natural state, in the white of an egg; whence it derives its name, (*album ovi*, the Latin for the white of an egg.)

Albumen exists in the animal system in two forms,—in the liquid and the solid state. The best example of fluid albumen is the white of an egg. In the solid state it forms the principal part of all the membranes, skin, muscle, and glands.

1106. Milk burns very easily when boiled: water will not do so. Explain this.

A. 1st. Milk contains solid organic substances, capable of burning, which water does not; and,

2d. The heat of the fire coagulates the albumen of the milk, which falls to the bottom and adheres to the boiler.

1107. Why are lamb and veal more tender than beef and mutton?

A. Because they contain more albumen and less muscular fibre.

1108. Why do lamb and veal taint more quickly than beef and mutton?

A. Because they contain a large quantity of albumen, which is very liable to putrefaction.

1109. Why is meat tough which has been boiled too long?

A. Because the albumen becomes hard like the white of a hard-boiled egg.

The best way of boiling meat to make it tender is thus: Put your joint in very brisk-boiling water, and after a few minutes add a little cold water. The boiling water will *fix* the albumen, which will prevent the water from soaking into the meat, keep all its juices in, and prevent the muscular fibre from contracting. The addition of cold water will secure the cooking of the inside of the meat as well as of the surface.

1110. Why is meat always tough if it be put into the boiler before the water boils?

A. Because the water is not hot enough to coagulate the albumen between the muscular fibres of the meat, which therefore runs into the water and rises to the surface as a scum.

1111. Why is the flesh of old animals tough?

A. Because it contains very little albumen and much muscular fibre.

1112. Is salted meat as nutritious as fresh meat?

A. No; because the albumen of the meat is separated from the flesh by the brine, as well as the alkaline phosphates, and some other substances of great value.

Phosphates are alkaline and mineral: alkaline phosphates are phosphoric acid combined with some alkali, such as soda, potash, magnesia, &c.

"Albumen of the meat,"—a substance resembling the white of an egg, which lies between the muscular fibres of all flesh and makes the meat tender.

"The alkaline phosphates of meat" are such as these: the phosphate of soda, the phosphate of potash, and the phosphate of magnesia, which are extracted from the meat by the acid reaction of the brine.

1113. Why does salt preserve meat?

A. 1st. Because it removes the water contained in the animal fibre, absorbing it and leaving the meat dry.

2d. Salt is composed of chlorine and sodium: the chlorine of the salt takes up the hydrogen of the meat as it is given off, and prevents the offensive taste and smell of decay;

3d. Brine draws away the albumen from

between the muscular fibres, which is very subject to putrefaction;

4th. The salt unites with the muscular fibre, and makes a new chemical compound much less subject to decay; and,

5th. It keeps the air, flies, &c. from the meat.

1114. Is albumen found only in animals?

A. No: it abounds also in vegetables. It makes the chief bulk of some seeds, as wheat, corn, &c.

1115. What is fibrine?

A. It is a compound which abounds in both animal and vegetable substances. The chief part of muscular flesh is formed of fibrine. It also exists in chyle, and enters into the composition of the blood.

1116. What is caseine?

A. A white substance which exists in milk, and constitutes the greater part of cheese made from skimmed milk.

It resembles coagulated but pulverulent albumen.

1117. Does caseine exist also in vegetables?

A. It is found in peas, beans, &c. They are crushed, mixed with water, and strained. In this way the caseine is procured, which has all the characteristics of skimmed milk.

1118. What is gelatine?

A. It is a jelly-like substance, formed by

boiling animal membranes, skin, and even bones. It does not exist in its natural state in the animal system, but is easily produced by means of hot water. The well-known substance called isinglass, and also calves'-feet jelly, are familiar examples of gelatine. Glue is a kind of gelatine dried in the air.

1119. Why does the use of salt beef produce scurvy?

A. Because the soluble salts are removed from the beef by brine; in consequence of which, it cannot restore to the human system those salts which are essential to preserve the blood in a healthy state.

Dr. Budd has shown that it is the absence of vegetables, and not the use of salt meat, which produces scurvy.

1120. Why does the use of vegetables generally prevent scurvy?

A. Because they contain the soluble salts removed from the beef by brine; which, being restored by the vegetables, preserve the blood in a healthy state.

1121. Why is lime-juice a perfect cure for scurvy?

A. Because it contains the very salts removed from the beef by the action of the brine,—namely, alkaline phosphates, and sulphate, chloride, and phosphate of lime.

1122. Why does currant-juice when boiled with sugar form a jelly?

A. Because the currant-juice contains pectine,—a gelatinous matter which abounds in many fruits. The consistence of currant and other fruit jellies is ascribed to this substance.

CHAPTER IV.—ANIMAL HEAT.

1123. WHAT is the cause of animal heat?

A. Animal heat is produced by the combustion of hydrogen and carbon in the capillary vessels.

1124. How do hydrogen gas and carbon get into these vessels?

A. The food we eat is converted into blood; and blood contains both hydrogen and carbon.

1125. Why is every part of the body warm?

A. Because the capillary vessels run through every part of the human body, and the combustion of blood takes place in the capillary vessels.

1126. What are the capillary vessels?

A. Vessels as small as hairs, running all over the body: they are called capillary from the Latin word "*capillaris*," (like a hair.)

1127. Prove that these capillary vessels run all over the human body.

A. Whenever blood flows from a wound, some vein or vessel must be divided; and, as you can bring blood from any part of the body by a very slight wound, these little vessels must run through every part of the human frame.

1128. How does combustion take place in the capillary vessels?

A. The carbon of the blood combines with the oxygen of the air we breathe, and forms into carbonic acid gas.

1129. What becomes of this carbonic acid gas formed in the human blood?

A. The lungs throw off almost all of it into the air, by the act of respiration.

1130. Does the heat of the human body arise from the same cause as the heat of fire?

A. Yes, precisely. The carbon of the blood combines with the oxygen of the air inhaled, and produces carbonic acid gas, which is attended with combustion.

1131. If animal heat is produced by combustion, why does not the human body burn up like a coal or candle?

A. It actually does so. Every muscle, nerve, and organ of the body actually wastes away like a burning candle, and, being reduced to air and ashes, is rejected from the system as useless.

1132. If every bone, muscle, nerve, and organ is thus consumed by combustion, why is not the body entirely consumed?

A. It would be so, unless the parts destroyed were perpetually renewed; but, as a lamp will not go out so long as it is supplied with fresh oil, neither will the body be consumed so long as it is supplied with sufficient food.

1133. What is the principal difference between the combustion of a fire or lamp and that of the human body?

A. In the human body the combustion is effected at a much lower temperature and is carried on more slowly than it is in a lamp or fire.

1134. What causes the heat of our body?

A. The carbon of our blood combines with the oxygen of the air inhaled, and produces carbonic acid gas; which evolves heat in a way similar to burning fuel.

1135. Why do oxygen and carbon so readily unite in the blood?

A. Because the atoms of carbon are so loosely attracted by the other materials of the blood that they unite very readily with the oxygen of the air inhaled.

1136. Is carbonic acid wholesome?

A. No: it is fatal to animal life, and, whenever it is inhaled, acts like a narcotic poison,—producing drowsiness, which sometimes ends in death.

1137. How is it that carbon can be made to burn at so low a temperature in the human body?

A. Because the carbon in the blood is reduced to very minute particles; and these particles are ready to undergo a rapid change as soon as oxygen is supplied.

1138. Why are very poor people instinctively averse to ventilation?

A. 1st. Because ventilation increases the oxygen of the air, the combustion of food, and the cravings of appetite; and,

2d. Ventilation cools the air of rooms: to poor people, therefore, who are ill clad, the warmth of an ill-ventilated apartment is agreeable.

1139. Why are the ill clad also instinctively averse to cleanliness?

A. Because dirt is warm: (thus, pigs, who love warmth, are fond of dirt:) to those, therefore, who are very ill clad, the warmth of dirt is agreeable.

1140. Why does flannel, &c. make us warm?

A. Flannel and warm clothing do not make us warm, but merely prevent our body from becoming cold.

1141. How does flannel, &c. prevent our body from becoming cold?

A. Flannel, being a bad conductor, will

neither carry off the heat of our body into the cold air, nor suffer the cold air to come in contact with our warm body.

1142. Why are frogs and fishes cold-blooded animals?

A. Because they consume very little air; and without a plentiful supply of air combustion is too slow to generate much animal heat.

1143. Why is a dead body cold?

A. Because air is no longer conveyed to the lungs after respiration has ceased, and therefore animal heat is no longer generated by combustion.

1144. Why do we need warmer clothing by night than by day?

A. 1st. Because the night is generally colder than the day; and,

2d. Our bodies are then colder also; because we breathe more slowly, and our animal combustion is retarded.

1145. Why do we perspire when very hot?

A. The pores of the body are like the safety-valves of a steam-engine: when the heat of the body is very great, some of the combustible matter of the blood is thrown off in perspiration, and the heat of the body kept more temperate.

1146. Why does running make us warm?

A. Because we inhale air more rapidly

when we run, and cause the blood to pass more rapidly through the lungs in contact with it. Running acts upon the capillary vessels as a pair of bellows on a common fire.

1147. Why does inhaling air rapidly make the body feel warm?

A. Because more oxygen is introduced into the body; in consequence of which, the combustion of the blood is more rapid, the blood itself is more heated, and every part of the body is made warmer.

1148. How does the combination of oxygen with the blood produce animal heat?

A. The principal element of the blood is carbon; and this carbon, combining with the oxygen of the air inhaled, produces carbonic acid gas, in the same way as burning fuel.

1149. What becomes of the nitrogen of the air after the oxygen enters the blood?

A. It is thrown out from the lungs unchanged, by the act of breathing, to be again mixed with oxygen and converted into common air.

1150. Explain how we breathe.

A. By a muscular action, we make an enlarged space in the chest; the pressure of the external atmosphere forces air into this space, so as to fill it. By a second muscular action, the lungs are compressed, and the air is forced out and escapes. The air which escapes is chiefly nitrogen.

1151. Why does the vitiated air, after the oxygen has been absorbed, come out of the mouth, and not sink into the stomach?

A. Because a mechanical provision is made in the upper part of the windpipe and gullet for this purpose.

The lungs are a hollow, spongy mass, capable of confining air and of being dilated by it. They are so situated in the thorax (or chest) that the air must enter into them whenever the cavities of the thorax are enlarged. The process of breathing is performed thus: When we *inhale*, the thorax is expanded; in consequence of which, a vacuum is formed round the lungs, and heavy external air instantly enters, through the mouth and throat, to supply this vacuum.

When we *exhale*, the thorax contracts again; in consequence of which, it can no longer contain the same quantity of air as it did before; and some of it is necessarily expelled. When this expulsion of air takes place, the lungs and muscular fibres of the windpipe and gullet contract in order to assist the process.

1152. If both in combustion and respiration the oxygen of the air is consumed and the nitrogen rejected, why are not the proportions of the air destroyed?

A. Because the under surface of vegetable leaves during the day gives out oxygen, and thus restores to the air the very element of which it has been deprived.

1153. Whence do leaves obtain the oxygen which they exhale?

A. From the carbonic acid absorbed by the roots from the soil and carried to the leaves by the rising sap.

Carbonic acid, it must be remembered, is a compound of carbon and oxygen.

1154. How do plants contrive to absorb carbonic acid from the soil?

A. It rises, by capillary attraction, through the small fibrous roots, after it has been dissolved in the soil by water.

1155. If leaves throw off the oxygen of the carbonic acid, what becomes of the carbon?

A. It is retained to give firmness and solidity to the plant itself.

1156. Show how God has made animal life dependent on that of vegetables.

A. Animals require oxygen to keep them alive, and draw it from the air by inspiration. The under surface of leaves gives out oxygen, and thus supplies the air with the very gas required for the use of animals.

1157. Show how God has made vegetable life dependent on that of animals.

A. Plants require carbonic acid, which is their principal food; and all animals exhale the same gas from their lungs. Thus plants supply animals with oxygen, and animals supply plants with carbonic acid.

SECTION I.—FOOD.

1158. What is the fuel of the body?

A. Food is the fuel of the body. The carbon of the food, mixing with the oxygen of the air, evolves heat, in the same way that a fire or candle does.

1159. How is food converted into blood?

A. After it is swallowed, it is dissolved

in the stomach into a gray pulp, called chyme; it then passes into the intestines, and is converted by the "bile" into a milky substance, called chyle.

1160. What becomes of the milky substance called chyle?

A. It is absorbed by vessels called "lacteals," and poured into the veins on the left side of the neck.

1161. What becomes of the chyle after it is poured into the veins?

A. It mingles with the blood, and is itself converted into blood also.

1162. How does the oxygen we inhale mingle with the blood?

A. The oxygen of the air mingles with the blood in the lungs, and converts it into a bright-red color.

1163. How does oxygen convert the color of blood into a bright red?

A. The coloring-matter of the blood is formed by very minute globules floating in it; the oxygen, uniting with the coats of these globules, makes them milky, and the dark coloring-matter of the blood, seen through this milky coat, appears of a bright red.

If you put some dark venous blood into a milky glass, and hold it up toward the light, it will appear of a bright florid color like arterial blood.

1164. What is the color of the blood before it is oxidized in the lungs?

A. A dark purple. The oxygen turns it to a bright red.

"Oxidized," impregnated with oxygen.

1165. Why are persons pale who live in close rooms and cities?

A. Because the blood derives its redness from the oxygen of the air inhaled; but, as the air in close rooms and cities is not fresh, it is deficient in oxygen, and cannot turn the blood to a beautiful bright red.

1166. Why are persons who live in the open air and in the country of a ruddy complexion?

A. Because they inhale fresh air which has its full proportion of oxygen; and the blood derives its bright-red color from the oxygen of the air inhaled.

1167. Why is not the air in cities so fresh as that in the country?

A. Because it is impregnated with the breath of its numerous inhabitants, the odor of its sewers, the smoke of its fires, and many other impurities.

1168. Why do we feel lazy and averse to activity in very hot weather?

A. 1st. Because muscular activity increases the heat of the body, by quickening the respiration; and,

2d. The food we eat in hot weather, not

being greasy, naturally abates our desire for bodily activity.

1169. Why are the Esquimaux passionately fond of train-oil and whale-blubber?

A. Because oil and blubber contain large quantities of carbon and hydrogen, which are exceedingly combustible; and, as these people live in climates of intense cold, the heat of their bodies is increased by the greasy nature of their food.

1170. Why do we like strong meat and greasy food when the weather is very cold?

A. Because strong meat and grease contain large portions of carbon and hydrogen, which, when burned in the blood, produce a larger amount of heat than any other kind of food.

1171. Why do persons eat more food in cold weather than in hot?

A. Because the body requires more fuel in cold weather to keep up the same amount of animal heat; and as we put more fuel on a fire on a cold day to keep our apartments warm, so we eat more food on a cold day to keep our body warm.

1172. Why do we like fruits and vegetables most in hot weather?

A. Because they contain less hydrogen and carbon than meat, and therefore produce both less blood, and blood of a less combustible nature.

1173. Why do we feel a dislike to strong meat and greasy food in very hot weather?

A. Because strong meat and grease contain so much carbon and hydrogen that they would make us intensely hot: we therefore instinctively refuse them in hot weather.

1174. Why do the inhabitants of tropical countries live chiefly upon rice and fruit?

A. Because rice and fruit by digestion are mainly converted into water, and, by cooling the blood, prevent the tropical heat from feeling so oppressive.

1175. Why is the blood of a less combustible nature if we live chiefly upon fruits and vegetables?

A. Because fruits and vegetables supply the blood with a very large amount of water,—which is not combustible, like the carbon and hydrogen of strong meat.

1176. How do fruits and vegetables cool the blood?

A. 1st. They diminish the amount of carbon and hydrogen in the blood, which are the chief causes of animal heat; and,

2d. They supply the blood with a large amount of water, which exudes through the skin and leaves the body cool.

SECTION II.—HUNGER.

1177. Why does cold produce hunger?

A. 1st. Because the air contains more oxygen in cold weather, and therefore fires burn more fiercely, and animal combustion is more rapid; and,

2d. As we are more active in cold weather, our increased respiration acts like a pair of bellows on the capillary combustion.

1178. Why does rapid digestion produce a craving appetite?

A. This is a wise providence to keep our bodies in health: they give notice, by hunger, that the capillary fires need replenishing, in order that the body itself may not be consumed.

1179. Why do we feel a desire for activity in cold weather?

A. 1st. Because activity increases the warmth of the body, by fanning the combustion of the blood; and,

2d. The strong food we eat creates a desire for muscular exertion.

1180. Why does reading aloud make us feel hungry?

A. Because it increases respiration; and, as more oxygen is introduced into the lungs, our food-fuel is more rapidly consumed.

1181. Why do we feel less hungry in the night than in the day?

A. Because we breathe more slowly during

sleep: therefore less oxygen is introduced into the lungs to consume our food-fuel.

1182. Why does hard work produce hunger?

A. Because it produces quicker respiration; by which means a larger amount of oxygen is introduced into the lungs, and the capillary combustion increased. Hunger is the notice given by our body to remind us that our food-fuel must be replenished.

1183. Why have persons who follow hard out-of-door occupations more appetite than those who are engaged in sedentary pursuits?

A. Hard bodily labor in the open air causes much oxygen to be conveyed into the lungs by inspiration; the combustion of the food is carried on quickly, animal heat increased, and need for nutritious food more quickly indicated by craving hunger.

1184. Why have persons who follow sedentary pursuits less appetite than ploughmen and masons?

A. 1st. Because the air they inhale is less pure, being deprived of some of its oxygen; and,

2d. Their respiration is neither so quick nor so strong; and therefore the combustion of their food is carried on more slowly.

1185. Why do persons feel lazy and averse to exercise when they are half starved or ill fed?

A. Animal food contains great nourishment, and produces a desire for active occupations;

but when the body is not supplied with strong food, this desire for muscular action ceases, and the person grows slothful.

1186. Why does a man shrink when starved?

A. Because the capillary fires feed upon the human body when they are not supplied with food-fuel. A starved man shrinks, just as a fire does when it is not supplied with fuel.

1187. When a man is starved, what parts of the body go first?

A. First, the fat, because it is the most combustible; then the muscles; last of all, the brain; and then the man dies, like a candle which is burnt out.

1188. Why does want of sufficient nourishment often produce madness?

A. Because after the fat and muscles of the body have been consumed by animal combustion the brain is attacked, and madness often ensues.

CHAPTER V.—SLEEP.

1189. What is sleep?

A. Sleep is the rest of the brain and nervous system.

1190. Why have dreamers no power of judgment or reason?

A. Because the "cerebrum" (or front of the brain) is inactive and at rest.

1191. Why can we not see when we are asleep with our eyes open?

A. Because the "retina of the eye" is inactive and at rest.

1192. Why can we not hear in sleep?

A. Because the nerve of hearing, seated within the tympanum of the ear, is at rest.

1193. Why can we not feel when we are asleep?

A. Because the extremities of the nerves situated in the skin are inactive and at rest.

1194. Why can we not taste when we are asleep?

A. Because the nerves at the end of the tongue are inactive and at rest.

1195. Why have persons in sleep no will of their own, but may be moved at the will of any one?

A. Because the "cerebellum" (or posterior part of .the brain) is inactive and at rest.

1196. Why does a person feel when he is touched?

A. Because the extremities of certain nerves situated in the skin are excited, and produce a nervous sensation called feeling.

1197. Why are persons able to taste different flavors?

A. Because the "papillæ" of the tongue and palate are excited when food touches them, and produce a nervous sensation called taste.

1198. Why is a dead man taller than a living one?

A. Because at death the cartilages are relaxed. So, also, after a night's rest a man is taller than when he went to bed.

CHAPTER VI.—ACIDS.

1199. What is an alkali?

A. The converse (or the opposite) to an acid.

The word alkali is compounded of the Arabic prefix *al*, and *kali*, the name of plant-ashes, from which potash is obtained.

1200. What are the fixed alkalies? and why are they so called?

A. The fixed alkalies are potash, soda, and lithia: they are called fixed alkalies because at a red-heat they will not fly off in vapor.

1201. What is the volatile alkali? and why is it so called?

A. Ammonia, or hartshorn,—a compound of nitrogen, hydrogen, and oxygen: it evaporates at even a low temperature, and is therefore called the volatile alkali.

1202. What are salts?

A. The combination of an acid with an alkali forms what is chemically termed a salt.

1203. What are acids?

A. Those chemical bodies called acids are usually, but not always, sour to the taste: they change most vegetable blue colors to red: they combine readily with alkalies and form salts.

1204. Why does hartshorn extract stains or spots in clothing caused by an acid?

A. Because hartshorn is an alkali; and the property of alkalies is to neutralize acids.

1205. Why does pyroligneous acid preserve meat and remove its taint?

A. Because it contains a small quantity of creasote, which is a great preservative of all animal substances.

Pyroligneous acid is vinegar obtained from wood.
Creasote,—from the Greek words κρεας, (creas,) *flesh*, and σωζω, (sozo,) *save*,—an extract from the oil of tar, and a powerful antiseptic.

1206. Why are unripe apples and gooseberries sour?

A. Because they contain malic acid.

"Malic," from the Latin word *malum*, an apple.

1207. Why does tanning hides convert them into leather?

A. Because oak-bark contains tannic acid, which with the gelatin of the hides forms an insoluble compound called leather.

1208. Why do old wine-casks smell offensively?

A. Because wine and whiskey contain an acid called œnanthic acid, which unites with the alcohol of the wine and forms a salt of an offensive smell.

This salt is called the œnanthate of ethyle,—that is, the winey acid of ether.
"Œnanthate," from the Greek word οινος, *wine;* and "ethyle," from the two Greek words αιθηρ-υλη, (aither-ule,) the basis or fundamental principle of ether.

1209. Why are limes, lemons, and unripe oranges sour?

A. Because they contain citric acid.

"Citric," from the Latin word *citrus*, a lemon or citron.

1210. Why are tamarinds and unripe grapes sour?

A. Because they contain tartaric acid.

Tartaric acid is the acid of tartar. Tartar is a substance deposited by wine, adhering like a hard crust to the sides of the casks.

1211. Why does rennet curdle milk?

A. Because it converts the sugar of milk into lactic acid, which mixes with the casein and coagulates it.

Rennet is the prepared inner membrane of the stomach of a calf, and is so called from the German word *rinnen*, to curdle.

1212. Why does sour milk curdle?

A. Milk consists of five ingredients: 1, casein, or curd; 2, butter; 3, sugar; 4, water; 5, certain salts.

The casein or curd of sweet milk is like the white of an egg before it is boiled; but the casein or curd of sour milk is like the white of an egg after it is boiled.

This casein or curd of milk is coagulated by acids. When milk is sour, the lactic acid of the sour milk, mixing with the casein, coagulates it; in consequence of which, it separates from the water and becomes an insoluble mass: in other words, the milk curdles.

"Lactic acid"—from the Latin word *lac*, milk—is the acid of sour milk. But it is found in several other substances, as in the fermented juice of beet-root, turnips, carrots, rice-water, tanning-bark, &c.

1213. Why is vinegar sour?

A. Because it contains acetic acid.

"Acetic," from the Saxon word *æced*, vinegar; whence also our word *acid*,—that is, like vinegar.

1214. If wine or beer be imperfectly corked, why does it rapidly turn sour?

A. Because air gets into the liquor; and the oxygen of the air, combining with the alcohol of the liquor, produces acetic acid, (or vinegar.)

CHAPTER VII.—OILS.

1215. Of what is soap made?

A. Soap is the product of any fatty matter combined with an alkali.

1216. Why does soap when laid on paint destroy it?

A. Because the soda or potash of which the soap is composed destroys or neutralizes the oil in the paint, and sets the coloring-matter free.

1217. Why does soapy water "lather"?

A. Because soap makes the water tenacious, and prevents its bubbles of air from bursting. "Lather" is only an accumulation of air-bubbles.

Any substance is said to be tenacious which holds fast or retains another: thus, the soapy water holds or retains the air-bubbles.

1218. Why is it impossible to write on greasy paper?

A. Because grease has no affinity for water or ink, and therefore will not mix with it.

1219. Why does turpentine take out grease-spots from cloth?

A. Because turpentine dissolves fixed oils.

The fixed oils are all greasy oils, such as sperm-oil, olive-oil, &c. The other sort of oils, called volatile or essential oils, are those used in perfumery, &c.

1220. Why is mutton-fat, &c. solid, and not liquid?

A. Because fat contains a predominance of solid stearine, and only a very small quantity of the liquid oily substance called oleine. On the other hand, oil contains more of the liquid oleine, and less of the solid matter called stearine.

1221. Why is butter hard in cold weather, and soft in warm?

A. Because in winter the weather is too cold to melt the stearine, and the butter is solid; but the heat of summer dissolves it, or holds it in solution in the oily substance called oleine, and the butter is soft and liquid.

1222. Why does oil become thick in winter-time?

A. 1st. Because it is condensed by the cold, and rendered more solid; and,

2d. Because the "stearine," which is held in solution in warm weather, is separated by the action of the cold, and deposited as a thick white and almost solid substance.

"Stearine"—from the Greek word *στεαρ*, (stear,) *suet*—is the solid or hard ingredient of all fat, suet, oil, &c. The soft or liquid part is called oleine,—from the Latin word *oleum*, oil.

1223. What is the difference in composition between hard and soft soap?

A. Hard soap is made of soda: soft soap is made of potash.

1224. Soap is made of oil or fat: how is it that oil and fat make water greasy, whereas soap destroys grease?

A. Oil contains two parts,—the solid part called stearine, and the liquid part called oleine.

Stearine of oil is not soluble in water; but when soda or potash is mixed with it, the oily principle flies off, and the stearine is converted into an oxide of potassium, which is quite soluble in water.

Oxide of potassium is the fundamental part of potash: it is what chemists call a metallic oxide.

1225. From what is salad-oil made?

A. It is expressed from the fruit of the olive-tree. The best olive or salad oil is extracted from the pulp of the fruit by gentle pressure in the cold.

There are other qualities inferior to this, in which heat aids the extraction of the oil.

1226. Why does churning cream convert it into butter?

A. Cream is the fat or butter of milk contained in little globular cases of albumen. By churning, this film or envelope of albumen is broken, and the butter or fat set free.

The globules are invisible to the naked eye, but may be distinctly seen floating about milk, by means of a tolerable microscope.

1227. What is Indian-rubber?

A. Indian-rubber, or caoutchouc, is a vegetable substance existing in the milky juices of several species of the *ficus*, and oxidized in contact with the air.

"Ficus," the fig-tribe, (a species of fig-tree.)

1228. What is gutta percha?

A. It is the juice of a tree which grows in Malacca, Borneo, and their vicinities, and becomes oxidized in contact with the air.

Like caoutchouc, it is highly elastic when heated to 145°, but hardens again when cold. It is so tenacious that a piece one-eighth of an inch in thickness, when cold, will suspend one hundred and forty pounds without breaking.

It is the product of a forest-tree called *Isonandra gutta.*

CHAPTER VIII.—ANTIDOTES FOR POISONS.

1229. If a person feels faint from the fumes of prussic acid, what is the best antidote?

A. To smell the vapors of strong ammonia, (hartshorn.)

1230. What is the best treatment for one who has swallowed prussic acid?

A. Apply diluted ammonia (hartshorn) to the nostrils, and let a stream of cold water from a pitcher fall from some height on the region of the spine.

Electrical shocks are said to be very beneficial also.

1231. If corrosive sublimate has been swallowed, what is the best antidote?

A. Albumen; that is, the white of an egg: the yolk of the egg also contains albumen, together with an oil which is a good antidote against this poison.

Flour and water mixed to the consistence of a smooth paste have proved efficacious.

1232. If an over-dose of laudanum has been taken, what is the best antidote?

A. Iodine, three grains; iodide of potassium, six grains; water, one pint: to be given in doses of a wineglassful.

Vomiting should be promoted by emetics.

Electro-magnetism is often efficacious in restoring the nervous sensibilities.

1233. If a person should swallow oxalic acid, what is the best antidote?

A. Chalk or magnesia mixed with a little water.

1234. What is the best antidote to verdigris?

A. Sugar, or the white of egg.

1235. If chlorine gas has been taken immoderately, what is the best antidote?

A. Removal to a current of fresh air, and the inhalation of ammonia, (hartshorn.)

1236. Why is strong green tea unwholesome?

A. Because it contains prussic acid, which injures the nervous system.

1237. Why will strong Souchong tea poison flies?

A. Because it contains prussic acid, which destroys their nervous system.

PART V.

METEOROLOGY.

CHAPTER I.—ATMOSPHERE.

1238. WHAT is meteorology?

A. It is a science which has for its object the investigation of the changes which are constantly taking place in the atmosphere. The knowledge of the alterations of the weather and of the laws which govern these alterations is styled Meteorology; that is, weather-wisdom.

1239. Of what is atmospheric air composed?

A. Principally of two gases, oxygen and nitrogen, mixed together in the following proportion,—viz. 1 part of oxygen to 4 of nitrogen.

It must not be forgotten that the air contains small quantities of other gaseous substances, as vapor of water, carbonic acid, and ammonia.

1240. What do you mean by a gas?

A. An elastic fluid resembling air.

Most gases are invisible or colorless, like air.

"Elastic:" in this respect gas differs from a liquid, which is almost inelastic, whereas gas is exceedingly elastic.

"Resembling air," or aeriform. The word *gas* means air; but air is a compound of two gases. Some few gases are visible,—as chlorine, which is a greenish yellow.

1241. How is the air heated?

A. By convection, thus:—The sun heats the earth, and the earth heats the air resting upon it: the air thus heated rises, and is succeeded by other air, which is heated in a similar way, till the whole volume is warmed by "convective currents."

1242. What is meant by "convective currents" of hot air?

A. Streams of air heated by the earth, which rise and carry heat with them.

1243. Does the sun heat the air as it does the earth?

A. No: the air is not heated by the rays of the sun, because air, like water, is a very bad conductor.

1244. How is the air made cold?

A. The air resting on the earth is made cold by contact: this cold air makes the air above it cold; and cold currents, or winds, agitate the whole till all becomes of one temperature.

1245. What effect is produced upon air by cold?

A. It is condensed, or shrunk into a smaller compass; in consequence of which, it becomes heavier, and descends toward the ground.

1246. Prove that air is condensed by cold.

A. Lay a bladder half full of air before a fire till it has become fully inflated: if it be now removed from the fire, the bladder will collapse, because the air condenses into its former bulk.

1247. How do you know that condensed air will descend?

A. Because a fire-balloon falls to the earth as soon as the spirit in the cotton is burnt out and the air of the balloon has become cold again.

1248. What is meant by the bladder "collapsing"?

A. The skin becoming wrinkled, shrivelled, and flabby, because there is not sufficient air inside to fill it.

1249. How are fishes able to ascend to the surface of water?

A. Fishes have an air-bladder near the abdomen: when this bladder is filled with air, the fish increases in size, and, being lighter, ascends through the water to its surface.

1250. How are fishes able to dive in a minute to the bottom of a stream?

A. They expel the air from their air-bladder; in consequence of which, their size is diminished, and they sink instantly.

1251. Why do persons who ascend in balloons feel pain in their eyes, ears, and chest?

A. Because the air in the upper regions of the atmosphere is more rare than the air in their bodies; and, till equilibrium is restored, pain will be felt in the more sensitive parts of the body,—more especially in the tympanum of the ear.

1252. Why do persons who descend in diving-bells feel pain in their eyes, ears, and chest?

A. Because the air in the diving-bell is compressed by the upward pressure of the water; in consequence of which, great pain is felt in the more sensitive parts of the body.

The pressure thus caused is sometimes sufficient to ruptur the membrane of the tympanum and produce deafness.

1253. Why do we feel oppressed just previous to a storm?

A. Because the air is greatly rarefied by heat and vapor, and the air within us, seeking to become of the same rarity, produces an oppressive and suffocating feeling.

1254. How do you know that the density of the air is lowered previous to a storm?

A. Because the mercury of a barometer rapidly falls.

1255. What is to be understood by the density of the air?

A. The quantity contained in a given bulk.

1256. Is there any law regulating the density of the atmosphere?

A. The density of the air decreases with the altitude.

1257. To what is this owing?

A. To the diminished pressure of the air and the decreasing force of gravity. Those portions directly incumbent upon the earth are most dense, because they bear the weight of the superincumbent portions: thus, the hay at the lower part of the stack bears the weight of that above, and is therefore more compact and dense.

Fig. 3.

In the accompanying engraving this idea may be conveyed by the gradual shading, which denotes the gradual diminution in the density of the atmosphere in proportion to its altitude.

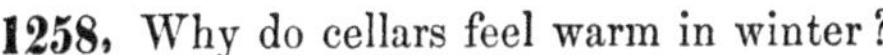

1258. Why do cellars feel warm in winter?

A. Because the external air has not free access into them; in consequence of which, they remain at an almost even temperature, —which in winter-time is warmer than the external air.

1259. Why do cellars feel cold in summer?

A. Because the external air has not free access into them; in consequence of which, they remain at an almost even temperature, —which in summer-time is colder than the external air.

1260. Why is it often painful and difficult to breathe on a mountain-top?

A. Because the pressure of air on the mountain-top is not so great as it is on the plain, and the air inside our bodies, seeking to become of the same rarity, bursts through the pores of the body and produces great pain.

1261. What effect has heat upon the air?

A. Heat rarefies the air and causes it to expand.

1262. How do you know that heat causes the air to expand?

A. Thus: if a bladder half full of air, tied tightly round the neck, be laid before a fire, the air will expand by the heat and fill the bladder.

1263. What is a barometer?

A. A weather-glass, or instrument to measure the variations in the weight of the air; by means of which variations we may judge what weather may be expected.

"Barometer" is a compound of two Greek words,—βαρος, (baros,) *weight*, and μετρον, (metron,) *a measure*.

1264. When, and by whom, was the barometer invented?

A. About the middle of the seventeenth century, by Torricelli, a friend and pupil of Galileo.

He selected for his experiment mercury, the heaviest known liquid. As this is 13½ times heavier than water, he argued that the column of mercury which would be sustained by a vacuum must be 13½ times less than the height of a column of water sustained in like manner, or about 30 inches. He procured a glass tube A B (fig. 4) more than 30 inches in length, open at one end, A, and closed at the other end, B. Placing this tube with the open end upward, he filled it with mercury, and applying his finger to the end A, so as to prevent the escape of the mercury, he inverted the tube, plunging the end A into the cistern

C D, (fig. 5,) containing mercury; the open end, A, being below the surface F of the mercury in the cistern, and no air having been al-

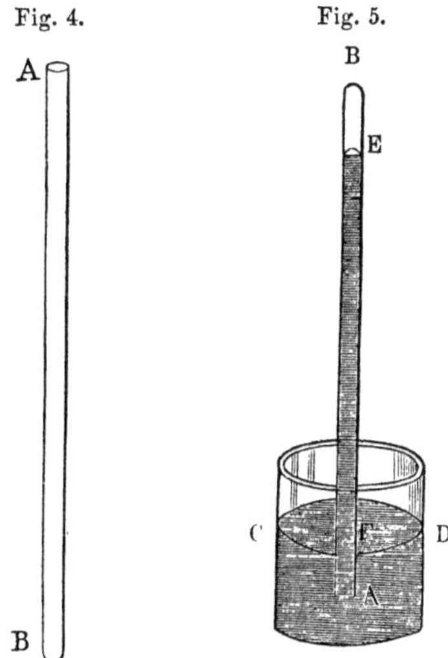

Fig. 4. Fig. 5.

lowed to communicate with it. Upon removing the finger, therefore, the mercury in the cistern came in immediate contact with the mercury in the tube. Immediately the mercury was observed to subside from the top of the tube and its surface gradually to descend to the level E, about 30 inches above the mercury in the cistern. The result was what Torricelli expected; and he soon perceived the true cause of the phenomenon. The atmospheric pressure, acting upon the surface F, while the surface E was protected from the pressure by the closed end, B, of the tube, supported the weight of the column E F. The pressure was transmitted by the liquid mercury in the cistern from the external surface F to the base of the column contained in the tube.

1265. How was the fact that the column of mercury was sustained by the pressure of the atmosphere further verified?

A. By an experiment made by Pascal, in France.

1266. How did these experiments lead to the invention of the barometer?

A. It was noticed that when the apparatus above described was kept in a fixed position, the height of the column fluctuated from day to day within certain small limits. The effect was of course to be attributed to the variation in the weight of the incumbent atmosphere, arising from various meteorological causes.

Fig. 6.

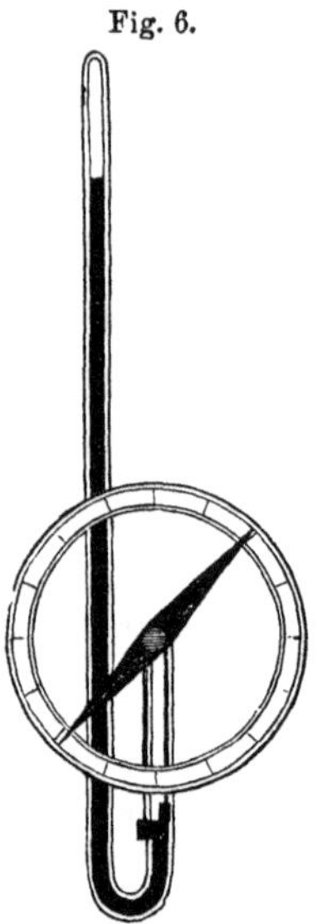

The wheel barometer consists of a bent tube filled with mercury, as represented in fig. 6, the column being sustained by the pressure of the atmosphere upon the surface of the mercury in the shorter arm, the end of which is open. A small float of iron or glass rests upon the mercury in the shorter arm of the tube, and is suspended by a slender thread, which is passed round a wheel carrying an index. As the level of the mercury is altered, and the weight raised or lowered in the tube, the index moves; and, as the divisions on the circumference of the circles within which it moves are much amplified, very slight changes are easily read off.

1267. Why is the tube of a barometer left open?

A. That the air may press upon it freely; and, as this pressure varies, the mercury rises or falls in the tube.

The top of the tube must be a "vacuum;" otherwise the pressure of the external air upon the lower part of the column cannot affect the mercury.

1268. How can a barometer, which measures the weight of air, be of service as a weather-glass?

A. When air is moist, or filled with vapor, it is lighter than usual, and the column of mercury stands low;

When air is dry and free from vapor, it is heavier than usual, and the mercury stands high.

Thus the barometer, by showing the variations in the weight of the air, indicates the changes of the weather also.

1269. The height of mountains may be ascertained by a barometer: explain this.

A. As we ascend a high mountain, the quantity of air above us becomes less and less every step we ascend, and requires less mercury to balance it; in consequence of which, the mercury in the tube of the barometer falls.

If a pile of books be placed on a table, the bottom book will sustain the most weight, and every book will sustain less and less as we get nearer and nearer to the top. The air somewhat resembles this pile. That on the surface of the earth resembles the bottom book of the pile; and as we ascend a mountain the quantity of air above keeps diminishing, and the weight to be sustained is in proportion less.

For general purposes, we may take this for a rule: for every one hundred feet of perpendicular height the barometer will fall one-tenth of an inch. If, therefore, the barometer has fallen one and a half inches, you know the mountain is fifteen hundred feet high.

1270. Why can you tell, by looking at a barometer, what kind of weather it will be?

A. Because the mercury in the tube rises and falls as the air becomes heavier or lighter; and we can generally tell by the weight of the air what kind of weather to expect.

1271. Of what use is a barometer to sailors?

A. It warns them to regulate their ships before squalls come on.

1272. How can a barometer warn sailors to regulate their ships?

A. As it indicates when wind, rain, and storm are at hand, the sailor can make his ship trim before they overtake him.

1273. Does water invariably boil when the thermometer indicates its temperature to be 212°?

A. No: its boiling-point is 212° when the barometer stands at 30 inches. If the barometer rises above 30 inches, the boiling-point of water is more than 212°.

1274. Suppose the barometer should fall below 30 inches: will the water boil before it is heated to 212°?

A. Yes: water has been known to boil at 180° of temperature. This occurred on the top of the Himalaya Mountains, at an elevation of 18,000 feet above the level of the sea.

1275. Is boiling water always equally hot?

A. No: in elevated places many substances cannot be cooked by boiling in water.

1276. Why cannot many substances be cooked by boiling water in elevated places?

A. Because the pressure of the atmosphere is diminished, and consequently the mercury in the barometer would stand below 30 inches. When this is the case, water boils before it is heated to 212°.

1277. Would water boil at a lower temperature than 212° if placed under the exhausted receiver of an air-pump?

A. Yes: water may be made to boil at a temperature about equal to that of summer weather, or about 72°.

1278. Do all liquids boil at a lower temperature when in vacuo?

A. Yes: under the exhausted receiver of an air-pump all liquids will, as a general rule, boil at a temperature 140° lower than in the open air.

"Vacuo," unoccupied space; a space containing nothing,—not even air.

1279. Why will they boil at a lower temperature when in vacuo?

A. Because the pressure of the atmosphere is diminished.

1280. What is the ordinary pressure of the atmosphere?

A. About 15 pounds on the square inch when the barometer stands at 30 inches.

1281. If the atmospheric pressure is equal to about 15 pounds on the square inch, to what weight is an ordinary-sized man exposed?

A. To a pressure of about fourteen tons.

1282. If he were oppressed with a weight of fourteen tons of iron, he would be crushed: why does not the pressure of the air kill us?

A. Because the air is inspired by the lungs and pervades the whole body: it presses equally in all directions, and therefore we suffer no inconvenience.

1283. Does the air press all bodies equally on all sides?

A. It does. Its upward pressure is equal to its downward or its lateral pressure.

"Lateral," at the sides, sideways.

1284. Why will not liquor run freely out of a barrel until the vent-peg is removed?

A. Because the upward pressure of the external air admitted through the vent-peg holds the liquor back, as it is not counterbalanced by any pressure of air on the surface of the liquid in the barrel.

The upward pressure of air is illustrated by the following simple experiment:—Fill a wineglass with water; cover the top of the glass with a piece of writing-paper; turn the glass upside down, and the water will not run out. The paper is used merely to give the air a medium sufficiently dense to act against.

1285. When liquor is decanted or poured from a bottle, why does it gurgle?

A. The bubbling noise is made by the air rushing into the bottle and the liquor bursting out.

The liquor, filling the neck of the bottle, prevents the air from getting freely in, and the air, pressing against the mouth of the bottle, prevents the liquor from getting freely out; in consequence of which, the air bursts into the neck of the bottle, and the liquor runs from the same, by fits and starts, as either is able to prevail: as this process is repeated, the noise produced is called a gurgle.

1286. If you insert a straw into a barrel of cider, wine, &c., you may suck the liquid at pleasure: explain this.

A. By sucking, all the air is exhausted or

drawn out of the straw: the weight of the surrounding air causes the liquid to rush in to fill the vacuum in the straw, and, of course, it flows into the mouth.

1287. If a flat piece of moist leather be put in close contact with a stone or other heavy body, and a cord be attached to the centre of the leather, the stone may be lifted by the cord: explain this.

A. The air is excluded between the leather and the stone; consequently, a vacuum is formed, and, owing to the pressure of the atmosphere, which is equal to 15 pounds for every square inch, the leather and stone are so firmly attached together that the weight of the stone is not sufficient to separate them.

1288. What is a thermometer?

A. An instrument to show the temperature of the air, water, or any substance whatever.

"Thermometer" is a compound of two Greek words,—*θερμος*, (thermos,) *heat*, and *μετρον*, (metron,) *measure*.

1289. What is the difference between a thermometer and a barometer?

A. In a thermometer the mercury is sealed up from the air, and rises or falls as the varying temperature of the air expands or contracts it; but

In a barometer the mercury is left exposed (or open) to the air at its lower extremity, and rises or falls as the varying weight of the air presses upon the open column.

1290. If the mercury of the thermometer be sealed up from the air, how can the air affect it?

A. The heat of the air passes through the glass tube into the mercury, which causes the metal to expand and rise in the tube.

1291. When, and by whom, was the thermometer invented?

A. The thermometer was invented about the year 1600; but, like many other inventions, the merit of its discovery is not to be ascribed to one person, but to be distributed among many.

1292. Why is the thermometer in general use in the United States, England, and Holland called Fahrenheit's thermometer?

A. Because thermometers having a like graduation were first manufactured by Fahrenheit, a Dutch philosophical-instrument-maker. The employment of mercury as the most suitable fluid for the thermometer is also usually attributed to him.

Fig. 7.

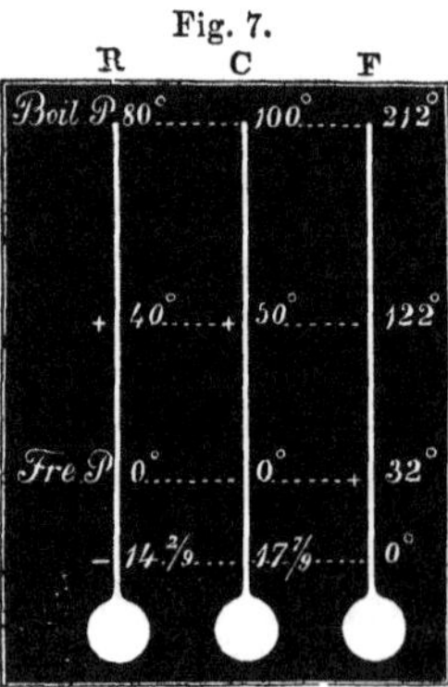

1293. How many kinds of thermometers are in general use?

A. Three,—Fahrenheit's, Reaumur's, and the Centigrade thermometer, or thermometer of Celsius.

1294. What constitutes the difference between these instruments?

A. The differences of graduation between the freezing and boiling points of water. Reaumur's is divided into eighty degrees, the Centigrade into one hundred, and Fahrenheit's into one hundred and eighty. According to Reaumur, water freezes at 0° and boils at 80°; according to Centigrade, it freezes at 0° and boils at 100°; and according to Fahrenheit, it freezes at 32° and boils at 212°.

CHAPTER II.—WINDS.

1295. WHAT is wind?

A. Wind is air in motion.

1296. What puts the air in motion, so as to produce wind?

A. The principal causes are the variations of heat and cold, produced by the succession of day and night and of the four seasons.

1297. What is the cause of wind?

A. The sun heats the earth, and the earth heats the air resting upon it: as the warm air ascends, the void is filled up by a rush of cold-air to the place; and this rush of air we call wind.

1298. Does the wind always blow?

A. Yes: there is always some motion in

the air; but the violence of the motion is perpetually varying.

1299. Does the rotation of the earth upon its axis affect the motion of the air?

A. Yes, in two ways: 1st. As the earth moves round its axis, the thin movable air is left somewhat behind, and therefore seems, to a stationary object, to be blowing in the opposite direction to the earth's motion; and,

2d. As the earth revolves, different portions of its surface are continually passing under the vertical rays of the sun.

1300. When are the rays of the sun called "vertical rays"?

A. When the sun is in a direct line above any place, his rays are said to be "vertical" to that place.

1301. Illustrate the manner in which the earth's surface passes under the vertical sun.

A. Suppose the brass meridian of a globe to represent the vertical rays of the sun: as you turn the globe round, different parts of it will pass under the brass rim in constant succession.

1302. Why is it noonday to the place over which the sun is vertical?

A. Because the sun is half-way between his rising and setting to that place.

1303. Show how this rotation of the earth affects the air.

A. If we suppose the brass meridian to be the vertical sun, the whole column of air beneath will be heated by the noonday rays: that part which the sun has left will become gradually colder and colder, and that part to which the sun is approaching will grow constantly warmer and warmer.

1304. Then there are three qualities of air about this spot?

A. Yes: the air over the place which has passed the meridian is cooling; the air under the vertical sun is the hottest; and the air which is over the place about to pass under the meridian is increasing in heat.

1305. Does air, like water, expand by heat?

A. It does; and this expansion is the cause of winds.

1306. How does this variety in the heat of air produce wind?

A. The air always seeks to preserve an equilibrium: therefore cold air rushes into the void made by the upward current of warm air.

1307. Why does not the wind always blow one way, following the direction of the sun?

A. Because the direction of the wind is subject to perpetual interruptions from hills and valleys, deserts, seas, &c.

1308. How can hills and mountains alter the course of the wind?

A. Suppose a wind blowing from the north strikes a mountain: as it cannot pass through it, it must either rush back again, or fly off at one side, (as a marble when it strikes against a wall.)

1309. Do mountains affect the wind in any other way?

A. Yes: many mountains are capped with snow, and the warm air is condensed when it comes in contact with them; but as soon as the temperature of the wind is changed, its direction may be changed also. (See Fig. 8.)

Fig. 8.

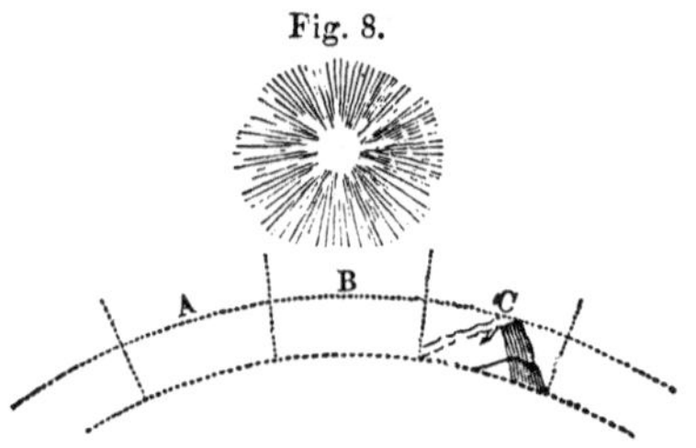

Suppose A, B, C to be three columns of air,—A, the column of air which is cooling down; B, the column to which the sun is vertical; and C, the column which is to be heated next. In this case the cold air of A will rush toward B C; because the air of B and C is hotter than A. But suppose, now, C to be a snow-capped mountain: as the hot air of B reaches C, it is chilled; and, being now colder than the air behind, it rushes back again toward A, instead of following the sun.

1310. How can the ocean affect the direction of the wind?

A. When the ocean rolls beneath the vertical sun, the water is not made so hot as the land; in consequence of which, the general direction of the wind is directed from tracts of ocean toward tracts of land.

1311. Why is not the water of the sea made so hot by the vertical sun as the surface of the land?

A. 1st. Because the evaporation of the sea is greater than that of the land;

2d. The constant motion of the water prevents the increase of temperature at the surface;

3d. The rays of the sun strike into the water; in consequence of which, the immediate surface is much less affected; and,

4th. Water is a bad conductor of heat.

1312. Why does the evaporation of the sea prevent its surface from being heated by the vertical sun?

A. Because its heat is absorbed in the generation of vapor and carried off into the air.

1313. Why does the motion of the sea prevent its surface from being heated by the vertical sun?

A. Because each portion rolls away as soon as it becomes heated, and is succeeded by another; and this constant motion prevents the surface of the sea from being much more heated than the water below the surface.

1314. Why are those winds which blow over large continents or tracts of land generally dry?

A. Because in their passage they absorb very little water, as they do not blow over large oceans.

1315. Why do our hands and lips chap in frosty and windy weather?

A. 1st. Because the wind or frost absorbs the moisture from the surface of the skin; and,

2d. The action of wind or frost produces a kind of inflammation on the skin.

1316. Why does wind dry damp linen?

A. Because dry wind (like a dry sponge) imbibes the particles of vapor from the surface of the linen as fast as they are formed.

1317. Why are the west winds in the Atlantic States generally dry?

A. Because they come over large tracts of land, and therefore absorb very little water; and, being thirsty, they readily imbibe moisture from the air and clouds, and therefore bring dry weather.

1318. Why is our north wind generally cold?

A. Because it comes from the polar regions, over mountains of snow and seas of ice.

1319. Why are our north winds generally dry?

A. Because they come from colder regions, and, being warmed by the heat of our climate, absorb moisture from every thing with which they come in contact; in consequence of which, they are generally dry.

1320. Why are our south winds generally warm?

A. Because they come over countries warmer than our own, where they are much heated.

1321. Why are winds which blow over a vast body of water generally rainy?

A. Because they come laden with vapor: if, therefore, they meet with the least chill, some of the vapor is deposited as rain.

1322. Do clouds affect the wind?

A. Yes. As passing clouds screen the direct heat of the sun from the earth, they diminish the rarefaction of the air also; and this is another cause why neither the strength nor direction of the wind is uniform.

SECTION I.—CONSTANT WINDS.

1323. Would the wind blow regularly from east to west if these obstructions were removed?

A. Without doubt. If the whole earth were covered with water, the winds would always follow the sun, and blow uniformly in one direction.

1324. Do winds ever blow regularly?

A. Yes: in those parts of the world which present a large surface of water, as in the Atlantic and Pacific Oceans.

1325. What are the winds which blow over the Atlantic and Pacific Oceans called?

A. They are called "trade-winds."

1326. Why are they called "trade-winds"?

A. Because they are very convenient to merchants who have to cross the ocean, inasmuch as they always blow in one direction.

1327. In what direction do the trade-winds blow?

A. That in the northern hemisphere blows from the northeast; that in the southern hemisphere, from the southeast.

1328. Why do they not blow from the full north and south?

A. Because currents of air flowing from the poles give them an easterly direction.

This effect is due in some measure to the rotation of the earth on its axis.

1329. What is the cause of these currents of air from the poles to the equator?

A. The air about the equator constantly ascends, in consequence of being rarefied by the heat of the sun; and, as the hot equatorial air ascends, cold air from the north and south flows toward the equator to restore the equilibrium.

1330. Is there an upper as well as a lower current in the atmosphere?

A. Yes: the upper current of rarefied air is from the equator to the poles,—where it is condensed, and then returns again to the equator, forming the lower current.

1331. These lower currents (from the poles to the equator) have an easterly tendency. Explain the cause of this.

A. All the atmosphere revolves with the earth; but when a current of air from the poles flows toward the equator, it comes to a part of the earth's surface which is moving faster than itself; in consequence of which, it is left behind, and thus produces the effect of a current moving in the opposite direction.

Thus, to a person in a carriage, the hedges and trees seem to be running in an opposite direction.

As the circumference of the earth at the equator is much larger than the circumference of the earth at the poles, every spot of the earth's equatorial surface must move much faster than the corresponding one at the poles.

As the earth revolves on its axis from west to east, the air which is carried with it will seem to blow from the west. As, however, the current of air from the poles seems to blow in the opposite direction, it will seem to blow from the east, (or to be an easterly wind.)

1332. By what means are the northeast and southeast trade-winds produced?

A. By a combination of the two motions of the polar currents; which produces the intermediate directions of the northeast and southeast.

1333. Are both these motions of the polar currents real?

A. No: the motion from the east to west is only apparent. As the earth revolves from west to east, the air carried with it will be a west wind; but the polar currents seem to blow in the opposite direction, merely because they have not acquired the same velocity.

1334. Do trade-winds blow from the northeast and southeast all the year round?

A. Yes, in the open sea; that is, in the Atlantic and Pacific Oceans, for about thirty degrees each side of the equator.

1335. What do the northeasterly and southeasterly trade-winds produce when they meet near the equator?

A. A region of calms, in which thick, foggy air prevails, with sudden showers and thunder-storms.

1336. Is this region of calms fixed in its position?

A. No: it shifts its place according to the sun's distance, and position in regard to the equator,—being sometimes entirely to the north of the equator, and occasionally reaching as far as two degrees south of it.

1337. Do the trade-winds blow uniformly from northeast and southeast in the Indian Ocean?

A. No; nor in those parts of the Atlantic and Pacific which verge on the continents.

1338. How do the trade-winds in the Indian Ocean blow?

A. From April to October a southwest wind prevails; from October to April, a northeast.

SECTION II.—PERIODIC WINDS.

1339. What are those periodical currents of air called which affect the neighborhood of the Arabian, Indian, and Chinese Seas?

A. They are called Monsoons.

1340. How far do the limits of the monsoons extend?

A. They extend from the African shore to the longitude of New Guinea, and are felt northward as far as the parallel of latitude which crosses the Loochoo Isles.

The Loochoo Isles are about 24° north latitude, and 130° east longitude.

1341. Are the monsoons as powerful as the trade-winds?

A. They are far more so, and very often amount to violent gales.

1342. Why do not the trade-winds in the Indian Ocean blow southwest from April to October?

A. Because the air of Arabia, Persia, India, and China is so rarefied by the excessive heat of their summer sun that the cold air from the south rushes toward these countries, across the equator, during these six months, and produces a southwest wind.

1343. To what distance does this southwest wind prevail?

A. From three degrees south of the equator, to the shores of the Arabian, Indian, and Chinese Seas.

1344. Why do the trade-winds in the Indian Ocean blow northeast from October to April?

A. Because the southern part of the torrid zone is most heated when the sun has left the northern side of the equator for the southern, and the cold air from the north, rushing toward the southern tropic, is diverted into the direction of northeast, where it continues for the other six months of the year.

1345. Why are the monsoons more useful to the mariner than the fixed trade-winds?

A. Because the mariner is able to avail himself of these periodic changes to go in one direction during one half of the year and to return in the opposite direction during the other half.

1346. How is the change of the monsoons marked?

A. By an interval of alternating calms and storms.

1347. Show the goodness and wisdom of God in the constant tendency of air to equilibrium.

A. If the torrid zone were not tempered by cold air from the polar regions, it would become so hot that no human being could endure it. If, on the other hand, the polar regions were never warmed by hot air from the torrid zone, they would soon become insufferably cold.

1348. In what other way does the mingling of the polar and equatorial atmosphere act beneficially?

A. In the equatorial regions the great abundance of vegetable life is productive of a very large amount of oxygen; in the colder regions, artificial fires and dense masses of animal life produce large quantities of carbonic acid. The mingling of the polar and equatorial atmosphere assists in supplying each of these regions with the very gas in which it would be otherwise deficient.

1349. Why does the expansion of air cause wind?

A. The heat of the sun heats that part of the surface of the earth over which it is vertical; the heat of the earth thus acquired by absorption is imparted to the lowest stratum of air, which, becoming expanded, rises and gives place to another, and in this manner an ascending current is established.

The colder and heavier air rushes in from the colder regions north and south to fill the vacuum thus occasioned, thus producing wind.

"Stratum," layer. The lowest stratum of air is that portion of air which is in contact with the surface of the earth.

1350. How does the mingling of the polar and equatorial atmosphere serve to supply each region with the gas it most requires?

A. The plants of the equatorial regions require carbonic acid; the animals of the colder regions require oxygen. The currents of air from the poles carry carbonic acid to the equatorial plants, and the currents of air from the equator carry oxygen to the animals which abound nearer the poles.

SECTION III.—VARIABLE WINDS.

1351. What are variable winds?

A. Those winds which are irregular as to their direction or time of continuance.

1352. Why is the rising sun in summer sometimes accompanied with a breeze?

A. Because the heat of the rising sun stops the radiation of heat from the earth, and warms its surface.

1353. How does this warmth produce a breeze?

A. The air resting on the earth's surface, being warmed by contact, ascends, and colder air, rushing in to fill up the void, produces the morning breeze.

1354. Why is there often an evening breeze during the summer months?

A. Because the earth radiates heat at sunset and the air is rapidly cooled down by contact: this condensation causes a motion in the air, called the evening breeze.

1355. Why are tropical islands subject to a sea-breeze every morning? that is, a breeze blowing from the sea to the land.

A. Because solar rays are unable to heat the surface of the sea, as they do the earth: therefore the air resting on the sea is less heated than the air resting on the earth, and the colder sea-air blows inland to restore the equilibrium.

1356. Why is a fine clear day sometimes overcast in a few minutes?

A. Because some sudden change of temperature has condensed the vapor of the air into clouds.

1357. Why are clouds sometimes dissipated very suddenly?

A. Because some dry wind, blowing over the clouds, imbibes their moisture and carries it off in invisible vapor.

1358. Why does wind sometimes bring rain and sometimes fine weather?

A. If the wind be colder than the clouds, it will condense their vapor into rain; but if the wind be warmer than the clouds, it will dissolve them and cause them to disappear.

1359. Why is a land-breeze unhealthy?

A. Because it is frequently laden with exhalations from putrefying animal and vegetable substances.

1360. Why is a sea-breeze fresh and healthy?

A. Becauses it passes over the sea, and is not laden with noxious exhalations.

1361. What is the cause of a sea-breeze?

A. When the land is more heated by the sun than the sea is, the land-air becomes hotter than that over the sea; in consequence of which, the cooler sea-air glides inland to restore the equilibrium.

1362. Why does a sea-breeze feel cool?

A. Because the sun cannot make the surface of the sea so hot as the land: therefore the air which blows from the sea is cooler than the air of the land.

1363. Why are tropical islands subject to a land-breeze every evening? that is, a breeze blowing from the land toward the sea.

A. Because the surface of the land cools down faster after sunset than the surface of the sea; in consequence of which, the air of the cold land is condensed, sinks down, and spreads itself into the warmer sea-air,—causing the land-breeze.

1364. Why is not the air which passes over water so cool as that which passes over land?

A. Because water does not cool down at sunset so fast as land does, and therefore the air in contact with it remains warmer.

1365. Why does not water cool down so fast as land?

A. 1st. Because the surface of water is perpetually changing, and as fast as one surface is made cold another is presented; and,

2d. The moment water is made cold it sinks, and warmer portions of water rise to occupy its place: therefore, before the surface of the water is cooled, the whole volume must be made cold,—which is not the case with land.

1366. Why is the land-breeze cool?

A. Because the surface of the land is cooled at sunset more rapidly than the surface of the sea: therefore seamen feel the air from the land to be chilly.

1367. Explain the cause of sea-waves.

A. The wind, acting on the surface of the sea, piles up ridges of water, leaving behind an indentation: as the water on all sides rushes to fill up this indentation, the disturbance spreads on all sides, and billow rolls after billow.

1368. Why does wind generally feel cold?

A. Because a constantly changing surface comes in contact with our body, to draw off its heat.

1369. How fast does wind travel?

A. A gentle breeze goes at the rate of about five miles an hour; a high wind, from twenty to sixty; a hurricane, from eighty to one hundred miles an hour.

1370. What is a hurricane?

A. A terrific storm of wind, which, while it passes over the surface of the earth or ocean, revolves on an axis, or turns upon itself.

1371. Explain this more fully.

A. It is the nature of a hurricane to travel round and round as well as forward, very much as a corkscrew travels through a cork, except that the circles are all flat, and described by a rotatory wind upon the surface of the water.

1372. What name do the Chinese give to hurricanes?

A. They call them typhoons.

1373. How is the velocity of winds ascertained?

A. By observing the velocity of the clouds, and by an instrument for the purpose, called an Anemometer.

Pronounced an-e-mom′e-ter. From two Greek words,—*ανεηος*, (anemos,) *wind*, and *μετρον*, (metron,) *a measure*. This term is applied more frequently to an instrument which measures the force of wind.

1374. How is the velocity of the clouds ascertained?

A. By observing the speed of their shadow along the ground,—which is found in a high wind to vary from twenty to sixty miles an hour.

1375. In what respect does a tornado differ from a hurricane?

A. Tornadoes may be regarded as hurricanes, differing chiefly in respect to their continuance and extent.

1376. How long do they usually last?

A. From fifteen to seventy seconds.

1377. What is their extent?

A. Their breadth varies from a few rods

to several hundred yards, and the length of their course rarely exceeds twenty miles.

1378. What phenomena generally attend them?

A. The tornado is generally preceded by a calm and sultry state of the atmosphere, when suddenly the whirlwind appears, prostrating every thing before it. Tornadoes are usually accompanied by thunder and lightning, and sometimes showers of hail.

1379. What is a waterspout?

A. A waterspout is a whirlwind over the surface of water, and differs from a whirlwind on land in the fact that water is subjected to the action of the wind, instead of objects on the surface of the earth.

1380. When an observer is near, are any sounds perceptible?

A. A loud hissing noise is heard, and the interior of the column seems to be traversed by a rushing stream.

1381. What is the breadth and height of waterspouts?

A. In diameter the spout at the base ranges from a few feet to several hundreds, and its altitude is supposed to be often upwards of a mile.

1382. What are its successive appearances?

A. At first it appears to be a dark cone, extending from the clouds to the water; then it becomes a column uniting with the water. After continuing for a little time, the column becomes disunited, the cone reappears, and is gradually drawn up into the clouds. (See fig. 9.)

Fig. 9.

1383. Is it supposed that water is sucked up from the ocean or lake by the waterspout?

A. It is a common belief that water is sucked up by the action of the spout into the clouds; but there is reason to suppose that water rather descends from the clouds, as water which has fallen from a spout upon the deck of a vessel has been found to be fresh. There is no evidence, furthermore, that a continuous column of water exists within the whirling pillar.

1384. What are sand-pillars?

A. They are gigantic columns of sand raised by whirlwinds in the deserts of Africa and other countries. They sometimes extend as high as the clouds, and move with various degrees of velocity, carrying destruction in their paths.

CHAPTER III.—CLOUDS.

1385. WHAT are clouds?

A. Moisture evaporated from the earth, and again partially condensed in the upper regions of the air.

1386. What is the difference between a fog and a cloud?

A. Clouds and fogs differ only in one respect:—clouds are elevated above our heads; but fogs come in contact with the surface of the earth.

1387. Why are clouds higher on a fine day?

A. Because they are lighter and more buoyant.

1388. Why are clouds lighter on a fine day?

A. 1st. Because the vapor of the clouds is less condensed; and,

2d. The air itself, on a fine day, retains much of its vapor in an invisible form.

1389. Why do clouds float so readily in the air?

A. Because they are composed of very minute globules, called vesicles, which, being lighter than air, float like soap-bubbles.

1390. Are all clouds alike?

A. No: they vary greatly in density, height, and color.

1391. What is the chief cause of fog and clouds?

A. The changes of the wind.

Many local circumstances, also, favor the formation of clouds.

1392. How can the changes of the wind affect the clouds?

A. If a cold current of wind blows suddenly over any region, it condenses the invisible vapor of the air into cloud or rain; but if a warm and dry current of wind blows over any region, it disperses the clouds, by absorbing their vapor.

1393. What countries are the most cloudy?

A. Those where the winds are most variable, as Great Britain.

1394. What countries are the least cloudy?

A. Those where the winds are least variable, as Egypt.

1395. At what distance are the clouds from the earth?

A. Some thin, light clouds are elevated above the highest mountain-tops; some heavy ones touch the steeples, trees, and even the earth; but the average height is between one and two miles.

Streaky, curling clouds, like hair, are often five or six miles high.

1396. What clouds are the lowest?

A. Those which are the most highly electrified: lightning-clouds are rarely more than about seven hundred yards above the ground, and often actually touch the earth with one of their edges.

1397. What is the size of the clouds?

A. Some clouds are twenty square miles in surface and above a mile in thickness, while others are only a few yards or inches thick.

1398. How can persons ascertain the thickness of a cloud?

A. As the tops of high mountains are generally above the clouds, travellers may pass quite through them into a clear blue firmament, when the clouds will be seen beneath their feet.

1399. What produces the great variety in the shape of the clouds?

A. Three things: 1st. The cause and manner of their formation;

2d. Their electrical condition; and,

3d. Their relations to currents of wind.

1400. How can electricity affect the shape of clouds?

A. If one cloud be full of electricity and another not, they will be attracted to each other, and either coalesce, diminish in size, or vanish altogether.

1401. What clouds assume the most fantastic shapes?

A. Those that are the most highly electrified.

1402. What effect have winds on the shape of clouds?

A. They sometimes absorb them entirely, sometimes increase their volume and density, and sometimes change the position of their parts.

1403. How can winds absorb clouds altogether?

A. Warm, dry winds will convert the substance of clouds into invisible vapor, which they will carry away in their own current.

1404. How can winds increase the bulk and density of clouds?

A. Cold currents of wind will condense the invisible vapor of the air and add it to the clouds with which they come in contact.

1405. How can winds change the shape of clouds by altering the position of their parts?

A. Clouds are so voluble and light that every breath of wind changes the position of their vesicles or bubbles.

1406. What are the general colors of the clouds?

A. White and gray when the sun is above the horizon, but red, orange, and yellow at sunrise and sunset.

The blue sky is not cloud at all.

1407. Why are the last clouds of evening generally of a red tinge?

A. Because red rays, being the least refrangible of all, are the last to disappear.

Fig. 10.

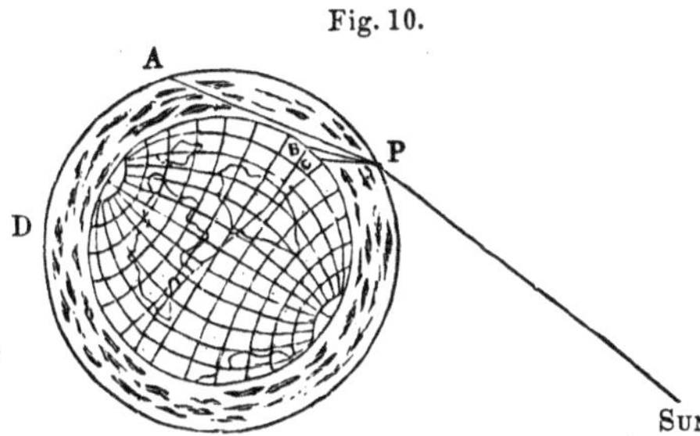

Suppose P A to be the red rays; P B, the yellow; P C, the blue. If the earth turns in the direction P A D, it is quite manifest that a spectator will see A (the red rays) some time after P C and P B have passed from sight.

1408. What is meant by being "less refrangible"?

A. Being less readily bent. Blue and yellow rays are more easily bent below the horizon by the resistance of the air; but red rays are not so much bent down, and therefore we see them later in the evening.

As at A, in Fig. 10.

1409. Why are morning clouds generally of a red tinge?

A. Because red rays are the least refrangible of all; and, not being bent so much as blue and yellow rays, we see them sooner in the morning.

Thus, (Fig. 10,) if the earth turned in the direction D A P, a spectator at D would see A (the red rays) long before he saw P B and P C.

1410. Why is not the color of clouds always alike?

A. Because their size, density, and situation in regard to the sun are perpetually varying; so that sometimes one color is reflected and sometimes another.

1411. What regulates the motion of the clouds?

A. Principally the winds; but sometimes electricity will influence their motion.

1412. How do you know that clouds move by other influences besides wind?

A. Because in calm weather we often see small clouds meeting each other from opposite directions.

1413. How do you know that electricity affects the motion of the clouds?

A. Because clouds often meet from opposite directions, and, having discharged their opposite electricities into each other, vanish altogether.

1414. What are the uses of clouds?

A. 1st. They act as screens to arrest the radiation of heat from the earth;

2d. They temper the heat of the sun's rays; and,

3d. They are the great storehouses of rain.

"Radiation of heat;" that is, the escape of heat when no conductor carries it away.

1415. Why is wind said to blow up the clouds?

A. Because a dry, warm wind which has travelled over seas, having absorbed a large quantity of moisture, deposits some of it in the visible form of clouds as soon as it reaches a colder region of air.

1416. Why does wind sometimes drive away the clouds?

A. Because it has travelled over dry lands or thirsty deserts, and become so dry that it absorbs vapor from the clouds and causes them to disappear.

1417. What is the cause of a red sunset?

A. The vapor of the air not being actually condensed into clouds, but only on the point of being condensed.

1418. Why is a red sunset an indication of a fine day to-morrow?

A. Because the vapors of the earth are not condensed into clouds by the cold of sunset. Our Lord referred to this prognostic in the following words:—"When it is evening, ye say, It will be fair weather, for the sky is red." (Matt. xvi. 2.)

1419. What is the cause of a coppery-yellow sunset?

A. The vapor of the air being actually condensed into clouds.

1420. Why do vapors not actually condensed refract red rays, while condensed vapors refract yellow?

A. Because the beams of light meet with very little resistance; in consequence of which, those rays are bent down to the eye which require the least refraction, such as red.

See Fig. 10, where it is evident that the red ray P A is less bent than the yellow and blue rays P B, P C.

1421. Why do condensed vapors refract yellow rays, whereas vapors not actually condensed refract red?

A. Because the beams of light meet with more resistance from the condensed vapor; in consequence of which, those rays are bent down to the eye which are more refracted than the red, such as yellow.

See Fig. 10, where it is evident that the yellow ray P B is more bent than the red ray. P A.

1422. Why is a yellow sunset an indication of wet weather?

A. Because it shows that the vapors of the air are already condensed into clouds: rain, therefore, may be shortly expected.

1423. What is the cause of a red sunrise?

A. Vapor in the upper region of the air just on the point of being condensed.

1424. Why is a red and lowering sky at sunrise an indication of a wet day?

A. Because the higher regions of the air are laden with vapor on the very point of condensation, which the rising sun cannot disperse. Hence our Lord's observation, "In the morning ye say, It will be foul weather to-day, for the sky is red and lowering." (Matt. xvi. 3.)

1425. Why is a gray morning an indication of a fine day?

A. Because only the air contiguous to the earth is damp and full of vapor: there are no vapors in the higher regions of the air to bend down to the eye even the red rays of any beam of light.

1426. What difference in the state of the air is required to make a gray and red sunrise?

A. In a gray sunrise, only that portion of air contiguous to the earth is filled with vapor: all the rest is clear and dry; but in a red sunrise, the air in the upper regions is so full of vapor that the rising sun cannot disperse it.

1427. Why is a gray sunset an indication of wet weather?

A. Because it shows that the air on the surface of the earth is very damp at sunset; which is a plain proof that the air is saturated with vapor; in consequence of which, wet weather may be soon expected. Hence the proverb—

"Evening red and morning gray
Will set the traveller on his way;
But evening gray and morning red
Will bring down rain upon his head."

1428. What is meant by an aurora borealis, or northern light?

A. Luminous clouds in the northern sky at night-time. Sometimes streaks of blue, purple, green, red, &c., and sometimes flashes of light, are seen.

1429. What is supposed to be the cause of the aurora borealis, or northern light?

A. Electricity in the higher regions of the atmosphere is undoubtedly an active agent in producing this phenomenon.

1430. Is the aurora ever seen in other parts of the heavens than toward the north?

A. It seems to originate at or near the poles of the earth, and is, consequently, seen in its greatest perfection within the arctic and antarctic circles; but auroras of great brilliancy are often seen in the temperate zones.

1431. Do auroras appear only at certain seasons of the year?

A. They appear at all seasons, but are only visible during the absence of sunlight.

1432. Do the auroras appear at any particular seasons and times?

A. They appear more frequently in the winter than in the summer, and are only seen at night.

1433. Do they occur in the daytime?

A. The aurora is known to affect the magnetic needle and the telegraph; and, as the effect upon these instruments is noticed by day as well as by night, there can be no doubt of the occurrence of the aurora at all hours. The intense light of the sun renders the auroral light invisible during the day.

1434. Of what utility are the auroral appearances in the polar regions?

A. During the long polar night, when the sun is below the horizon, the aurora appears with a magnificence unknown in other regions, and affords light sufficient for many of the ordinary out-door employments.

Fig. 11.

The accompanying figure represents one of the most beautiful of the auroral phenomena.

1435. Why does a haze around the sun indicate rain?

A. Because the haze is caused by vapor in the upper regions of the air.

1436. Why is a halo around the moon a sure indication of rain?

A. Because it is caused by vapor in the upper regions of the air. The larger the halo the nearer the rain-clouds, and the sooner may rain be expected.

1437. Why do we feel almost suffocated in a hot cloudy night?

A. Because the heat of the earth cannot escape into the upper regions of the air, but is pent in by the clouds and confined to the surface of the earth.

1438. Why do we feel sprightly in a clear, bright night?

A. Because the heat of the earth can readily escape into the upper regions of the air, and is not confined and pent in by thick clouds.

1439. Why do we feel depressed in spirits on a wet, murky day?

A. 1st. Because the air is laden with vapor and has (proportionally) less oxygen;

2d. The air, being lighter than usual, does not balance the air in our body; and,

3d. Moist air has a tendency to depress the nervous system.

1440. What is meant by the "air balancing the air in our body"?

A. The human body contains air of a given density: if, therefore, we ascend into a rarer air or descend into a denser, the balance is destroyed, and we feel oppressed.

1441. Why do we feel oppressed if the air around is not of the same density as that in our body?

A. Because, if the air be more dense than

our body, it will produce a feeling of oppression: if it be less dense, the air in our body will produce a feeling of distension.

SECTION I.—MODIFICATION OF CLOUDS.

1442. Into how many classes are the different sorts of clouds generally divided?

A. Into three classes, viz.: Simple, Intermediate, and Compound.

1443. How are simple clouds subdivided?

A. Into—1. Cirrus; 2. Cumulus; and, 3. Stratus clouds. (See Fig. 12.)

1444. What sort of clouds are called cirrus?

A. Clouds like fibres, loose hair, or thin streaks, are called "cirrus clouds."

1445. Why are these clouds called cirrus?

A. From the Latin word *cirrus*, a lock of hair, or curl. Cirrus clouds are the most elevated of all.

1446. What do cirrus clouds portend?

A. When the streamers point upward, the clouds are falling, and rain is at hand; but when the streamers point downward, drought may be expected.

1447. What sort of clouds are called cumulus?

A. Cumulus clouds are lumps, like great sugar-loaves, volumes of smoke, or mountains towering over mountains.

Fig. 12 illustrates the appearance of the cirrus, cumulus, and stratus clouds.

Fig. 12.

Cirrus, *a*; cumulus, *b*; and stratus, *c*.

1448. Why are these monster masses called cumulus clouds?

A. From the Latin word *cumulus*, a mass or pile.

1449. What do cumulus clouds foreshow?

A. When these piles of cloud are fleecy and sail against the wind, they indicate rain; but when their outline is very hard, and they come up with the wind, they foretell fine weather.

Cumulus clouds should be smaller toward evening than they are at noon. If they increase in size at sunset, a thunder-storm may be expected in the night.

1450. What sort of clouds are called stratus?

A. Creeping mists, especially prevalent in a summer evening: these clouds rise at sunset in low, damp places, and are always nearer the earth than any other sort of cloud.

1451. Why are these mists called stratus clouds?

A. From the Latin word *stratus,* laid low, or that which lies low.

1452. What produces cirrus clouds?

A. Moisture, in a visible form, deposited in the higher regions of the atmosphere by ascending currents of heated air.

1453. What produces cumulus clouds?

A. Masses of visible vapor passing from the places where they were formed to other places where they are about to be either dissolved or deposited as falling rain.

1454. What produces stratus clouds?

A. Beds of visible moisture, formed by some chilling effects acting along the direct surface of the earth.

1455. How are the intermediate clouds subdivided?

A. Into two sorts:—1. The Cirro-Cumulus; and, 2. The Cirro-Stratus.

1456. What are cirro-cumulus clouds?

A. Cirro-cumulus clouds are cirrus clouds springing from a massy centre, or heavy masses edged with long streaks, generally called "mares' tails."

A system of small round clouds may be called cirro-cumulus.

1457. What do cirro-cumulus clouds generally forebode?

A. Continued drought, or hot, dry weather.

1458. What are cirro-stratus clouds?

A. They compose what is generally called a "mackerel sky." This class of clouds invariably indicates rain and wind: hence the proverb—

"Mackerels' scales and mares' tails
Make lofty ships to carry low sails."

1459. What produces cirro-cumulus clouds?

A. Cumulus clouds dissolving away into cirrus produce the intermediate class, called cirro-cumulus.

1460. What produces cirro-stratus clouds?

A. Cirrus clouds accumulating into denser masses produce the intermediate class, called cirro-stratus.

1461. How are compound clouds subdivided?

A. Compound clouds are also subdivided

into two sorts:—1. The Cumulo-Stratus; and, 2. The Nimbus clouds.

Fig. 13 illustrates the appearance of the cirro-stratus, the cirro-cumulus, the nimbus, and the cumulo-stratus.

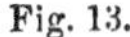

Fig. 13.

Cirro-stratus, *b*, *c*, *d*; cirro-cumulus, *a*; nimbus, *e*; cumulo-stratus, *f*.

1462. What is meant by cumulo-stratus clouds?

A. Those clouds which assume all sorts of gigantic forms,—such as vast towers and rocks, huge whales and dragons, scenes of battle, and cloudy giants. This class of clouds is the most romantic and strange of all.

1463. What do the cumulo-stratus clouds foretell?

A. A change of weather,—either from fine weather to rain, or from rain to fine weather.

1464. What are nimbus clouds?

A. All clouds from which rain falls. *Nimbus* is the Latin word for "clouds which bring a storm." (See Fig. 13.)

1465. By what particular character may the nimbus or rain cloud be at once distinguished?

A. By the want of a defined outline: its edge is gradually shaded off from the deep gray mass into transparency.

1466. What appearance takes place in the clouds at the approach of rain?

A. The cumulus cloud becomes stationary, and cirrus-streaks settle upon it, forming cumulo-stratus clouds, black at first, but afterward of a gray color.

1467. Why do clouds gather around mountain-tops?

A. Because the air, being chilled by the cold mountain-tops, deposits its vapor there in a visible form or cloud.

SECTION II.—DEW.

1468. What is dew?

A. Dew is the vapor of the air condensed by coming in contact with bodies colder than itself.

1469. Why is the ground sometimes covered with dew?

A. Because the surface of the earth at sunset is made so very cold by radiation that the warm vapor of the air is chilled by contact and condensed into dew.

1470. What is the difference between dew and rain?

A. In dew the condensation is made near the earth's surface.

In rain the drops fall from a considerable height.

1471. What is the cause of both dew and rain?

A. Cold condensing the vapor of the air when near the point of saturation.

1472. Why do mist and fog vanish at sunrise?

A. Because the condensed particles are again changed into invisible vapor by the heat of the sun.

1473. Why is the earth made colder than the air after the sun has set?

A. Because the earth radiates heat very freely, but the air does not; in consequence of which, the earth is often five or ten degrees colder than the air after sunset, although it was much warmer than the air during the whole day.

1474. Why is the earth warmer than the air during the day?

A. Because the earth absorbs solar heat very freely, but the air does not; in consequence of which, it is often many degrees warmer than the air during the day.

1475. Why is the surface of the ground colder in a fine, clear night than in a cloudy one?

A. Because on a fine, clear starlight night heat radiates from the earth freely and is lost in open space, but on a dull night the clouds arrest the process of radiation.

1476. Why is dew deposited only on a fine, clear night?

A. Because the surface of the ground radiates heat most freely on a fine night, and, being cooled down by this loss of heat, chills the vapor of the air into dew.

1477. Why does abundance of dew in the morning indicate that the day will be fine?

A. Because dew is never deposited in dull, cloudy weather, but only in very clear, calm nights, when the cold currents of air are not mixed with those of a warmer temperature.

1478. Why is there no dew on a dull, cloudy night?

A. Because the clouds arrest the radiation

of heat from the earth; and, as the heat cannot freely escape, the surface is not sufficiently cooled down to chill the vapor of the air into dew.

1479. Why is a cloudy night warmer than a fine one?

A. Because the clouds prevent the radiation of heat from the earth; in consequence of which, the surface of the earth remains warmer.

1480. Why is dew most abundant in situations most exposed?

A. Because the radiation of heat is not arrested by houses, trees, hedges, or any other thing.

1481. Why is there scarcely any dew under trees or shrubbery?

A. 1st. Because the thick foliage of trees or shrubbery arrests the radiation of heat from the earth; and,

2d. Foliage radiates some of its own heat toward the earth; in consequence of which, the ground underneath a tree or bush is not sufficiently cooled down to chill the vapor of the air into dew.

1482. Dust very rarely flies by night: why is this?

A. 1st. Because the dews of night moisten the dust and prevent its rising into the air; and,

2d. As the surface of the earth is colder than the air after sunset, the current of the wind will incline downward, and tend rather to press the dust down than to buoy it up.

1483. Why is there no dew in the morning after a windy night?

A. 1st. Because the wind evaporates the moisture as fast as it is deposited; and,

2d. It disturbs the radiation of heat, and thus diminishes the deposition of dew.

1484. Why are valleys and hollows often thickly covered with dew, although they are sheltered?

A. Because the surrounding hills prevent the repose of air from being disturbed, but do not overhang and screen the valleys sufficiently to arrest their radiation.

1485. Why does dew fall more abundantly on some things than on others?

A. Because some things radiate heat more freely than others, and therefore become much cooler in the night.

1486. Why are things which radiate heat most freely always the most thickly covered with dew?

A. Because the vapor of the air is chilled into dew the moment it comes in contact with them.

1487. What kind of things radiate heat most freely?

A. Grass, wood, and the leaves of plants radiate heat very freely; but polished metal, smooth stones, and woollen cloth part with their heat very tardily.

1488. Do the leaves of all plants radiate heat equally well?

A. No: rough, woolly leaves, like those of a hollyhock, radiate heat much more freely than the hard, smooth, polished leaves of a common laurel.

1489. Show the wisdom of God in making grass, the leaves of trees, and all vegetables, excellent radiators of heat.

A. As vegetables require much moisture, and would often perish without a plentiful deposit of dew, He wisely made them to radiate heat freely, so as to chill the vapor which touches them into dew.

1490. Will polished metal, smooth stones, and woollen cloth readily collect dew?

A. No: while grass and leaves of plants are completely drenched with dew, a piece of polished metal or woollen cloth lying on the same spot will be almost dry.

1491. Why would polished metal and woollen cloth be dry while grass and leaves are drenched with dew?

A. Because the polished metal and woollen cloth part with their heat so slowly that the vapor of the air is not chilled into dew as it passes over them.

1492. Why is a gravel-walk almost dry when a grass plat is covered thickly with dew?

A. Because grass is a good radiator, and throws off its heat very freely; but gravel is a very bad radiator, and parts with its heat very slowly.

1493. Is that the reason why the grass is saturated with dew and the gravel is not?

A. Yes. When the vapor of warm air comes in contact with the cold grass, it is instantly chilled into dew; but it is not so freely condensed as it passes over gravel, because gravel is not so cold as the grass.

1494. Why does dew rarely fall upon rocks and barren lands?

A. Because rocks and barren lands are so compact and hard that they can neither absorb nor radiate much heat; and, as their temperature varies but slightly, very little dew distils upon them.

1495. Why does dew fall more abundantly on cultivated soils than on barren lands?

A. Because cultivated soils, being loose and porous, very freely radiate by night the heat which they absorbed by day; in consequence of which, they are much cooled down, and plentifully condense the vapor of the passing air into dew.

1496. Show the wisdom of God in this arrangement.

A. Every plant and inch of land which needs the moisture of dew is adapted to collect it; but not a single drop is wasted where its refreshing moisture is not required.

1497. Show the wisdom in having polished metal and woolen cloth bad radiators of heat.

A. If polished metal collected dew as easily as grass, it could never be kept dry and free from rust. Again, if woollen garments collected dew as readily as the leaves of trees, we should be often soaking wet, and subject to constant colds.

1498. Show how this affords a beautiful illustration of Gideon's miracle, recorded in Judges vi. 37, 38.

A. The fleece of wool, which is a very bad radiator of heat, was soaking wet with dew when the grass, which is a most excellent radiator, was quite dry.

1499. Was this not contrary to the laws of nature?

A. Yes, and it was, therefore, a plain demonstration of the power of God, who could thus change the very nature of things at his will.

1500. Why do our clothes feel damp after walking in a fine evening in spring or autumn?

A. Because the vapor condensed by the cold earth rests upon them like dew.

1501. When is dew most copiously distilled?

A. After a hot day in summer or autumn,—especially if the wind blow over a body of water.

1502. Why is dew distilled most copiously after a hot day?

A. Because the surface of the hot earth

radiates heat very freely at sunset, and, being made much colder than the air, chills the passing vapor and condenses it into dew.

1503. Why is there less dew when the wind blows across the land than when it blows over a body of water?

A. Because the winds which blow across the land are dry and arid, but those which cross the water are moist and full of vapor.

1504. How does the dryness of the wind prevent the fall of dew?

A. As winds which blow over the land are very dry, they imbibe the moisture of the air; in consequence of which, there is very little left to be condensed into dew.

1505. How does the moisture of the wind promote the fall of dew?

A. As winds which blow over water are saturated with vapor, they require very little reduction of heat to cause a copious deposition of dew.

1506. Does not air radiate heat, as well as the earth and its various plants?

A. No: the air never radiates heat; nor is the air made hot by the rays of the sun.

1507. Why will dew-drops roll about cabbage-plants, poppies, &c. without wetting the surface?

A. Because the leaves of cabbages and poppies are covered with a very fine waxen powder, over which the dew-drop rolls without wetting the surface, as a drop of rain would over dust.

1508. Why does not a drop of rain wet the dust over which it rolls?

A. Because dust has no affinity for water, and therefore repels it.

1509. Why does not the dew-drop wet the powder of the cabbage-plant?

A. Because the fine powder which covers the cabbage-leaves has no affinity for water, and therefore repels it.

1510. Why will dew-drops roll over a rose, &c. without wetting the petals?

A. Because the leaves of a rose contain an essential oil, which has no affinity for water, and therefore repels it.

1511. Why can swans and ducks dive under water without being wetted?

A. Because their feathers are covered with an oily secretion, which has no affinity for water, and therefore repels it.

SECTION XII.—RAIN, SNOW, HAIL.

1512. What is rain?

A. Rain is the vapor of the clouds or air, condensed and precipitated to the earth.

1513. Does rain-water possess any fertilizing properties besides that of mere moisture?

A. Yes: rain-water contains an abundance of carbonic acid, and a small quantity of ammonia; to which much of its fertilizing power may be attributed.

Ammonia is a compound of nitrogen and hydrogen. Common artshorn is ammonia and water.

1514. In what part of the world does rain fall most abundantly?

A. Near the equator; and the quantity of rain decreases as we approach the poles.

It should be observed that there are fewer rainy days, although more rain actually falls during the wet season of the equator than falls in twelve months at any other part of the globe.

1515. Why does rain fall in drops?

A. Because the vapory particles in their descent attract each other, and those which are sufficiently near unite and form into drops.

1516. Why does not the cold of night always cause rain?

A. Because the air is not always near saturation; and, unless this be the case, it will be able to hold its vapor in solution even after it is condensed by the chilly night.

1517. Why does a passing cloud often drop rain?

A. Because the cloud, blown by the wind, encounters a current of cold air, which condenses its vapor and causes it to fall to the earth in rain.

1518. Why are rain-drops sometimes much larger than at other times?

A. Because the rain-cloud is floating nearer the earth: when this is the case, the drops are large, because such a cloud is much more dense than one more elevated.

The size of the rain-drop is also increased according to the rapidity with which the vapors are condensed.

1519. Does not wind sometimes increase the size of rain-drops?

A. Yes,—by blowing two or more drops into one.

1520. Why do clouds fall in rainy weather?

A. 1st. Because they are heavy with abundant vapor; and,

2d. The density of the air being diminished, it is less able to buoy the clouds up.

1521. How do you know that the density of the air is diminished in rainy weather?

A. Because the mercury of a barometer falls.

1522. Why is rain-water more fertilizing than pump-water?

A. 1st. Because it contains more carbonic acid; and,

2d. It contains also a small quantity of ammonia, with which it supplies the young plants.

1523. Why does rain purify the air?

A. 1st. Because it beats down the noxious exhalations collected in the air, and dissolves them;

2d. It mixes the air of the upper regions with that of the lower regions; and,

3d. It washes the earth, and sets in motion the stagnant contents of sewers and ditches.

1524. Why are mountainous countries more rainy than flat ones?

A. Because the air, striking against the sides of the mountains, is carried up the inclined plane, and brought in contact with the cold air of the higher regions; in consequence of which, its vapor is condensed and deposited in rain.

1525. Why does a sponge swell when it is wetted?

A. Because the water penetrates the pores of the sponge by capillary attraction, and drives the particles farther from each other; in consequence of which, the bulk of the sponge is greatly increased.

1526. Why do violin-strings snap in wet weather?

A. Because the moisture of the air, penetrating the string, causes it to swell, and as the cord thickens, its tension is increased, and the string snaps.

1527. Why does paper pucker when it is dampened?

A. Because the moisture, penetrating the paper, drives its particles farther apart; and, as the moisture is absorbed unequally by the paper, some parts are more enlarged than others; in consequence of which, the paper blisters or puckers.

1528. In which part of the day does the most rain fall?

A. More rain falls by night than by day; because the cold night condenses the air and diminishes its capacity for holding vapor in solution.

1529. What beneficial effect has rain upon fallen leaves?

A. It hastens the putrefaction of the fallen leaves; and this makes the earth fertile.

1530. Why do swallows fly low when rain is at hand?

A. Because the insects of which they are in pursuit have fled from the cold, upper regions of the air to the warm air near the earth; and, as their food is low, the swallows fly low.

1531. Why do these insects seek the lower regions of the air in wet weather more than in fine weather?

A. Because in wet weather the upper regions of the air are colder than the lower; and, as insects enjoy warmth, they seek it near the earth.

1532. Why do sea-gulls fly about the sea in fine weather?

A. Because they live upon the fishes which are found near the surface of the sea in fine weather.

1533. Why may we expect stormy rains when sea-gulls assemble on the land?

A. Because the fishes on which they live leave the surface ot the sea in stormy weather, and are beyond the reach of the sea-gulls; in consequence of which, they are obliged to feed on the worms and larvæ which are driven out of the ground at such times.

"Larvæ," little grubs and caterpillars.

1534. Why do petrels fly to the sea during a storm?

A. Because they live upon sea-insects, which are always to be found in abundance about the spray of swelling waves.

Petrels are birds of the duck-kind, which live in the open sea. They run on the top of the waves, and are called Petrels—or rather Peterels—from "St. Peter," in allusion to his walking on the sea to go to Jesus.

1535. What is snow?

A. The condensed vapor of the air frozen and precipitated to the earth.

1536. What is the cause of snow?

A. When the air is nearly saturated with vapor, and condensed by a current of air below the freezing-point, some of the vapor is condensed, and frozen into snow.

A few years ago, some fishermen who wintered at Nova Zembla, after they had been shut up in a hut for several days, opened the window, and the cold external air, rushing in, instantly condensed the air of the hut, and its vapor fell on the floor in a shower of snow.

1537. Why does snow fall in winter-time?

A. Because the sun's rays are too oblique to heat the surface of the earth; and, as the earth has no heat to radiate into the air, the air is very cold.

1538. What is the cause of sleet?

A. When flakes of snow in their descent pass through a stratum of air above the freezing-point, they partially melt, and fall to the earth as half-melted snow, or sleet.

1539. What is the use of snow?

A. To keep the earth warm, and to nourish it.

1540. Does snow keep the earth warm?

A. Yes,—because it is a very bad conductor of heat; in consequence of which, when the earth is covered with snow, its temperature very rarely descends below the freezing-point, even when the air is fifteen or twenty degrees colder.

1541. Why is snow a bad conductor of heat and cold?

A. Because air is confined among the crystals; and air is a very bad conductor: when, therefore, the earth is covered with snow, it cannot throw off its heat by radiation.

1542. Tell me the words of the Psalmist (cxlvii. 16) respecting snow, and explain what he means.

A. The Psalmist says, "The Lord giveth snow like wool;" and he means, not only that snow is as white as wool, but that it is also as warm as wool.

1543. Why is wool warm?

A. Because air is among the fibres of the wool; and air is a very bad conductor of heat.

1544. Why does snow nourish the earth?

A. Because it supplies moisture containing carbonic acid, which penetrates slowly into the soil and insinuates itself through every clod, ridge, and furrow.

1545. Why is there no snow in summer-time?

A. Because the heat of the earth melts it in its descent, and prevents it from reaching the surface of the earth.

1546. Why are some mountains always covered with snow?

A. 1st. Because the air on a high mountain is more rarefied; and rarefied air retains much heat in a latent state; and,

2d. Mountain-tops are not surrounded by earth, to radiate heat into the air; and therefore the snow is not melted in its descent, but falls on the mountain and lies there.

1547. Why is snow white?

A. Because it is formed of an infinite number of very minute crystals and prisms, which reflect all the colors of the rays of light from different points; and these colors, uniting before they meet the eye, cause snow to appear white.

The same answer applies to salt, loaf-sugar, &c.

1548. What is hail?

A. Rain which has passed in its descent through some cold stratum of air and has been frozen into drops of ice.

1549. What makes one stratum of air colder than another?

A. It is frequently caused by electricity unequally distributed in the air.

1550. Why is hail frequently accompanied by thunder and lightning?

A. 1st. Because the congelation of water into hail disturbs the electricity of the air; and,

2d. The friction produced by the fall of hail excites it still more.

1551. Why does hail fall generally in summer and autumn?

A. 1st. Because the air is more highly electrified in summer and autumn than in winter and spring; and,

2d. The vapors in summer and autumn, being rarefied, ascend to more elevated regions, which are colder than those nearer the earth.

1552. What things are essential to cause hail?

A. Two strata of clouds having opposite electricities, and two currents of wind. The lower cloud, being negative, is the one precipitated in hail.

1553. When is the vapor of the air or clouds precipitated in hail, rain, or snow?

A. When the air is saturated with vapor and a cold current condenses it: it is then no longer able to hold all its vapor in solution, and some of it falls as rain

SECTION IV.—MIST, FOG, FROST.

1554. What is the cause of mist?

A. Currents of air from the water coming in contact with colder land-currents.

1555. Why are the currents of air from the land colder than those blowing over water?

A. Because the earth radiates heat after sunset more freely than water; consequently, the air which comes in contact with the land is colder than that which comes in contact with the water.

1556. Why are windows often covered with thick mist, and the frames wet with standing water?

A. Because the temperature of the external air usually falls at sunset, and chills the window-glass with which it comes in contact.

1557. How does this account for the mist and water on a window?

A. As the warm vapor of the room touches the cold glass, it is chilled and condensed into mist, and the mist, collecting into drops, rolls down the window-frame in little streams of water.

1558. Does the glass of a window cool down more rapidly than the air of the room itself?

A. Yes; because the air is kept warm by fires, and by the animal heat of the people in the room; in consequence of which, the air of a room suffers very little diminution of heat from the setting of the sun.

1559. Whence arises the vapor of a room?

A. 1st. The very air of the room contains vapor;

2d. The breath and insensible perspiration of the inmates increase this vapor; and,

3d. The steam of food increases it still more.

1560. What is meant by "the insensible perspiration"?

A. From every part of the human body an insensible and invisible perspiration issues all night and day, not only in the hot weather of summer, but also in the coldest day of winter.

1561. If the perspiration be both insensible and invisible, how is it known that there is any such perspiration?

A. If you put your naked arm into a clean, dry glass tube, the perspiration will condense on the glass like mist.

1562. Why are carriage-windows very soon covered with thick mist?

A. Because the warm vapor of the carriage is condensed by the cold glass, and covers it with a thick mist.

1563. Why is the glass window cold enough to condense the vapor of the carriage?

A. Because the inside of a carriage is much warmer than the outside; and the glass window is made cold by contact with the external air.

1564. Where does the warm vapor of the carriage come from?

A. The warm breath and insensible perspiration of the persons riding load the air of the carriage with warm vapor.

1565. What is the cause of the pretty frost-work seen on bedroom-windows in winter-time?

A. The breath and insensible perspiration of the sleeper, coming in contact with the ice-cold window, are frozen by the cold glass, and form those beautiful appearances seen in our bedrooms or a winter morning.

1566. Why is the glass of a window colder than the walls of a room?

A. Because glass is so excellent a radiator that it parts with its heat more rapidly than the walls do.

1567. Why is a tumbler of cold water made quite dull with mist when brought into a room full of people?

A. Because the hot vapor of the room is condensed upon the cold tumbler, with which it comes in contact, and its invisible and gaseous form is changed into that of a thick mist.

1568. Why is a glass made quite dull by laying a hot hand upon it?

A. Because the insensible perspiration of the hot hand is condensed upon the cold glass, and made perceptible.

1569. Why does this misty appearance go off, after a little time?

A. Because the glass becomes of the same

temperature as the air of the room, and it will no longer chill the vapor which touches it, and condense it into mist.

1570. Why does breathing on a glass make it quite dull?

A. Because the hot breath is condensed by the cold glass, and therefore covers it with a thick mist.

1571. Why are the walls of a house often damp in a sudden thaw?

A. Because the walls, being thick, cannot change their temperature so fast as the air; in consequence of which, they retain their coldness after the thaw has set in.

1572. How does "retaining their coldness" account for their being so damp?

A. As the vapor of the warm air touches the cold walls, it is chilled and condensed into water, which either adheres to the walls or trickles down in little streams.

1573. Why are balusters, &c. damp after a thaw?

A. Because they are made of some very close-grained varnished wood, which cannot change its temperature so fast as the air.

1574. How does this account for the balusters being damp?

A. The vapor of the warm air, coming in contact with the cold balusters, is chilled and condensed into water upon them.

1575. Why is our breath visible in winter and not in summer?

A. Because the intense cold condenses our breath into visible vapor; but in summer the air is not cold enough to do so.

1576. Why are our hair and the brim of our hat often covered with little drops of pearly dew in winter-time?

A. Because our breath is condensed as soon as it comes in contact with our cold hair or hat, and hangs there in little dew-drops.

1577. What is fog?

A. Fog is only very thick mist.

1578. What is the cause of fog?

A. If the night has been very calm, the radiation of heat from the earth has been very abundant; in consequence of which, the air resting on the earth has been chilled, and its vapor condensed into a thick mist.

1579. Why does not the mist become dew?

A. Because the chill of the air is so rapid that vapor is condensed faster than it can be deposited, and, covering the earth in a mist, prevents any further radiation of heat from the earth.

1580. When the earth can no longer radiate heat upwards, does it continue to condense the vapor of the air?

A. No: the air in contact with the earth becomes about equal in temperature with the surface of the earth itself; for which reason the mist is not condensed into dew, but remains floating above the earth as a thick cloud.

1581. This mist seems to rise higher and higher, and yet remains quite as dense below as at first. Explain this.

A. The air resting on the earth is first chilled, and chills the air resting on it; the air which touches this new layer of mist being also condensed, layer is added to layer; and thus the mist seems to be rising, when in fact it is only deepening.

1582. Why do mist and dew vanish as the sun rises?

A. Because the air becomes warmer at sunrise, and absorbs the vapor.

1583. What is the cause of a London fog?

A. These fogs (which occur generally in the winter-time) are occasioned thus:—Some current of air, being suddenly cooled, descends into the warm streets, forcing back the smoke in a mass towards the earth.

1584. Why are there not fogs every night?

A. Because the air will always hold in solution a certain quantity of vapor, (which varies according to its temperature;) and when the air is not saturated, it may be cooled without parting with its vapor.

1585. When do fogs occur at night?

A. When the air is saturated with vapor during the day. When this is the case, it deposits some of its superabundant moisture in the form of dew or fog as soon as its capacity for holding vapor is lessened by the cold night.

1586. Why is there very often a fog over marshes and rivers at night-time?

A. Because the air of marshes is almost always near saturation; and therefore the least depression of temperature will compel it to relinquish some of its moisture in the form of dew or fog.

1587. Why does vapor sometimes form into clouds, and sometimes rest upon the earth as mist or fog?

A. This depends on the temperature of the air. When the surface of the earth is warmer than the air, the vapor of the earth, being condensed by the chill air, becomes mist or fog; but when the air is warmer than the earth, the vapor rises through the air, and becomes cloud.

1588. Why do hills, &c. appear larger in a fog?

A. Because the air is laden with vapor, which causes the rays of light to diverge more; in consequence of which, they produce on the eye larger images of objects.

1589. Why do trees, &c. in a fog appear farther off than they really are?

A. Because the fog or mist diminishes the

light reflected from the object; and as the object becomes more dim, it seems to be farther off.

Dr. Kane, the great Arctic navigator, says, "The effects of fogs upon our estimation of dimension and distance are well known: men are magnified to giants, and brigs 'loom up,' as the sailors term it, into ships of the line."

1590. If cold air produces fog, why is it not foggy on a frosty morning?

A. 1st. Because less vapor is formed on a frosty day; and,

2d. The vapor is frozen upon the ground before it can rise from the earth, and becomes hoar-frost.

1591. Why are fogs more general in autumn than in spring?

A. The earth in spring is not so hot as it is in autumn; in consequence of which, its vapor is not chilled into fog as it issues into the air.

1592. Why are fogs more common in valleys than on hills?

A. 1st. Because valleys contain more moisture than hills; and,

2d. They are not exposed to sufficient wind to dissipate the vapor.

1593. How does wind dissipate fogs?

A. Either by blowing them away, or by dissolving them into vapor again.

1594. What is hoar-frost?

A. There are two sorts of hoar-frost: 1. Frozen dew; and, 2. Frozen fog.

1595. What is the cause of the ground hoar-frost, or frozen dew?

A. Very rapid radiation of heat from the earth; in consequence of which, the surface is so cooled down that it freezes the dew condensed upon it.

1596. Why is hoar-frost seen only after a very clear night?

A. Because the earth will not have thrown off heat enough by radiation to freeze the vapor condensed upon its surface unless the night was very clear.

1597. What is the cause of that hoar-frost which arises from frozen fog?

A. The thick fog which invested the earth during the night, being condensed by the cold frost of early morning, is congealed upon every object with which it comes in contact.

1598. Why does hoar-frost very often cover the ground and trees, when the water of rivers is not frozen?

A. Because it is not the effect of cold in the air, but cold on the surface of the earth (produced by excessive radiation) which freezes the dew condensed upon it.

1599. Why is the hoar-frost upon grass and vegetables much thicker than that upon lofty trees?

A. Because the air resting on the surface of the ground is much colder after sunset than the air higher up; in consequence of which, more vapor is condensed and frozen there.

CHAPTER IV.—ICE.

1600. What is freezing?

A. The solidification of fluid bodies by the abstraction of the heat necessary to their fluid form.

1601. What is ice?

A. Frozen water. When water is reduced to thirty-two degrees of heat, it will no longer remain in a fluid state.

1602. Why is solid ice lighter than water?

A. Because water expands by freezing, and, as the bulk is increased, the gravity must be less.

1603. When does water begin to expand from cold?

A. When it is reduced to thirty-eight degrees and eight-tenths. Water is wisely ordained by God to be an exception to a very general rule; it contracts till it is reduced to thirty-eight degrees and eight-tenths, and then it expands till it freezes.

1604. Why does water expand when it freezes?

A. Because it is converted into solid crystals which do not fit so closely as particles of water do.

1605. Why do water-pipes frequently burst in frosty weather?

A. Because the water in them freezes, and, expanding by frost, bursts the pipes to make room for its increased volume.

1606. Does not water expand by heat as well as by cold?

A. Yes: it expands as soon as it is more than thirty-eight degrees and eight-tenths, till it boils; after which time it flies off in steam.

1607. Why does not water when freezing expand upwards, like boiling water, and run over?

A. Because the surface is frozen first, which prevents the overflowing of the water.

1608. Why do tiles, stones, and rocks often split in winter?

A. Because the moisture in them freezes, and, expanding by frost, splits the solid mass.

1609. In winter-time, foot-marks and wheel-ruts are often covered with an icy net-work, through the interstices of which the soil is clearly seen: why does the water freeze in net-work?

A. Because it freezes first at the sides of the foot-prints; other crystals gradually shoot across, and would cover the whole surface, if the earth did not absorb the water before it had time to freeze.

1610. In winter-time, these foot-marks and wheel-ruts are sometimes covered with a perfect sheet of ice, and not an icy net-work: why is this?

A. Because the air is colder and the earth harder than in the former case; in consequence of which, the entire surface of the foot-print is frozen over before the earth has had time to absorb the water.

1611. Why is not the ice solid in these ruts? why is there only a very thin film or net-work of ice?

A. Because the earth absorbs most of the water, and leaves only the icy film behind.

Fig. 14.
Freezing water, 32°. 212°, boiling water.

Here A B measures the bulk of a portion of water at 42°. It goes on increasing in bulk to C D, when it boils. It also goes on increasing in bulk to E F, when it freezes.

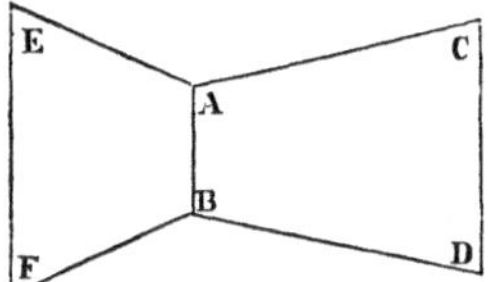

1612. Why is the bottom of a river seldom frozen?

A. Because water ascends to the surface as soon as it becomes colder than forty-two degrees, and, if it freezes, floats there till it is melted.

Ice is sometimes formed at the bottom of rivers. It is then called ground-ice.

1613. Show the wisdom of God in this wonderful exception to a general law.

A. If ice were heavier than water, it would sink; and a river would soon become a solid block of ice.

The general rule is, that all substances become heavier from condensation; but ice is lighter than water.

1614. Why does not the ice on the surface of a river chill the water beneath and make it freeze?

A. 1st. Because water is a very bad conductor, and is heated or chilled by convection only;

2d. If the ice on the surface were to communicate its coldness to the water beneath, the water beneath would communicate its heat to the ice, and the ice would instantly melt; and,

3d. The ice on the surface acts as a shield, to prevent the cold air from penetrating through the river, to freeze the water below the surface.

1615. Why does water freeze at the surface first?

A. Because the surface is in contact with the air, and the air carries away its heat.

1616. Why does the coat of ice grow thicker and thicker if the frost continues?

A. Because the heat of the water immediately below the frozen surface passes through the pores of the ice into the cold air.

1617. Why are not whole rivers frozen, layer by layer, till they become solid ice?

A. Because water is so slow a conductor that our frosts never continue long enough to convert a whole river into a solid mass of ice.

1618. Why does not running water freeze so fast as still water?

A. 1st. Because the motion of the current disturbs the crystals, and prevents their forming into a continuous surface; and,

2d. The heat of the under surface is communicated to the upper surface by the rolling of the water.

1619. When running water is frozen, why is the ice generally very rough?

A. Because little flakes of ice are first formed and carried down the stream, till they meet some obstacle to stop them; other flakes of ice, impinging against them, are arrested in like manner; and the edges of the different flakes, overlapping each other, make the surface rough.

1620. Why do some parts of a river freeze less than others?

A. Because springs issue from the bottom, and, as they bubble upward, thaw the ice, or make it thin.

1621. When persons fall into a river in winter-time, why does the water feel remarkably warm?

A. Because the frosty air is at least ten or twelve degrees colder than the water is.

The temperature of the water below the surface is at least 38°; but that of the air is 12°, or even less.

1622. Why is shallow water frozen more quickly than deep water?

A. Because the whole volume of water must be cooled to thirty-eight degrees before the surface can be frozen; and it takes a longer time to cool down a deep bed of water than a shallow one.

1623. Why is sea-water rarely frozen?

A. 1st. Because the mass of water is so

great that it requires a very long time to cool the whole volume down to 38°;

2d. The ebb and flow of the sea interfere with the cooling influence of the air; and,

3d. Salt water never freezes till the surface is cooled down twenty-five degrees below the freezing-point.

1624. Why do some lakes rarely, if ever, freeze?

A. 1st. Because they are very deep; and,

2d. Because their water is supplied by springs which bubble from the bottom.

1625. Why does the depth of water retard its freezing?

A. Because the temperature of the whole volume of water must be reduced to 38° before the surface will freeze; and the deeper the water the longer will it be before the whole volume is thus reduced.

1626. Why do springs at the bottom of a lake prevent its freezing?

A. Because they are continually sending forth fresh water, which prevents the lake from being reduced to the necessary degree of coldness.

1627. It is colder in a thaw than in a frost. Explain the reason of this.

A. When frozen water is thawed, it absorbs heat from the air, &c. to melt the ice; in consequence of which, the heat of the air is greatly reduced.

1628. It is warmer in a frost than in a thaw. Explain the reason of this.

A. When water freezes, it gives out latent heat, in order that it may be converted into solid ice; and, as much heat is liberated from the water to the atmosphere, the air feels warmer.

1629. Salt dissolves ice. Explain the reason of this.

A. Water freezes at 32°, but salt and water will not freeze till the air is twenty-five degrees colder: if, therefore, salt be added to frozen water, it dissolves it.

1630. Why does pure water freeze more quickly than milk?

A. Because milk contains certain salts in solution; in consequence of which, it requires a greater degree of cold to congeal it than water.

Water freezes at 32°, but salt and water will not freeze unless the thermometer sinks below 7°.

1631. Will any thing dissolve ice except salt?

A. Yes; any acid will, such as sulphuric acid, nitric acid, &c.

1632. Why is a mixture of salt and snow colder than snow itself?

A. Because salt dissolves the crystals of snow into a fluid; and whenever a solid is converted into a fluid, heat is absorbed, and the cold made more intense.

1633. Why does frost make the earth crack?

A. Because the water absorbed by the

earth in warm weather, expanding by the frost, thrusts the particles of earth apart from each other, and leaves a chink or crack between.

1634. Show the wisdom of God in this arrangement.

A. These cracks in the earth let in air, dew, rain, and many gases favorable to vegetation.

1635. Why does the earth crumble in spring?

A. Because the ice of the clods dissolves; and the particles of earth which had been thrust apart by the frost, being left unsupported, tumble into minute parts, because their cement of ice is dissolved.

1636. Why does mortar crumble away in frost?

A. Because it was not dried in the warm weather: therefore its moisture freezes, expands, and thrusts the particles of the mortar away from each other; but as soon as the frost goes the water condenses, and leaves the mortar full of cracks and chinks.

1637. Why does stucco peel from a wall in frosty weather?

A. Because the stucco was not dried in the warm weather: therefore its moisture freezes, expands, and thrusts its particles away from the wall; but as soon as the water condenses again by the thaw, the stucco, being unsupported, falls by its own weight.

1638. Why cannot bricklayers and plasterers work in frosty weather?

A. Because frost expands mortar, and causes the bricks and plaster to start from their position.

1639. Why do bricklayers cover their work with straw in spring and autumn?

A. Because straw is a non-conductor, and prevents the mortar of their new work from freezing during the cold nights of spring and autumn.

1640. Why are water-pipes often covered with straw in winter-time?

A. Because straw, being a non-conductor, prevents the water of the pipes from freezing, and the pipes from bursting.

1641. Can water be frozen in any way except by frosty weather?

A. Yes; in many ways. For example, a bottle of water wrapped in cotton and frequently wetted with ether will soon freeze.

1642. Why would water freeze if the bottle were kept constantly wetted with ether?

A. Because evaporation would carry off the heat of the water and reduce it to the freezing-point.

1643. Why does ether freeze under the receiver of an air-pump when the air is exhausted?

A. Because evaporation is greatly increased

by the diminution of atmospheric pressure; and the ether freezes by evaporation.

FREEZING-MIXTURES.

Equal weights of fresh snow (or pounded ice) and common salt will produce a temperature of 4° below zero.

A mixture of three parts of crystallized chloride of calcium and two parts of snow will create a temperature sufficiently cold to freeze mercury.

The most powerful freezing-mixture now known is formed by dissolving solid carbonic acid or solid nitrous oxide in sulphuric ether. In this way temperatures from 120° to 146° below zero have been obtained.

1644. Is a mixture of salt and snow really colder than snow?

A. Yes, many degrees colder; so that if the hand be dipped into the mixture first, and into snow afterward, the snow will seem to be comparatively warm.

PART VI.

OPTICS.

CHAPTER I.—LIGHT.

1645. WHAT is light?

A. Rapid undulations of a fluid called ether, made sensible to the eye by striking on the optic nerve.

1646. In what manner is light propagated?

A. In right lines from every luminous point, every such line being called a ray of light.

1647. What is meant by a pencil of light?

A. A collection of radiating lines or rays, as seen in fig. 15.

Fig. 15.

1648. What is a focus of light?

A. When rays of light continually approach each other, as in moving to a point, they are said to converge, and the point at which the converging rays meet is called the "focus."

1649. How fast does light travel?

A. Light travels so fast that it would go eight times round the earth while a person counts "one."

Light travels about 200,000 miles in one second of time.

1650. What is ether?

A. A very subtle fluid, which pervades all space.

1651. How can undulations of ether produce light?

A. As sound is produced by undulations of air striking on the ear, so light is produced by undulations of ether striking on the eye.

1652. How does combustion make undulations of light?

A. The atoms of matter set in motion by heat, striking against this ether, produce undulations in it, as a stone thrown into a stream produces undulations in the water.

1653. Does all light travel equally fast?

A. Yes: the light of the sun or the light of a candle travels at the rate of about 200,000 miles in a second.

1654. Where does the light of houses, trees, and fields come from?

A. The light of the sun, or of some lamp or candle, is reflected from their surfaces.

1655. Why are some surfaces brilliant, like glass and steel, and others dull, like lead?

A. Those surfaces which reflect the most

light are the most brilliant; and those which absorb light are dull.

1656. What is meant by reflecting light?

A. Throwing the rays of light back again from the surface on which they fall.

1657. What is meant by absorbing light?

A. Retaining the rays of light on the surface on which they fall; in consequence of which, their presence is not made sensible by reflection.

1658. Why can a thousand persons see the same object at the same time?

A. Because it throws off from its surface an infinite number of rays in all directions; and one person sees one portion of these rays, and another person another.

1659. Why is the eye pained by a sudden light?

A. Because the nerve of the eye is burdened with rays before the pupil has had time to contract.

1660. Why does it give us pain if a candle be brought suddenly toward our bed in the night-time?

A. Because the pupil of the eye dilates very much in the dark, in order to admit more rays. When, therefore, a candle is brought suddenly before us, the enlarged pupils overload the optic nerves with rays, which causes pain.

1661. Why can we bear the candle-light after a few moments?

A. Because the pupils contract again almost instantly, and adjust themselves to the quantity of light which falls upon them.

1662. Why can we see nothing when we leave a well-lighted room and go into the darker road or street?

A. Because the pupil, which contracted in the bright room, does not dilate instantaneously; and the contracted pupil is not able to collect rays enough from the darker road or street to enable us to see objects before us.

1663. Why do we see better when we get used to the dark?

A. Because the pupil dilates again, and allows more rays to pass through its aperture; in consequence of which, we see more distinctly.

"Thus, when the lamp that lighted
The traveller at first goes out,
He feels a while benighted,
And lingers on in fear and doubt.

"But soon, the prospect clearing,
In cloudless starlight on he treads,
And finds no lamp so cheering
As that light which heaven sheds."

1664. If we look at the sun for a few moments, why do all other things appear dark?

A. Because the pupil of the eye becomes so much contracted by looking at the sun that it is too small to collect sufficient rays from other objects to enable us to distinguish their colors. (See Accidental Colors.)

1665. Why can we see the proper colors of every object again, after a few minutes?

A. Because the pupil dilates again, and accommodates itself to the light around.

1666. Why can tigers, cats, and owls see in the dark?

A. Because they have the power of enlarging the pupil of their eyes so as to collect the scattered rays of light; in consequence of which, they can see distinctly when it is not light enough for us to see any thing at all.

1667. Why do cats keep winking when they sit before a fire?

A. Because the pupil of their eye is very broad, and the light of the fire is painful: so they keep shutting their eyes to relieve the sensation of too much light.

1668. Why do glow-worms and fire-flies glisten by night only?

A. Because the light of day is so strong that it eclipses the feeble light of a glow-worm or fire-fly; in consequence of which, glow-worms are invisible by day.

1669. Why can we not see the stars in the daytime?

A. Because the light of day is so powerful that it eclipses the feeble light of the stars; in consequence of which, they are invisible by day.

1670. Why can we see the stars, even at mid-day, from the bottom of a deep well?

A. Because the light of the stars is not

overpowered by the rays of the sun, which are lost in the numerous reflections which they undergo in the well.

The rays of the sun will enter the well very obliquely; whereas many stars will shine directly over the well.

1671. Why do we not see things double, with two eyes?

A. 1st. Because the axis of both eyes is turned to one object, and therefore the same impression is made on the retina of each eye; and,

2d. Because the nerves which receive the impression have one point of union before they reach the brain.

This is not altogether satisfactory,—although it is the explanation generally given. The phenomenon, probably, is rather psychological than material.

1672. Why do we see ourselves in a glass?

A. Because the rays of light from our face strike against the surface of the glass, and, instead of being absorbed, are reflected, or sent back again to our eye.

1673. Why are the rays of light reflected by a mirror?

A. Because they cannot pass through the impenetrable metal with which the back of the glass is covered: so they bound back, just as a marble would do if it were thrown against a wall.

1674. When a marble is rolled toward a wall, what is the path through which it runs called?

A. The line of incidence.

1675. When a marble bounds back again, what is the path it then describes called?

A. The line of reflection.

(See Fig. 16.) If A B be the line of incidence, B E is the line of reflection; and *vice versa.*

1676. When the light of our face goes to the glass, what is the path through which it goes called?

A. The line of incidence.

1677. When the light of our face is reflected back again from the mirror, what is this returning path called?

A. The line of reflection.

1678. What is the angle of incidence?

A. The angle between the line of incidence and the perpendicular.

1679. What is the angle of reflection?

A. The angle between the line of reflection and the perpendicular.

Fig. 16.

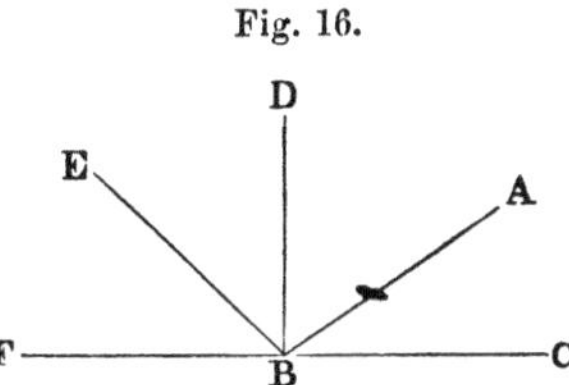

Let F C be any surface, D B a perpendicular to it. If a marble were thrown from E to B, and bounded back to A, then E B D would be called the angle of incidence, and A B D the angle of reflection.

1680. Why does our reflection in a mirror seem to approach us as we walk toward it, and to retire from us as we retire?

A. Because the lines and angles of incidence are always equal to the lines and angles of reflection; in consequence of which, the image will always seem to be as far behind the mirror as the real object is before it.

Fig. 17.

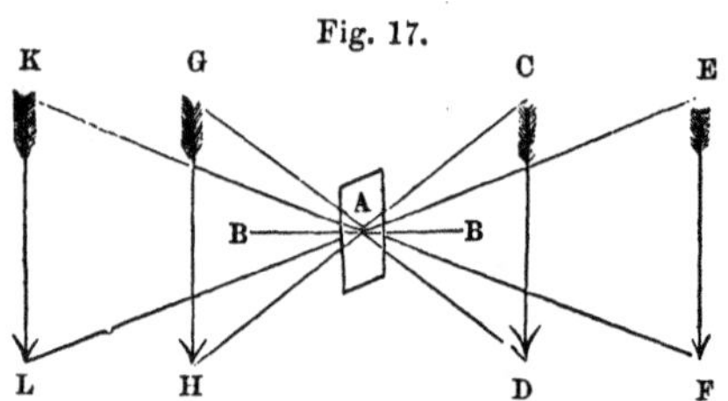

Suppose A to be a mirror, C A, E A, and D A, F A, the lines of incidence; then G A, K A, and H A, L A, are the lines of reflection. When the arrow is at C D, its image will appear at G H, because line C A = G A, and line D A = H A; and also angle C A B = angle G A B, and angle D A B = angle H A B. For a similar reason, if the arrow were at E F, the image would seem to be at K L.

1681. Why does the image of any object in water always appear inverted?

A. Because the angles of incidence are always equal to the angles of reflection.

Fig. 18.

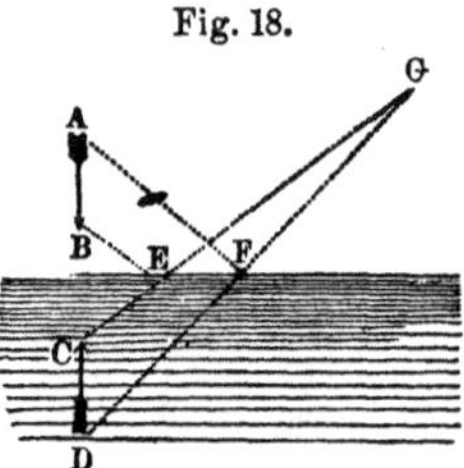

Here the arrow-head A strikes the water at F, and is reflected to D, and the barb B strikes the water at E, and is reflected to C.

If a spectator stands at G, he will see the reflected lines C E and D F produced as far as G.

It is very plain that A (the more elevated object) will strike the water and be projected from it more perpendicularly than the point B; and therefore the image will seem inverted.

1682. When we see our reflection in water, why do we seem to stand on our head?

A. Because the angles of incidence are always equal to the angles of reflection.

Suppose our head to be at A, and our feet at B; then the shadow of our head will be seen at D, and the shadow of our feet at C. (See fig. 18.)

1683. Why do windows seem to blaze at sunrise and sunset?

A. Because glass is a good reflector of light; and the rays of the sun, striking against the window-glass, are reflected, or thrown back.

1684. Why do not windows reflect the noonday rays also?

A. They do; but the reflection is not seen.

1685. Why is the reflection of the rising and setting sun seen in the window, and not that of the noonday sun?

A. Because the rays of the noonday sun enter the glass too obliquely for their reflection to be seen.

Sun near noon. Fig. 19.

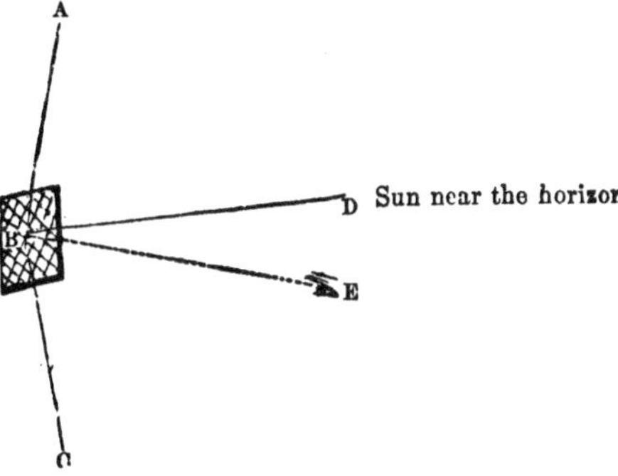

In the preceding cut, A B represents a ray of the noonday sun striking the window at B; its reflection will be at C.

But D B (a ray of the rising or setting sun) will be reflected to E, (the eye of the spectator.)

1686. Why can we not see the reflection of the sun in a well during the daytime?

A. Because the rays of the sun fall so obliquely that they never reach the surface of the water at all, but strike against the sides.

Fig. 20. The Sun.

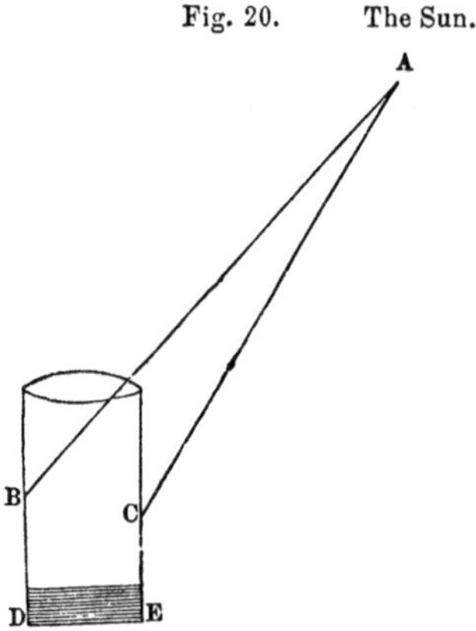

Let B D E C be the well, and D E, the water.

The ray A B strikes against the brick-work inside the well; and the ray A C strikes against the brick-work outside the well.

None will ever touch the water D E.

1687. Why are stars reflected in a well, although the sun is not?

A. Because the rays of those stars which pass nearly overhead will not fall so obliquely into the well as the rays of the sun.

Fig. 21.

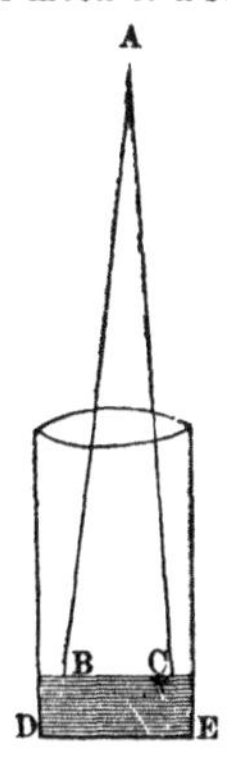

Here the star's rays A B, A C, both strike the water D E, and are reflected by it.

1688. Why are more stars visible from a mountain than from a plain?

A. Because the light has less air to pass through, and the atmosphere on a mountain is more clear. As air absorbs and diminishes light, the higher we ascend the less light will be absorbed.

1689. In a sheet of water at noon, the sun appears to shine upon only one spot, and all the rest of the water seems dark: why is this?

A. Because the rays fall at various degrees of obliquity on the water, and are reflected at similar angles; but, as only those which meet the eye of the spectator are visible, all the water will appear dark except that one spot. (See fig. 22.)

Fig. 22

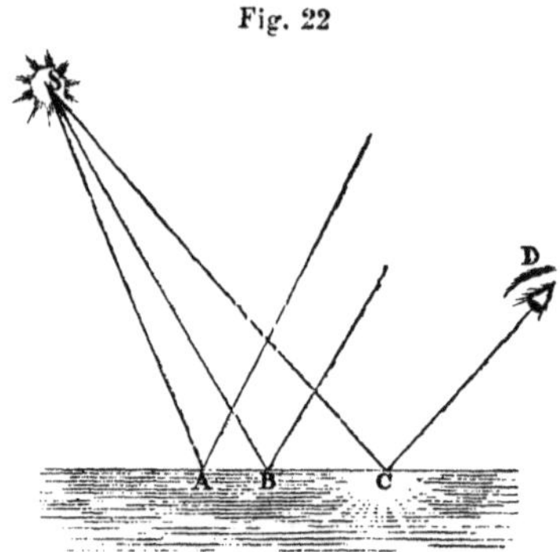

Here, of the rays S A, S B, and S C, only the ray S C meets the eye of the spectator D.

The spot C, therefore, will appear luminous to the spectator D, but no other spot of the water A B C.

1690. Why can we not see into the street or road when candles are lighted?

A. 1st. Because glass is a reflector, and throws the candle-light back into the room again; and,

2d. The pupil of the eye, having become contracted by the light of the room, is too small to collect rays enough from the dark street to enable us to see into it.

1691. Why do we often see the fire reflected in our parlor-window in winter-time?

A. Because glass is a good reflector; and the rays of the fire, striking against the window-glass, are reflected back into the room again.

1692. Why is this reflection more clear if the external air be dark?

A. Because the reflection is not eclipsed by the brighter rays of the sun striking on the other side of the window.

1693. If the shadow of an object be thrown on a wall, the closer the object is held to the candle the larger will be its shadow. Why is this?

A. Because the rays of light diverge from the flame of the candle in straight lines, like lines drawn from the centre of a circle.

Fig. 23.

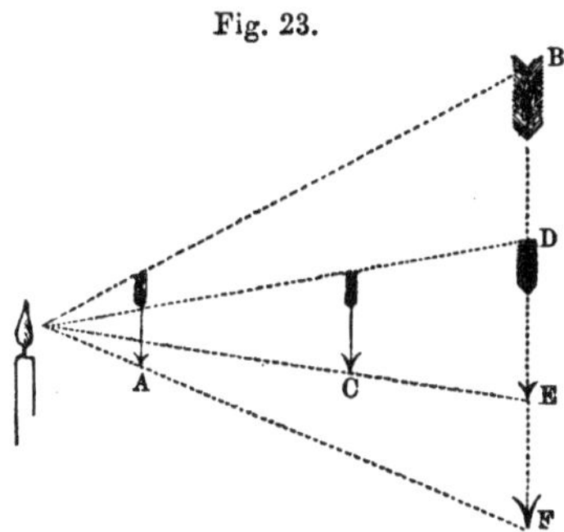

Here the arrow A, held close to the candle, will cast the shadow B F on a wall; while the same arrow held at C would cast only the little shadow D E.

1694. When we enter a long avenue of trees, why does the avenue seem to get narrower and narrower, till the two sides appear to meet?

A. Because the farther the trees are off, the more acute will be the angle that any opposite two make with our eye. (See Fig. 24.)

Fig. 24.

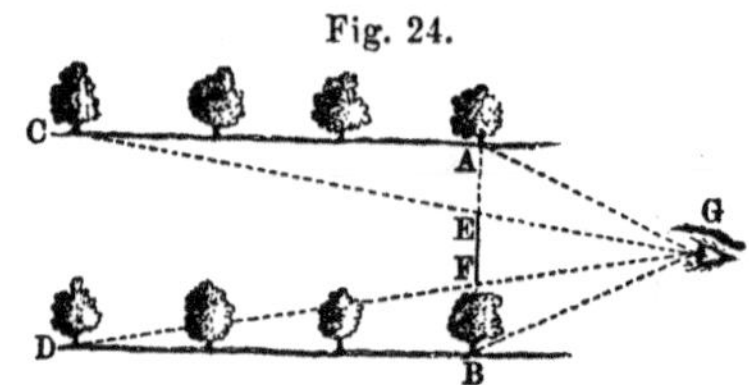

Here the width between the trees A and B will seem to be as great as the line A B; but the width between the trees C and D will seem to be no more than E F.

1695. In a long, straight street, why do the houses on the opposite sides seem to approach nearer together as they are more distant?

A. Because the more distant the houses are, the more acute will be the angle which any opposite two make with our eye.

Thus, in fig. 24, if A and B were two houses at the top of the street, the street would seem to be as wide as the line A B; and if C and D were two houses at the bottom of the street, the street there would seem to be no wider than E F.

1696. In an avenue, why do the trees seem to be smaller as their distance increases?

A. Because the farther the trees are off, the more acute will be the angle made by their perpendicular height with our eye.

Fig. 25.

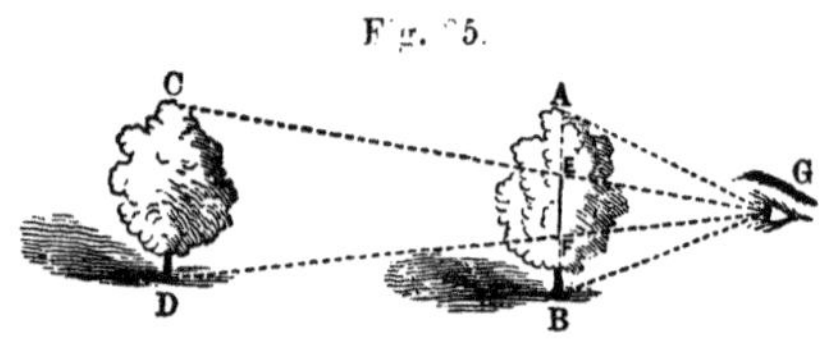

Here the first tree A B will appear the height of the line A B; but the last tree C D will appear only as high as the line E F.

1697. Why does a man on the top of a mountain or church-spire appear so small?

A. Because the angle made in our eye by the perpendicular height of the man at that distance is no larger than that made by a crow close by.

Fig. 26.

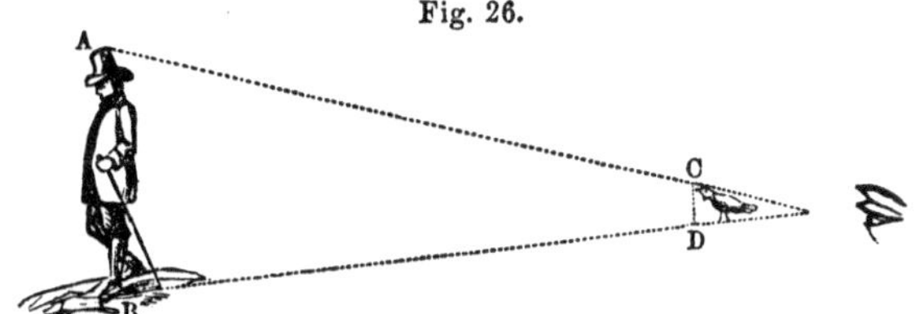

Let A B be a man on a distant mountain or spire, and C D, a crow close by.

The man will appear only as high as the line C D, which is the height of the crow.

1698. Why does the moon appear to us so much larger than the stars, though in fact it is a great deal smaller?

A. Because the moon is very much nearer to us than any of the stars.

Fig. 27.

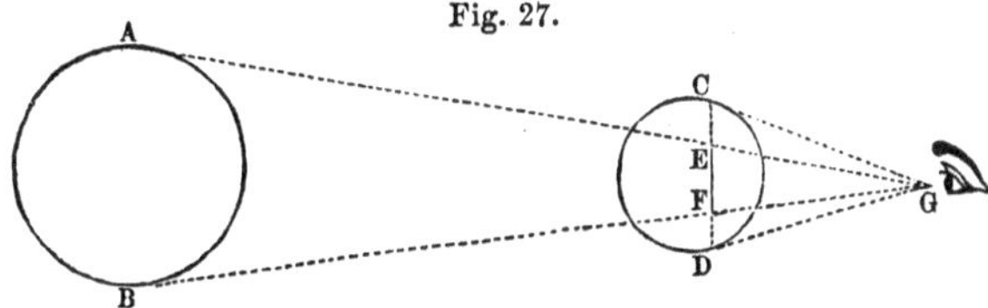

Let A B represent a fixed star, and C D, the moon.

A B, though much the larger body, will appear no larger than E F; whereas the moon (C D) will appear as large as the line C D to the spectator G.

The moon is 240,000 miles from the earth,—not quite a quarter of a million of miles. The nearest fixed stars are 20,000,000,000,000. (that is, twenty billions.)

If a ball were to travel 500 miles an hour, it would reach the moon in twenty days; but it would not reach the nearest fixed star in 4,500,000 years. Had it begun, therefore, when Adam was created, it would have been now no farther on its journey than a coach which has to go from the Land's End, Cornwall, to the most northern parts of Scotland, will be after it has passed about three-quarters of a mile.

1699. Why does the moon, which is a sphere, appear to be a flat surface?

A. Because it is so far off that we cannot distinguish any difference between the length of the rays issuing from the edge and those which issue from the centre.

Fig. 28.

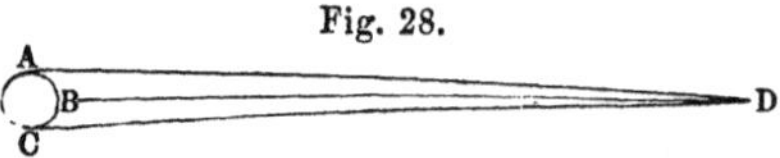

The rays A D and C D appear to be no longer than the ray B D; but if all the rays seem of the same length, the part B will not seem to be nearer to us than A and C; and therefore A B C will look like a flat or straight line.

The rays A D and C D are 240,000 miles long; the ray B D is 238,910 miles long.

1700. Why does distance make an object invisible?

A. Because no visible perpendicular can be inserted between the lines which form the angle, or because the lines actually cross before they meet our eye.

Fig. 29.

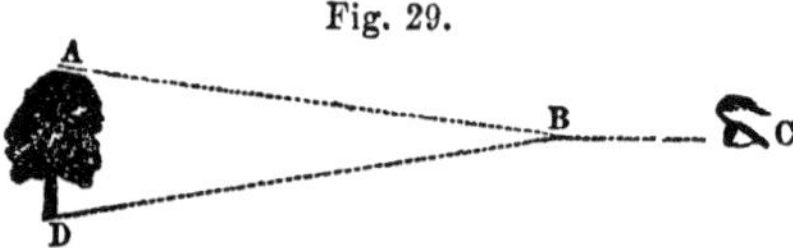

Here the tree A D would not be visible to the spectator C, even if he were to approach as far as B; because no visible perpendicular can be inserted between the two lines A C, D C, at the point B, and after B the lines would cross: therefore the tree would be invisible from C till after the spectator had passed B.

1701. What is the meaning of perspective?

A. The science of perspective teaches to draw on a plane surface true pictures of objects as they appear to the eye from any distance and in any position.

"Plane surface," a flat or even surface. The word "perspective" is from the Latin *per*, through, and *specio*, to look.

1702. What is the use of telescopes?

A. They gather together the rays of light, and a greater quantity are brought to the eye.

1703. How can these rays be gathered together?

A. Rays of light diverge—that is, spread out in all directions—from a luminous object. The number of these diverging rays which will enter the eye is limited by the size of the pupil. But, before they reach the eye, they may be received upon a glass lens of a convex form, which will have the effect of collecting them into a space less in magnitude than the pupil of the eye. If the eye be placed where the rays are thus collected, all the light will enter the pupil.

1704. Why do telescopes enable us to see objects invisible to the naked eye?

A. Because they gather together more luminous rays from obscure objects than the eye can, and form a bright image of them in the tube of the telescope where they are magnified.

1705. When a ship out at sea is approaching the shore, why do we see the small masts before we see the bulky hull?

A. Because the earth is round; and the curve of the sea hides the hull from our eyes after the tall masts have become visible.

Fig. 30.

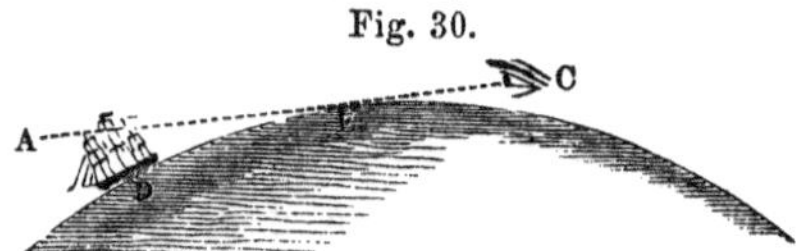

Here only that part of the ship above the line A C can be seen by the spectator A: the rest of the ship is hidden by the swell of the curve D E.

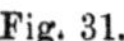
Fig. 31.

The diminution of the size of a ship seen at sea, owing to the convexity of the earth and the distance of the observer, is also illustrated in fig. 31.

1706. Horn is transparent: why are not horn shavings transparent also?

A. Because the surface of the shaving has been torn and rendered rough; and the rays of light are too much reflected and refracted by the rough surface to be transmitted through the shaving, so as to produce transparency.

1707. Why does wetting a cornelian make it more transparent?

A. Because the pores of the cornelian are then filled with water; and, as the density of the mass is rendered somewhat more uniform than when those pores were filled with air, the stone becomes more transparent.

Transparency depends on the uniformity of the parts.

If the parts of any substance are not pretty uniform, the rays of light are refracted and absorbed so frequently that no part of them can emerge on the opposite side.

SECTION I.—THE EYE, THE SEAT OF VISION.

1708. What is meant by the "retina of the eye"?

A. The net-work which lines the back of the eye is called the retina.

Fig. 32.

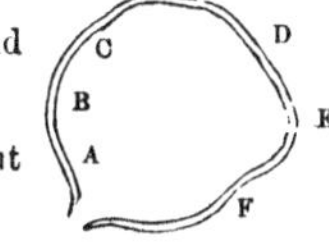

The net-work A B C is called the retina, and the projecting part D E F is called the cornea.

This net-work is composed of a spreading out of the fibres of the nerve of vision.

1709. Does light admitted through the pupil to the retina produce vision?

A. Yes; provided the light enter in sufficient quantity.

1710. What is that portion of the eye called which in some persons is blue, in others gray or nazel?

A. It is called the iris.

1711. In the centre of the iris is a circular black spot: what is this called?

A. It is called the pupil. This spot, however, is not a black substance, but an aperture, which appears black only because the chamber within it is dark. It is, properly speaking, the window of the eye, through which light is admitted, which strikes on the retina.

1712. Why are some persons near-sighted?

A. Because the cornea of their eye is so prominent that the image of distant objects is formed before it reaches the retina, and, therefore, is not distinctly seen.

Fig. 33.

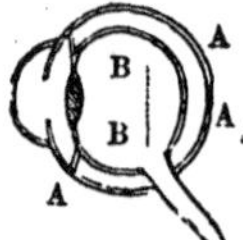

Thus, as in figure 33, the image is formed at B B before it reaches the retina A A A.

1713. What is meant by the "cornea of the eye"?

A. All the outside of the visible part of the eyeball.

Fig. 34.

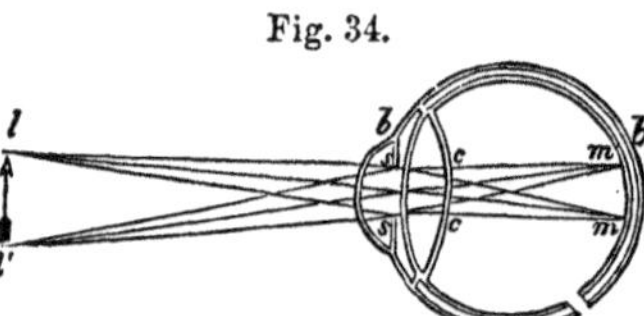

The eye, being nearly spherical in form, is composed, in the first place, of a tough, opaque membrane *b b*, called the *sclerotic* coat, constituting the white of the eye; lining this is the *choroid membrane*, which terminates near the iris in a series of filaments forming the *ciliary ligament.* The *cornea s s* is an exceedingly tough membrane, although clear and transparent: it is firmly united to the sclerotic coat,—fixed into it, indeed, like the glass into the case of a watch, and supported by several adhering layers. The centre of the cornea is a circular opening, the *pupil;* and within it is *c c*, the *crystalline lens,* a transparent capsule containing the *vitreous humor.* Within the choroid coat is a very delicate black pigment, and immediately within this the *retina,* which forms the innermost coating of the visual chamber. The *retina* is a delicate reticulated membrane, which appears to be an extension of the optic nerve.

1714. What is a lens?

A. A piece of glass or other transparent substance, bounded on both sides by polished spherical surfaces, or on the one side by a spherical and on the other by a plane surface.

1715. How many varieties of lenses are generally recognized?

A. Two: convex and concave.

Fig. 35.

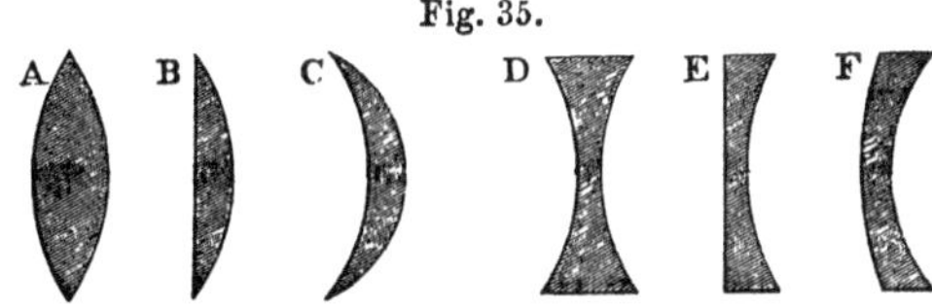

Among convex lenses are the double convex, A, (fig. 109,) to which the appellation "lens" was originally applied from its resemblance to a lentil-seed, (*lens* in Latin,) being bounded by two convex spherical surfaces whose centres are on opposite sides of the lens; the plano-convex, B, having one side bounded by a plane surface and the other by a convex surface; and the meniscus or concavo-convex, C, bounded on one side by a concave and on the other by a convex surface,—the former being a portion of a larger circle than the latter, and therefore the surfaces meet when produced.

There are also three principal varieties of concave glasses; as the double concave, D, bounded by two concave surfaces, forming portions of spheres whose centres are on opposite sides of the lens; the plano-concave, E, bounded on one side by a plane and on the other by a concave surface; and the convexo-concave, F, bounded by a convex surface on one side, and by a concave one on the other,—but these surfaces, when produced, do not meet.

1716. What sort of glasses do near-sighted persons wear?

A. If the cornea be too convex, (or projecting,) the person must wear double concave glasses to counteract it.

1717. What is meant by "double concave glasses"?

A. Glasses hollowed in on both sides.

1718. Where is the image of objects formed, if the cornea be too convex?

A. If the cornea be too convex, the image of a distant object is formed in the vitreous humors of the eye, and not on the retina.

Fig. 36.

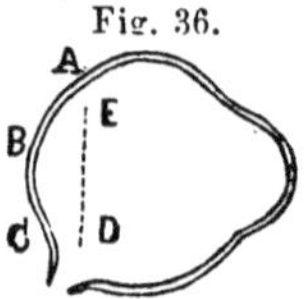

Thus, the image is formed at D E, and not on A B C, (the retina.)

1719. What is the use of double concave spectacle-glasses?

A. To cast the image farther back, in order that it may be thrown upon the retina and become visible.

1720. Why are old people far-sighted?

A. Because the humors of their eyes are dried up by age; in consequence of which, the cornea sinks in, or becomes flattened.

1721. Why does the flattening of the cornea prevent persons seeing objects which are near?

A. Because the cornea is too flat, and the image of near objects is not completely formed when their rays reach the retina; in consequence of which, the image is imperfect and confused.

Fig. 37.

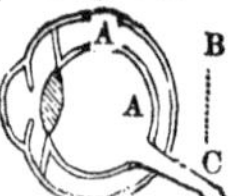

Thus, as in fig. 37, if the cornea is too flat, a perfect image would be formed at some distance behind the retina A A A, at the point B C, and not upon the retina, the point necessary to produce perfect vision.

1722. What sort of glasses do old people wear?

A. As their cornea is not sufficiently convex, they must use double convex glasses, to enable them to see objects near at hand.

1723. What sort of glasses are "double convex" spectacle-glasses?

A. Glasses which curve outwards on both sides.

1724. What is the use of double convex spectacle-glasses?

A. To shorten the focus of the eye, and bring the image of distant objects upon the retina.

1725. Why do near-sighted persons bring objects close to the eye in order to see them?

A. Because the distance between the front and back of the eye is so great that the image of distant objects is formed in front of the retina; but when objects are brought near to the eye, their image is thrown farther back, and made to fall on the retina.

1726. Why do old people hold objects far off in order to see them better?

A. Because the distance between the front and back of their eyes is not great enough; when, however, objects are held farther off, it compensates for this defect, and a perfect image is formed on the retina.

1727. Why are hawks able to see at such great dis tances?

A. Because they have a muscle in the eye which enables them to flatten their cornea, by drawing back the crystalline lens. (See fig. 34.)

This muscle is called the Marsupium.

1728. Why can hawks see objects within half an inch of their eye, as well as those at a great distance?

A. Because their eyes are furnished with a flexible bony rim, which throws the cornea forward and makes the hawk near-sighted.

SECTION II.—DECEPTIONS OF VISION.

1729. Why cannot we count the posts of a fence when we are riding rapidly in a railroad-car?

A. Because the light from each post falls upon the eye in such rapid succession that the vibration of the rays of light from one post does not cease until the rays from the succeeding post fall on the eye.

1730. How can the apparent magnitude of the sun at the time of his rising, and again at noonday, be measured?

A. This may be accomplished by extending two threads of fine silk, fastened in a frame, parallel to each other. The frame should be placed in such a position, and at such a distance from the eye, that, when presented to the sun or moon in the horizon, the threads will appear exactly to touch its upper and lower limb, or, in other words, be just sufficiently separated to admit of the disk of the sun or moon to appear between them and touch.

Now, if the sun or moon be viewed in the same manner at noonday, it will be found that they are just far enough apart to admit of the disk between them,—showing that the apparent increased magnitude at rising and setting is an optical deception, or, rather, an error in judgment.

1731. If you move a stick burning at one end pretty briskly around, it seems to make a circle of fire: why is this?

A. Because the eye retains the image of any bright object after the object itself is withdrawn; and, as the spark of the stick returns before the image has faded from the eye, it seems to form a complete circle.

The light proceeding from the stick enters the eye, and causes certain vibrations, which are so exceedingly rapid that the action of the light is not retarded for a sufficient length of time to perceive the motion of the stick.

1732. If separate figures (as of a man and a horse) be drawn on separate sides of a card, and the card twirled quickly, the man will seem to be seated on the horse: why is this?

A. Because the image of the horse remains upon the eye till the man appears.

The thaumatrope is constructed on this principle.

CHAPTER II.—REFRACTION.

1733. WHAT is meant by refraction?

A. Bending a ray of light, as it passes from one medium to another.

Fig. 38.

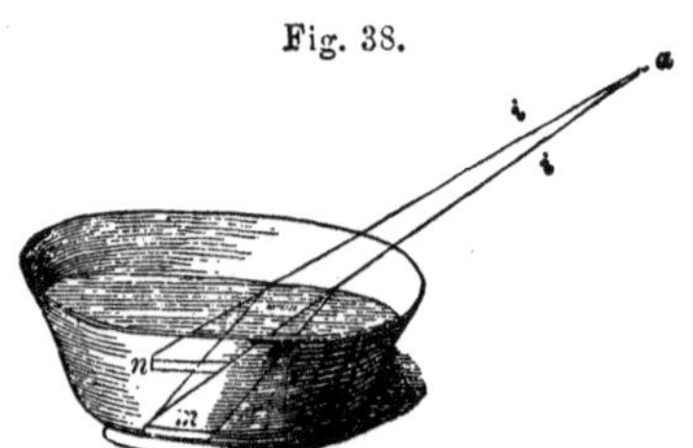

Place a silver coin *m* at the bottom of a basin, (fig. 38.) The rays *i i* proceeding to the eye from the silver surface render the coin visible. The point *a*, the eye, is then moved farther back, so that the edge of the basin obstructs the direct rays, and of course the coin is no longer seen. If an attendant carefully pours water into the basin, so that the object is not moved, it will presently, as the water rises in the basin, again become visible. This arises from the refraction of the rays by the water, the image, indeed, appearing at *n* instead of at *m*.

1734. Does air possess the property of refracting light?

A. Yes: the more dense the air, the greater is its refractive power. Consequently, that portion of the atmosphere at the earth's surface possesses the greatest refractive power, its density gradually diminishing, according to its distance from the earth, till it becomes so rare as scarcely to produce any refraction upon light.

1735. How is a ray of light bent, as it passes from one medium to another?

A. When a ray of light passes into a

denser medium, it is bent *toward* the perpendicular; when it passes into a rarer medium, it is bent *from* the perpendicular.

Fig. 39.

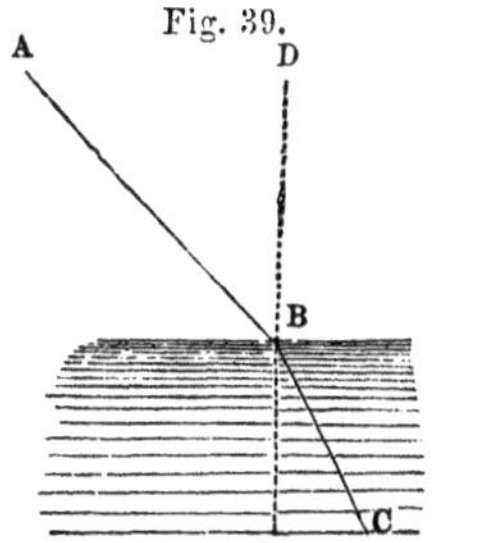

Fig. 40.

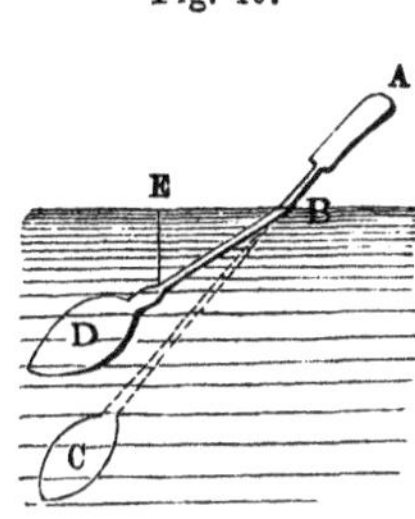

Suppose D E to be a perpendicular line.

If A B (a ray of light) enters the water, it will be bent toward the perpendicular to C.

If, on the other hand, C B (a ray of light) emerges from the water, it will be bent away from the perpendicular toward A.

1736. Why does an oar in water appear bent?

A. Because the part out of the water is seen in a different medium to the part in the water; and the rays of these two parts, meeting together at the surface of the river, form an angle, or, in other words, make the oar look as if it were bent.

As all rays of light are refracted (or bent) more in their passage through water than in their passage through air, they will tend to cross each other at the surface of the water, and, of course, form an elbow or angle.

1737. Why does a spoon in a glass of water always appear bent?

A. Because the light reflected from the spoon is refracted as it emerges from the water.

(See Fig. 40.) The spoon A B C will appear bent like A B D.

1738. Why does a river always appear more shallow than it really is?

A. Because the light of the bottom of the river is refracted as it emerges from the water.

(See fig. 40.) The bottom of the river will appear elevated, like the bowl of the spoon D.

1739. How much deeper is a river than it seems to be?

A. About one-third. If, therefore, a river seems only four feet deep, it is really nearly six feet deep.

The exact apparent depth would be $4\frac{1}{2}$. To find the real depth, multiply by 4 and divide by 3: thus, $4\frac{1}{2} \times 4 \div 3 = 6$, real depth.

Many boys get out of their depth in bathing, in consequence of this deception. Remember, a river is always one-third deeper than it appears to be: thus, if a river seems to be 4 feet deep, it is in reality nearly 6 feet deep; and so on.

1740. Why do fishes seem to be nearer the surface of a river than they really are?

A. Because the rays of light from the fish are refracted as they emerge from the water: and, as a bent stick is not so far from end to end as a straight one, so the fishes appear nearer to our eye than they really are. (See fig. 40.)

1741. Into how many parts may a ray of light be divided?

A. Into three parts,—blue, yellow, and red.

These three colors, by combination, make seven:—1. Red; 2. Orange (or red and yellow); 3. Yellow; 4. Green (or yellow and blue); 5. Blue; 6. Indigo (a shade of blue); and, 7. Violet (or blue and red).

1742. How is it known that a ray of light consists of several different colors?

A. Because, if a ray of light be cast upon a triangular piece of glass, (called a prism,) it will be distinctly divided into seven colors:—1. Red; 2. Orange; 3. Yellow; 4. Green; 5. Blue; 6. Indigo; and, 7. Violet.

1743. Why does a prism divide a ray of light into various colors?

A. Because all these colors have different refractive susceptibilities. Red is refracted least, and blue the most: therefore the blue color of the ray will be bent to the top of the prism, and the red will remain at the bottom.

Fig. 41.

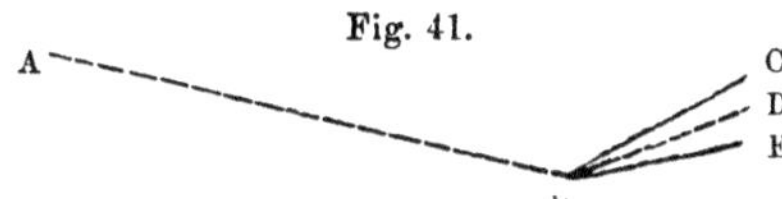

Here the ray A B (received on a prism at B) would have the blue part bent up to C, the yellow part to D, and the red part no farther than E.

Fig. 42.

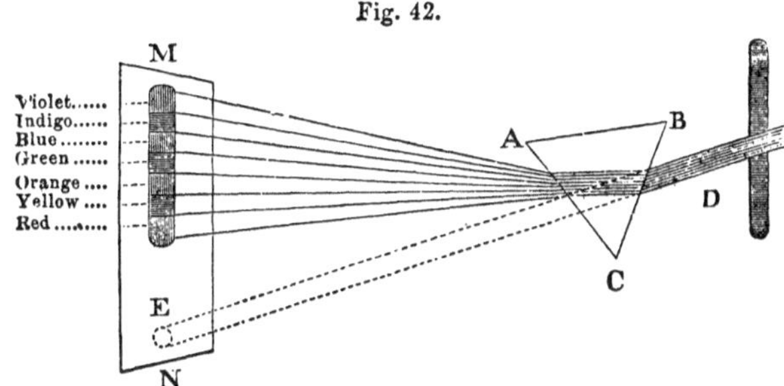

The separation of a ray of solar light into different colors by refraction may be more accurately displayed by admitting a ray through an aperture in a window-shutter into a darkened chamber, and causing it to fall on a diaphanous prism A B C, as represented in the preceding figure. A ray D thus entering, and suffered to pass unobstructed, would form on a plane surface a circular disk of white light E; but, the prism being so placed that the ray may enter and quit it at equal angles, it will be refracted in such a manner as to form on a screen M N, properly placed, an oblong image, called the solar spectrum, and divided horizontally into seven colored spaces or bands of unequal extent, succeeding each other in the order represented:—red, orange, yellow, green, blue, indigo, violet.

1744. Are the colored rays, once separated and refracted by the prism, capable of being separated and refracted again?

A. They are not, and are hence designated primary colors.

1745. What is meant by the refraction of a ray?

A. Bending it from its straight line.

Thus, the ray A B of fig. 41 is refracted at B into three courses, C, D, and E.

1746. What is a rainbow?

A. The rainbow is a semicircular band or arc, composed of the different colors generally exhibited upon the clouds during the occurrence of rain in sunshine.

1747. What is the cause of a rainbow?

A. When the clouds opposite the sun are very dark, and rain is still falling from them, the rays of the sun are divided by the raindrops as they would be by a prism.

Let A, B, and C (fig. 43) be three drops of rain; S A, S B, and S C, three rays of the sun. S A is divided into the three colors; the blue and yellow are bent above the eye D, and the red enters it.

The ray S B is divided into the three colors; the blue is bent above the eye, and the red falls below the eye D, but the yellow enters it.

Fig. 43.

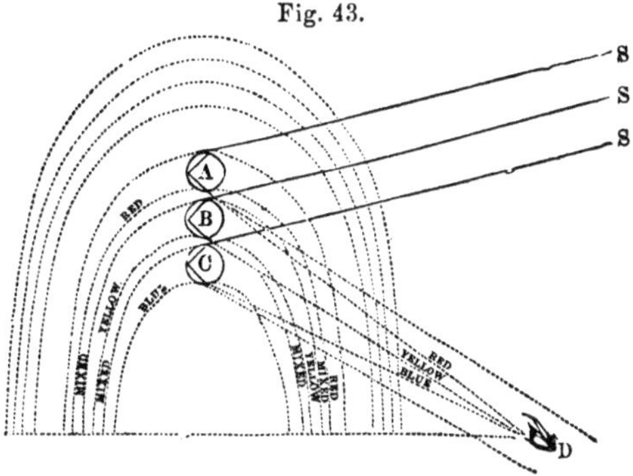

The ray S C is also divided into the three colors. The blue (which is bent most) enters the eye; and the other two fall below it. Thus, the eye sees the blue of C, and of all drops in the position of C; the yellow of B, and of all drops in the position of B; and the red of A, and of all drops in the position of A: and thus it sees a rainbow.

1748. Does every person see the same colors from the same drops?

A. No: no two persons see the same rainbow.

To another spectator, the rays from S B might be red instead of yellow; the ray from S C, yellow; and the blue might be reflected from some drop below C. To a third person, the red might issue from a drop above A, and then A would reflect the yellow, B the blue, and so on.

1749. Why are there often two rainbows at the same time?

A. The first (or primary) bow is formed by two refractions of the solar ray and one reflection, the rays of the sun entering the drops at the top and being reflected to the eye from the bottom. (See figs. 44, 45.)

Fig. 44.

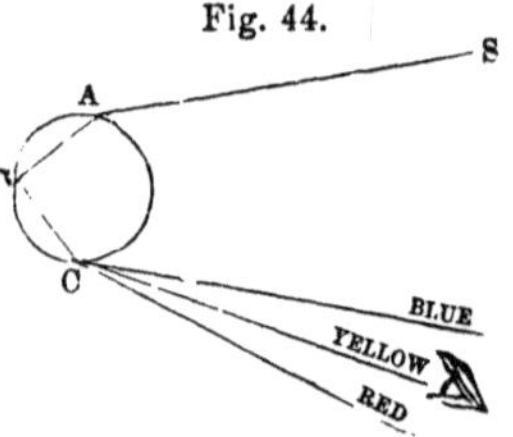

Thus, in fig. 44, the ray S A of the primary rainbow strikes the drop at A, is refracted or bent to B, the back part of the inner surface of the drop, then refracted to C, the lower part of the drop, when it is refracted again, and so bent as to come directly to the eye of the spectator.

The secondary (or outer) bow is produced, on the contrary, by two refractions and two reflections, the ray of light entering the drops from the bottom and being reflected to the eye from the top.

Fig. 45.

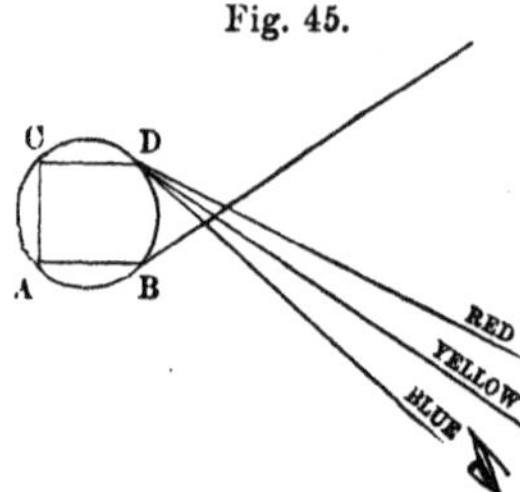

Thus, in fig. 45, the ray S B of the secondary bow strikes the bottom of the drop at B, is refracted to A, is then reflected to C, is again reflected to D, when it is again refracted or bent, till it reaches the eye of the spectator.

1750. Why are the colors of the second bow reversed?

A. Because in one bow we see the rays which enter at the top of the rain-drops refracted from the bottom; but in the other bow we see the rays which enter at the bottom of the rain-drops (after two reflections) refracted from the top.

(See fig. 46.) Here A B C represents three drops of rain in the secondary (or upper) rainbow.

The least refracted line is red, and blue the most.

So the red (or least refracted rays) of all the drops in the position of A—the yellow of those in the position of B—and the blue (or the *most* refracted rays) of the lowest drops, all meet the eye D, and form a rainbow to the spectator.

The reason why the primary bow exhibits the stronger colors is that the colors are seen after *one* reflection and *two* refractions; but the colors of the secondary (or upper) rainbow undergo *two* reflections and *two* refractions.

Fig. 46.

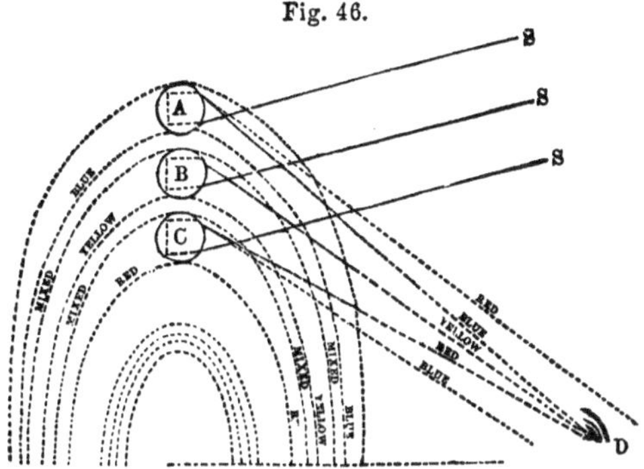

1751. Why does a soap-bubble exhibit such a variety of colors?

A. Because the thickness of the film through which the rays pass is constantly varying.

1752. How does the thickness of the film affect the color of the soap-bubble?

A. Different degrees of thickness in the film produce different powers of refraction; and, as the thickness of the film varies, different colors reach the eye.

1753. Why is a soap-bubble constantly changing its thickness?

A. Because the water runs down from the top to the bottom of the bubble, till the crown becomes so thin as to burst.

1754. Why are the late evening clouds red?

A. Because red rays, being the least refrangible, are the last to disappear.

Fig. 47.

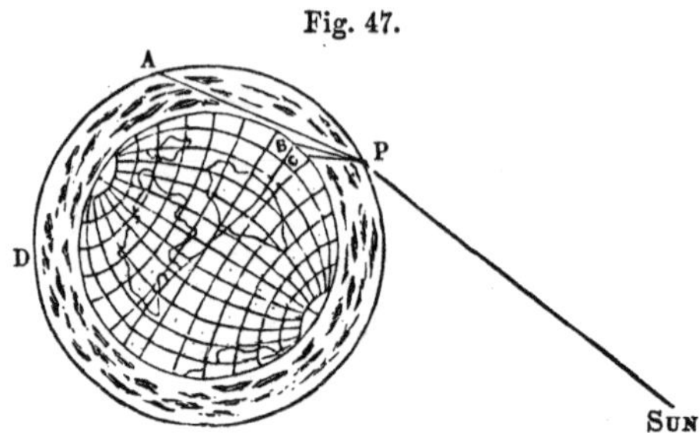

Suppose P A to be a red ray, P B, yellow, and P C, blue: if the earth turns in the direction of C B D, it is quite manifest that a spectator standing at C or B (carried round in the same direction) would lose sight of the red rays (A) last of all.

1755. Why are the early morning clouds red?

A. Because red rays, being the least refrangible, are the first to appear.

(See fig. 47.) We must suppose the sun to be on the left side of the diagram, or (what will answer the same purpose) suppose the earth to be turning in the direction of D A P: then it is quite clear that every person on the earth's surface will pass under A (the red rays) before he passes under B or C; and therefore the sun's early morning rays will be red.

1756. Why does the sun look red in a fog?

A. Because red rays have a greater momentum than any other rays; and this superior momentum enables them to penetrate the dense atmosphere more readily than either blue or yellow rays, which are either absorbed or reflected by the fog.

1757. Why are the edges of clouds more luminous than their centres?

A. Because the body of vapor is thinnest at the edges of the clouds.

1758. Why is it light when the sky is covered with thick clouds?

A. Although the sun's rays are refracted and absorbed in a measure by the clouds, a sufficient number reach the earth to give light.

1759. What is the cause of morning and evening twilight?

A. When the sun is below the horizon, the rays which strike upon the atmosphere or clouds are bent down toward the earth, and produce a little light, called twilight.

(See fig. 47.) Here the rays of P A will give some light.

1760. Sometimes ships are distinctly seen by an observer on shore before they are actually above the horizon: explain this.

A. This is owing to the refracting power of the atmosphere at the time. The different strata of air being of unequal density, the rays of light from the ship to the eye of the observer are bent in a curve; so that the vessel is visible before it is really above the horizon.

It is owing to this refracting power of the atmosphere that the sun appears to us before he rises, and that we see him after he has actually set.

1761. Can you relate how Captain Scoresby, when navigating the Greenland Seas, saw a ship at a great distance below the horizon?

A. He saw the inverted image of a ship in the air, although it was below the horizon, and on observing it attentively he discovered it to be his father's ship Fame, which at that moment was seventeen miles below the horizon, and thirty miles distant.

1762. How can you account for the inverted image of the ship? Why did he not see it in its proper position, with its hull next the water?

A. In this instance the stratum of air nearest the earth's surface was less dense than that immediately above it, and therefore the refractive power of the upper stratum was greater than that of the lower.

Dr. Kane mentions a beautiful display of refraction in the Arctic regions, when the coast thirty miles off was seen to assume the most fantastic shapes.

1763. Why does mother-of-pearl show so many colors?

A. Mother-of-pearl consists of a vast number of very thin, half-transparent layers of unequal thickness, overlapping each other like the scales of a fish.

Where these layers terminate, there are very small grooves or streaks running in all directions, which act like prisms.

It is these streakings, or grooves, which cause the various and changing colors of mother-of-pearl.

The same thing may very easily be imitated, and is frequently done in what are called "iris ornaments," first invented by John Barton, Esq., of the Royal Mint, England. These iris ornaments are made of steel, and have about 30,000 grooves per inch: they are used for buttons, sword-handles, etc., and are very brilliant.

Mother-of-pearl may also be imitated by taking impressions of it in wax, balsam of tolu, isinglass, or gum: these impressions will exhibit all the shades and colors of mother-of-pearl, merely because the impression will be streaked or grooved in a similar way.

1764. Why do the stars twinkle?

A. Because the inequalities and undulations in the atmosphere produce unequal refractions of light; and these unequal refractions cause the twinkling or irregular brilliancy of the stars.

1765. Why do stars twinkle more than usual just previous to a rain?

A. Because the air is unequally filled with vapor, which offers constant and unequal obstructions to the passage of the rays of light.

1766. Why are some things transparent?

A. Because every part between the two surfaces has a uniform refracting power,—in other words, has in every place the same density; and therefore the rays of light emerge on the opposite side.

1767. Why are some things not transparent?

A. Because the particles which compose them are separated by minute pores or spaces, which have a different density from the particles themselves: therefore the rays of light are reflected and refracted too often to emerge.

1768. Why are dry paper and calico, which are opaque, made transparent by being oiled?

A. Because the pores are filled by the oil, which has nearly the same density as the substance of the paper itself,—by which means a uniform density is effected, and the substance becomes transparent.

1769. Why is glass, which is transparent, rendered opaque by being ground or pulverized?

A. Because the whole substance from surface to surface is no longer of a uniform density.

CHAPTER III.—REFLECTION.

1770. What is meant by reflection of light?

A. Reflection, in Optics, means the rebounding of light from the surfaces on which it falls.

1771. An object in the shade is not so bright and apparent as an object in the sun: why is it not?

A. Because objects in the shade are seen by reflected light reflected; that is, the light is twice reflected; and, as the rays of light are always absorbed in some measure by every substance on which they fall, some light is lost,—1st, before the second reflection is made, and, 2d, in the object that makes the second reflection.

Part of the rays are absorbed, and part are scattered in all directions by irregular reflections; so that rarely more than half is reflected, even from the most highly-polished metals.

1772. If a picture be highly varnished, or covered with a glass, it cannot be seen in certain positions: why not?

A. 1st. Because the glass or varnish is a reflector; and, whenever a strong light is reflected from the glass to the eye of the spectator, the glass or varnish becomes very luminous, and the picture remains in comparative darkness; and,

2d. When the spectator is so placed as to catch the rays of light reflected from the glass or varnish, his eye is dazzled and cannot see the more faintly illuminated picture.

1773. Why do you see the reflection of two candles, or two fires, in a looking-glass or window-pane, though there be only one candle or fire in the room?

A. Because each surface of the looking-glass or window-pane makes a reflection.

In order to get these two reflections, you must not stand directly before the glass, but a little on one side.

1774. Why is the shadow of the moon stronger than the shadow of the sun?

A. Because the light of the moon is not so strong as the light of the sun; in consequence of which, the dispersed and reflected rays of the moon cannot reduce the opacity of shadow so much as the more intense rays of dispersed and reflected daylight.

"The opacity of shadow,"—that is, the darkness of shadow.

1775. Why is an ink-spot on linen black when first made?

A. Because the ink produces a chemical change in the internal condition of the fibres of the linen, by which it loses its power of reflecting light; and, as it absorbs the rays of the sun, the spot seems black.

The black color of ink is a compound of tannic acid, sesquioxide of iron, and water.

1776. Why does the black ink-spot on linen turn yellow after a few days?

A. Because the compound which composes the blackness of ink is destroyed by exposure to air; and the linen partially recovers its power of reflecting colors, but with a preference to yellow rays.

The tannic acid and water are in a measure taken up by the air, and the oxide of iron leaves a yellow iron-mould behind.

1777. What surfaces reflect light best?

A. Smooth and polished surfaces are the best reflectors of light.

1778. Glass is a smooth and polished surface: is it a good reflector of light?

A. Glass is transparent, and therefore transmits light; .but if one of its surfaces be covered with amalgam, the light cannot pass through it, and is consequently reflected.

1779. Why are some substances shining, and others dull?

A. Because some substances reflect rays, and are bright, but others absorb them.

1780. Why do deserts dazzle from sunshine?

A. Because each grain of sand reflects the rays of the sun like a mirror.

CHAPTER IV.—COLOR.

1781. WHY is a ray of light composed of various colors?

A. To vary the color of different objects. If solar light were of one color only, all objects would appear of that one color, or else black.

1782. Some things are of one color, and some of another: explain the cause of this.

A. Every ray of light is composed of all the colors of the rainbow, and some substances reflect one of these colors, and some another.

1783. Why do some substances reflect one color, and some another?

A. Because the surfaces are differently constructed, both physically and chemically.

1784. Why is a rose red?

A. Because the surface of a rose absorbs the blue and yellow rays of light, and reflects only the red.

1785. Why are some things black?

A. Because they absorb all the rays of light, and reflect none.

1786. Why are some things white?

A. Because they absorb none of the rays of light, but reflect them all.

1787. Why are the leaves of plants green?

A. Because a peculiar chemical principle, called chlorophyll, formed within their cells, has the property of absorbing the red rays and of reflecting the blue and yellow,—which mixture produces green.

Chlorophyll (χλωρον φυλλον, (chloron phullon,) a *green leaf*) is the green matter of vegetable substances.

1788. Why are leaves light-green in spring?

A. Because the chlorophyll is not fully formed.

1789. Why do leaves turn brown in autumn?

A. Because the chlorophyll undergoes decay, and is not replaced as it is in the spring.

1790. Why do the lustres of a chandelier seem tinted with various brilliant colors?

A. Because each "drop" of the chandelier is so cut as to act like a prism. It decomposes the light, and reflects the different rays from its different points or angles.

1791. Why do all things appear black in the dark?

A. In the dark there is no color, because there is no light to be absorbed or reflected, and, therefore, none to be decomposed.

"Colors are but phantoms of the day:
With that they're born, with that they fade away:
Like beauty's charms, they but amuse the sight,
Dark in themselves, till by reflection bright.
With the sun's aid, to rival him they boast,
But, light withdrawn, in their own shades are lost."

Of course, in certain degrees of darkness all objects are actually invisible. The question refers to that peculiar degree of darkness when the forms of objects may be seen, but not their hues.

1792. Why does a blue dress appear green by candle-light?

A. Because the light of a candle is tinged with yellow; and this yellow tinge, mixing with the blue color of the dress, produces green.

1793. Why are some plants white which are kept in the dark?

A. Because chlorophyll can be formed only by the agency of the sun's rays; and it is this peculiar chemical principle which gives the green tinge to healthy leaves and plants.

Some plants are yellowish green from the same cause.

1794. Why does the sun generally fade artificial colors?

A. Generally, the loss of color arises from the oxidation of the substances used in dyeing; as tarnish and rust are an oxidation of metals.

Sometimes, however, the ingredients of the dye are otherwise decomposed by the sun; and the color (which is due to a combination of ingredients) undergoes a change as soon as the sun deranges or destroys that combination.

1795. If we look at a red-hot fire for a few minutes, why does every thing seem tinged with a bluish-green color?

A. Because bluish green is the "accidental color" of red; and if we fix our eye upon any color whatsoever, we see every object tinged with its accidental color when we turn aside.

The accidental color is the color which would be required to be added in order to make up white light. For this reason it is sometimes called *complementary* color.

The accidental color of red is bluish green.
" " orange is blue.
" " yellow is dark violet.
" " green is reddish violet.
" " blue is orange red.
" " indigo is orange yellow.
" " violet is yellow green.
" " black is white.
" " white is black.

1796. Why does the eye perceive the accidental color when the fundamental one is removed?

A. Because the nerve of the eye has become tired of the one, but still remains fresh for the perception of the other.

1797. If we wear blue glasses, why does every thing appear tinged with orange when we take them off?

A. Because orange is the "accidental color" of blue; and if we look through blue glasses, we shall see its "accidental color" when we lay our glasses aside.

1798. If we look at the sun for a few moments, every thing seems tinged with a dark violet color: why is this?

A. Because dark violet is the "accidental color" of yellow; and, as the sun is yellow, we shall see its "accidental color," dark violet, when we turn from gazing at it.

1799. Does not the dark shadow which seems to hang over every thing after we turn from looking at the sun arise from our eyes being dazzled?

A. Partly so: the pupil of the eye is very much contracted by the brilliant light of the sun, and does not adjust itself immediately to the feebler light of terrestrial objects; but, independent of this, the "accidental color" of the sun, being dark violet, would tend to throw a shadow upon all things. (See Q. 1791.)

The law of accidental color is this:—The accidental color is always half the spectrum. Thus, if we take half the length of the spectrum by a pair of compasses, and fix one leg in any color, the other leg will hit upon its accidental color.

The spectrum means the seven colors, (red, orange, yellow, green, blue, indigo, and violet,) divided into seven equal bands, and placed side by side in the order just mentioned.

PART VII.

SOUND, AND ATTRACTION.

CHAPTER I.—TRANSMISSION OF SOUND.

1800. How is sound produced?

A. The vibration of some sonorous substance produces motion in the air, called sound-waves, which strike upon the ear and give the sensation of sound.

1801. How fast does sound travel?

A. About 13 miles in a minute, or 1125 feet in a second of time.

Light would go 480 times round the whole earth while sound was going 13 miles.

1802. What are sonorous bodies?

A. Bodies which produce sound are called sonorous bodies.

1803. Why are some things sonorous, and others not?

A. The sonorous quality of any substance depends upon its hardness and elasticity.

1804. What surfaces are best adapted for the transmission of sound?

A. Smooth surfaces, such as ice, water, or hard ground.

1805. What plan do savages adopt to hear the approach of an enemy or beasts of prey?

A. They place their ears to the ground, and by this means can distinguish clearly the approach of an enemy.

1806. Why do windows rattle when carts pass by a house?

A. 1st. Because glass is sonorous, and the air communicates its vibrations to the glass, which echoes the same sound; and,

2d. The window-frame being shaken, contributes to the noise.

Window-frames are shaken—1. By sound-waves impinging against them; 2. By a vibratory motion communicated to them by the walls of the house.

1807. Why are copper and iron sonorous, and not lead?

A. Copper and iron are hard and elastic; but, as lead is neither hard nor elastic, it is not sonorous.

1808. Of what is bell-metal made?

A. Of copper and tin.

1809. Why is a mixture of tin and copper used for bell-metal?

A. Because it is much harder and more elastic than either of the pure metals.

1810. Why do we hear a bell if it be struck?

A. The bell vibrates, and in its agitation

compresses the air to a certain distance around it, at each vibration. The compressed air instantly expands, and in doing so repeats the pressure on the air next in contact with it, and so on,—as a pebble thrown into still water makes waves all around it,—diminishing in force the more distant they are from the original stroke. The air thus agitated reaches the ear, where a similar impulse is given to a very delicate membrane, and the mind then receives the impression of sound.

1811. How can a bell, which is solid, be said to vibrate?

A. Although the metal of which the bell is composed is solid, it actually changes its form every time it is struck, and its particles are thereby thrown into motion.

1812. Why is the sound of a bell stopped by touching the bell with our finger?

A. Because the weight of our finger stops the vibrations of the bell; and as soon as the bell ceases to vibrate, it ceases to make sound-waves in the air.

1813. After striking a finger-glass, why is the sound silenced upon touching the glass with the finger?

A. Because the pressure of the finger stops the vibrations of the glass; and as soon as the finger-glass ceases to vibrate, it ceases to make sound-waves in the air.

1814. Why does a split bell make a harsh, disagreeable sound?

A. Because the split of the bell causes a double vibration; and, as the sound-waves clash and jar, they impede each other's motion and produce discordant sounds.

1815. Why can persons living a mile or two from a town hear the bells of the town-churches sometimes, and not at others?

A. Because fogs, rain, and snow obstruct the passage of sound by interfering with the undulations of the sound-waves; but when the air is cold and clear, sound is propagated more easily.

1816. Why can we hear distant clocks most distinctly in clear, cold weather?

A. Because the air is of more uniform density, and there are fewer currents of air of unequal temperature to interrupt the sound-waves.

Besides, dense air can propagate sound-waves more readily than rarer air.

1817. Why can persons near the poles hear the voices of men in conversation for a mile distant in winter-time?

A. Because the air is very cold, clear, and still; in consequence of which, there are but few currents of air of unequal temperature to interrupt the sound-waves.

Captain Ross heard the voices of his men in conversation a mile and a half from the spot where they stood.

1818. Why are not sounds such as those of distant church-bells heard so distinctly on a hot day as in frosty weather?

A. 1st. Because the density of the air is less uniform in very hot weather;

2d. The air is more rarefied, and, consequently, a worse conductor of sound; and,

3d. It is more liable to accidental currents, which impede the progress of sound.

1819. How do you know that rarefied air cannot transmit sound so well as dense air?

A. Because the sound of a bell in the receiver of an air-pump can scarcely be heard after the air has been partially exhausted; and the report of a pistol fired on a high mountain would be scarcely audible.

1820. Why does the sea heave and sigh just previous to a storm?

A. Because the density of the air is very suddenly diminished, and therefore its power to transmit sound is diminished also; in consequence of which, the roar of the sea is less audible, and seems like heavy sighs.

1821. Why is the air so universally quiet just previous to a tempest?

A. Because the air is suddenly and very greatly rarefied, and therefore its power to transmit sound is diminished.

1822. Why do we hear sounds better by night than by day?

A. 1st. Because night air is of more uniform density, and less liable to accidental currents; and,

2d. Night is more still, from the suspension of business.

1823. Why is the air of more uniform density by night than it is by day?

A. Because it is less liable to accidental currents; inasmuch as the breezes (created by the action of the sun's rays) generally cease during the night.

1824. How should partition-walls be made, in order to prevent the voices in adjoining rooms from being heard?

A. The space between the laths should be filled with shavings or saw-dust; and then no sound would ever pass from one room to another.

1825. Why would shavings or saw-dust prevent the transmission of sound from room to room?

A. Because there would be several different media for the sound to pass through:—1st, the air; 2d, the laths and plaster; 3d, the saw-dust or shavings; 4th, lath and plaster again; 5th, the air in the adjoining room: every change of medium diminishes the strength of the sound-waves.

1826. Why can deaf people hear through an ear-trumpet?

A. Because the ear-trumpet contracts the

diameter of the sound-waves; in consequence of which, their strength is increased.

1827. What is a stethoscope?

A. It is an instrument, resembling a small trumpet, used for ascertaining the action of the lungs. The wide mouth is applied to the body, and the other end is held to the ear of the physician, who can hear distinctly the action of the lungs, and judge whether they be healthy or the reverse.

1828. Why does sound seem louder in caves than on a plain?

A. Because the sides of the cave confine the sound-waves and prevent their spreading; in consequence of which, their strength is greatly increased.

1829. Why are the summits of high mountains more quiet than plains?

A. Because the air is greatly rarefied at some distance above the general surface of the earth, and, as the air becomes rarefied, sound becomes less intense.

1830. How do you know that the rarity of air diminishes the intensity of sound?

A. If a bell be rung in the receiver of an air-pump, the sound becomes fainter and fainter as the air is exhausted, till at last it is almost inaudible.

1831. A person situated at the extremity of a wire

600 feet in length will hear the same sound twice. Explain this.

A. The sound is transmitted through the wire and through the air; but the air is not so good a conductor of sound as the iron wire: therefore, while it passes along the wire almost instantaneously, it requires some time to travel the same distance through air.

1832. Can sound be heard through water?

A. Yes: a bell rung under water can be heard above; and if the head of the auditor be under water at the time, it can be still more distinctly heard. It is not, however, so loud and clear as when rung in the air.

1833. If from an eminence you look down upon a long column of soldiers marching to a band of music in front, those in the rear will be seen to step a little later than those some distance before them. Can you explain the reason of this?

A. Each rank steps, not when the sound is made, but when, in its progress down the column at the rate of 1125 feet in a second of time, it reaches their ears. Those who are near the music hear it first, while those at the end of the column must wait until it has travelled to their ears at the above rate.

1834. Why does a railway-train make more noise when it passes over a bridge than when it runs over solid ground?

A. Because the bridge is elastic, and vibrates much more from the weight of the train than the solid earth; in consequence of which, it produces more definite sound-waves.

The bridge acts as a sounding-board; and the water or earth below the bridge repeats the sound.

1835. Why can sounds be heard in a calm day at a greater distance on the sea than on land?

A. 1st. Because the air over the sea is generally denser and more laden with moisture than the air over the land;

2d. The density is more uniform; and,

3d. Water being more elastic than land, it is a better propagator of sound.

SECTION I.—MUSICAL SOUNDS.

1836. What are musical sounds?

A. Regular and uniform successions of vibrations.

1837. What is the difference between a musical sound and a mere noise?

A. All mere noises are occasioned by irregular impulses communicated to the ear; but, in order to produce a musical sound, the impulses, and, consequently, the undulations of the air, must be all exactly similar in duration and intensity, and must recur after exactly equal intervals of time.

1838. Do all persons hear sounds alike?

A. No: that faculty seems to depend upon the sensibility of the auditory nerves.

"Auditory,"—having the power of hearing.

1839. What are the boundaries of human hearing?

A. The whole range of human hearing, from the lowest note of the organ to the highest known cry of insects,—as of the cricket,—includes about nine octaves.

All ears, however, are by no means gifted with so great a range of hearing: many persons, though not at all deaf, are quite insensible to the highest notes of some insects.

1840. How many vibrations of a musical chord are necessary to produce a definite sound?

A. When the vibrations are less than sixteen in a second of time, a continued sound cannot be communicated to the ear.

1841. How many vibrations is the human ear able to appreciate?

A. The human ear is capable of appreciating as many as twenty-four thousand vibrations in a second of time, and is, consequently, able to hear a sound which only lasts the twenty-four thousandth part of a second!

1842. Why are some notes bass, and some treble?

A. Because slow vibrations produce bass or deep sounds; but quick vibrations produce shrill or treble ones.

1843. Why do flutes, &c. produce musical sounds?

A. Because the breath of the performer causes the air in the flute to vibrate; and this vibration sets in motion the sound-waves of the air.

1844. Why is an instrument flat when the strings are unstrung?

A. Because the vibrations are too slow; in consequence of which, the sounds produced are not shrill or sharp enough.

SECTION II.—ECHO.

1845. What is echo?

A. Echo is reflected sound.

1846. What is the cause of echo?

A. Whenever a sound-wave strikes against any obstacle, such as a wall or hill, it is reflected, or thrown back; and this reflected sound is called an echo.

1847. What places are most noted for echoes?

A. Caverns, grottoes, and ruined abbeys; the areas of halls; the windings of long passages; the aisles of cathedral-churches; mountains and icebergs.

1848. Why are caverns, grottoes, and ruins noted for echoes?

A. Because the sound-waves cannot pass beyond the cavern or grotto, and therefore must flow back.

1849. Why do halls, winding passages, and cathedral-aisles produce echoes?

A. Because the sound-waves cannot flow freely forward, but perpetually strike against the walls, and are beaten back.

1850. Why are mountains and icebergs noted for echoes?

A. Because they present a barrier to the sound-waves, which they cannot pass, and are sufficiently elastic to throw them back.

1851. Why do not the walls of a small room produce echoes?

A. Because sound travels with such velocity that the echo is blended with the original sound, and the two produce but one impression on the ear.

Sound travels thirteen miles in a minute; and no echo is heard unless the surface against which the sound strikes is sixty-five feet from the place whence the sound originally proceeded.

1852. Why do very large buildings (as cathedrals) often reverberate the voice of the speaker?

A. Because the walls are so far off from the speaker that the echo does not return in time to blend with the original sound, and therefore each sound is heard separately.

1853. Why do some echoes repeat only one syllable?

A. Because the echoing body is very near. The farther the echoing body is off, the more sound it will reflect: if, therefore, it be very near, it will repeat but one syllable.

1854. Why does an echo sometimes repeat two or more syllables?

A. Because the echoing body is far off, and therefore there is time for one reflection to pass away before another reaches the ear.

All the syllables must be uttered before the echo of the first syllable reaches the ear: if, therefore, a person repeats seven syllables in two seconds of time, and hears them all echoed, the reflecting object is 1125 feet distant,—because sound travels 1125 feet in a second, and the words take one second to go to the reflecting object, and one second to return.

1855. Why are two or more echoes sometimes heard?

A. Because separate reverberating surfaces receive the sound and reflect it in succession.

Seventeen miles above Glasgow, (Scotland,) near a mansion called Rosneath, is a very remarkable echo. If a trumpeter plays a tune and stops, the echo will begin the same tune and repeat it all accurately; as soon as this echo has ceased, another will echo the same tune in a lower tone; and after the second echo has ceased, a third will succeed with equal fidelity, though in a much feebler tone.

At the Lake of Killarney, in Ireland, there is an echo which plays an excellent "second" to any simple tune played on a bugle.

1856. What causes the murmuring sound produced by the discharge of great guns?

A. The murmuring sound is a succession of echoes from the particles of vapor floating in the atmosphere; and when the discharge is effected under a dense cloud, the echoes are stronger, resembling rolling thunder.

CHAPTER II.—ATTRACTION.

1857. What is the meaning of the word attraction?

A. It denotes the power or principle by which all bodies mutually tend toward each other.

1858. How many kinds of attraction are there?

A. There are two kinds of attraction,—that which acts at all distances, however great, and that which acts at very small or insensible distances.

SECTION I.—GRAVITATION.

1859. What is that attraction called which acts at great distances?

A. The attraction of gravitation.

Electrical and magnetic attractions also act at considerable distances.

1860. All bodies tend toward, or are attracted by, the earth: is the earth attracted by them also?

A. Yes: the attraction is mutual; but, as the earth is so much larger than any body on, or near, its surface, the only perceptible attraction is that produced by the earth.

1861. What is this attraction called?

A. It is called the attraction of gravitation.

It is the attraction of gravitation, combined with other causes, which carries the earth and planets round the sun.

SECTION II.—CENTRE OF GRAVITY.

1862. What is the centre of gravity?

A. The centre of weight; in other words, that point on which if supported the body would balance itself.

1863. Where is the centre of gravity in man?

A. The centre of gravity in man lies between the hips. The base is the space between his feet.

1864. Why does an old man use a cane when he walks?

A. To enlarge his base, and prevent the line of direction from falling outside the base.

1865. What is meant by the base of a body?

A. The lowest part or side of a body.

1866. What is the line of direction?

A. The line drawn from the centre of gravity toward the centre of the earth.

1867. How can you find the centre of gravity in an irregularly-shaped body?

A. First suspend it from a point, as at *a*, (fig 48,) and at the same point suspend a plumb-line *c*, when both board and line will hang in the position represented in the figure. Having marked this line, let it be suspended from another and different point, as in fig. 49, and the perpendicular line indicated by the plumb again marked. The point where these two lines so marked cross each other is the centre of gravity of the body, as seen in fig. 50.

Fig. 48. Fig. 49. Fig. 50.

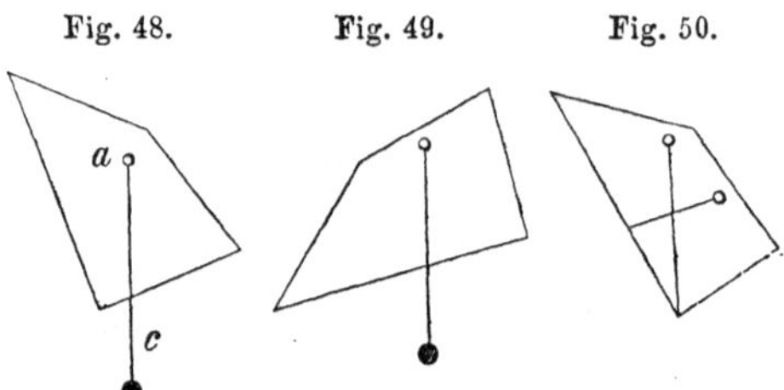

When two or more bodies are connected, the centre of gravity of the two is the point on which they will balance without falling. Thus, if two balls, each weighing four pounds, be connected by a bar, the centre of gravity will be a point on the bar equally distant from each. But if one of the balls be heavier than the other, the centre of gravity will, in proportion, approach the larger ball. This is illustrated by fig. 51, in which the centre of gravity about which the two balls support themselves is seen to be nearest the heaviest and largest ball.

Fig. 51.

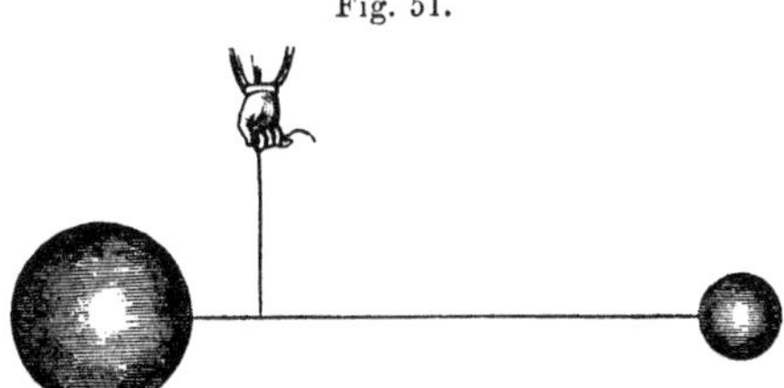

1868. Why does a person in rising from a chair bend forward?

A. When a person is sitting, the centre of gravity is supported by the chair; in an erect position, the centre of gravity is supported by the feet: therefore before rising it is necessary to change the centre of gravity, and by bending forward we transfer it from the chair to a point over the feet.

1869. Why does a quadruped never raise both feet on the same side simultaneously?

A. Because, if it did, the centre of gravity would be unsupported, and the animal would fall over.

1870. Why is a turtle placed upon its back unable to move?

A. Because the centre of gravity of the turtle is, in this position, at the lowest point, and the animal is unable to change it: therefore it is obliged to remain at rest.

1871. Why does a person carrying a weight upon his back stoop forward?

A. In order to bring the centre of gravity of his body and the load over his feet.

If he carried the load in the position of the figure at A, he would fall backwards, as the direction of the centre of gravity would fall beyond his heels: to bring the centre of gravity over his feet, he assumes the position indicated by the figure B.

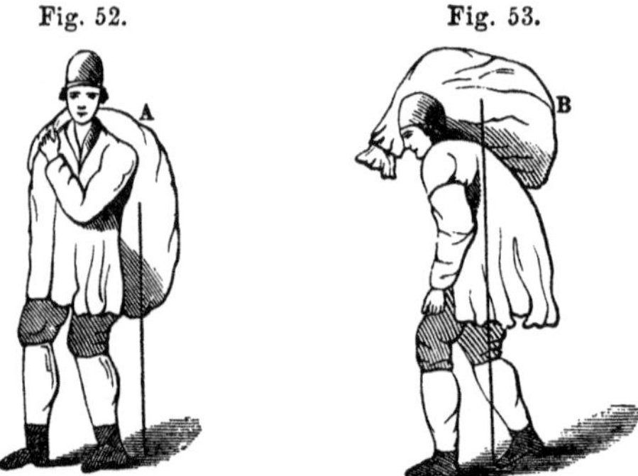

Fig. 52. Fig. 53.

1872. Why is it more difficult to overthrow a body having a broad base than one resting upon a narrow basis?

A. Because a body cannot fall over so long as a line directed from the centre of gravity vertically toward the surface upon which the body rests, falls within the figure formed by the base of the body in question. Hence, the broader the base of a body, the more securely it will stand.

1873. How long will a wall or tower stand securely?

A. So long as the perpendicular line drawn through its centre of gravity falls within its base.

The celebrated Leaning Tower of Pisa, three hundred and fifteen feet high, with an inclination from the perpendicular of twelve feet, is an example of this law. For instance, the line in fig. 54, from the summit to the ground, passing through the centre of gravity, falls within the base, and the tower stands securely; but suppose an attempt

Fig. 54.

was made to carry it a little higher, the perpendicular line passing through the centre of gravity would then fall without the base, and the structure could no longer support itself.

SECTION II.—COHESION AND ADHESION.

1874. What is that attraction called which acts only at small distances?

A. The attraction of cohesion,—which is the attraction between particles of the same substance. For example, the particles of the table or inkstand are attracted or united by cohesion.

1875. When particles of different substances are attracted to each other, what is that attraction called?

A. It is called adhesion.

1876. Give an example of adhesion.

A. When water is poured on a piece of glass, it is said to adhere to the glass,—the water and glass being different substances.

1877. Why is mortar used in building walls of brick or stone?

A. Because the wet mortar adheres to the bricks, and when it becomes dry its particles cohere so strongly as to become one solid mass.

1878. Why could not blocks of iron or any other metal be cemented together by mortar?

A. Because all metals, being good conductors of heat, readily expand and contract with changes of temperature. This expansion and contraction breaks the mortar and prevents its adhesion.

1879. Why does not the mortar break between bricks?

A. Because bricks are bad conductors of heat, and do not expand so much as blocks of metal.

1880. Why do the bubbles in a cup of tea follow the spoon?

A. Because the spoon, being the superior mass, attracts them. The bubbles will also be attracted to the sides of the cup.

1881. Why are the sides of a pond often covered with leaves?

A. Because the shore attracts them.

1882. Why can you fill a glass with water above its brim?

A. Because the particles of water are kept from flowing over by the attraction of cohesion exerted between them.

SECTION III.—CAPILLARY ATTRACTION.

1883. What is capillary attraction?

A. The power which very minute tubes possess of causing a liquid to rise in them above its level.

Fig. 55.

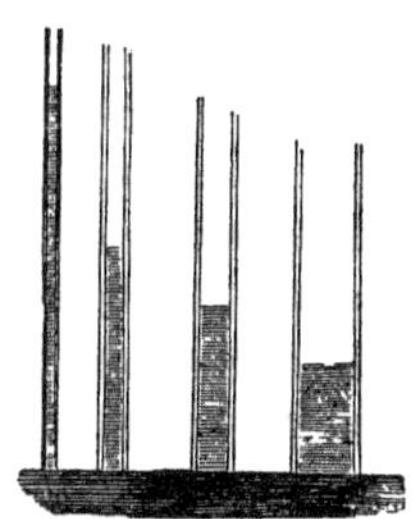

Capillary, from the Latin *capillus*, a hair,—the tubes referred to being almost as fine as a hair. The smaller the tube, the higher the fluid will rise in it. Fig. 55 illustrates the manner in which water will rise in tubes of different diameters.

1884. Why does water melt salt and sugar?

A. Because the water insinuates itself into the pores of the sugar and salt by capillary attraction, and forces the particles of sugar or salt to separate.

1885. Why is vegetation on the margin of a river more luxuriant than in an open field?

A. Because the porous earth on the bank draws up the water by capillary attraction, and by that means nourishes the roots of the plants.

1886. Why will water poured into the saucer of a flower-pot resuscitate the plant in the pot?

A. Because the water in the saucer is drawn up into the earth in the pot by capillary attraction. The same attraction also conveys the moisture into the stem and leaves of the plant.

1887. If a drop of liquid be spilled on the table-cloth, why will it spread in all directions?

A. Because the threads of the cloth absorb the water by capillary attraction.

1888. If a bowl be filled with water, how may it be emptied of its contents by capillary attraction?

A. By placing the corner of a towel of sufficient size into the bowl: the liquid will rise through the threads of the towel by capillary attraction, and after a time the bowl will be empty.

1889. Why does blotting-paper absorb ink?

A. Because, owing to the loose texture of the paper, the minute fibres draw up the ink by capillary attraction.

1890. Why will not common writing-paper absorb ink as well as blotting-paper?

A. Because the sizing which is put on the surface of writing-paper fills up the interstices between the fibres, and prevents capillary attraction.

1891. What occasions the rise of water or other liquids in small tubes?

A. The attraction between the liquid and the walls of the tube.

1892. Why does the water rise higher in a tube of small diameter than in a large one?

A. Because in a small tube the sides, being

Fig. 57.

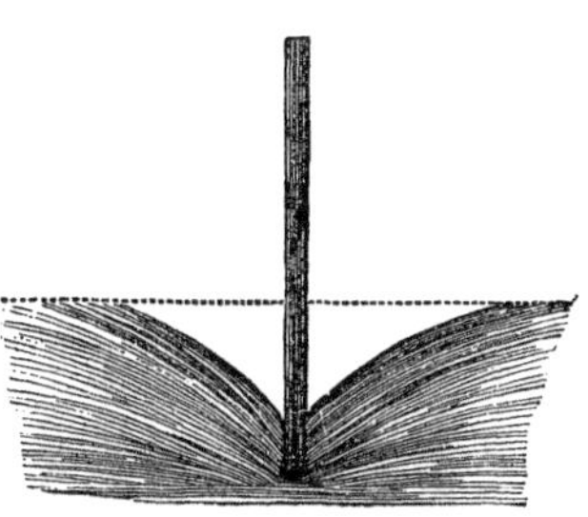

1896. Why, in a barometer, is the top of the column of mercury convex or oval?

Fig. 58.

A. Because, owing to the repulsion between the glass and the mercury, the latter, when it comes in contact with the glass, is depressed; which leaves the central part of the top of the column of mercury the highest, as is shown in fig. 58.

1897. Why will water, ink, or oil, coming in contact with the edge of a book, soak farther in than if spilled upon the sides?

A. Because the space between the leaves acts in the same manner as a small tube would,—attracts the fluid, and causes it to penetrate far inward. The fluid penetrates with more difficulty upon the side of the leaf, because the pores in the paper are irregular, and not continuous from leaf to leaf.

great, and that which acts at very small or insensible distances.

SECTION I.—GRAVITATION.

1859. What is that attraction called which acts at great distances?

A. The attraction of gravitation.

Electrical and magnetic attractions also act at considerable distances.

1860. All bodies tend toward, or are attracted by, the earth: is the earth attracted by them also?

A. Yes: the attraction is mutual; but, as the earth is so much larger than any body on, or near, its surface, the only perceptible attraction is that produced by the earth.

1861. What is this attraction called?

A. It is called the attraction of gravitation.

It is the attraction of gravitation, combined with other causes, which carries the earth and planets round the sun.

SECTION II.—CENTRE OF GRAVITY.

1862. What is the centre of gravity?

A. The centre of weight; in other words, that point on which if supported the body would balance itself.

1863. Where is the centre of gravity in man?

A. The centre of gravity in man lies between the hips. The base is the space between his feet.

1864. Why does an old man use a cane when he walks?

A. To enlarge his base, and prevent the line of direction from falling outside the base.

1898. Why does dry wood swell when immersed in water?

A. Because the water enters the pores of wood by capillary attraction, and forces the particles farther apart from each other.

1899. Why may an immense mass, suspended by a dry rope, be raised a little way by merely wetting the rope?

A. Because the moisture imbibed into the substance of the rope by capillary attraction causes it to swell laterally, and to become shorter.

CHAPTER II.—SPECIFIC GRAVITY.

1900. WHAT is meant by specific gravity?

A. It denotes the weight of a body, as compared with the weight of an equal bulk of some other body taken as a standard.

1901. What body is commonly used as a standard?

A. The standard commonly used is distilled water at the temperature of 60° of Fahrenheit. A cubic foot of water of this temperature weighs exactly one thousand ounces.

A cubic foot of any liquid is the quantity which could be contained in a vessel whose inner surface would measure exactly one foot in height, one foot in length, and one foot in depth.

1902. Why will a piece of cork float on water?

A. Because the specific gravity of the cork

is less than that of the water. In other words, a quantity of water equal in bulk to the piece of cork would weigh heavier than the cork.

1903. Does any portion of the cork sink below the surface of the water?

A. Yes: about one-fourth part of the cork will sink below the surface of the water; that is, the cork will displace a portion of water equal in weight to the whole piece of cork. The bulk of water thus displaced would measure about one-fourth part the bulk of the cork.

1904. A lump of tin weighing a pound, if thrown into the water, would sink: how could the same quantity of tin be made to swim?

A. By increasing the extent of its surface, or, in other words, its bulk.

On this principle large iron steamers are made to float. The weight of the vessel and its contents is less than that of an equal bulk of water.

1905. Does a body weigh as much in water as in air?

A. No: the water buoys the body up, and it weighs just as much less in water as the weight of the bulk of water it displaces.

For this reason a person can lift a stone under water which he could not raise when out of the water.

1906. Why does cream rise to the surface of milk?

A. Because the specific gravity of the cream is less than that of the milk. For the same reason, oil floats on water.

If the neck of a bottle of pure water be inserted in the bung-hole of a cask filled with brandy, the water will run out of the bottle by its own weight, and the brandy will ascend into the bottle. The reason of this is, the specific gravity of the brandy is less than that of the water. But if the bottle be filled with ether instead of water, the brandy would not fill the bottle, because ether is specifically lighter than brandy.

1907. Why is it more easy to swim in salt water than in fresh?

A. Because the specific gravity of salt water is greater than that of fresh, and the swimmer is buoyed up.

1908. Why does a cook throw an egg into brine to try if it be strong enough for pickling?

A. Because if the brine be strong enough, its specific gravity will be greater than that of the egg, and the egg will float.

1909. Why can fat persons swim more easily than those who are not fat?

A. Because fat is specifically lighter than water: therefore the fatter a man is, the more easily he can swim.

1910. How are fishes able to ascend to the surface of the water?

A. Fishes are endowed with an organ called an air-bladder. When the bladder is filled with air, their bulk is increased, and they rise to the surface; but when the air is expelled, their bulk contracts, and they sink.

PART VIII.

MISCELLANEOUS.

1911. How can a sick-room be kept free from unhealthy effluvia?

A. By sprinkling it with vinegar boiled with myrrh or camphor, or by putting some chloride of lime in a flat dish, dampening it a little, and placing it in the apartment.

1912. When infectious diseases prevail, how can the contagious matter be removed from bedrooms, hospitals, houses, &c.?

A. By using a solution of chlorine or of sulphurous acid; which will not only remove the contagious matter, but also the offensive smell of a sick-room.

1913. Why does chloride of lime fumigate a sick-room?

A. Because the chlorine absorbs the hydrogen of the confined air, and by this means removes both the offensive smell and the infection of a sick-room.

1914. Why should bedrooms, cottages, hospitals, and stables be occasionally whitewashed?

A. Because the lime which composes the

whitewash is very caustic, and removes all organic matters adhering to the walls.

1915. Why does lime destroy the offensive smells of bins, sewers, &c.

A. Because it decomposes the offensive gases upon which the smell depends, and destroys them.

1916. Why is guano valuable as a manure?

A. Because it contains ammonia, potash, soda, lime, &c., which are all essential to the growth of plants.

Guano is found upon the coasts of Peru, in the islands of Chinche, near Pisco, and at several other places more to the south; also on the coasts of Africa. It forms a deposit fifty or sixty feet thick, and of considerable extent, and appears to be the accumulation of the excrements of innumerable flocks of birds, especially herons and flamands, which inhabit these islands. It is an excellent manure, and forms the object of a most extensive and profitable trade.

1917. What is the use of lime, marl, &c., as manure?

A. 1st. They decompose vegetable substances; and,

2d. They liberate the alkalies in union with the silica of the soil.

1918. The soil contains carbonic acid: whence is this derived?

A. 1st. From the air; from which it is driven by falling showers;

2d. From the decomposition of vegetable and animal matters, which always produces this gas in abundance; and,

3d. All limestone, chalk, and calcareous

stones contain quantities of carbonic acid in a solid state.

"Calcareous," that is, of a limy nature.

1919. What causes the disease commonly called the itch?

A. It is produced by an insect called the "itch-insect," which burrows in the skin, and is greatly encouraged by filth. Sulphur, corrosive sublimate, &c. will destroy the insect, and cure the disease.

1920. When wine is spilled on a table-cloth or napkin, how can the stain be removed?

A. By dipping it in a weak solution of chlorine.

Chlorine is a principal ingredient in bleaching-powder.

1921. When wine is spilled on a table-cloth, &c., why do persons generally cover the part immediately with salt?

A. Because salt is a compound of chlorine and sodium; and the chlorine of the salt acts as a bleaching-powder.

1922. Why are books discolored by age or damp?

A. Because the fibre of the paper becomes partially decomposed, and various impurities from the atmosphere (or other sources) become mixed with it.

1923. Why does waxing cotton or thread make it stronger?

A. Because it cements the loose filaments

to the cord, and makes the strands of the thread more compact.

The "filaments" are the loose fibres of the cotton.
The "strands" are the twists or single yarns twisted into a thread.

1924. Some sweet cakes are crisp and hard when baked, but if sal-æratus be mixed with the dough they will be soft. Why is this?

A. Sal-æratus has an affinity for moisture, which it absorbs from the atmosphere, and this moisture tends to keep the cakes soft.

1925. How does starch assist in giving a smooth glazed surface to linen?

A. It fills the interstices between the threads, and makes the fabric of more uniform density.

"Interstices between the threads,"—that is, the small spaces between the threads.

1926. How does starch stiffen linen?

A. By filling the interstices of the linen, by which means it is rendered more rigid and firm.

1927. The hooked top of walking-sticks is made by boiling the end of the stick and then bending it into an arch. Why is a stick made flexible by boiling?

A. Wood contains many substances soluble in hot water, as starch, sugar, gum, &c., and several others which are softened by it: as, therefore, several substances are dissolved, and others softened, by boiling water, the stick is rendered flexible.

Cellular fibre and woody matter, when boiled in water, become soft and gelatinous.

1928. Why does the sun or fire warp wood?

A. Because heat draws out the moisture from that surface of the wood which faces it, and causes it to shrink: as, therefore, the heated surface of the wood shrinks, and is smaller than the other surface, it draws it into a curve, and the wood is warped.

1929. If you scrape a slip of paper with a knife, why will the paper curl?

A. Because the under surface of the paper is contracted by scraping, which brings the particles closer together; this contraction of the under surface bends the slip of paper into a curl or arch.

1930. Why do plants which are kept at a window bend toward the glass?

A. Because the side away from the light grows faster than the side facing the light, and pushes the top of the plant over in a curve.

Woody tissue is deposited in the stem most abundantly on the side nearest the light; and where wood is formed most, growth is slowest, because the part is less succulent.

Wood is warped by the fire, because the under surface is smaller than the upper; and paper is made to curl by scraping the under surface with a knife, for the same reason.

1931. When a candle is blown out, whence arises the offensive odor?

A. The tallow distils a substance in the smoke, called acryle, which has a very offensive smell.

"Acryle," from two Greek words *ακρη-υλη*, (akre-ule,) the basis, or principle, of a wick or end; that is, the odor which issues from a wick-end after it has been blown out.

1932. If a silver spoon which has been tarnished by an egg be rubbed with a little salt, why will the tarnish disappear?

A. The tarnish in this case is sulphuret of silver, produced by the sulphur of the egg combining with the silver spoon. Salt acts upon this sulphuret of silver thus:—

The sodium of the salt combines with the sulphur, and produces sulphate of soda. The sulphur being thus taken away from the silver, the tarnish disappears.

1933. Why does a black hat at the sea-side become a rusty brown?

A. Because the muriatic acid of the sea-water disturbs the gallic acid of the black dye, and turns it a reddish brown.

1934. What is an excellent remedy against rats and mice?

A. Sulphuretted hydrogen. All that is necessary is to introduce the beak of a retort into a rat-hole while sulphuretted hydrogen is being given off. It will destroy the rats, and make the hole unfit for others to frequent.

Sulphuretted hydrogen is made thus: Put into a retort or glass bottle a quantity of sulphuret of iron, prepared by heating a rod of iron to white heat; bring it in contact with a roll of sulphur: this will form sulphuret of iron, which let drop into water; pour over it a small portion of water, and then add an equal quantity of sulphuric acid: sulphuretted hydrogen will be given off copiously.

1935. Why are hams preserved by smoking them?

A. Because the smoke of a wood fire contains creasote, which is a great preservative of all animal substances.

1936. What is common marking-ink?

A. There are generally two bottles,—one containing a solution of the carbonate of soda, and another containing a solution of nitrate of silver. The cloth is first moistened with the carbonate of soda, dried, smoothed, and then written on with a pen dipped in the nitrate of silver. An oxide of silver is thus precipitated, and leaves a black mark upon the fabric.

1937. Why is sorrel sometimes used to remove ink-spots from linen?

A. Because it contains oxalic acid.

Oxalic, from the Greek word *οξαλις*, (oxalis,) *sorrel.* Oxalic acid is sometimes erroneously called "salt of lemons."

1938. Why does oxalic acid take out ink-spots?

A. Because it dissolves the tannate of iron, of which the black portion of the ink consists.

"Tannate of iron" is tannic acid combined with iron. Tannic acid is the acid of tan, or oak-bark.

1939. Why do laundresses put their linen in the sun to whiten?

A. This question is rather difficult to solve. The most probable solution is, that air and moisture, (arising from rain, dew, or artificial sprinkling,) influenced by solar light, oxidize the color on the fibre without the assistance of alkali.

1940. Why do bricks turn green on being exposed for some time to the weather, especially if deprived of the rays of the sun?

A. The "green" is a moss, or lichen, which grows on the bricks, and thrives better in the shade than in the sun. The seeds of this moss are supposed to be scattered by the winds.

1941. The white of egg is generally mixed with ground coffee before it is put over the fire to boil: why is this done?

A. Because the albumen contained in the white of the egg coagulates while boiling, and entangles the small particles of coffee, called "grounds," with it, which fall to the bottom of the pot, and leave the liquid clear.

1942. Why does water rot wood? and why does air rot wood?

A. Because the solid part of the wood is converted into what is called *humus*, by oxidation: thus,—

1st. The carbon of the wood is oxidized into carbonic acid; and,

2d. The hydrogen of the wood is oxidized into water. The residue becomes *humus*, or mould.

The black mould of our gardens is called humus, and is produced by the decay of vegetable matter by the action of air and water.

1943. Why does bread become mouldy after it has been kept for some time?

A. Because the spores of the mould-fungus,

floating in the air, fix themselves in the decaying bread and germinate.

Fungi germinate only in decaying bodies.

Spores, or sporules, from the Greek word σπορα, *seed*, is a word used by botanists to indicate the seed of cryptogamic (or flowerless) plants. They differ from seeds in this respect: every part of the spore shoots into a plant, and not one particular point alone, as in common seeds.

1944. Why does the expansion of air at the end of an egg make it feel warm to the tongue?

A. Because air is a very bad conductor, and the more air an egg contains, the less heat will be drawn from the tongue when it touches the shell.

1945. Why will a new-laid egg feel colder to the tongue at the end than a stale one?

A. Because it contains more white and less air; and, as the white of an egg is a better conductor than air, the heat of the tongue will be drawn off more rapidly, and the egg will feel colder.

1946. Of what is gunpowder composed?

A. Saltpetre, charcoal, and sulphur, in the proportion of 76 parts of saltpetre, 14 of charcoal, and 10 of sulphur.

1947. What is the combustible ingredient?

A. Charcoal.

1948. Of what use is the saltpetre?

A. When heated, it is decomposed, and furnishes oxygen, which combines with the charcoal and supports flame.

1949. What is the cause of the expansive force of gunpowder?

A. When the match is applied, the ignition of the powder increases its temperature and liberates nitrogen and carbonic acid gases.

At the moment of explosion gunpowder is expanded about 4000 times.

1950. Why is gunpowder grained?

A. In order to facilitate the transmission of the flame to all parts of the mass.

SCIENTIFIC AMUSEMENTS

FOR

YOUNG PEOPLE.

COMPRISING

CHEMISTRY.
CRYSTALLIZATION.
COLORED FIRES.
CURIOUS EXPERIMENTS.
OPTICS.
CAMERA OBSCURA.
MICROSCOPE.
KALEIDOSCOPE.
MAGIC LANTERN.
ELECTRICITY.
GALVANISM.
MAGNETISM.
AEROSTATION.
ARITHMETIC, ETC.

BY JOHN HENRY PEPPER,

F.C.S., A. INST. C.E., LATE PROFESSOR OF CHEMISTRY AT THE ROYAL POLYTECHNIC

With One Hundred Illustrations.

37 433

SCIENTIFIC AMUSEMENTS.

Fig. 1.

INTRODUCTION.

Many years ago, a little boy, with his face most unpleasantly speckled with a number of small scars, (just healing,) happened to meet that awful personage, the "family doctor," who was coming down-stairs from a grand medical consultation with mamma and the assembled inmates of the nursery. The grave son of Æsculapius at once and most tenderly inquired (oh, that dreadful physic-bill!) after the health of the juvenile, with a view, no doubt, to correct the excessive heat of blood which had caused so frightful an eruption on his youthful countenance.

"And pray, sir," asked the doctor, "what is the matter with you?" The boy, half frightened at the distant prospect of bolus and draught, replied, in the usual lucid manner, "Nothing, sir." "Nothing!" said the doctor: "why, what an inflammatory state your skin is in! I must send you some cooling medicine immediately, my *dear* boy." "Oh, sir, please sir, don't: its phosphorus!" The doctor forgot his dignity, and stared with amazement. He was clever, but of the very old school. He waited one moment, felt the boy's pulse, and looked hard in his face again, as if to count the spots, and at last his pent-up feelings found vent. "Take care, sir! take care, or you'll blow your head off with your chemical pranks. And now tell me how it happened." The youthful philosopher was not long in relating that he had read, in a book on chemistry, that if phosphorus and chlorate of potash were rubbed together in a mortar, they made a "*bang*," which he had tried accordingly in his bedroom, secretly, with the help of the kitchen mortar; that the *stuff* would not go off at first, and whilst he gathered up all his strength and gave the blow that produced the *stunning* effect, his face, somehow or other, came over the mortar, and all the phosphorus blew up into it. "And a lucky fellow," rejoined the doctor, "you are to escape the penalty of *injured eyes!*" and so will every one say who reads this account. But the moral of our story is, the *caution* to all would-be *juvenile philosophers* not to attempt experiments they do not thoroughly understand, and especially to avoid those results that merely end in explosions, and try only those combinations of chemical substances which are *pleasing* and *without danger*, such as will now be described in the following popular sketch of the Science of Chemistry.

Fig. 2.—The danger of experiments with explosive bodies.

CHEMISTRY.

In the history of nations, we read of a very brave and talented people, who, under the name of the "Moors," and sometimes called the "Saracens," helped to rescue the rude Romano-German population of Europe from the Gothic brutishness and ignorance into which they had lapsed. The warlike Moors originally came from Arabia, and are, therefore, the descendants of Ishmael; and although, when conquerors, they were at first quite as ready to destroy as to create, and, in pursuit of the former evil passion, even burnt the magnificent library of Alexandria, yet when they had conquered and gained wealth they cultivated learning of every kind, and became highly civilized; so that when they ruled Spain they introduced into Europe the science of astronomy, the principles of numeral notation, algebra, and the noble science of chemistry, which derives its name (according to the Rev. Mr. Palmer, Professor of Arabic) from the word "alchemy," or, more properly, "al-kemy," *the knowledge of the substance or composition of bodies*, so named from the substantive *kyamon*, that is, *the constitution of any thing*, derived from the root *kama*.

It is pretended by some that the words "chemistry" and "alchemy" are derived from the name of Shem, or Chem, the son of Noah, who is said to have been an adept in the art; and to this day there are persons who assert that the Jews still possess the art of making gold, or they could not possess such fabulous wealth. Others say the art was derived from the Egyptians, among whom it was founded by Hermes Trismegistus. The Jesuit Father Martini, in his "Historia Sinica," says it was practised by the Chinese two thousand five hundred years before the birth of Christ; but, as he does not produce any proofs or data upon which this statement is founded, his assertion is worth very little, or nothing. There can be no doubt that impostors, who deceived the unwary with the pretence of making gold and silver, existed in Rome in the first centuries after the Christian era, and that when discovered they were liable to punishment as knaves and swindlers.

Fig. 3.—An alembic, or alambic, employed by the alchemists for the process of distillation and sublimation.

At Constantinople, in the fourth century, the art of transmutation was fully believed in, and many Greek ecclesiastics wrote learned treatises thereon. Of these and other distant periods the information respecting alchemy must be considered doubtful; but it is certain that in the eighth century the art reappeared among the Arabians. Now there are many words in common use which are derived, like the word "alchemy," from the Arabic language, such as "Al-manack," "Al-koran;" and hence it is not surprising to find chemical words which have the like origin. Thus, the word "al-kali," derived from *kali*, a plant, *al-kali*, of a plant, representing an important class of chemical bodies having opposite qualities to acids, is clearly of Arabic origin: so, again, with the names of apparatus, such as the alembic, or alambic. This is compounded of the Arabic particle *al*, the, and the Greek word *ambix*, a kind of cup or cover of a pot. It is now used to denote the whole of an apparatus for distilling, as in Fig. 3; but it formerly denoted, according to Bishop Watson, only one part of it,—viz., the head, or that part in which the distilled matter was collected.

Fig. 4.—A signifies the candlestick, which must be hollow and full of *water*.
B. The top of the candlestick, which must be wide, to contain good store of water, *for* to fill up the candlestick as the candle riseth up.
C. The candle, which must be as long as the candlestick.
D. The vessel that contains either water, sand, or ashes for any vessel to be set into.
E. A glass vessel standing in *digestion.*

Astrology preceded astronomy, and alchemy paved the way for the science of chemistry. Much valuable time and money were thrown away by learned but misguided men, who, groping their way in the dark, and not having the advantage of perusing books written by shining lights such as Sir Humphry Davy or Faraday, stumbled on many valuable truths in their pursuit of the ever-attractive "Philosopher's Stone," which was to turn lead into gold, or, as a magical potation, under the name of the "Elixir of Life," was not only to impart longevity, but continual life, so that the maker of the gold should not lose it in the grim clutch of King Death. The worldly desire to *have* and *enjoy* is well depicted in these dreams of the alchemists, whilst the most intense nonsense is apparent in many of their notions. Thus, in a "Discourse on divers Spagyrical [*i.e.* chemical] Experiments and Curiosities, and of the Anatomy of Gold and Silver," by one John French, "Doctor of Physick," and printed as late as 1651, in the time of the "Commonwealth" of Oliver Cromwell, we are gravely told how "*To extract a white milkie substance from the rayes of the moon.*" At the same time, in this discourse there is much that is useful, and we learn that distillation may be conducted by a lamp; and this statement is accompanied with a diagram, of which a copy is given, (Fig. 4,) where we see the germ—the principle—of Palmer's celebrated spring candlestick, in which the candle is maintained at one height by the compression and elasticity of a spring.

Grave and honest men continued their studies in alchemy with amazing industry. The clever chemist—not alchemist—Boerhaave distilled mercury one thousand and nine times, in order, as he says in his paper addressed to the Royal Society, "to subvert the high pretensions of other alchemists that mercury could never be freed from its original impurity but by being joined to some purer body of the same nature with itself, such as gold or silver," as also to prove "the unchangeableness both of mercury and gold, how often soever they were distilled together."

During the time that the true believers continued their

Fig. 5.—The death of *Bombastes* Paracelsus by drinking alcohol, being his alleged *Elixir of Life.*

experiments, there was another class of men who, with consummate impudence, possessed themselves of a few chemical terms and hard words, and astonished the ignorant with juggling tricks, which passed for true alchemy. They had only to consult the works of clever, perhaps honest, alchemists, to learn the magniloquent style of describing experiments. There was Paracelsus, who was undoubtedly a most learned man, and called by Naudé "the zenith and rising sun of all the alchemists:" he indulged in a rampant style of puffing himself. In the year 1526 he was chosen Professor of Physics and Natural Philosophy in the University of Basle, where his lectures attracted vast numbers of students. He treated the physicians of his time with the most absurd vanity and illiberal insolence, telling them "that the very down of his bald pate had more knowledge than all their writers, the buckles of his shoes more learning than Galen and Avicenna, and his beard more experience than all their universities;" he revived the extravagant doctrines of Raymond Lully concerning a universal medicine, and boasted himself to be in possession of secrets able to prolong the present period of human life to that of the antediluvians: he had, in fact, made the discovery of alcohol, and thought that in it he had found the long-sought elixir of life. Paracelsus determined to put it to the test, and, drinking copiously of his alcohol, (with a daring worthy of a better cause,) sank dead on the floor of his laboratory,—a type, as Cumming says, "of man's effort to save himself—that is, to live forever."

Fig. 6.—A. Real gold. B. Common iron. The whole being painted over with a reddish color, would have the appearance of a rusty nail.

The swindlers and cheats did not propose to themselves such tragic experiments, but studied carefully the art of deceiving fools (of whom, it is said, the human race is chiefly composed) by first awakening the passion of avarice: thus, they would invest a little of the precious metal in the construction of a nail half gold and half iron, and, meeting with a victim of the required softness, they would then carelessly remove it from their pockets in company with other nails, and, producing a phial of the elixir, would expend the *last drop* in changing the nail into gold; the elixir, of course, being colored water that could wash off the paint with which the nail was covered.

The *last drop* of elixir being expended, it was, of course, necessary for the alchemist to prepare *some more*, and, presenting the nail as an earnest of his power, he would be at free quarters for many months with his patron, who would incur, at the alchemist's suggestion, unheard of expenses for chemicals, glasses, furnaces, &c., until, tired out with repeated failures, he would send the alchemist (not empty) away, to repeat in some other locality the same impertinent trick on the wisdom of his fellow-creatures. There is nothing that better demonstrates the shrewdness of Queen Elizabeth than her dealings with Dr. Dee. Like our own beloved sovereign, she was the patron of learned men, and, having been presented with a round piece of silver which Dr. Dee pretended he had made of a portion of brass cut out of a warming-pan, the said pan being afterward sent to her majesty that she might convince herself that the piece of silver exactly corresponded with the hole which was cut into the brass, did receive him most favorably, at least so far as words went, and gave orders that he should not be molested in his pursuits of chemistry and philosophy, at the same time, with most sensible queen-craft, intimating that the man who could make silver must be *perfectly independent* of her exchequer.

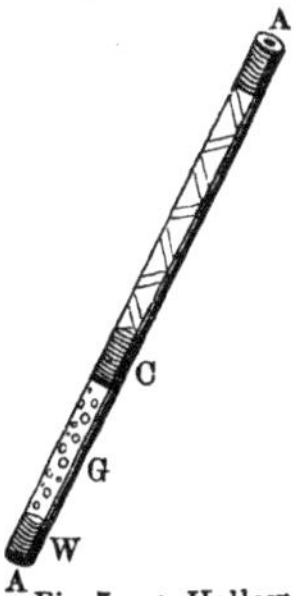

Fig. 7.—A. Hollow metal rod, in which W represents the wax, to close one end. G. The grains of gold. C. A cork, to prevent the grains of gold making a noise in the tube.

There were other mendicant rogues who pretended to transmute vulgar lead and copper into royal gold by certain powders, which they projected and always *stirred* into the baser metal, to the wondering delight and edification of all concerned. In fact, the *stirrer* was the *primum mobile* in this amusing fraud; and, after the fashion of the wonderful miracle of producing the omelet in the empty frying-pan, as narrated by all truth-loving chroniclers of Spain and her mendicant monks, these cunning jugglers previously conveyed their atom of gold into the hollow of the *stirrer*, and by the help of a little powdered charcoal, sulphur, and nitre, which made a great deflagration or fizz when thrown into the red-hot crucible, the eyes of the curious were dazzled, and the conjurors passed themselves off as the possessors of the true philosopher's stone, and rewarded the believers and reproved the incredulous by the production of a modicum of gold.

Fig. 8.—Alchemist using his hollow rod.

It were tedious to give the names of all the alchemists who have distracted the peace of mind of others who succeeded them by their insane ravings after the mysterious chemical which was, by multiplication on the largest scale, to produce a mountain of gold from a molehill of *the quintessence:* it is sufficient to know that, so far as our modern chemistry enlightens us, it is impossible to change one element into another. There are certain substances which are called *allatropic;* that is to say, they are capable of assuming one or more physical states, and putting on such disguises that even the best-devised masquerade dress cannot approach them in the perfection of concealment.

Thus, charcoal, which possesses almost the property of ubiquity, is to be found as the very corner-stone in the fabric of the fairest faces of Eve's daughters. It lurks in the sweetened cup of tea; and a quarter of a pound of nice white lump sugar put into a breakfast-cup with the smallest possible dash of boiling water, and then the addition of plenty of oil of vitriol, is a truly wonderful spectacle, and more instructive than much reading, to see the white sugar turn black, then boil spontaneously, and now, rising out of the cup in solemn black, it heaves and throbs as the oil of vitriol continues its work in the lower part of the cup, emitting volumes of steam, and reminding one of some of those remarkable upheavings of the earth which geologists delight to paint and talk about, till the acid has spent its fury. The elements forming water in the sugar have been attracted, and are now united to the oil of vitriol, (scientifically called sulphuric acid;) a divorce has taken place between the water and the charcoal, which latter now tumbles over the sides of the cup.

Fig. 9.—Breakfast-cup containing a quarter of a pound of lump sugar, upon which a little boiling water has been poured, and then plenty of sulphuric acid.

In describing this experiment the other state of charcoal (the allatropic condition) must not be forgotten. The breakfast-cup is full of—no! not diamonds!—it only contains a porous sort of black charcoal; and yet, in Nature's hand, this common black matter is moulded into the costly diamond, and, glancing from the ring on the finger to the solid contents of the cup, it is difficult to trace out any analogy; but this is the point of the argument, and is the nearest approach to the alchemical fantasy of our forefathers. A substance may take two or three forms, as already described. but it is impossible, so far as experience teaches us, to change one *element* into another. We may have charcoal, as coke, the diamond, plumbago, anthracite, a smokeless coal; but we cannot change it, or lead, or copper, into gold, unless we adopt the time-honored and most successful mode of transmutation, and become coal, lead, or diamond merchants.

Speaking of elements brings us to the consideration of chemistry as a modern science. Just eighty-seven years ago Dr. Priestley began his famous experiments with the preparation and examination of various gaseous bodies, one important result of which was the discovery of "oxygen gas," the foundation of the present classified and embodied series of facts that record the labors of so many talented men. Thus, oxygen deservedly stands at the head of the list of the elements which form every animate and inanimate thing within, upon, or about the world. There is nothing more encouraging to a beginner in chemistry, such as the youthful philosopher who expends his shillings and sixpences in chemicals and apparatus, who disdains to play out his half-holidays, and, enraptured with the wonders of which he is the magician, is better pleased experimenting in the secluded garret-room than in the noisy playground,—there is nothing more satisfactory than the statement that the highest mountain and the lowest valley, the most beautiful summer-cloud or the grandest cataract of water, the ugliest reptile or the most graceful form, the noblest palace erected by the hand of man, with its pictures, statuary, paintings, carpets, furniture, silks, satins, velvets, its costly jewels, diamonds, pearls, rubies, and sapphires, or the poorer hovel, with its shivering tenants in rags, can each and all be referred in composition to some sixty-two or sixty-three elements, which are easily classified, viz.:—

Three permanent gases:—oxygen, nitrogen, hydrogen.

Four elements having many similar characteristics:—chlorine, bromine, iodine, fluorine.

Five solids which do not possess the usual metallic properties: —carbon, boron, selenium, sulphur, phosphorus.

Fifty metals, only one of which is a liquid,—viz., quicksilver, or mercury,—all the others being solid.

In this list there is the alpha, beta, gamma, delta of chemistry, puzzled out by the laborious work of some of the most talented and gifted of men, and, once grasped, this chemical alphabet is the stepping-stone to compound words of one or more syllables, or containing one or more elements. Thus, oxygen and hydrogen combined spell *water;* charcoal, oxygen, and calcium, chemically united, spell *the marble arch;* carbonate of lime, sulphur, oxygen, aluminium, potassium, spell *alum.* The word *spell* is pressed into the service, and is intended, of course, to be a synonym for the verb *to form* or *produce:* at all events, having been once used in this way to help an analogy, we may lay it on one side, and now begin to describe some of these experimental lessons, commencing with

THE ATMOSPHERE.

Nitrogen is the principal constituent of the air of the atmosphere which surrounds our globe, extending to a height of about forty-five miles above it, and playing a most important part in the economy of nature, inorganic as well as organic.

This atmospheric air consists of nearly four-fifths of nitrogen, and rather more than one-fifth of oxygen, about seventy-nine of the former to twenty-one of the latter, and generally contains also a variable proportion of the vapor of water, and a very small quantity of carbonic acid gas, scarcely amounting to one part in one thousand. Its constituent parts are so easily separated that it appears to be rather an intimate mixture than a chemical compound, though the mixture is so complete that chemists have not been able to ascertain any difference in the composition of air taken from all parts of the world, and from different heights, up to the highest point which has to this time been attained.

This atmosphere presses on the surface of the globe and every being on it, with a force of about fifteen pounds to every square inch of surface; but, as it presses equally in all directions, upwards as well as downwards, its weight cannot be perceived unless the pressure be removed from one surface by some artificial means.

EXPERIMENTS.

1. Place a cylinder of strong glass, open at both ends, on the plate of the air-pump, and put your hand on the other end, and you will, of course, be able to remove it at pleasure. Now exhaust the air from the interior of the cylinder, and at each stroke of the pump you will feel your hand pressed tighter and tighter on the cylinder, until you will not be able to remove it; as soon as the air is again admitted to the interior of the cylinder, the pressure within will be restored, and the hand again be at liberty.

2. Tie a piece of moistened bladder very firmly over one end of a similar glass cylinder, and place the open end on the plate of the pump. As soon as you begin to exhaust the air from the interior, the bladder, which was previously quite

horizontal, will begin to bulge inwards, the concavity increasing as the exhaustion proceeds, until the bladder, no longer able to bear the weight of the superincumbent air, breaks with a loud report.

3. The elasticity of air, or indeed of any gaseous body, may be shown by introducing under the air-pump receiver a bladder containing a very small quantity of air, its mouth being closely tied. As you exhaust the air from the receiver, that portion contained in the bladder, being no longer pressed upon by the atmosphere, will gradually expand, distending the bladder until it appears nearly full; on readmitting the air into the receiver, the bladder will at once shrink to its former dimensions.

A shrivelled apple, placed under the same conditions, will appear plump when the air is removed from the receiver, and resume its former appearance on the readmission of the air.

4. There is a very pretty apparatus made for the purpose of showing the pressure of the atmosphere, consisting of a hollow globe of brass, about three inches in diameter, divided into two equal parts, which fit very accurately together; it is furnished with two handles, one of them screwed into a hollow stem communicating with the interior of the globe and fitting on to the air-pump; the other is attached to a short stem on the opposite side of the globe. In the natural state, the globe may easily be separated into its two hemispheres by one person pulling the handles; but after the air has been exhausted from the interior, it requires two very strong men to separate the parts, and they will often fail. By turning the stopcock, and readmitting the air into the interior of the globe, it will come asunder as easily as at first.

THE BAROMETER.

We are indebted to the weight of the atmosphere for the power we possess of raising water by the common pump; for the piston of the pump withdrawing the air from the interior of the pipe, which terminates in water, the pressure of the atmosphere forces the water up the pipe to supply the place of the air withdrawn. It was soon found, however, that when the column of water in the pipe was more than thirty feet high, the pump became useless, for the water refused to rise higher. Why? It was found that a column of water about thirty feet high exerted a pressure equal to the weight of the atmosphere, thus establishing an equilibrium between the water in the pipe and the atmospheric pressure.

This is the principle on which the barometer, or *measurer of weight*, as its name imports, is constructed. The metal mercury is about twelve times heavier than water: consequently, if a column of water thirty *feet* high balances the pressure of the atmosphere, a column of mercury thirty *inches* high ought to do so also; and this is in fact the case. If you take a glass tube nearly three feet long, and closed at one end, fill it with mercury, then, placing your finger on the open end, invert the tube into a basin or saucer containing some of the same metal, upon removing your finger (which must be done carefully, while the mouth of the tube is completely covered by the mercury) it will be seen that the fluid will fall a few inches, leaving the upper part of the tube empty. Such a tube, with a graduated scale attached, is in truth a barometer, and as the weight of the atmosphere increases or decreases, so the mercury rises or falls in the tube. This instrument is of the greatest value to the seaman, for a sudden fall of the barometer will often give notice of an impending storm when all is fine and calm, and thus enable the mariner to make the preparations necessary to meet the danger.

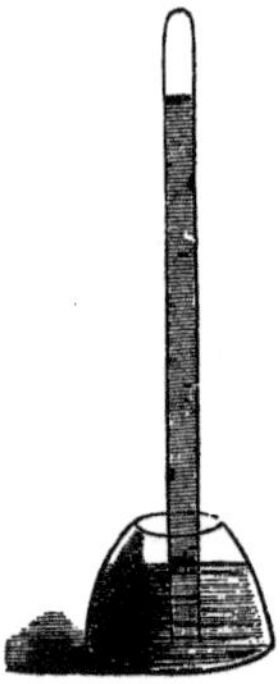

Fig. 10.

This instrument was discovered by an Italian philosopher, named Torricelli, and from him the vacuum formed in the upper end of the tube above the surface of the mercury has been called the Torricellian vacuum. It is by far the most perfect vacuum that can be obtained, containing necessarily nothing but a minute quantity of the vapor of mercury.

EXPERIMENT.

Pass a little ether through the mercury in the tube, and as soon as it reaches the empty space it will boil violently, depressing the mercury until the pressure of its own vapor is sufficient to prevent its ebullition. If you now cool the upper part of the tube, so as to condense the vapor, the pressure being thus removed, the ether will again begin to boil, and so alternately, as often as you please. In order to show this fact with effect, the bore of the tube should not be less than half an inch in diameter.

ATMOSPHERIC AIR.

Atmospheric air contains, besides the oxygen and nitrogen, its principal constituents, a small proportion of carbonic acid gas, as has been mentioned; and this may be shown by filling a tube about half full of lime-water, and shaking it with the air contained in the other half, when it will become slightly turbid from the insoluble carbonate of lime formed.

When we consider that every living animal is constantly consuming oxygen and replacing it by carbonic acid gas, and that all burning bodies, fires in our dwellings, furnaces, artificial lights of all kinds, act in the same way in abstracting the oxygen from the air and replacing it by immense quantities of carbonic acid gas, which is a poison to all animals who breathe or attempt to breathe it, we must wonder what becomes of this irrespirable gas, as it is found to exist in the air in quantities so minute, and by what means the oxygen is restored and the air again made fit for respiration. This is effected by one of those laws which the wisdom of the Creator has impressed upon matter, by which one part of creation as it were balances another, and all proceeds in an endless circle of change. This carbonic acid, which is so poisonous to animal life, is the food of the vegetable world, plants having the power of taking up the carbonic acid into their pores, converting the carbon into their own substance, and rejecting the oxygen, which is again respired by animals, &c. In the same way, all animal refuse is the food of vegetables, and is used under the name of manures.

The atmosphere contains also a variable quantity of vapor of water, invisible so long as it is in the state of vapor, but it may be rendered obvious by bringing any very cold body into warm air, when the vapor will condense on the cold body in the form of small drops of water. A tumbler of fresh-pumped water brought into a crowded room is almost immediately covered with moisture, and it may also be seen on bottles of wine which have been put into ice before coming to table. Fogs are occasioned by the condensation of vapor produced by mixing a current of warm air with a colder air. The Banks of Newfoundland are notorious for dense fogs, occasioned by the warm air brought from the south by the great Gulf Stream mixing with the cold air from the Arctic regions, and thus precipitating the vapor in a visible form, rendering every thing but itself *in*visible. The famous London fogs depend upon the same precipitation of the vapor of water, with the addition of the smoke from the numerous sea-coal fires, which give it that interesting yellow tinge for which it is so remarkable.

Aqueous vapor, being lighter and more transparent than air, permits objects to be seen more distinctly in proportion to its quantity: hence, when distant hills appear nearer and objects upon them more distinct than usual, rain may be expected, the air being fully charged with vapor ready to be deposited on the slightest cause.

THE VARIOUS MODES OF PREPARING OXYGEN GAS.

Procure an old gun-barrel, and plug up the touch-hole with wire, or, if a larger quantity of oxygen is required, obtain an empty iron quicksilver bottle. In the first place, fit into the gun-barrel a cork with a pewter tube, or stretch a piece of vulcanized India-rubber tube over the end of the gun-barrel, having previously poured in some black oxide of manganese, in grain, not powder, as the latter contains water, which, expanding into steam, has a tendency to blow out the powdered manganese, causing it to clog the pewter tube or vulcanized India-rubber tubing. If the touch-hole end be now placed between the bars on an ordinary fire, and the tube conveyed an inch or so beneath the surface of some water in a pail or foot-tub, bubbles of gas will soon escape, which can be collected in a bottle previously filled with water and held over the end of the pipe; the gas ascends into the bottle, gradually displacing the water, and, when filled, the bottle is corked, or stoppered, under water, and removed for use.

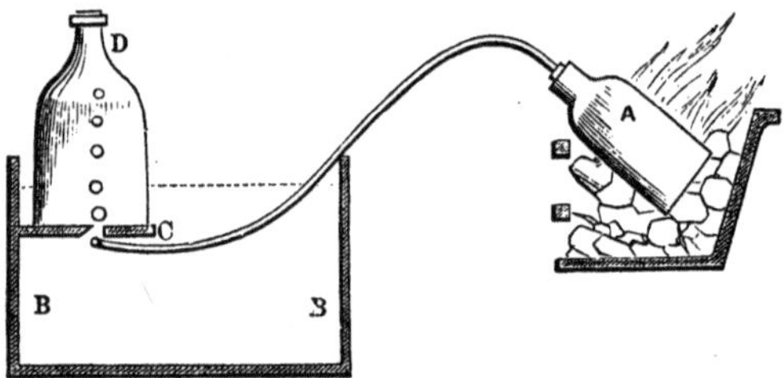

Fig. 11.—A, the iron bottle containing the black oxide of manganese, with pipe passing to the pneumatic trough, B B, in which is fixed a shelf, C, perforated with a hole, under which the end of the pipe is adjusted, and the gas passes into the gas-jar, D.

If the large mercury-bottle is used, an iron pipe is screwed into the orifice, from which the plug is removed, and when the pipe is fixed, the bottle is filled with grain manganese and placed in a proper furnace, whilst the gas can be conveyed to a pneumatic trough by means of vulcanized India-rubber tubing, which is remarkably useful for all experiments connected with the gases.

ANOTHER MODE OF MAKING OXYGEN GAS.

Obtain a Florence oil flask, and, having cleaned out the oil by means of some bits of soap and boiling water, and thoroughly washing the flask, let the vessel dry, and then take away the wicker-work,—which need not be wasted, as it can be coiled round and bound, and answers admirably for a stand to support the flask upright. Into the flask place a mixture of two ounces of powdered chlorate of potash and one ounce of powdered black oxide of manganese, both of which should be dry and well mixed before they are placed in the flask; then fit a cork and pewter tube. The cork can be easily bored, either with a *rat-tail* file, or, what is still better, a *cork-borer*, which can be purchased at any of the chemical-apparatus shops. Now place the flask and bent tube on a ring-stand, and apply the heat of a spirit-lamp, when torrents of gas will escape. The oxygen may be collected in gas-jars or bottles over the pneumatic trough, and pictures of all the apparatus used are given here, to assist the manipulation of the youthful chemist, who will, of course, be most desirous to begin by making oxygen gas.

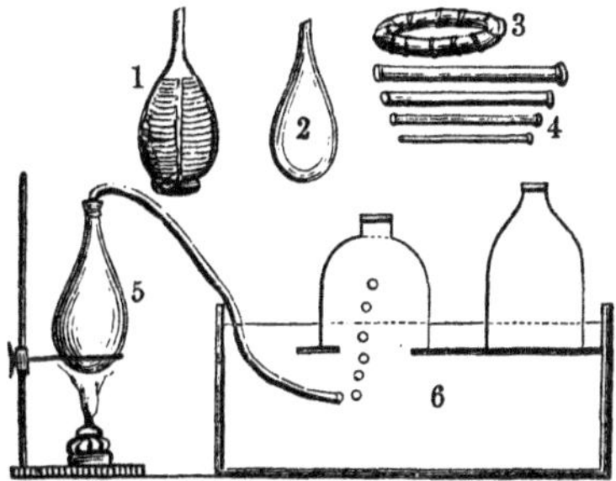

Fig. 12.—1. Florence oil flask with wicker-work.
2. Ditto cleaned and dried.
3. The wicker converted into a pad to rest the flask on.
4. Cork borers fitting into each other, and of all sizes.
5. Flask fitted with cork and bent tube, and containing the chlorate of potash and black oxide of manganese, with spirit-lamp. The pewter pipe leads to No. 6.
6. Pneumatic trough. The gas-jar standing on the shelf, and receiving the bubbles of gas from No. 5.
N.B. With the above arrangement nearly all the most interesting gases may be prepared.

EXPERIMENTS WITH OXYGEN GAS.

If a lighted taper is blown out so as to leave a part of the *snuff* (so called, *i.e.* the wick) in a state of ignition, and then plunged into oxygen gas, the taper relights with a slight pop or noise, being a good example of the power of oxygen to *support combustion.*

CURIOUS COLORED LIGHT OBTAINED BY BURNING SULPHUR IN OXYGEN.

Into a deflagrating spoon (which is a little cup made of brass or copper screwed on to the end of a copper or iron wire) place a little sulphur; when set on fire, and plunged into oxygen, it emits a most remarkable colored light. After the combustion is over, some amusing experiments can be made with the product.

TO BLEACH A RED ROSE AND OTHER FLOWERS.

If a red rose be placed inside the jar where the sulphur has been burnt, the color is discharged, and the rose rendered nearly white.

Many variegated dahlias, blue heartsease, or a bunch of blue violets, have their colors curiously modified, if not bleached, by the acid produced, which is called sulphurous acid, and is most largely employed for bleaching straw hats and bonnets. The same acid is exceedingly valuable as a disinfectant, and also for arresting fermentation. Many casks of *home-made wine* become *home-made vinegar* in consequence of the rapidity of the fermentation in warm weather; and the fumes of sulphur, obtained either by burning that substance in air or oxygen, have the remarkable power of stopping the too rapid conversion of sugar into alcohol. The sulphurous acid described is one of the most ancient bleaching agents, and it is even mentioned by Pliny as used for whitening woollen fleeces.

TO OBTAIN A WHITE SOLID FROM THE WATER IN WHICH THE GAS-JAR CONTAINING THE SULPHUROUS ACID STANDS.

After trying the bleaching experiments explained, let the gas jar and the remaining fumes stand for some little time in a dish with water containing a little nitric acid, when the acid and some sulphuric acid will gradually fall into and mix with the water, which should be pure and distilled. If a piece of paper colored blue with tincture of litmus be dipped into the water, it changes red, demonstrating the presence of an acid body; and, on the addition of a solution of nitrate of baryta, a white precipitate falls, called sulphate of baryta, or *heavy white*. This is a pigment largely used for enamelled papers, and is also sometimes employed to adulterate white lead. Experiments can always be made instructive as well as entertaining; and the production of the *heavy white* is a good example of chemical affinity, as well as of the indestructibility of matter, for it now contains the greater part of the sulphur originally burnt in the oxygen gas,—sulphate of baryta consisting of 16 parts sulphur, 82 parts oxygen, and 68½ parts of the metal barium.

TO MAKE TEST-PAPERS.

Test-papers are exceedingly valuable to the experimental chemist for the purpose of detecting the presence of acids and alkalies; and they may be prepared in the most simple manner. Take an ounce of litmus and place it in a ten-ounce bottle, pour upon it a mixture of five ounces of alcohol (methylated spirit will do very well) and five ounces of water; continually shake the ingredients during several days, when a deep blue tincture will be obtained, which may be poured off clear into another bottle, or filtered through blotting-paper. To use the *tincture* of litmus, (for all solutions of vegetable substances in alcohol are generally called tinctures, especially when employed in medicine,) pour a little into a soup-plate, and then take some strips of blotting-paper, pass them through the tincture, when they will absorb sufficient to color the paper a lovely blue, which is now to be hung up, and when dry placed in a well corked or stoppered wide-mouthed bottle in a dark place. The paper is now called litmus paper, and is an exceedingly delicate test for acid bodies soluble in water.

TURMERIC PAPER.

This test is used to detect alkalies, and, in contact with a solution of potash, soda, or ammonia, changes to a reddish-brown; it is prepared in precisely the same manner as the litmus paper, by using one ounce of powdered turmeric root to five ounces spirit and five ounces water.

ANOTHER DELICATE TEST FOR ALKALIES.

Take some litmus paper and pass it through very weak vinegar, and hang it up to dry. The paper is now red; but in the presence of an alkali it immediately changes to a blue, as may be noticed in trying some other amusing experiments with oxygen gas.

INTENSE HEAT AND LIGHT PRODUCED BY BURNING PHOSPHORUS IN OXYGEN.

If this experiment is tried with the precautions mentioned, the gas-jar may be usually saved; but, if carelessly performed, the heat produced is so great that it generally cracks the glass. Take a moderate-sized piece of phosphorus and dry thoroughly by pressing it gently in blotting-paper; place this in a deflagrating spoon, and, having previously removed the stopper of the gas-jar containing the oxygen, place the spoon and its contents in the neck of the jar, and then ignite the phosphorus by touching it with a hot wire. Now place the spoon in the centre of the jar, when a dazzling bright light is obtained. This experiment is made still more amusing by first showing some flowers in pots and colored silks by a monochromatic light, and afterward lighting up the phosphorus, when all the colors are shown with great brilliancy. In this case the gas-jar should be screened from the eyes of the spectators, so that they may be able to appreciate the changes of color in the articles displayed by the two lights.

A MONOCHROMATIC LIGHT.

Into a pint-bottle of methylated spirit place two ounces of common salt, which must be constantly shaken; after agitation, pour some on a cloth or some cotton-wool tied round a stick and placed in the nozzle of a common candlestick. If flowers or colored shawls are exhibited by the light obtained from the burning spirit containing the salt, they present a most dreary and monotonous appearance, and the contrast is very marked when the jar of oxygen is produced and the phosphorus burnt: the colors appear to be restored as if by magic. Of course, these experiments must be prepared in a darkened room: a room with shutters is very convenient for these experiments.

Fig. 13.—Table set out in a darkened room.
A. The candlestick and cotton saturated with spirit and salt, burning and producing a yellow light.
B. The phosphorus in oxygen.
F. Flowers of various colors in centre of table.

AN ACID OBTAINED BY BURNING PHOSPHORUS IN OXYGEN.

If the phosphorus is burnt in a jar containing dry oxygen gas, the phosphoric acid deposits in white flakes, which, if mixed rapidly with lime and a little water, constitute a useful material for stopping teeth, as the lime and phosphoric acid unite and form phosphate of lime; this substance is perfectly harmless, and, unlike the dangerous mercurial amalgams placed in hollow teeth, cannot injure the health of persons using it. If the jar of oxygen stands in a plate containing water, the white flakes of phosphoric acid rapidly dissolve, and, when tested by the litmus paper, betray the presence of the acid by the change of the blue to red. This experiment contrasts curiously with the next.

AN ALKALI PRODUCED BY BURNING A METAL IN OXYGEN, AND THE CHAMELEON EXPERIMENT.

Potassium is lighter than water, and when placed in a spoon and heated by a spirit-lamp, and then plunged into a jar of oxygen, it glows with an intense and sudden heat. If the product contained in the spoon is now dissolved in water, the solution changes the color of the turmeric from a yellow to a reddish brown, showing that oxygen can not only produce an acid but an alkali; and a very interesting result is obtained by taking the litmus paper changed to red from the phosphoric acid, and restoring the blue by dipping it into the solution from the potassium, or by taking the turmeric paper, already changed to a reddish brown by the alkali, and bringing back the bright yellow by placing it into the phosphoric-acid solution. This experiment, which is quite chameleon in its character, is very easily performed, and furnishes a striking example of the difference between acids and alkalies.

COMBUSTION OF STEEL SPRING IN OXYGEN.

Take a bit of watch-spring, and *soften* the *end* by means of the flame of a spirit-lamp. When cold, twist round it a piece of waxed thread or waxed taper. If this is set on fire, and introduced into a jar of oxygen, the steel spring burns with great intensity, throwing out sparks in every direction; and, as these are extremely hot, they strike against and melt themselves into the body of the glass; other portions fall into the water below, and frequently pass through the stratum of water, melting the glaze and adhering firmly to it. In this experiment the result is neither acid nor alkaline, but a mixture of the oxides of iron, a neutral compound being formed; and it is very curious here to mark the elasticity, hardness, and toughness of the steel as compared with the product of combustion, which is so brittle that it may be crushed by the fingers in the palm of the hand.

FIRE FROM WATER, OR THE MODERN GREEK FIRE.

Potassium will burn very readily in oxygen gas, the combustion being retarded chiefly from the formation of a crust of oxide or potash covering the metal. This does not occur if potassium is thrown on water: the metal oxidizes rapidly, and so much heat is generated during the change, that the hydrogen escaping around the ignited ball takes fire, whilst the potash formed on the surface is rapidly cleared off, and the whole mass being converted into potash is at the last a red-hot ball of that substance, and, being no longer able to maintain its high temperature, comes in contact with the water, and bursts with a sharp crack; and for that reason the vessel in which potassium is burnt must not be approached at the last stage of the combustion too closely, as the particles from the red-hot ball of potash would cause intense agony if they happened to enter the eye.

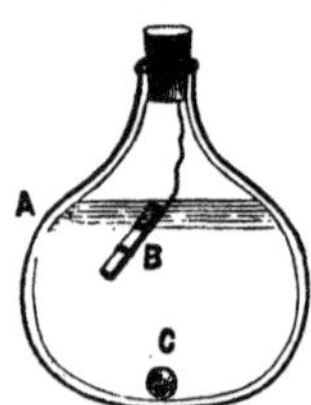

Fig. 14.—A. The globe full of naphtha or ether.
B. Slender tube tied to a bit of thread attached to the cork, containing the potassium.
C. The bullet, to insure the fracture of the glass.

Advantage is taken of this property in the popular experiment called the "Modern Greek Fire." Globes of glass are filled with ether or naphtha, and a thin glass tube placed inside, containing some small pellets of the metal potassium. If a bullet or a marble is placed in the glass globe, and it is dashed on the surface of the water, the globe, with the slender tube containing the potassium, breaks, the contents are discharged on the water upon which the ether and potassium float, and as the latter takes fire instantaneously, it communicates to the ether or naphtha, and a perfect sheet of fire covers the tank, pond, or lake in which the experiment is performed.

FIRE FROM ICE.

Make a hole in a thick piece of ice, dry it out with some cotton, and place into the hole a bit of potassium, when the metal immediately takes fire, and sometimes is discharged from the hole with great violence, especially if the potassium has been held some time in the fingers and become warm. Care must always be taken not to lean over the ice or water during experiments with potassium; and it should be remembered that it very nearly always explodes when held in the fingers or warmed before use.

THE ANALYSIS OF AIR.

One of the most pleasing and simple experiments is that of analyzing air, or separating it into its constituent parts: thus, if a lighted taper be placed in a bottle, it burns at first with its ordinary brilliancy; in a short time, however, the flame diminishes and the work of combustion is brought to an end. It might be thought that the carbon of the taper had removed all the oxygen and converted it into carbonic acid; and, to prove that this is not the case, a little burning sulphur in a spoon is now introduced, which is not extinguished till some time has elapsed. After this burning phosphorus may be placed into the same bottle, and when the latter substance has ceased burning, no other combustible will continue to burn, as the oxygen is wholly removed, and nitrogen with the white smoke of the phosphoric acid alone remain; the latter soon dissolves away in the presence of a little water, leaving the nitrogen behind.

Nitrogen or azote instantly extinguishes a lighted taper, and is lighter than oxygen, as may be proved by the next experiment.

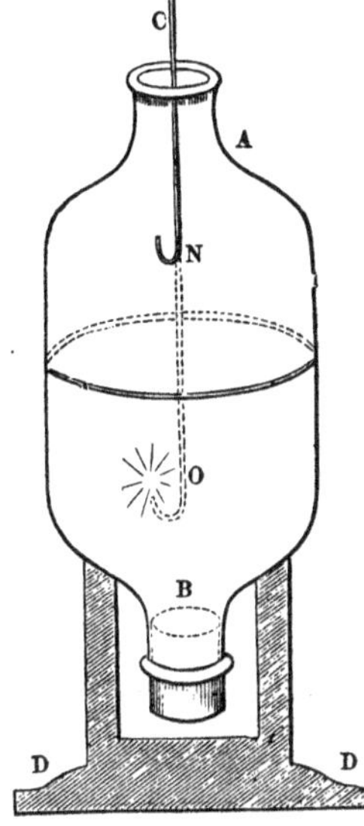

Fig. 15.—A, gas-jar, containing nitrogen; N, standing on B, another jar full of oxygen, O. The taper C is extinguished at N and re-lighted at O. D, D, stand, supporting the jars.

A LIGHT GAS WILL FLOAT ON A HEAVY GAS LIKE ALCOHOL UPON WATER.

If alcohol, colored blue with litmus, be placed into a phial, some water may be introduced beneath it by means of a tube, and the former floats on the latter. The same principle may be displayed with the gases: thus, if a jar containing oxygen is inverted, and placed with the mouth upwards, and covered with a glass plate, and another jar, containing nitrogen gas, (with a similar glass plate,) in the upright position, be placed upon it, the two glass plates can be withdrawn; and a lighted taper being introduced is first extinguished in the top gas-jar, containing the nitrogen, whilst it is immediately relighted on being thrust into the lower jar, containing the oxygen.

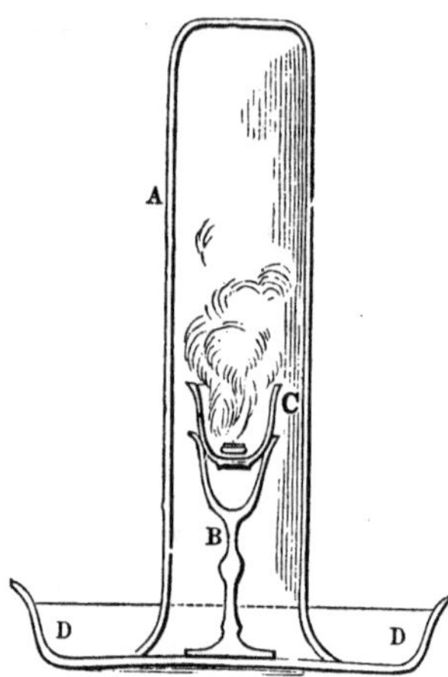

Fig 16.—A. The gas-jar, containing atmospheric air.
C. The cup containing the phosphorus.
B. The wineglass supporting it.
D D. The plate or dish containing water, in which the whole stands.

TO PREPARE NITROGEN.

Into a little porcelain cup, supported on a small wineglass or other convenient stand placed in a dish with some water, put a piece of phosphorus; set this on fire and invert a jar of air over it, and, as the water rises in the jar, pour more into the dish; or, if the stand, &c. be placed on the shelf of the pneumatic trough, the water will absorb the phosphoric acid and rise in the jar in consequence of the removal of one-fifth of the volume,—viz., oxygen gas. After the white smoke has disappeared, the residual gas is nitrogen.

TO MAKE ATMOSPHERIC AIR.

Take four measures of nitrogen and pass them into a tall jar, or, what is better, graduate or divide a long jar into five equal parts, and fill four of the parts with nitrogen gas, which extinguishes flame; then pass in some oxygen gas, to fill up the remaining one-fifth in the graduated long glass; finally, slide a glass plate over the orifice of the jar, and agitate the vessel so as to mix the two gases. A lighted taper introduced into this mixture burns precisely as it would do in common air; and the experiment is very instructive, and shows the synthesis of the chief constituents of common air.

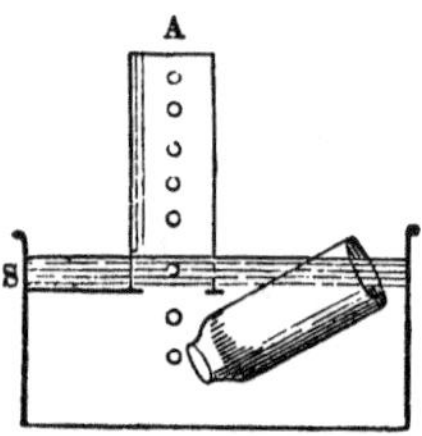

Fig. 17.—Gas-jar, A, on the shelf, S, of the pneumatic trough, full of water, and mode of passing gas into it from bottle, B.

HEAT, OR CALORIC.

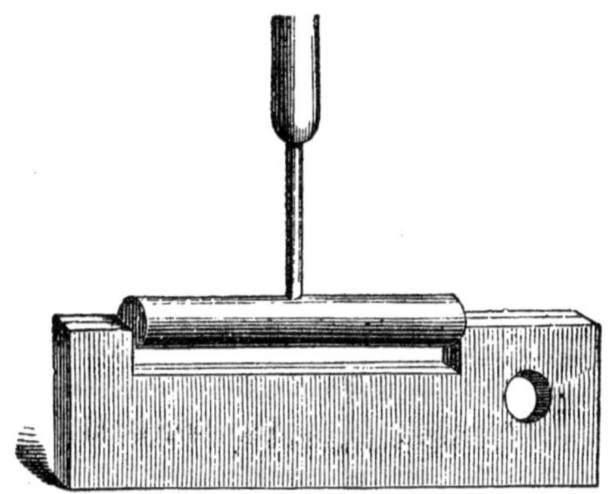

Fig. 18.—A B, cylinder of brass. C D, iron gauge, admitting A B longitudinally, and also in the hole E when cold, but excluding A B when the latter is heated and expanded.

The chief agent in causing the repulsion or separation of the particles of bodies from each other is heat, or more correctly *caloric*, by which is understood the unknown *cause* of the effect called heat. Philosophers are not agreed upon the nature of this wonderful agent. It pervades all nature, is the cause of nearly all the changes that take place, whether in organic or inorganic matter, and has great influence in the meteorological phenomena which we observe in the atmosphere that surrounds our planet. It appears to be intimately connected with light, electricity, and magnetism, subjects which the genius of Faraday and others is investigating, and by their discoveries bringing us nearer to the knowledge of the real nature of these most wonderful forces.

Caloric, then, exists in all bodies, and has a constant tendency to equalize itself, as far at least as its outward manifestation, called temperature, is concerned; for if a *hot* body be brought near colder ones it will give up heat to them, until by its loss and their gain they all become of the same temperature; and this proceeds more or less rapidly according as the original difference of temperature was greater or less. Some other circumstances also influence this equalization. The converse will take place on introducing a cold body among warmer ones, when heat will be abstracted from all the bodies within reach of its influence, until it has absorbed sufficient caloric to bring its own temperature to an equality with theirs. This is the true explanation of the apparent production of *cold.* When, for instance, an iceberg comes across a ship's course, it appears to *give out* cold, whereas, it has abstracted the heat from the air and sea in its neighborhood, and they in turn act upon the ship and every thing in it, until one common temperature is produced in all the neighboring bodies.

It does not follow that the bodies thus equalized in temperature contain equal quantities of caloric; far from it. Each body requires a particular quantity of caloric to raise its temperature through a certain number of degrees; and such quantity is called its *specific* caloric. A pound of water, for instance, will take just twice as much caloric as a pound of olive oil to raise its temperature through the same number of degrees: the *specific* caloric of water is, therefore, double that of oil. Mix any quantity of oil at 60° of temperature with an equal weight of water at 90°, and you will find the temperature of the mixture to be nearly 80°, instead of only 74° or 75°, showing that while the water has lost only 10° of caloric, the mixture has risen 20°. If the oil be at 90°, and the water at 60°, the resulting temperature will be only 70°, or thereabouts, instead of 75°, the mean: thus, here the hot oil has lost 20°, while the mixture has risen only 10°; the water, then, contains at the same temperature *twice* as much caloric as the oil; its specific caloric is *double* that of the oil. This mean temperature does result when equal weights of the *same* body at different temperatures are mixed together.

The sensations called heat and cold are by no means accurate measures of the real temperature of any substances, for many causes influence these sensations, some belonging to the substances themselves, others to the state of our organs at the time. Every one has remarked that metals in a warm room feel warmer, and in a cold room colder, than wooden articles, and these again than woollen or cotton articles of dress or furniture: this arises from metals being what is termed better *conductors* of heat than wood, and this better than wool, &c.; that is, they give out or absorb caloric more rapidly than these last. Some philosophers, wishing to ascertain how much heat the human body could endure, had a room heated with stoves, every crevice being carefully stopped, until the temperature rose so high that a beefsteak placed on the table was sufficiently cooked to be eaten. They were dressed in flannel, and could with impunity touch the carpets, curtains, &c., in the room; but the iron handles, fire-irons, and all metallic substances, burnt their fingers; and one who wore silver spectacles was obliged to remove them to save his nose. The fallacy of our sensations may be easily shown by taking two basins, placing in one some water at 100°, in another some water at as low a temperature as can easily be procured; hold the right hand in one, the left in the other, for a few minutes, and then mix them, and place both hands in the mixture; it will feel quite *cold* to the hand that had been in the hotter water, and *hot* to the other.

In order to arrive at a correct estimate of the temperature of bodies, instruments are made use of, called thermometers, or measurers of heat, which show increase or diminution of temperature by the rising or falling of a column of some fluid in a tube of glass, one end of which is expanded into a bulb, and the other hermetically sealed. This effect is produced by the expansion or swelling of the fluid as caloric is added to, and its contraction when caloric is abstracted from it. Colored spirits of wine, or quicksilver, are the most usual thermometric fluids, and the tube containing them is fixed to a wooden or metallic frame, on which certain divisions are marked, called degrees.

That in general use in England is called Fahrenheit's, from the name of the person who first introduced that particular scale. In this thermometer, the point at which the mercury in the tube stands when plunged into melting ice is marked 32°, and the distance between that point, and the point to which the mercury rises in boiling water, is divided into 180 equal parts, called degrees; so that water is said to boil at 212° = 180° + 32°. There are two other scales of temperature used in different parts of the world, but it is not worth while to notice them here.

Not only do different bodies at the same degree of temperature contain very different quantities of caloric, but this also is the case with the same body in different forms. Ice, water, and steam, are three forms of the same body, but ice at 32° contains much less caloric than water at the same temperature, and water at 212° contains much less caloric than steam (or water in a state of vapor) at that temperature.

Place in a jar any given quantity of snow, or small pieces of ice, at 32°, and in another the same weight of water at 32°, pour on each an equal weight of water at 172°, and you will find that in the first case the ice will be melted, but the temperature will remain at 32° or thereabouts, while the temperature of the water in the other vessel will have risen to 100° or thereabouts, being as near as possible the half of the excess of the temperature of the hot water, 140° over that of the cold, namely 70° added to 32°, the original temperature. Now, what has become of the heat which was added to the ice, and is apparently lost?—it is *absorbed* by the ice in its passage to the fluid state: so that water may be said to be a compound of ice and caloric.

Again, take ten ounces of water at about 50°, and add one ounce of water at 212°, and the temperature of the mixture will be about 66°; then condense some steam at 212° into another ten ounces of water until it has become eleven ounces, and you will

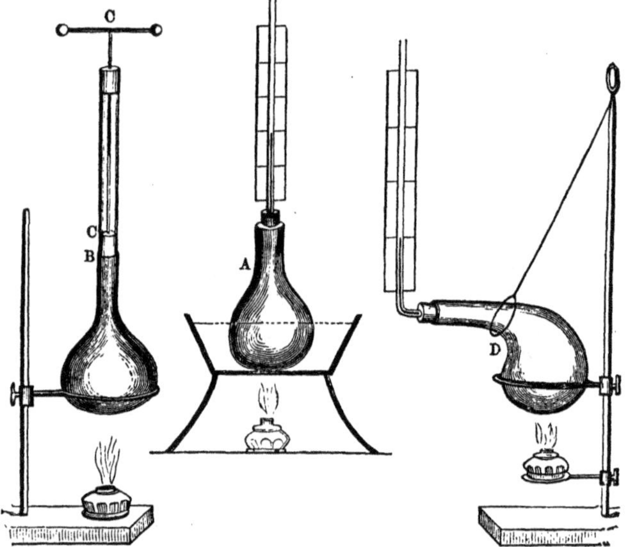

Fig. 19.—Expansion of liquids is shown at A by the colored water rising in the tube from the flask, which is quite full of liquid, and heated by boiling water. B. The expansion of the water heated by the spirit-lamp is shown by the rising of the piston and rod C C. D represents a retort filled up like A to show the expansion of a liquid by heat.

find the temperature will be nearly 212°. Why does the ounce of steam at 212° raise the temperature of the water so much higher than the ounce of water at the same temperature? Obviously, because it contains hidden in its substance a vast quantity of caloric, not to be detected by the thermometer; in fact, that steam is a compound of *water* and caloric, as water is a compound of *ice* and caloric; and this caloric which exists, more or less, in all bodies without producing any obvious effect, is called *latent* caloric, from the Latin verb *lateo*, to lie hidden. The quantity of caloric thus absorbed as it were by various bodies differs for each body, and for the same body in different forms, as mentioned above.

EXPANSION.

As a general rule, all bodies, whether solid, liquid, or gaseous, are expanded by caloric. This may be shown by experiments in each form of matter.

Have a small iron rod made, which when cold just passes through a hole in a plate of metal; heat it, and it will no longer pass; after a time the rod will return to its former temperature, and then will go through the hole as before. The rod increases in length as well as width; if you have a gauge divided into $\frac{1}{100}$ of an inch, and place the rod in it when cold, noting its position, on heating, it will extend to a greater length in the gauge, returning to its former place when cool. (See Fig. 18, p. 457.)

The effect of caloric in causing fluids to expand is actually employed as a measure of quantity in the thermometer, the rise of the fluid in the tube when heated depending on the increased bulk of the fluid occasioned by the addition of caloric. The same fact is to be noticed every day when the cook fills the kettle and places it on the fire. As the water becomes warmer it expands, that is, takes up more room than it did before, and the water escapes by slow degrees, increasing as the heat increases, up to the point of boiling, when a sudden commotion takes place from a condensation of a portion of the water into steam.

But it is in the form of vapor or gas (which, by-the-by, is not the same thing*) that the expansive force of caloric is most obvious. The gigantic powers of the steam-engine depend entirely on the tendency of vapor to expand on the addition of caloric; and this force of expansion appears to have no limit; boilers made of iron plates an inch or even more in thickness, and the buildings or ships containing them, having

---

* It may be well to state here, that by *vapor* is generally understood the aerial form of a substance usually existing in a solid or fluid form at ordinary temperatures; as the vapor of iodine, a solid; of mercury, water, spirits, and other fluids; while the term *gas* is applied to those bodies usually known in the aerial state; thus, oxygen, nitrogen, carbonic acid, hydrogen &c. &c., are called gases. It is, however, but an arbitrary distinction: for many of these gases have, by the combined influence of cold and powerful pressure, been converted into fluids, and even solids,—carbonic acid gas, for instance!

been torn to pieces and scattered in all directions by the expansive power of steam. Take a bladder, and fill it about half full of air, and tie the neck securely; upon holding it to the fire it will swell out, and become quite tense from the expansion of the contained air.

The principal source of caloric is the sun, whose beams, diffused through all nature by the refractive property of the atmosphere, are the source of vitality both to vegetables and animals, and, when concentrated by a large convex lens, produce the most intense heat, sufficient to light a piece of diamond and melt platinum. Caloric is also produced or evolved by combustion, by friction, percussion, chemical combination, electricity, and galvanism.

The evolution of heat by friction may be witnessed daily in a thousand instances. Lucifer matches are lighted by rubbing the highly inflammable substances with which they are tipped against a piece of sandpaper. Nearly all savage people procure fire by rubbing a piece of hard wood violently against a softer piece. The axle-trees of steam-engines, and even of carriages, have been known to be so heated by friction as to endanger burning the carriage; and it is very usual to be

Fig. 20.—C. The steel. B. The flint. E. The tinder. D. The matches of the old-fashioned tinder-box, A.

obliged to pour a quantity of cold water on the iron axle of the carriages of an express train after an hour of constant and rapid work. If you merely rub the blade of a knife rapidly on a piece of wood, it will become hot enough to burn your hand.

Percussion is merely a more energetic kind of friction, and is often resorted to by the blacksmith to light his furnace. He places a nail or other piece of soft iron on his anvil, and beats it rapidly with the hammer, when it becomes actually red hot. The production of sparks by striking flint against steel, or two pieces of flint one against the other, is a familiar instance of heat produced by percussion.

One of the most powerful means of producing heat is the process of combustion.

Combustion, as the word imports, is the *burning together* of two or more substances, a chemical union of oxygen generally with carbon and hydrogen in some shape or other. In our ordinary fires we burn coal, a hydro-carbon as it is called; and the gas which is now so universally used for the purpose of illumination is a compound of the same bodies; so wax, tallow, oil of various kinds, both of animal and vegetable origin, are all hydro-carbons.

On the application of a sufficient heat, and a free access of atmospheric air, or of some other gas containing oxygen in a certain state of combination, these bodies take fire, and continue to burn either with flame, or a red or even white heat without flame, until they are consumed; that is, until they have entered into new combinations with the oxygen, and are converted into carbonic acid and water, the carbon forming the first product, the hydrogen the other.

EXPERIMENTS PRODUCING HEAT AND COLD.

Water is presented to us by nature in three forms,—viz., in the conditions of ice, water, and steam; and many beautiful experiments can be made with it in either of these states.

CRYSTALS OF SNOW.

Very few persons have any idea of the lovely forms they tread under foot when walking over fresh-fallen snow, or remember that frozen water is capable of assuming the three states of snow, hail, and ordinary ice.

The atmosphere always contains a considerable quantity of aqueous vapor, or invisible steam, which collects in the form of clouds, and in cold weather, in extra-tropical latitudes, descends in the form of snow, and covers the surface of the earth with a mantle of virgin white.

Fig. 21.—Snow crystals.

Snow has not only been seen in Europe, but has even visited China; and some years ago, a correspondent at Canton, writing to a friend, says, "The elders of our European society are, at this moment, in the ecstasy of revived associations, pelting each other with snow-balls from the house-tops with all their might."

WATER DOES NOT CONTRACT WHEN REDUCED TO THE FREEZING-POINT.

It is well known that solids usually expand by heat and contract by cold. This is proved by fitting a cold bar of metal into a gauge, and then heating it, when the bar will no longer enter the same space, and has therefore expanded.

Liquids, such as alcohol and mercury, follow the same law, as shown in the useful instrument called the thermometer; but water is a curious exception, and, after falling to a temperature of 40° F., begins to expand till it reaches a temperature of 32°, when it floats upon the surface of the warmer water, and thus protects the lower strata, containing the living insects, plants, and fish, from the dangerous action of intense cold. The fact itself is proved by taking a long glass and nearly filling it with water. If a thermometer is placed at the bottom, the temperature may be, say 40°; whilst if a lump or two of ice be placed on the top, it floats and partly melts, reducing the temperature of the water to 32° Fahr. Now, if the water contracted as it became colder, the particles would become more condensed or heavier, and hence they would sink to the bottom, and, being succeeded by fresh quantities of warmer water, the whole volume would sink to the freezing-point, or 32° Fahr.; whereas they expand, become lighter, and swim on the surface of the warmer part of the fluid, like oil upon water.

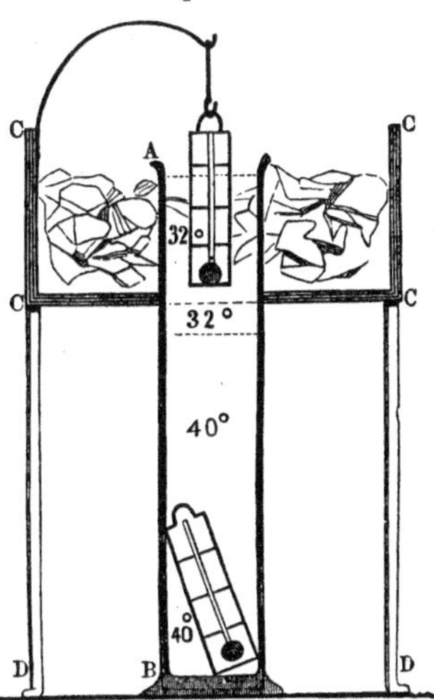

Fig. 22.—A. Top of glass of water at a temperature of 32°, with lumps of ice floating. B. Bottom of water, and temperature at 40°. C C C C. Box, on legs, D D, containing a freezing-mixture.

FUSIBLE METAL EXPANDS UP TO A CERTAIN TEMPERATURE, AND CONTRACTS IF THE HEAT IS INCREASED.

Rose's fusible metal is made by melting one part of lead and mixing with it one part of tin and two parts of bismuth. A bar of this alloy expands till it attains a temperature of 111° Fahrenheit; it then rapidly contracts by the addition of heat, and at 156° attains its greatest density or contraction. After passing this temperature, the metal again expands, and melts at 201°, being eleven degrees below the boiling point of water. For that reason certain persons, of course wags, have taken the trouble to make spoons of it, and one may easily imagine the surprise of any grave person quietly stirring his or her tea, to see the spoon gradually disappear from their vision and sink in the liquid state to the bottom of the cup.

HOW TO EXAMINE THE VARIED CRYSTALLINE FORMS OF SNOW.

By collecting some snow on a black hat or a piece of black velvet and examining it by means of a magnifying glass, it is distinctly seen that they are not mere shapeless flakes, but possess crystalline forms of extreme beauty and of very great variety. In the Polar regions snow assumes the most beautiful and varied forms. Scoresby has figured ninety-six varieties, distributed into three classes: viz.: *Lamellar*, or disposed in thin plates; *Spicular*, or dart-like, or sharp-pointed; and *Pyramidal* crystals. The snow crystals constantly vary, like the pictures of a kaleidoscope, and sometimes resemble parallel fillets, leaves, and spines with rosette terminations, as in Fig. 21, p. 464.

TO MAKE ICE IN SUMMER, AND LOWER THE TEMPERATURE OF WATER BY THE SUDDEN LIQUEFACTION OF A SOLID.

1st. Dissolve powdered nitre rapidly in water, when the temperature will fall from 50° to 35°. This fact is well known to experienced officers in hot climates, who thoroughly appreciate the value of a cartridge shaken gently over the neck of a bottle of wine standing in a pail of water. The cartridge contains nitre, which liquefies rapidly and cools the wine.

2d. Two hundred and seven parts of lead, 118 of tin, and 284 of bismuth melted together and granulated (*i.e.* poured whilst liquid into water) will produce a temperature of 16° below the freezing-point of water, if added rapidly to 1617 parts of quicksilver.

3d. Four ounces of nitrate of ammonia, four ounces of carbonate of soda, dissolved in four ounces of water, will freeze water contained in a convenient thin metallic vessel surrounded with it.

HEAT PRODUCED BY THE SOLIDIFICATION OF A LIQUID.

Take some blue vitriol and heat it to redness in a crucible; when cold, place it in a well-stoppered bottle for use. If a little be put on a plate and sprinkled with cold water, steam issues in considerable quantity; and if a slice of phosphorus is placed on the surface of the blue vitriol, it will take fire in consequence of the latent heat set free by the chemical union of the water with the dry sulphate of copper or blue vitriol, when the water is in effect solidified. Ships laden with lime have taken fire from the leakage of the water, which combine- with the lime and produces a great heat.

HEAT PRODUCED BY THE CONDENSATION OF WATER.

A pint of water mixed with one pint of oil of vitriol generates a large amount of heat, and when cold does not measure two pints, showing that condensation has taken place.

DIFFERENCE BETWEEN LATENT AND SENSIBLE HEAT.

If a nail is made red hot, it glows with the ignition, and throws off heat, which is apparent to the senses; but if a cold horseshoe-nail is examined, there is no direct evidence of the presence of heat; when, however, the same *cold* nail is rapidly hammered on an anvil, enough heat is obtained to set fire to a piece of phosphorus. The heat thus squeezed out by compression is called latent heat.

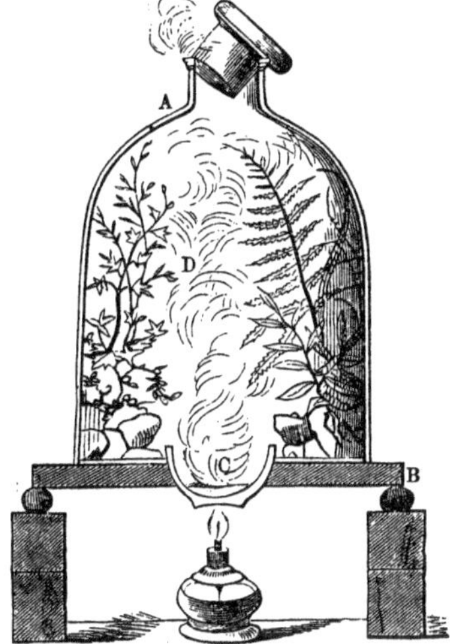

Fig. 23.—Circular wooden stand, B, with sprigs of holly, &c., inserted.
A. The gas-jar, with stopper left sufficiently open to allow the benzoic acid vapor to escape a little.
C. The evaporating-dish, containing the benzoic acid, and heated by the spirit-lamp.
D. The sprigs of holly, rock-work, shells, &c.

TO IMITATE HOAR-FROST.

Hoar-frost is caused by the freezing of the dew deposited on the branches and twigs of trees and bushes, and may be perfectly imitated by arranging some sprigs of holly or other plants on a wooden stand, in the centre of which is fitted a small evaporating-dish containing some benzoic acid. On the application of heat, the acid is sublimed, and may be collected in a gas-jar placed over the stand and bits of holly: and, as the vapor cools, a beautiful deposit of the crystals of benzoic acid on the miniature trees takes place. This experiment admits of a very tasteful arrangement, and after completion will last a long time, if protected by a glass shade.

THE BOILING OF ONE LIQUID MAY FREEZE ANOTHER.

To show that the heat abstracted by the boiling of one liquid will freeze another, fill a tall narrow glass about half full of cold water, (the colder the better,) and place in it a thin glass tube containing some ether. Put them under the receiver of an air-pump. As you exhaust the air, the ether will begin to boil, until at length, by continuing the exhaustion, the water immediately surrounding the tube of ether will freeze, and a tolerably large piece of ice may thus be obtained.

Ether evaporates so rapidly even under the pressure of the atmosphere, that a small animal, such as a mouse, may be actually frozen to death by constantly dropping ether upon it. If poured on the hand, it produces a degree of cold that soon becomes, to say the least, unpleasant.

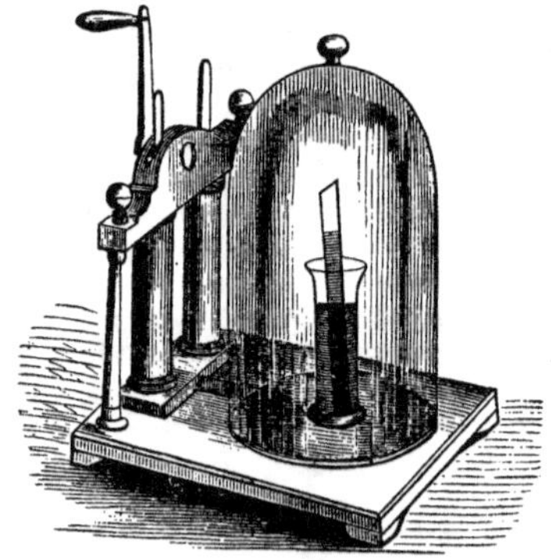

Fig. 24.

EXPERIMENT.

Place a flat saucer, containing about a pound of oil of vitriol, under the receiver of the air-pump, and set in it a watch-glass containing a little water, supported on a stand with *glass* legs. Exhaust the receiver, when the water will evaporate, but without boiling, and the vapor being absorbed as it forms by the oil of vitriol, the vacuum is preserved, and the evaporation continues, until the vapor has abstracted so much caloric from the remainder of the water that it is all at once converted into ice.

In most elementary works on chemistry may be found a long table of freezing-mixtures, as they are called, some with and others without ice or snow. I have selected a few from each division.

FREEZING-MIXTURES WITH ICE OR SNOW.

{ Snow or powdered ice	2	parts.
{ Powdered common salt	1	"
{ Snow	5	"
{ Powdered common salt	2	"
{ Powdered sal ammoniac	1	"
{ Snow	3	"
{ Dilute sulphuric acid	2	"
{ Snow	2	"
{ Crystallized muriate of lime	3	

WITHOUT SNOW OR ICE.

{ Sulphate of soda	3	parts.
{ Dilute nitric acid	2	"
{ Nitrate of ammonia	1	"
{ Water	1	"
{ Phosphate of soda	2	"
{ Dilute nitric acid	1	"
{ Sulphate of soda	2	"
{ Muriatic acid	1	"

The effects of most of these mixtures may be considerably increased by previously cooling the ingredients *separately* in other freezing-mixtures.

CRYSTALLIZATION.

THE ancients were unacquainted with the nature of crystals, and very far from having any just idea of the phenomena of crystallization; for Pliny, who flourished in the first century of the Christian era, speaks of the rock-crystal as a piece of ice frozen to the point of acquiring a permanent consistency and durability; when, in fact, the rock crystal is composed of a mineral called silica, which crystallizes in six-sided prisms, terminating with six-sided pyramids.

The phenomena of crystallization, so replete with beauties,

and so marvellous in their results, often take place within the reach of our observation, without, however, attracting it, from our ignorance of the circumstance. The substance which in cold and dry winter nights covers the panes of glass, exhibiting various fantastic and elegant ramifications, is the human breath crystallized. The pellucid and transparent coating which in the depth of winter covers and so elegantly decks the branches of trees and leaves of evergreens is no more than crystallized water. The snow which falls and accumulates before our eyes, is a congeries or mass of an immense number of separate and transparent crystals of ice.

ALUM BASKETS.

Fig. 25.

A common willow or wire basket may be covered with beautiful crystals, by immersing it in a solution of alum prepared for the purpose. The water used for the solution must be twice the quantity required to cover the basket, and sufficient alum put in to make a saturated solution, which you must filter through a piece of brown paper into a saucepan or pipkin. But if you wish your basket to be colored, the dye must be added to the solution before it is filtered. To produce *crimson* crystals, it is necessary to use an infusion of madder and cochineal; *yellow*, muriate of iron or turmeric; *black*, Japan ink thickened with gum; *blue*, a solution of indigo in sulphuric acid; *pale blue*, equal portions of alum and blue vitriol; and to produce *green*, you have only to add to these last ingredients a few drops of muriate of iron. Of course, all these colors are more or less deep, according to the quantity of coloring-matter employed.

The solution being filtered, boil it gently until half the quantity has been evaporated, then put it into a jar, or any other vessel in which the basket may be immersed, and remove it with its contents to a dry place, where it may cool without being disturbed.

It is to be observed that, if you make use of a wire basket, the wire must be filed, or covered all over with worsted, as the surface of whatever is incrusted must be equally rough.

STAR-LIKE CRYSTALS.

Pour three ounces of diluted nitric acid into a glass vessel, and add to it gradually two ounces of bismuth broken by a hammer into small pieces. The metal will be attacked with great energy, and nitrate of bismuth will be formed. Crystallize the solution by a gentle heat, and preserve the crystals, which possess great beauty, under a glass.

BEAUTIFUL GROUPS OF CRYSTALS.

Dissolve in seven different tumblers, each containing warm water, half-ounces of the sulphates of iron, copper, zinc, soda, alumina, magnesia, and potash. Pour them all, when completely dissolved, into a large evaporating-dish of Wedgwood ware, and stir the whole with a glass rod; set the dish in a warm place, where it cannot be affected by the dust, and where it may not be agitated. When the necessary evaporation has taken place, the whole will shoot out into crystals. These will be interspersed in small groups and single crystals among each other. Their color and peculiar form of crystallization will distinguish each crystal separately, and the whole together, remaining in the respective places where they were deposited, will display a very curious and beautiful appearance. Preserve it carefully from dust.

CRYSTALS OF ALUM.

Dissolve a pound and a half of alum in a quart of boiling water, and suspend in it a piece of coke; set it aside to cool, and a beautiful crystallization, resembling a mineralogical specimen, will be obtained.

METALLIC CRYSTALLIZATION.

Melt a ladleful of bismuth, and let it cool gradually till a thin crust has formed on its surface; then, by means of a pointed iron, make two small apertures through the crust; quickly pour out by one of the openings the fluid portion, as carefully and with as little motion of the mass as possible, whilst the air enters at the other. On removing the upper crust by means of a chisel, when the vessel has become cold, a cup-shaped concavity will appear, studded with very brilliant crystals, more or less regular, according to the quantity of bismuth employed, the tranquillity and slowness with which it cooled, and the dexterity with which the fluid portion, at the moment it began to harden, was decanted from the crystallized part The same effect may be produced by fusing the substance in a small crucible which has a hole at its bottom, lightly closed by an iron rod or stopper, which is to be drawn out when the mass begins to congeal: by this means the superior portion, which is fluid, is made to run off, and a cake studded over with crystals is obtained.

CRYSTALS OF BLUE VITRIOL.

Boil a few copper filings in concentrated sulphuric acid, to which a small portion of nitric acid has been added, and, when the copper is dissolved, dilute the mixture with a little water, and then leave it where it can cool gradually. If the mixture be then suffered to remain a few hours undisturbed, beautiful crystals of blue vitriol will be found at the bottom of the vessel, as hard as some minerals.

CRYSTALLIZATION ON INSECTS, FLOWERS, MOSSES, ETC.

The application of aluminous crystallization to objects of natural history and botany has opened a wide field of amusement in a subject heretofore possessing little variety, inasmuch as baskets have been nearly the only articles subjected to the process of crystallization.

Put eighteen ounces of alum into a quart of water, (keeping the same proportions for a greater or less quantity,) and dissolve it by simmering it gently in a close tinned vessel over a moderate fire, stirring it frequently with a wooden spoon.

When the solution is completed, it must be poured into a deep glazed jar, and, as it cools, the subjects intended to be crystallized should be suspended in it by a piece of thread or twine, from a stick laid across the mouth of the jar,—where they must be suffered to remain for twenty-four hours. When taken out of the solution, they are to be hung up in a shady, cool situation, till perfectly dry. Care must be taken that the solution is neither too hot nor quite cold, as in the one case the crystals will be very small, and in the other much too large.

The insects adapted for crystallization are spiders, beetles, and grasshoppers; and among the vegetable productions the common moss-rose, bunches of hops, ears of corn, the daisy, hyacinth, pink, furze blossoms, lichens, and mosses are some of the most suitable subjects; the nests of small birds, with their eggs, particularly if fastened on the branch of a tree, are exceedingly interesting. It is necessary to observe that much attention must be paid to the deposition of the alum, to see that too great a quantity does not settle upon some parts and too little upon others.

OXY-CHLORIDE OF LEAD.

Melt in the bowl of a tobacco-pipe, or in a small crucible, a mixture of an ounce of litharge of lead, and a drachm of pulverized muriate of ammonia: when well incorporated by exposure to a red heat, pour it into a metallic cup, and allow it to cool: the result will be oxy-chloride of lead of a bright yellow color, which, when broken, will present a most beautiful crystalline appearance.

CRYSTALS OF GLAUBER SALTS.

On a solution of common soda pour, by small quantities at a time, diluted sulphuric acid, until the effervescence ceases; by gently evaporating the solution in a saucer near a fire, crystals of sulphate of soda (Glauber salts) will be obtained.

COMMON SALT.

Take some muriatic acid, and mix it with thrice its bulk of water, adding thereto as much soda as it will dissolve; by slowly evaporating the solution before the fire, muriate of soda (common table-salt) will be obtained.

TO MAKE LARGE CRYSTALS.

The salt to be crystallized is to be dissolved in water, and evaporated to such a consistency that it shall crystallize on cooling. Set it by, and when quite cold pour the liquid part from the mass of crystals at the bottom, and put it into a flat-bottomed vessel. Solitary crystals will form at some distance from each other, and gradually increase in size. Pick out the most regular, put them into another flat-bottomed vessel, a little apart from each other, and pour over them a quantity of fresh solution of the salt evaporated, till it crystallizes on cooling. Alter the position of every crystal once at least every day, with a glass rod, that all the faces may be alternately exposed to the action of the liquid; for the face on which the crystal rests never receives any increase. By this process the crystals will gradually augment in size. When they have acquired such a magnitude that their forms can easily be distinguished, the most regular are to be chosen, or those which have the exact shape which you wish to obtain. Each of them should be put separately into a vessel filled with a portion of the same liquid, and turned by the glass rod several times a day, and by this treatment you may obtain them almost of any size desired. Whenever it is observed that the angles and edges of the crystals become blunted, the liquid must immediately be poured off, and fresh liquid put in its place; otherwise the crystals will be infallibly destroyed.

LEAD TREE.

Dissolve two drachms of acetate of lead in a quart of water, and set it aside for a day or two, decant the clear solution into a large phial, and in the centre suspend a piece of zinc, by means of a silk thread fixed to the cork. If the whole be left undisturbed, the lead will arrange itself around the zinc in beautiful metallic plates resembling a shrub.

ARBOR DIANÆ, OR SILVER TREE.

Let six drachms of a saturated solution of pure silver in nitric acid, and four drachms of a similar solution of mercury in the same acid, be diluted with five ounces of distilled water, and poured into a small decanter or glass phial; then compose an amalgam, by mixing one part of finely-divided silver with seven parts of mercury, and place a small lump of it at the bottom of the bottle, which must be kept quite still. In a short time the surface of the amalgam will be covered with minute filaments of silver, and after standing about forty-eight hours, the solution will deposit all its silver, in the form of brilliant, arborescent crystals, springing like a glittering shrub from the bottom of the vessel.

Fig. 26.—Engraver's globe, with arborescent precipitate of silver.

THE CHEMISTRY OF WATER.

HOW TO TEST THE PURITY OF WATER.

Ordinary spring-water contains carbonic acid gas, which imparts an agreeable freshness and makes it agreeable to the taste. It is easily detected by adding a solution of lime-water, when the carbonic acid unites with the lime and forms carbonate of lime, which is precipitated as a white substance and is in fact common chalk.

Spring-water also contains generally sulphuric acid and

chlorine in combination with lime, magnesia, soda, or potash; these salts, with some organic matter, oxide of iron, silica, and alumina, usually constitute the residue left after evaporating a gallon of water to dryness, and hence the formation of what is called deposit or incrustation in boilers, or *fur* in tea-kettles.

To half a pint of water add a solution of nitrate of silver with some pure nitric acid. Chloride of silver is thrown down, which is a white precipitate that gradually blackens when exposed to light, and is evidence of the presence of chlorides such as common salt.

To another portion add some solution of nitrate of baryta with a little more nitric acid; a white precipitate of sulphate of baryta is formed, and shows the presence of sulphuric acid, most likely in combination with the lime, forming sulphate of lime or gypsum.

To a third portion add some oxalate of ammonia, and white oxalate of lime will be produced, if the water contains lime.

To detect the oxide of iron in water, a pint should be evaporated to dryness in a porcelain dish; to the residue some hydrochloric acid should be carefully added in very small quantity, and the excess gently evaporated away; then, on the addition of a little water and a solution of ferrocyanide of potassium, a splendid blue is produced, called Prussian blue, if oxide of iron be present.

The detection of the other substances in the water will require more practical skill than can be obtained by reading this little work; and the reader is referred to Abel and Bloxam's "Hand-Book of Chemistry."

PURE WATER IS NOT AFFECTED BY THE TESTS.

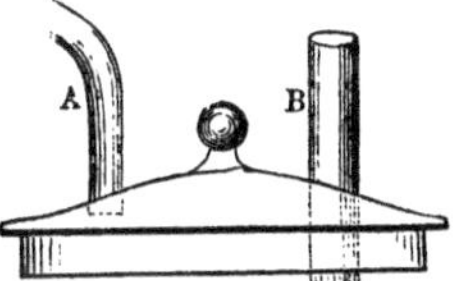

Fig. 27.—The lid to fit into tea-kettle. A is the pipe to which the pewter condensing-pipe will be attached. B is the supply-pipe for putting in fresh water, and, when steam issues from it, more water must be poured into the kettle.

Put some spring-water into an ordinary kettle, the spout of which has been closed by a cork. Get the tinman to make another lid, as shown at Fig. 27, and to fit a piece of pewter pipe into the top of it. Having placed the kettle on the fire, arrange the pipe as shown at Fig. 28, and wind round it a piece of cotton cloth; keep this constantly moist, and as the steam rises it is condensed in the pipe and runs down into a bottle, when it is now called aqua pura, or distilled water. Let the first quantity that distils over be thrown away, as the inside of the pipe is generally dirty.

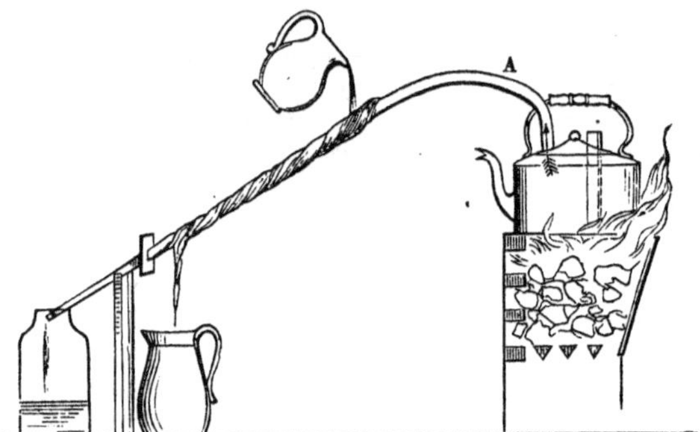

Fig. 28.—The tea-kettle still at work: the kettle is shown in section: the arrow shows the direction of the steam.

TO PROCURE HYDROGEN GAS.

Into a common wine-bottle, provided with a cork and pewter tube, place some granulated zinc or zinc cuttings; fill the bottle about half full with water, and add some oil of vitriol,—when effervescence takes place from the escape of hydrogen gas, which may be collected in gas-jars on the pneumatic trough, the same as oxygen gas, by fitting in the cork and tube.

CARE MUST BE TAKEN IN BURNING HYDROGEN FROM THE GENERATING-BOTTLE.

If it is desired to see the hydrogen burn from the end of the pewter pipe, it should be turned up straight, and before applying flame the first portion of the gas must be allowed to escape, or else the air already in the bottle mixes with the hydrogen and forms an explosive mixture, and, if this is fired, the cork and pewter pipe are blown to the ceiling, whilst the bottle is frequently broken and the acid spilled about. A case occurred where some boys, making hydrogen in their bedroom in an ink-bottle, with a tobacco-pipe stem for a jet, incautiously applied the flame, when the whole exploded, and one of the poor boys lost his eyesight.

FIRE ON WATER.

Take a finger-glass, and, after putting in plenty of granulated zinc, pour on some water and oil of vitriol, when a powerful effervescence takes place, and the liquid boils over the sides of the glass, which should stand in a soup-plate. Flame applied sets fire to the bubbles of escaping hydrogen, that dart over the whole surface and produce a number of slight explosions. This experiment should be performed under a chimney or in the open air, as the acid smoke, or rather steam, is very disagreeable.

Fig. 29.—The jar of hydrogen and the toy in hand.

EXPERIMENTS WITH HYDROGEN.

When a gas-jar is filled with hydrogen, it may be lifted carefully from the pneumatic trough without fear of any gas escaping, and placed on a stand sufficiently high to admit of the hand being inserted into the jar; if one of the squeaking toys be first worked in the air and then in the jar of hydrogen, the effect is very laughable, as the sound becomes so shrill, in consequence of the levity of the gas. A bell sounded in air and afterward in hydrogen is also an amusing experiment.

CURIOUS SOUNDS EMITTED BY BURNING HYDROGEN FROM A JET OVER WHICH GLASS TUBES OF VARIOUS SIZES ARE PLACED.

Take the generating hydrogen bottle, and fit a long jet with a small orifice; if the hydrogen is set on fire, and a tube placed over it at a certain place, the hydrogen flame begins to flicker and emit a sharp sound, which is varied according to the length and diameter of the glass tubes. Sometimes many tubes may be tried before the sound can be obtained.

SYNTHESIS OF HYDROGEN AND OXYGEN, AND FORMATION OF WATER.

If the jet over which hydrogen is burning is held under a cold glass jar, the steam is very soon condensed, and trickles down the sides in drops of water, produced by the combination of the hydrogen with the oxygen of the air, as every nine pounds of water consist of eight of oxygen and one of hydrogen.

EXPERIMENTS WITH OTHER GASES.

NITROUS OXIDE, OR LAUGHING-GAS, AND NITRIC OXIDE GAS.

Take two or three ounces of pure nitrate of ammonia in crystals, and put them into a retort, then apply the heat of a lamp to the retort, and take care that the heat does not exceed 500°. When the crystals begin to melt, nitrous oxide gas will be evolved in considerable quantities. Nitric oxide gas may be produced by pouring nitric acid, diluted with six times its weight of water, on copper filings, or small pieces of tin. The gas is evolved until the acid is saturated with oxide of copper, when the process may be stopped.

To inhale laughing-gas.—Procure an oiled or varnished silk bag, or a bladder furnished with a stop-cock; fill it with pure nitrous oxide, and, after emptying the lungs of common air, take the stop-cock into the mouth, and at the same time hold the nostrils; the sensations produced will be of a highly pleasing nature. A great propensity to laughter, a rapid flow of vivid ideas, and an unusual fitness for muscular exertion, are the ordinary feelings which it generally produces. The sensations produced by breathing this gas are not the same in all persons, but they are always of an agreeable nature, and not followed by any depression of spirits, like those occasioned by fermented liquors. Although no accident has yet happened to any one while inhaling laughing-gas, it is perhaps better to leave such experiments to be performed by experienced persons only. Nitric oxide gas nearly caused the death of Sir H. Davy, who tried to inhale it: the orange-red fumes of nitrous acids formed when it comes in contact with the air almost suffocated him.

COAL GAS.

Fill the bowl of a large tobacco-pipe with pulverized coal, and stop it close with a mixture of pipe-clay and sand; then put it into a clear fire, and in a few minutes carburetted hydrogen gas will issue from the end of the pipe, which may be ignited, and will burn like a taper, affording an example of the production of gaslight.

VIOLET-COLORED VAPOR.

Put three or four grains of iodine into a small test-tube, and seal the other end of it hermetically. If the tube be gently warmed, by holding it over a candle, the iodine will become converted into a beautiful violet-colored gas or vapor, which, when the tube is suffered to cool, condenses again into minute brilliant metallic crystals of a bluish color. This experiment may be repeated with the same tube and iodine for any number of times.

CHLORINE.

The other simple gas called a supporter of combustion is named chlorine, from a Greek word signifying yellowish green.

This gas was formerly called "oxymuriatic acid," being supposed to be a compound of oxygen and muriatic acid gases, until Sir H. Davy, in a series of masterly experiments carried on during the years 1808–11, proved that it contained no oxygen or muriatic acid, and that it was in fact a simple or undecompounded substance, and changed its name to chlorine, which name was, after some discussion, accepted by the scientific world, and is still in use.

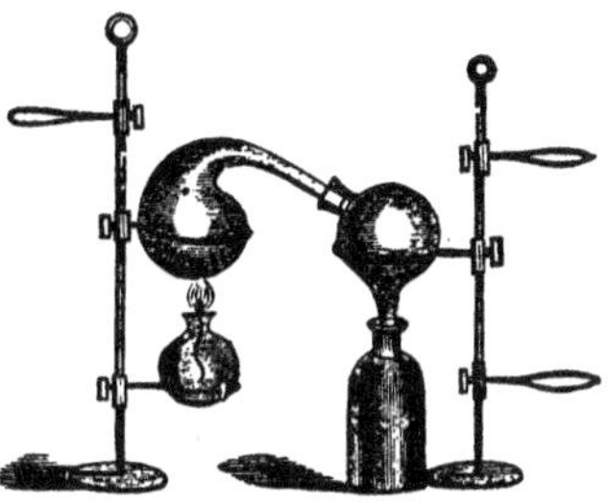

Fig. 30.

This gas may be obtained for experiment by gently heating in a retort a mixture of muriatic or hydrochloric acid, as it is now called, with some black oxide of manganese: the muriatic acid, a compound of chlorine and hydrogen, is decomposed, and so is the oxide of manganese, giving out some of its oxygen, which takes the hydrogen from the muriatic acid to form water, while the chlorine gas, with which the hydrogen had been united, is set at liberty, and may be collected in jars over water.

Chlorine gas is transparent, of a greenish-yellow color, has a peculiar disagreeable taste and smell, and, if breathed even in small quantities, occasions a sensation of suffocation, of tightness in the chest, and violent coughing, attended with great prostration. I have been compelled to retire to bed from having upset a bottle containing some of this gas. It destroys most vegetable colors when moist, and is in fact the agent now universally employed for bleaching-purposes.

It has also the power of combining with and destroying all noxious smells, and is invaluable as a purifier of foul rooms and a destroyer of infection. For these latter purposes it is used in combination with lime, either in substance or solution, under the name of "Chloride of Lime."

Sir W. Burnett has lately discovered that the chloride of zinc answers the same purposes as the chloride of lime, and has the advantage of being itself destitute of smell, and his fluid is frequently substituted for the other.

Chlorine gas is a powerful supporter of combustion, many of the metals taking fire spontaneously when introduced in a fine state of division into the gas.

EXPERIMENTS.

1. Into a jar of chlorine gas introduce a few sheets of copper-leaf, sold under the name of Dutch foil, when it will burn with a dull red light.

2. If some metallic antimony in a state of powder be poured into a jar of this gas, it will take fire as it falls, and burn with a bright white light.

3. A small piece of the metal potassium may be introduced, and will also take fire.

4. A piece of phosphorus will also generally take fire spontaneously when introduced into this gas. In all these cases direct compounds of the substances with chlorine are produced, called chlorides.

5. If a lighted taper be plunged quickly into the gas, it will continue to burn with a dull light, giving off a very large quantity of smoke, being in fact the carbon of the wax taper, with which the chlorine does not unite; while the other constituent of the taper, the hydrogen, forms muriatic acid by union with the chlorine.

6. This substance has the property of destroying most vegetable colors, and is used in large quantities for bleaching calico, linen, and the rags of which paper is made. It is a curious fact that it shows this property only when water is present, for if a piece of colored cloth is introduced dry into a jar of the gas, also dry, no effect will be produced; wet the cloth, and re-introduce it, and in a very short time its color will be discharged.

7. Introduce a quantity of the infusion of the common red cabbage, which is of a beautiful blue color, into a jar of this gas, and it will instantly become nearly as pale as water, retaining a slight tinge of yellow.

EXPERIMENTS WITH CARBON AND OXYGEN.

Carbon forms two gaseous compounds with oxygen: the first, called carbonic oxide, is not difficult to procure, but possesses no interesting properties. It is inflammable.

The other compound, carbonic acid, is transparent, colorless, much heavier than atmospheric air, has an agreeable taste, has the power of irritating the mucous membrane of the nose, (as any one can tell who has drunk soda-water,) without possessing any particular odor, is absorbed by water, does not support respiration, and extinguishes burning bodies.

Carbonic acid gas may be obtained with the greatest facility by pouring some sulphuric acid, diluted with about six parts of water, upon some pieces of marble or limestone in a bottle with a tube attached, when the gas comes over in torrents. It may be collected over water, or allowed to fall into a bottle.

EXPERIMENTS.

1. To show the great comparative weight of this gas, place a lighted taper at the bottom of a tall glass jar, then take a jar full of carbonic acid gas, and pour it as you would pour water into the jar containing the lighted taper; you will soon find the taper will be extinguished as effectually as if you had poured water on it, and the smoke of the taper will float on the surface of the gas in very beautiful wavy forms.

2. Heat a piece of the metal potassium in a metal spoon, (platinum is best,) and, if introduced in a state of ignition into the gas, it will continue burning brilliantly, producing a quantity of dense smoke, which is the carbon from the carbonic acid, the potassium having seized the oxygen and being converted by it into potash.

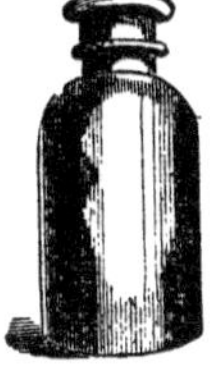

Fig. 31.—Stoppered bottle for holding gas.

3. If a mouse, bird, or other small animal be placed in a jar of this gas, it becomes insensible almost immediately, but if speedily removed it will occasionally recover.

4. Shake up some water with some of this gas in a bottle; the greater part of the gas will be absorbed by the water, which acquires a sparkling appearance and a pleasant sharp taste; with the addition of a little soda, this becomes the well-known beverage called soda-water, so famous for removing the morning headaches caused by "*that salmon*" having disagreed at yesterday's dinner.

CARBONIC ACID GAS.

It is the presence of this gas which renders it so dangerous to descend into deep wells, for by its great weight it collects at the bottom, and instantly suffocates any unfortunate person who incautiously subjects himself to it. Hence, it is prudent always to let down a lighted candle before any one descends into a well or other deep excavation, and if the candle is extinguished, it is necessary to throw down several pails of water, lime-water if possible, and again to try the candle, which must burn freely before it is safe for any one to descend.

It is this same gas, under the name of "choke-damp," which proves so dangerous to miners, particularly after an explosion of "fire-damp;" for it is the principal product of the explosion, and by its weight settles at the bottom of the mine, whence it is by no means an easy matter to dislodge it.

Carbonic acid gas has been condensed into the fluid form by causing it to be disengaged under great pressure; the fluid acid has the appearance of water. When the pressure is removed, as by allowing some of the fluid acid to escape from the vessel in which it has been condensed, it instantly reassumes the gaseous form, and in so doing absorbs so much latent caloric that a portion of the acid is actually solidified, and appears in the shape of *snow*, which may be collected and preserved for a short time. After a lecture by Mr. Addams before the Ashmolean Society of Oxford, a kind of *snow-ball* of carbonic acid was carried for a distance of 500 or 600 yards, and placed in a saucer in a room. It evaporated very rapidly, and left no residue, not even a mark where it had lain. It was too *cold* to be touched by the naked hand without pain.

Carbonic acid and lime are mutually tests for each other. If a jar containing a little lime-water be put into a jar of this gas, it speedily becomes turbid, the gas uniting with the lime, and producing chalk, (the carbonate of lime,) which is insoluble in water.

This gas is produced in large quantities by the respiration of animals, as may be proved by respiring through a tube immersed in lime-water, when the water will be instantly rendered turbid from the formation of chalk.

CARBON AND HYDROGEN.

To the combination of these elements in various proportions, and with the occasional addition of other substances, we are indebted for all, or nearly all, our means of obtaining light and heat. Coal, wood, spirit, oil, and all the varieties of fats, are composed principally of carbon and hydrogen, and may easily be converted into the gas with which our houses and streets are lighted, which is nearly pure carburetted hydrogen.

There are but two definite gaseous compounds of these two elements, the carburetted hydrogen, and bicarburetted or olefiant gas. The first is easily procured by stirring the bottom of stagnant water in a hot summer's day, and collecting the bubbles in a bottle filled with water and inverted over the place where the bubbles rise. This gas burns with a yellowish flame, and when mixed with a certain proportion of air, or oxygen gas, explodes with great violence on the application of a flame. It is the much-dreaded fire-damp generated so profusely in some coal-mines, and causing such fearful destruction to life and property when accidentally inflamed. It is this gas also, in a state of low combustion, which produces the lambent flame frequently seen in the evenings hovering over marshes, and called the "Will-o'-the-wisp." This appearance is still regarded with superstitious horror by the uneducated countryman.

The other compound, the bicarburetted hydrogen, forms by far the principal part of the gas used for illumination; and, in fact, whatever substance is employed for artificial light, whether oil, tallow, wax, &c. &c., it is converted into this gas by heat, and then furnishes the light by its own combustion.

This gas has some very curious properties, and may be obtained nearly pure by mixing in a retort, *very carefully*, one part of spirits of wine and four of sulphuric acid. The heat produced by the mixture being insufficient to decompose the spirit, a lamp must be placed under the retort, when the gas will speedily be disengaged, and will come over in great abundance: it may be collected over water.

This gas is transparent, colorless, will not support combustion, but is itself inflammable, burning with a brilliant white light, and being converted into carbonic acid and water. If mixed with three or four times its bulk of oxygen, or with common atmospheric air in much larger proportions, it explodes with great violence.

This gas is sometimes called "olefiant gas," from the property it possesses of forming an oily substance when mixed with chlorine.

EXPERIMENT.

Into a jar standing over water half-full of this gas, pass an equal quantity of chlorine gas. The gases will speedily unite and form an oily-looking liquid, which may be collected from the sides of the jar as it trickles down. By continually supplying the jar with the two gases as they combine, a considerable quantity of this substance may be collected. Care should be taken that the olefiant gas is rather in excess.

Fig. 32.

The substance produced is insoluble in water, with which it should be washed by shaking them together in a tube, and has a pleasant sweetish taste and aromatic smell, somewhat resembling ether.

COAL GAS.

The gas so universally employed for the purposes of illumination is a mixture of the carburetted and bicarburetted hydrogen, with minute portions of other gases scarcely worth mentioning. It is procured by submitting coals to a red heat in iron retorts, having a tube passing from one end, along which passes all the fluid and gaseous matter separated from the coal,—namely, gas tar, ammoniacal liquor, and various gases, carburetted hydrogen, carbonic acid, sulphuretted hydrogen, sulphurous acid, &c. &c. The tar and ammoniacal liquor remain in the vessel in which the tubes from the retorts terminate, and the gaseous productions are conveyed through water and lime to separate the impurities; the remaining gas, now fit for use, passes into large iron vessels, called gasometers, inverted over water, (like the jars in a pneumatic trough,) whence it is sent through pipes and distributed where required. What remains in the retorts is called coke. It consists principally of charcoal, mixed with the earthy and metallic particles contained in the coal.

EXPERIMENT.

If you possess an iron bottle, fill it with powdered coal, and attach a flexible tube to it, and put it in the fire: as soon as it becomes red hot, large quantities of smoke will escape from the end of the tube, being the gas mixed with all its impurities. By passing it through water (if mixed with lime it will be better) the gas may be collected in jars standing over water, and submitted to experiment. If you do not possess a bottle, take a tobacco-pipe with a large bowl; fill the bowl with small coal, cover it with clay or putty, and when dry put it into the fire, and the gas will soon appear at the other end of the pipe, when it may be lighted, or the gas may be collected over water, as in the former experiment.

This gas is given off spontaneously in some coal-mines, and, as it forms explosive mixtures with atmospheric air, the mines where it abounds could not be worked, except at the greatest risk, until about the beginning of the present century, when Sir H. Davy, while prosecuting some researches on the nature of flame, found that flame would not pass through metallic tubes; and he gradually reduced the length of the tubes, until he found that fine iron-wire gauze formed an effectual barrier against the passage of flame. He then thought that if the light in a lantern were surrounded with this gauze it might safely be used in an inflammable atmosphere where a naked light would instantly cause an explosion. Upon submitting the lamp to experiment, he found that by passing coal gas by degrees into a vessel in which one of his lamps was suspended, the flame first became much larger, and then was extinguished, the cylinder of gauze being filled with a pale flame, and though the gauze sometimes became red-hot it did not ignite the gas outside. As the supply of coal gas was diminished, the wick of the lamp was rekindled, and all went on as at first. A coil of platinum wire was afterward suspended in the lamps, which becomes intensely heated by the burning gas, and gives out sufficient light to enable the miner to see to work. As long as the gauze is perfect, it is impossible for the external air to be kindled by the wick of the lamp; but the miners are so careless that they will often remove the gauze to get a better light, to look for a tool, or some cause equally trivial, and many lives have been lost in consequence of such carelessness.

The effect of fine wire gauze in preventing the passage of flame may be shown by bringing a piece of the gauze gradually over the flame of a spirit-lamp until it nearly touches the wick, when the flame will be nearly extinguished, but the vapor of the spirit passes through, and may be lighted on the upper side of the gauze, which will thus have a flame on either side, though totally unconnected with each other. The flame from a gas-burner will answer as well as the spirit-lamp.

Nearly all the fluids, and solids also, used for procuring artificial light, such as naphtha, various oils, tallow, wax, spermaceti, spirits of wine, ether, &c. &c., are compounds of carbon and hydrogen in different proportions, with the occasional addition of some other elements, especially oxygen and hydrogen, in the proportions to form water: as a general rule, those bodies containing the greatest proportion of carbon give the most light, though not necessarily the most heat.

MISCELLANEOUS EXPERIMENTS.

HEAT.

1. Put some water into a glass or cup, and pour upon it about half the quantity of sulphuric acid; upon stirring them together, the temperature will rise to many degrees above boiling water. In mixing the acid with the water, the greatest care should be taken not to do it too suddenly, as the vessel

may break from the sudden heat, and the acid be spilt on the hands, clothes, &c. The greatest caution is also necessary in using it, as it will attack nearly every organic thing it is dropped on.—If a piece of iron is hammered smartly on an anvil, its latent heat will be evolved in a short time to such a degree that the iron will become almost red hot.—Pour a little clear water into a small glass tumbler, and put one or two pieces of phosphuret of lime into it. In a short time, flashes of fire will dart from the surface of the water, and terminate in ringlets of smoke, ascending in regular succession.

2. Thinly spread some dry nitrate of copper on a piece of tin-foil, three or four inches square, and wrap it up; there will not be any effect produced. Unfold the tin-foil, and sprinkle a very small quantity of water on the nitrate of copper, wrap it up again as quickly as possible, and press down the edges closely. Considerable heat, attended with fumes, will now be evolved; and, if the experiment be dexterously managed, it will ignite. This shows that nitrate of copper has not any effect on tin till in a state of solution.—Fill a saucer with water, and drop a small piece of potassium into it; the instant it touches the water it will burst, with a slight explosion, into a brilliant, violet-colored flame. It will continue burning for a short time on the surface of the water, darting from one side of the vessel to the other with great violence, like a beautiful fire-ball. If the potassium is thrown upon ice, it will likewise instantly take fire.—Pulverize separately one ounce of crystallized muriate of ammonia, an equal quantity of nitrate of potash, and two ounces of sulphate of soda; mix them together in a goblet with four ounces of cold water, and immediately immerse in the mixture a thin glass tube containing cold water; in a short time it will freeze, even in a warm room, or in the midst of summer.

3. Take a very thin glass bulb, half-filled with water, and continue to drop ether so slowly upon it that it may evaporate, and not fall from the surface of the glass; the water inside will quickly be frozen, and this effect will take place sooner if the bulb is held in a current of air.

4. Water expands by cold as well as by heat, and to prove this it is only necessary to expose a phial filled with water, closely corked, in a frosty night; when the water is frozen, the glass will burst.—Put into a wineglass a few teaspoonfuls of a concentrated solution of silicate of potash, and add to it gradually, drop by drop, sulphuric acid. If these two liquids be stirred together with a glass rod, they will become converted into an opaque, white, and almost solid mass.

. Pour a small quantity of water in some muriate of lime.

just sufficient to saturate, not liquefy it; then let some concentrated sulphuric acid fall gradually upon this solution, and a solid compound, called sulphate of lime, will be produced.

PRINCE RUPERT'S DROPS.

Fig. 33.

Glass is an extremely bad conductor of heat, and the reason why tumblers and other vessels made of glass crack when hot water is suddenly poured into them is, that the interior of the glass expands before the heat can penetrate through the particles on the outside, which are consequently then riven asunder. Small glass toys called Prince Rupert's drops, which may be obtained at a glass-blower's, show very clearly the effect of heat on bad conductors. They are made by dropping a small quantity of glass, while almost in a liquid state, into water, by which means a globule with a spiral tail is instantly formed; the outside of the globule cools and solidifies the instant it comes into contact with the water, before the inner part changes, and this, as it gradually hardens, would contract, were it not retained and kept in its form by its adherence to the outer crust. If the tail is broken off, or any other injury done to the globule, it will burst with a slight noise and fall to pieces. In order that glass-ware may be durable, it is annealed; that is to say, it is put into an oven the temperature of which is allowed to decrease gradually.

ATTRACTION AND DECOMPOSITION.

1. Add a little water impregnated with carbonic acid to a wineglass of clear lime-water: these two liquids will combine and form a white substance, which is called carbonate of lime. —Throw a piece of copper into a wineglass, and pour upon it some nitric acid; these two substances will combine, and a solution of clear blue color will be produced. If you plunge it into a piece of iron, (the blade of a knife will answer,) the acid will combine with this new body, and the copper will be precipitated on the blade of the knife in its original state. Should the solution be allowed to remain undisturbed for some days, it will crystallize, and salts of copper will be produced.

2. Pour a little of the infusion of litmus, or of red cabbage, into a wineglass, and add to it a single drop of nitric or sulphuric acid, and it will be instantly changed into a beautiful red color.

3. Take a little of the liquid mentioned in the above experiment. either before or after it has been converted to red, add·

to it a few drops of the solution of potash, or soda, and, upon stirring it up, a fine green color will be produced.

4. Let a drop of nitrate of copper fall into a glass, and then fill it up with water: it will be perfectly colorless; but upon putting a drop of liquid ammonia, which is also without color, into the glass, the liquid will change into a beautiful deep blue.

5. Take some of the blue liquid left by the former experiment, and let a drop or two of nitric acid fall into it, and it will become clear as crystal.

6. A drop of nitrate of copper poured into a glass of water will not produce any change in the color of the fluid; but if a small crystal or a drop of the solution of prussiate of potash be added, the water will become a dark brown.

7. Mix some powdered manganese with a little nitre, and throw the mixture into a red-hot crucible, and a compound will be obtained possessed of the singular property of changing to different colors according to the quantity of water that is added to it. A small quantity gives a green solution, whilst a greater quantity changes it to a beautiful rich purple. The last experiment may be varied by putting equal quantities of this substance into separate glasses, and pouring hot water in the one and a portion of cold water in the other. The hot solution will assume a beautiful green color, and the cold one a deep purple.

8. By pouring lime-water on to some juice of beet-root, a colorless liquid is obtained; but if a white cloth be dipped in the liquid and dried, in a few hours it will become quite red, by the mere contact of the air.

9. Spirits of hartshorn dropped into a solution of copper so weak as to be almost colorless will produce an intense blue, which disappears by adding an acid.

10. *To make Soap.*—Pour a little water into a phial containing about an ounce of olive oil; shake the phial, and if the contents are examined it will be found that no union has taken place; but if some solution of caustic potash is added, and the phial then shaken, an intimate combination of the materials occurs, and soap is produced.

11. Pour a little nitro-muriatic acid upon a small piece of gold, or gold-leaf, and in a short time it will be completely dissolved, and the solution will assume a beautiful yellow color.

12. Pour a small quantity of nitric acid upon a little bit of pure silver, or silver-leaf, and it will dissolve in a few minutes.

13. Pour a little sulphuric acid, diluted with about four times its bulk of water, upon a few iron-filings; a strong effervescence, caused by the escape of hydrogen gas, will take place, and in a little time the filings will disappear.

14. Pour some diluted nitric acid on a piece of copper, and in a little while the copper will be dissolved, and the solution will become of a beautiful blue tint.

15. Into a solution of nitrate of silver immerse a small bar of polished copper: on withdrawing the bar, it will be found to be covered with a fine coating of metallic silver.

16. A small bar of polished iron immersed in like manner in a solution of nitrate of copper will receive a coating of metallic copper.

17. A piece of silver immersed in the above solution will remain unchanged; but if immersed in contact with a piece of iron, both, when withdrawn, will be found to be covered with a coating of metallic copper.

18. Pour half an ounce of diluted nitro-muriate of gold into an ale-glass, and put in it a piece of very smooth charcoal. Expose the glass to the rays of the sun, in a warm place; and in a short time the charcoal will be covered over with a beautiful golden coat. Take it out with a pair of pincers, and enclose it in a glass for show.

TO MELT A COIN IN A NUT-SHELL.

Mix three parts of dried nitre, one of sulphur, and one of fine dry sawdust, and pound them well in a mortar. Press a portion of this powder into a walnut-shell, and also enclose within the shell a thin piece of silver or copper rolled up; then fill the shell with some more powder, press it down closely, and set fire to it; the piece of metal will soon be melted, whilst the nut-shell is merely blackened.

TO RENDER THE SURFACE OF WATER PHOSPHORESCENT.

Wet a lump of fine loaf sugar with phosphorized ether, and throw it into a basin of water; the surface of the water will become luminous, and show beautifully in the dark; by gently blowing upon it, phosphorescent undulations will be formed, which will illumine the air above the fluid for a considerable space. In winter the water must be rendered blood-warm. If the phosphorized ether be applied to the hands, (which may be done with safety,) it renders them luminous in the dark.

LUMINOUS WRITING IN THE DARK.

Put a small piece of solid phosphorus into a quill, and write with it upon paper; if carried into a dark room, the writing will appear luminous, and have a beautiful effect. Should the phosphorus take fire by the friction, it must be pluuged immediately under the surface of water and extinguished. If any burning phosphorus falls upon the hands, the painful effects of the severe burn are greatly mitigated by plunging them under the surface of water to which a very little solution of ammonia has been added.

SEMBLANCE OF PERPETUAL MOTION.

Into a basin of clean water put a few pieces of camphor; they will commence a peculiar motion, traversing every part of the surface of the water, but may instantly be stopped by dropping into the water the minutest quantity of an oily substance.

ARTIFICIAL PETRIFACTIONS.

Put into a retort a quantity of pounded fluor spar and sand, and pour upon it some sulphuric acid; fluosilicic acid gas will be disengaged, holding silex in solution. The subjects that you wish to resemble petrifactions must next be moistened with water, and placed in a vessel connected with the neck of the retort. The fluosilicic acid gas will be absorbed by the moisture adhering to the substances, and the silex will be precipitated upon them like a sort of hoar-frost, which will have a beautiful appearance, and be tolerably durable.

BEAUTIFUL EXPERIMENT WITH PHOSPHORUS.

Put half a drachm of solid phosphorus into a Florence oil-flask, holding the flask slantingly, that the phosphorus may not break the glass; pour upon it a gill and a half of water, and place the whole over a teakettle-lamp, or any common lamp, filled with spirits of wine; light the wick, which should be about half an inch from the flask, and as soon as the water is boiling hot, streams of fire resembling sky-rockets will burst at intervals from the water; some particles will also adhere to the sides of the glass, and immediately display brilliant rays, and thus continue until the water begins to simmer, when a beautiful imitation of the aurora borealis will commence, and gradually ascend until it collects into a pointed cone at the mouth of the flask; when it has continued for half a minute, blow out the flame of the lamp, and the apex of fire that was

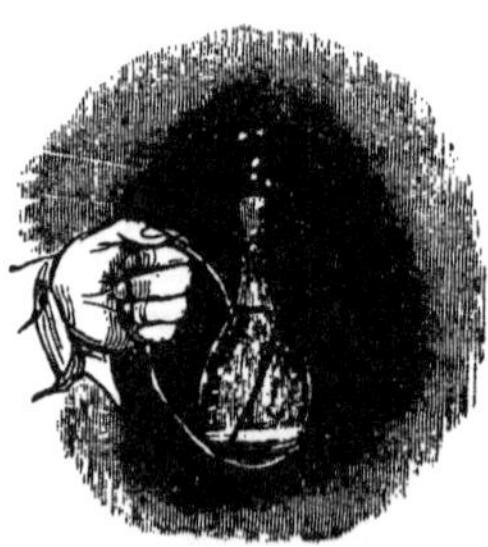

Fig. 34.

formed at the mouth of the flask will rush down, forming beautiful illumined clouds of fire rolling over each other for some time, and when these disappear, a splendid hemisphere of stars will present itself. After waiting a minute or two, light the lamp again, and nearly the same phenomena will be displayed as from the beginning. Let a repetition of lighting and blowing out the lamp be made for three or four times, so that the number of stars may be increased, and after the third or fourth time of blowing out the lamp, the internal surface of the flask will be dry. Many of the stars will shoot with great splendor from side to side, whilst others will appear and burst at the mouth of the flask. What liquid remains in the flask will serve for the same experiment three or four times, without adding any more water. Care should be taken, after the operation is over, to put the flask in a secure place.

SYMPATHETIC INKS.

All writings or drawings executed with sympathetic inks are illegible until, by the action of heat or some chemical agents upon a peculiar acid or substance which forms the basis of the ink, a change is effected, and a color produced from that which was before colorless.

1. Write with a weak solution of sulphate of iron, and it will be invisible; when dry, wash it over with a solution of prussiate of potash, and the writing will be restored, and turned to a beautiful blue.

2. Write with some of the above solution, and it will, as before stated, become invisible, but if a brush which has been dipped in a decoction of oak-bark, or tincture of galls, be slightly passed over it, it will turn black.

3. Write with the nitro-muriate of gold, and brush the letters over with muriate of tin in a diluted state. The writing, before invisible, will then appear of an exquisitely beautiful purple color.

4. The most curious of all kinds of sympathetic ink is that procured from cobalt. It is a very singular phenomenon, peculiar to this ink, that the characters of figures traced out with it may be made to appear and disappear at pleasure; all other kinds of sympathetic ink are at first invisible, until some fluid has been applied to cause their reappearance, but when once they are developed they remain permanent. To make this ink, take zaffre, and dissolve it in nitro-muriatic acid, until the acid extracts from it the metallic part, or cobalt, which communicates to the zaffre its blue color; then dilute the solution, which is very acrid, with common water. If you

write with this preparation, the characters will be invisible, but when exposed to a moderate degree of heat, they will become green, and on the paper cooling again they will vanish. However, if the paper is overheated the writing will not disappear.

5. Write with a diluted solution of muriate of copper, and the writing will be invisible, when dry; but on being held to the fire it will be of a yellowish-green color.

COLORED FIRES.

RED FIRE.

One ounce and a half of dry nitrate of strontia, three drachms and six grains of powdered sulphur, one drachm and twelve grains of chlorate of potash, two drachms of the sulphuret of antimony, and one scruple of charcoal, will make a most beautiful and intense red fire. Pound the chlorate of potash and sulphuret of antimony each separately in a mortar, and afterward mix them together on paper, then add them to the other ingredients. In mixing these ingredients, it must always be remembered that chlorate of potash and sulphur explode when rubbed together.

GREEN FIRE.

For green fire, take twenty-seven parts of nitrate of baryta, thirteen of flowers of sulphur, five of nitrate of potash, three of charcoal, and two of metallic arsenic. Let the nitrate of baryta be well dried and powdered; pulverize the other ingredients completely, mix them carefully together, and then grind them with a muller on a stone slab, taking especial care to incorporate them thoroughly.

A BLUISH-WHITE FIRE.

Take of nitrate of baryta twenty-seven parts by weight, of sulphur thirteen, of chloride of potassium five, of realgar two, and of charcoal three parts; incorporate them completely, and when inflamed they will emit that peculiar whitish-blue light accompanied by much smoke which is employed in fairy-scenes at theatres.

BENGAL LIGHT.

Mix together sixteen parts of nitre, four of sulphur, and one of orpiment; place it on a tile, and apply a match: it will burn with a bluish flame, and diffuse a most intense light.

ORANGE-COLORED FIRE.

If some muriate of magnesia be mixed with a little alcohol, and then set on fire, a very beautiful orange-colored flame will be produced.

SPUR FIRE.

This fire, the most beautiful of any composition yet known, is termed spur fire, from the sparks bearing a great resemblance to the rowel of a spur. It is generally made of saltpetre two pounds, sulphur one pound, and lampblack three-quarters of a pound, incorporated thoroughly together; it should then be put into cases about six inches in length, but not driven very hard. This composition is very difficult to mix. The saltpetre and brimstone must be first sifted together, then put into a marble mortar and the lampblack added to them; incorporate the ingredients with a wooden pestle till the mixture appears of a dark gray color; then drive some into a case for trial, and fire it in a dark place; if the sparks, which are called stars or pinks, come out in clusters, and afterward spread well without any other sparks, it is a sign of its being good; if any drossy sparks appear, and the stars are imperfect, the composition is not mixed enough; and if the pinks are very small and soon break, it is a sign that you have rubbed it too much. This fire has a better effect in a room than in the open air, and may be fired in a chamber without any danger; indeed, it is of so innocent a nature that, although it seems an improper phrase, it may truly be termed a cold fire, for, if well mixed, the sparks will not burn a handkerchief when held in the midst of them; you may hold the cases in your hand while the fire jets out with as much safety as a candle; and if you put your hand within a foot of the case, you will feel the sparks fall like drops of rain

---

CONCLUDING REMARKS.

Our limits warn us to close this highly interesting subject, and in so doing we shall observe that the experiments we have selected to elucidate the principles of chemistry are mostly very easy of attainment, and can be tried without incurring much expense: indeed, the smallest quantities sold of some of the more expensive articles will be amply sufficient for the purpose of displaying their effects, whilst a trifling quantity—three or four pennyworths, for instance—of the more common ones will do, as the effects are as beautifully apparent in small as in large quantities. Neither is it necessary to purchase many glasses or vessels in which to make the mixtures, as some slips of common window-glass will serve the purpose, if only a few drops of the liquids are mixed together. This economical plan has been adopted by Dr. Reid, of Edinburgh, with the greatest success; and tyros in chemistry would do well to bear in mind that Sir Humphry Davy taught himself with an apparatus which cost but a few shillings.

Fig. 35.—Globules of sodium rolling down and burning on wet blotting-paper placed on an inclined board provided with ledges at the sides to prevent the metal rolling off.

OPTICAL EXPERIMENTS.

Fig. 36.

"Hail, holy LIGHT! Offspring of heaven, first-born.
. . . . . . Before the sun,
Before the heavens, thou wert; and at the voice
Of God, as with a mantle didst invest
The rising world of waters dark and deep."

MILTON.

"Oh, what a noble heavenly gift is light!
By light, that blessed being, all things live."

SCHILLER'S *William Tell.*

IT may be said without exaggeration that the chief facts in the science of chemistry have been discovered within the last eighty-five years, and a similar remark may be made with respect to the beautiful phenomena of light, viz.: that the greatest refinements and improvements in the science of optics have been discovered and practised within about the same period.

although, of course, much was effected and reduced to system at least two hundred years ago. No other branch of science has given larger scope for the exercise of the highest order of reasoning than the gorgeous and magnificent effects of light; and the study of its nature was pursued with the greatest diligence and success by the philosophers of antiquity. If the earth was always flooded with light, probably its nature would not have excited so much curiosity; but the very fact of its being the precursor of man's daily toil, the first greeting of each day, would induce a greater amount of thought to be devoted to its origin and existence: hence light was typified in various ways in heathen mythology, and Eos or Aurora was the name of the goddess of the dawn, who at the close of every night rose from her couch, and in a chariot drawn by swift horses ascended up to heaven to announce the coming light of the sun; whilst Helios or Sol, the god of the sun, was fancifully supposed to start in a chariot drawn by four horses from his magnificent palace in the east, to speed to his second royal abode in the west, where his horses fed upon herbs growing in the Islands of the Blessed. Such fanciful creations of imagination indicate that the thoughts of the ancients were turned to the consideration of invisible, imponderable light, and they endeavored to give this "quintessence pure" a formal existence. The ancient Greeks were acquainted with the properties of the burning-glass, which was sold as a curiosity in the toy-shops, just as the kaleidoscopes and the magic-lanterns are to be obtained in the bazaars at the present day. In order to comprehend the principles of these optical contrivances, it is necessary to speak of the nature of light, beginning with the enumeration of the sources from which it may be derived.

THE SOURCES OF LIGHT.

Light emanates from, at least, six different sources. The first, the greatest and the grandest, is the sun, the centre of our planetary system, and the great source of light and heat to the earth. The magnificence of this celestial light-giving agent can only be appreciated by considering the gigantic size of the sun as compared with the earth, the former having a diameter of 770,800 geographical miles, and being 112 times greater than that of the earth.

The sun's volume is 1,407,124 times that of the earth, and 600 times greater than all the planets united. Sir John Herschel says, if a globe representing the sun, and two feet in diameter, be placed in the centre of a well-levelled field, and a circle described round it having a diameter of 430 feet, the representation of the earth placed on the circumference of this circle would not be larger than *a pea*, whilst the circumference would represent the orbit or path of the earth. Arago says, "It is no exaggeration to assert that the electric light is comparable to the solar light; the former is not effaced in the presence of that of the latter." According to the energy of the battery employed, the electric light varies from the fifth part to the fourth of that of the sun; and, supposing it to be equivalent to about three or four thousand wax-candles, the light of the sun, *at the surface of the earth*, would be equal to about twenty thousand candles on the same area as would be illuminated by a single electric light

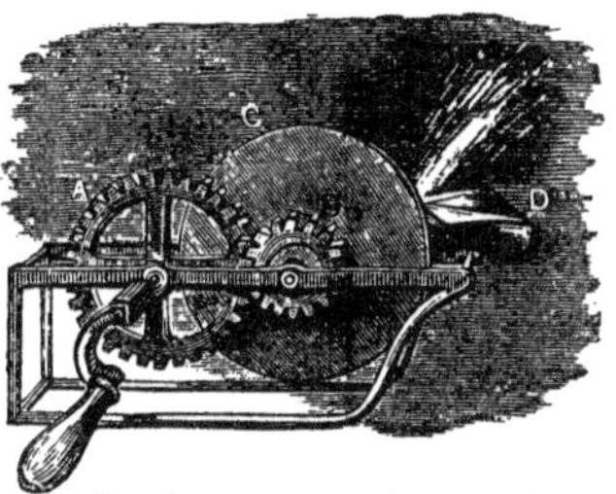

Fig. 37.—Miner's steel mill. A B, Large and small cog wheels.
The cog wheel A has a handle attached.
B is on the same shaft that carries the steel wheel C.
The flint is shown at D.

Fig. 38.—Miner at work in the coal-mine by the light of the sparks from the steel mill.

of great energy. Comparison is always a useful mode of instruction, and therefore it may be worth while to mention that the solar light is at least 300,000 times greater than that of the full moon; consequently the firmament must be gemmed with more than 300,000 full moons to produce a light equal to that of the sun. Light emanates from terrestrial matter, as when two substances are rubbed one against the other; and hence the use of the flint and steel: here minute particles of iron are rubbed off, the very act of friction being sufficient to produce the heat which helps their combustion in the air. Before the invention of the safety-lamp, and its use in coal-mines, steel mills were in constant requisition in dangerous pits, and every coal-hewer was provided with a little boy, whose monotonous duty consisted in turning a little steel wheel against a piece of flint, at the risk of continually rubbing off the skin from his fingers, or projecting the small particles of the flint or steel into his eyes; to say nothing of the occasional brutality of the coal-hewer, who would allow no relaxation to the tired little fingers which helped to produce the light.

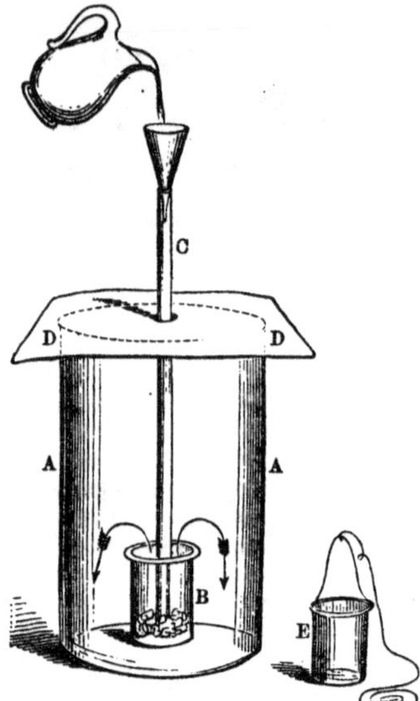

Fig. 39.—A A, Large glass jar.
B, Small ditto, containing the chlorinated lime.
C, Tube and funnel conveying the acid to B.
D D, Sheet of paper, with hole in centre to admit tube.
E, Small glass, used as a bucket.
The arrows show the direction of the heavy gas chlorine, and, when sufficient is obtained, the Dutch metal may be dipped in.

The friction of a railway-axle has occasionally been so great as even to set fire to the carriage to which it belonged.

Friction is, therefore, an important source of light, whether it be applied by civilized races to the ignition of a lucifer-match, or in the more troublesome and laborious efforts of a savage with his dried pieces of wood.

A third source of light is chemical action,—undoubtedly (next to the sun) the most valuable means of obtaining illuminating power without the exercise of physical strength. Light is procured from the mere contact of certain chemical agents. Thus, if some chlorinated lime, called chloride of lime, be moistened with water, and placed in a beaker-glass standing at the bottom of a deep jar, and some acid be poured upon it by means of a tube and funnel, the acid being hydrochloric or sulphuric acid, effervescence takes place; a heavy gas, called chlorine, is disengaged, which falls to the bottom of the jar; and if a little Dutch metal—*i.e.* copper-leaf—is now dropped into it, light is produced by the sudden combination of the metal with the gas.

In performing this experiment, great care must be taken not to inhale the chlorine gas, as it produces a most painful and irritating cough, which would last a considerable time. After performing the experiment, either place the glass on the chimney-hob till the gas has all passed up the chimney, or put it outside the window and shut down the sash; and after the acid has been poured in, put a plate over the top, to prevent any gas being carried out of the jar by accidental currents of air in the room.

A powder composed of chlorate of potash and sugar represents solidity. At the ordinary temperature of the atmosphere, these materials might remain in contact for years without evolving light, until touched with the smallest quantity (a drop) of oil of vitriol, when suddenly a little crackling noise is heard, a large flame flashes upwards, and the heap of powder is gone,—burnt up,—changed into carbonic acid and aqueous vapor, which pass into the air; while a small quantity of a white matter, and perhaps a few specks of charcoal, remain behind. Before the extended manufacture and application of phosphorus in the preparation of lucifer-matches, the same mixture, combined with a small quantity of red lead and gum, was attached to the ends of little bits of pine-wood, and these, when dipped into a bottle containing asbestos moistened with oil of vitriol, immediately took fire, as already explained.

A third and excellent illustration of chemical action as a source of light is shown in the combustion of all oil, tallow, wax, and gas in the production of artificial illumination; the perfection of the light depending, in a great measure, on the ignition of the solid charcoal, which introduces us to

The fourth mode of procuring light; viz.: *by the increase of heat in solid bodies*, or what is called ignition in contradistinction to combustion, which means the actual burning of a substance.

For instance, if a deep jar is filled with carbonic acid gas, and a piece of dry gun-cotton is dropped into it, a flame representing *combustion* will not fire the cotton, as the lighted taper is extinguished before reaching the explosive substance, because carbonic acid gas extinguishes flame; but if a piece of iron wire be heated—*i.e.* ignited—this may be passed through the carbonic acid gas unaltered, and, coming in contact with the gun-cotton, immediately causes it to burn.

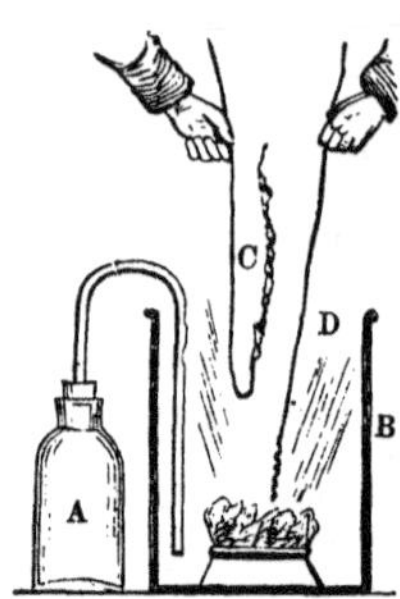

Fig. 40.—A, Bottle containing marble and hydrochloric acid, generating carbonic acid gas, which passes by the bent tube into

B B, Large beaker-glass, containing a little stand with gun-cotton.

C, Taper extinguished by carbonic acid.

D, Ignited wire, which fires the gun-cotton.

The increase of heat in solid bodies producing light is admirably illustrated in the dissection of the elements concerned in the combustion of ordinary gas, which consists chiefly of hydrogen gas and carbon: if the former is burned, it combines with the oxygen of the air, water is formed, and much heat, but little or no light, obtained. If, however, a coil of platinum wire is placed in the burning hydrogen, it becomes intensely ignited, and light is obtained; the metal is not consumed, or changed, or oxidized, only ignited, and if some powdered charcoal is substituted for the platinum wire and dusted in the flame, light is also obtained. To dust charcoal powder into a hydrogen flame would be a very tedious business: hence coal gas, which already contains the charcoal, supplies the element required, and, being in excess, is not wholly and at once burnt up by union with the oxygen of the air, but is deposited in the body of the flame, where, becoming ignited or incandescent, the light is produced, and this is the principle of the illuminating power of oil, tallow, wax, &c.

A fifth source of light, and one that may alarm or delight us according to the manner of its production, is Electricity,—that wondrous power which man has rendered subservient to his command, and employs to convey his thoughts almost as quickly as they are conceived, by the electric telegraph. In many other ways, and especially as a light-giving agent, electricity promises in due time to become second only to the sun in utility and brilliancy.

On a dark stormy night there is nothing more awful (in consequence of the suddenness of the appearance and disappearance of the excessively brilliant light) than a flash of lightning. In vain do the nervous try to exclude the bright gleams of light by closing shutters or hiding heads under the bedclothes: the light has come and gone ere the words which chronicle its existence have escaped us, and by the time we have remarked, "How blue the lightning is!" the cause of the color has vanished: the impression only remains upon the optic nerve.

The electric light is obtained either by passing a stream of sparks from the prime conductor of an electrical machine, or by the use of a powerful voltaic battery of at least thirty pairs, on Professor Grove's principle, which must be connected with the charcoal points arranged on the ends of the instrument called the universal discharge.

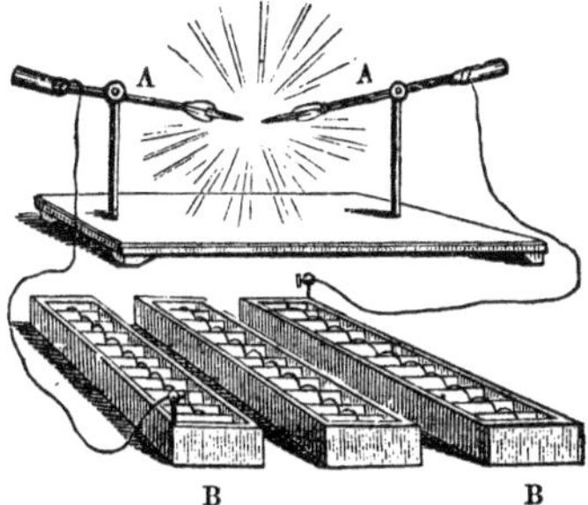

Fig. 41.—A A, The universal discharge with charcoal points.
B B, Three batteries of ten cells each.

The points must be constantly brought together, as the positive pole is always losing charcoal, which deposits partly on the negative pole; the carbon so deposited is not in a perfect state of aggregation, and soon burns away; otherwise the light is not caused by the combustion of the charcoal, and is produced by the ignition of the points, and the passage of the current of electricity from pole to pole.

The passage of the charcoal from one point to the other is perfectly and beautifully displayed on a screen to a number of persons at the same time, by using Duboscq's elegant arrangement, in which the electric lamp is placed inside a lantern with a plano-convex lens, and provided with a disk perforated with holes gradually decreasing in size. By adjusting the proper orifice to the lens, and connecting Duboscq's lamp with the battery of thirty cells, a picture of the charcoal points is projected on to the screen; the passage of the electric current, (shown by a bluish light,) with the transfer of the charcoal from the positive to the negative pole, is very perfectly seen.

Professor Pepper's Duboscq cascade will long be remembered by the *habitués* of the Polytechnic.

The sixth source of light is perhaps more curious than all the others which have been enumerated, and is called "*Phosphorescence.*" This term must not be confounded with the use of the highly combustible substance called phosphorus, as the luminous effects are obtained from bodies which do not contain any of that element. Moreover, a phosphorescent light is evolved from living insects, and therefore it must (in this case) be the result of some remarkable organic process.

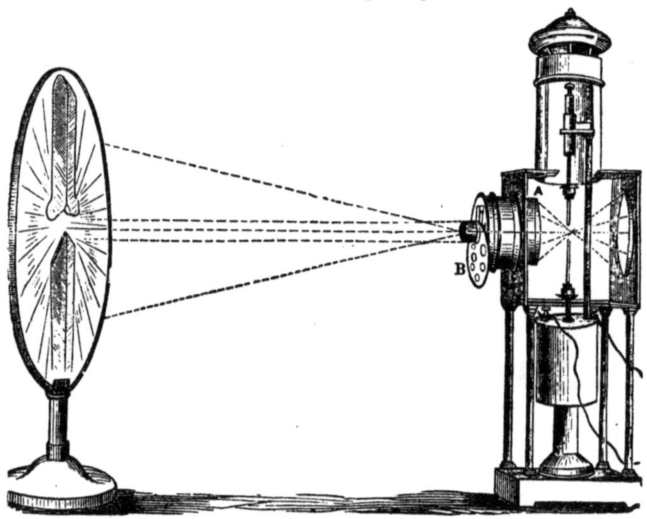

Fig. 42.—Duboscq's Electric Lamp, Lantern, and Screen. The lamp is placed in the lantern, and the door removed, to show the inside.
A. The plano-convex lens.
B. The diaphragm, perforated with holes of various sizes.
The picture of the positive and negative poles is shown on the white paper screen facing the diaphragm.

PHOSPHORESCENCE.

There are at least seven distinct means by which this kind of light is produced.

NO. I.—SOLAR PHOSPHORI.

Attention was first directed to this mode of causing bodies to shine in the dark by the experiments of a shoemaker of Bologna, who, being engaged in alchemical mysteries, had occasion to calcine some native sulphate of baryta, or what is commonly termed heavy spar, and he remarked that whenever this substance was exposed to the sun's rays after being heated red-hot, it possessed the curious property of shining when taken into a darkened chamber. The shoemaker, in looking for the philosopher's stone, missed the golden prize, but discovered this substance, which soon began to be in great demand among the curious under the name of Bolognian phosphorus, and after the death of Vincenzio Cascariolo, the clever shoe maker, a family of the name of Zagoni retained the secret of the preparation, and supplied the philosophers and dilettanti of Europe with this prepared substance.

Canton's phosphorus possesses similar properties, and is prepared by taking a dozen large oyster-shells and placing them in an open fire for half an hour, after which the whitest and largest pieces are selected, mixed with about one-third of their weight of flowers of sulphur, pressed into a crucible with a closely-luted cover, and heated red-hot for an hour. It should be remembered that the oyster-shells alone, when heated for about an hour in contact with charcoal, *i.e.* placed in an open fire surrounded with coke, become luminous when exposed to the sun's rays, and emit curious prismatic colors in a darkened room.

Nitrate of lime, prepared by saturating nitric acid with lime from chalk, evaporating to dryness, and melting at a low red heat, evolves light in a dark room after exposure to the sun's rays.

The conditions of success in the use of these solar phosphori consist in a great measure in the warmth and dryness of the weather, as a cold or damp state of the atmosphere decreases the power of shining.

NO. II.—PHOSPHORESCENCE BY HEAT.

In this case it is only necessary to take various substances in the powdered state, and to sprinkle them on a heated surface, such as a platinum spoon, held over the flame of a spirit-lamp, and an iron shovel, just red-hot, taking care of course to perform the experiment in a dark room or a cupboard lined with black calico.

The powdered substances which become luminous in this manner are—

- Fetid carbonate of lime, called stinkstone, which is rather plentiful at Bristol.
- Compact phosphate of lime.
- Calcareous spar.
- Heavy spar.
- Powdered quartz.
- Fluor or Derbyshire spar.

Mr. Pearsall has shown (in a very interesting series of experiments) that the luminosity of these substances is greatly increased by electrical discharges, and he found that it conferred the property upon many substances which did not otherwise possess it.

NO. III.—BODIES SPONTANEOUSLY PHOSPHORESCENT.

Various animal substances become luminous before putrescence has commenced, and especially the flesh of certain fish, of which the most remarkable are tench, carp, sole; and herring, lobsters, and crabs, when perfectly fit for the table, will sometimes emit a phosphorescent light.

One of the most remarkable instances on record is that described by the late Mr. Daniel Cooper, and witnessed by the author, viz., the phosphorescence of the whole of the human bodies which were undergoing dissection at the Webb Street School of Medicine. The phosphorescence commenced in one of the subjects, and a portion transferred by a scalpel to the other dead bodies conferred the same property upon them. The effect was extremely wonderful, not to say fearful; it reminded one of the ghostly story of "Frankenstein," and suggested the fanciful notion of the resuscitation of these poor remains of human mortality.

NO. IV.—PHOSPHORESCENT LIVING ANIMALS.

The glowworm (described, with many other "Common Objects of the Country," by the Rev. J. C. Wood) is not a worm, but a beetle.

Fig. 43.—Male and female glowworm.

The hundred-legged worm found in decayed poplar wood, or under lime, bricks, and pots in the garden, emits flashes of light when irritated by a little warm water. Whilst in tropical climates, the Lantern and Firefly have been the theme of admiration of every traveller.

NO. V.—THE PHOSPHORESCENCE OF THE SEA.

Dr. Young and others are of opinion that it is caused by microscopic mollusks. "Every time," says the doctor, "I threw a net into the water, I withdrew it full of biphores, beroës, and medusæ. In one single drop I discovered myriads of small beings moving rapidly about, and at every contraction of these animalculæ the emission of light became more intense. . . . I had placed in a glass vase some gigantic biphores; I saw them alternately rise and fall in the water, and all their movements were accompanied by a jet of fire, which increased the luminous intensity of the liquid fourfold."

The French Minister of Marine lately received a report from Captain Trébuchet, of the *Capricieuse* corvette, dated Amboyna, August 28, 1860, in which he states that on the night of the 26th of that month, while tacking to reach Amboyna, lying at about twenty miles E.N.E., he and his crew witnessed the curious spectacle of the Milky Sea, which the Dutch call the Winter Sea, because both the sky and the waters present the appearance of fields covered with snow. The phenomenon lasted from seven P.M. until the return of daylight. They at first attributed it to the reflection of the moon, then only three days old; but, as the appearance continued after the moon had set, this explanation had to be discarded. A bucketful of sea-water being drawn up and examined, it was found to contain about 200 groups of animalculæ of the same thickness (that of a hair), but of different lengths, varying between one and two tenths of a millimetre, and adhering to each other by tens and twenties, like strings of beads. These insects emitted a fixed light similar to that of the firefly or glowworm, and it was admitted on all hands that the white appearance of the sea could only be attributed to these minute creatures, the numbers of which must therefore exceed all imagination.

In a paper read before the Royal Society, written by Father Bourges, he speaks of the phosphorescence of the sea-water in the wake of the ship, and says, "One day we took in our ship a fish, which some thought was a boneta; the inside of the mouth of this fish appeared in the night like a burning coal, so that, without any other light, I could read by it the same characters that I read by the *light* in the *wake of the ship*. Its mouth being full of a viscous matter, we rubbed a piece of wood with it, which immediately became all over luminous; but as soon as the moisture was dried up, the light was extinguished." This phosphorescent light may be one of the inscrutable won ders of creation, and serve possibly to illumine the eternal darkness of the great ocean-depths to which the rays of the sun never penetrate, giving light to those animals which take their food near these valleys of the bed of the ocean.

NO. VI.—PHOSPHORESCENCE FROM VEGETABLE SUBSTANCES.

Decayed wood, and especially peat, has occasionally been observed to evolve a faint light, and even some flowers have been remarked to give out brilliant flashes of light during a warm summer's evening. The names of the flowers are the tuberose, nasturtium, and marigold; also the leaves of the phytolacca decandra, and certain mosses, with some species of rhizomorpha, have been observed to be luminous in mines.

NO. VII.—EMISSION OF LIGHT DURING CRYSTALLIZATION.

Mr. H. Rose notices a remarkable instance of this property in the solution of vitreous arsenious acid in hydrochloric acid; one ounce of the arsenious acid should be dissolved in three ounces of the hydrochloric acid diluted with one ounce of water, and the whole boiled for fifteen minutes in a flask; when very slowly cooled the arsenious acid gradually crystallizes, and nearly every crystal as it forms emits a bright flash of light in a darkened room.

The cause of phosphorescence does not yet seem to be perfectly understood; by the vibratory or undulatory theory of light, it is possible to conceive that vibrations may be commenced in phosphorescent bodies and communicated to the surrounding ether. The glowworm and firefly may be naturally endowed with the power to produce these rapid vibrations, the principle being, that as vibrations of the air produce sound, so the vibrations of the theoretical ether, which is supposed to fill all space, would generate light.

Phosphorescence is quite independent of combustion; it may arise in some cases from electrical disturbance, but, taking it as a whole, scientific men are obliged to confess their ignorance of the causes which produce the leading cases of phosphorescence already enumerated.

PHENOMENA OF LIGHT.

Hitherto the experiments and remarks in this article have applied merely to self-luminous bodies, but yet we see every other shape and form on the surface of the globe, although the bodies may not be self-luminous. The cause is very simple, and depends chiefly on the property possessed by all bodies of reflecting or throwing off the rays of light.

For instance, we might enter in imagination the cavern of the Forty Thieves in the tale of Ali Baba; the countless riches are comparatively useless, because we cannot see them, they do not shine and make themselves apparent in the dark; but a lighted taper or torch very soon throws its rays in every direction, and these falling on the surrounding objects are reflected to the eye and there produce the phenomena of vision.

A bright beam of light may be passed from the Duboscq lantern across a darkened chamber, and if it falls upon a piece of black velvet and the face is turned away from it, hardly any light is perceptible in the room; but if the rays be received on a sheet of card-board, then the secondary reflection illumines the room. It is this reflection of light by clouds and masses of vapor that produces the diffused light of day. If the globe was not surrounded by an atmosphere, the sun would look like a huge electric light in a perfectly black sky. Hence the important connection between luminous and non-luminous bodies. For the purpose of reasoning on the properties of light, it is usual to consider a beam of light as made up of rays, and when a ray of light remains in the same medium of the same density, it pursues a perfectly straight line, but if it passes out of that medium into another of a different density, or into any other solid, fluid, or gaseous body, it may be disposed of in four different ways. It may be

1. Reflected.
2. Refracted.
3. Polarized.
4. Absorbed.

The limits of this very popular article will not allow us to discuss Nos. 3 and 4, but there are many entertaining experiments to be performed with light in the use of various reflecting and refracting substances.

THE REFLECTION OF LIGHT.

Nature supplies us with bodies of all degrees of reflecting power, and it is a property which is influenced rather by the condition of the surface than the nature of the material, as we may destroy the brilliancy of a bright mirror by breathing upon it, and we may also confer a reflecting surface on black charcoal by applying the thinnest film of gold or silver leaf.

Concave mirrors, in which the surface corresponds with the inside of a watch-glass, have the property of collecting the rays of light, while convex mirrors, in which the surface resembles the exterior of a watch-glass, scatter the rays in all directions. Flat surfaces afford plain reflections, and one of the prettiest applications of flat-reflecting surfaces is shown in that beautiful invention of Sir David Brewster called

THE KALEIDOSCOPE.

This interesting instrument is of modern invention, and forms a toy of the most pleasing kind. Rough, though effective, kaleidoscopes may be purchased for a very moderate price at most toy-shops, but, for the instruction of those of our readers who would like to make them, we proceed to give some instructions by which they may construct very passable specimens for a trifling expense. Get a tube of tin or pasteboard of eight or ten inches in length and one and a half or two inches in diameter; have one end stopped up with a piece of tin firmly soldered in, and let there be a slight hole made exactly in the centre of this end-piece. Next procure two pieces of looking-glass of nearly the length of the tube, for reflectors; but if looking-glass is not easily obtained, strips of good new crown glass will answer the purpose, if the lower surfaces are blackened with lamp-black or black wax. These plates of glass must be put into the tube in the manner shown at B C B D in the marginal figure; they must be quite parallel and close to each other at the lower part B, and kept asunder at the upper part by a piece of cork or any other substance E; the polished sides of the glasses must be uppermost, as at *b b;* A indicates the sight-hole at the farther end, and close to this the reflectors must be fitted. The reflectors being put in, a piece of glass of the same diameter as the tube is to be pushed into the tube so as to touch the reflectors, sundry bits of different-colored glass are to be laid on it, and a ring of brass or copper placed round its edge, and then another piece of glass, one side of which has been ground with fine emery, laid upon that; the edges of the tin tube are then to be burnished down round the last-mentioned piece of glass, by which plan the glasses are firmly secured in their places and the instrument completed. If a piece of marbled or tinted paper is afterward nicely pasted over it, the kaleidoscope will look very neat and workmanlike.

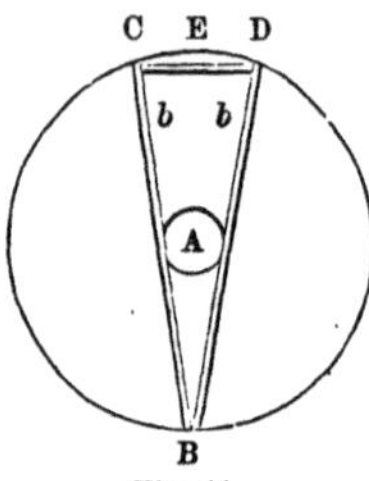

Fig. 44.

THE MYRIAMOSCOPE, OR MAGIC DESIGNER.

This instrument is a variation of the kaleidoscope, possessing much of the beautiful effect of that pleasing invention, without its liability to be affected by a shake, so as to derange the elegant forms which it produces.

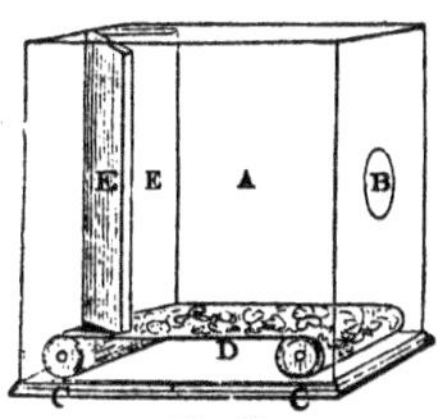

Fig. 45.

A is a square box, in the front of which the sight-hole B is made; two rollers, C C, are placed at the bottom of the box, and in order that they may be made to move round with facility, knobs or handles should be fixed to the ends of their axles at the sides of the box. On these rollers a piece of calico, D, must be wound, and upon which fanciful borders, flowers, and ornaments cut out from pieces of paper-hangings, must be pasted. Two plane mirrors, E E, joined together by a strip of leather, hinge-fashion, are then to be put on the calico, as shown in the margin, and, of course, all the objects thereon make a very pretty display in the glasses when viewed through the sight-hole B. The mirrors must be so constructed that they may be put to any inclination by means of two small pieces of wood fastened to them and passing through the sides of the box. An opening should be made in the box for the convenience of renewing the subjects, and the top of it be covered with muslin, strained tight, or some other semi-transparent medium.

THE REFRACTION OF LIGHT.

Light is refracted, or bent out of its course, when it passes obliquely through a medium of greater density than that which it has been traversing so as to fall quite in a different place to what it would have done had it not passed into that medium; and the amount of this refraction or bending of the light is always governed by its obliquity, and the nature of the substance through which it progresses. There are some substances or media which are of greater density and refract light better than others, as, for instance, alcohol refracts it more than water, oil more than alcohol, and glass even more than oil. Among the many useful inventions which the progress of civilization and knowledge has brought forward, there are few which are of so much utility as those which depend upon the refractive powers of glass for their effect; and these are the telescope, microscope, camera obscura, magic lantern, &c. &c. The pieces of glass used in these instruments are termed *lenses*, from their being made in the shape of a flat bean or lentil; this shape, from being rounded outwards on both sides, forms what is called a convex lens, and in addition, the concave, or *hollow* on both sides, with the various modifications of both kinds of lenses, are employed for optical purposes. The convex lenses cause the different rays which pass through them from any given point or object, to bend and unite together again at another point beyond them. The more convex the lens is, the nearer is its focus, for it has been ascertained that the focus of a double convex lens is exactly where the centre of the sphere would be, of which the surface of the lens is a portion; consequently, in proportion to the convexity of the lens, so will the nearness of its focus be, as it then forms a part of a smaller sphere. When the light proceeding from all points of any object placed before a lens is collected at a certain point beyond it, and received on a white screen or other medium in a darkened room, it produces the well-known effects of the magic lantern, the solar and oxy-hydrogen microscopes, and the camera obscura; and when the image beyond a lens is viewed in the air, in a particular direction, it then shows the disposition of parts which form the telescope, common microscope, &c. The concave lens acts exactly the reverse of the convex; that is, instead of converging the rays to a point, it expands them, and causes them to fill a space considerably larger than the size of the lens itself.

Some of the most striking of celestial appearances, and which are of very frequent occurrence, are the result of the reflection and refraction of the rays of light. The serene mild glow of twilight, which so softly and sweetly ends the day, and diminishes the transition from the burning glare of the sun to the cold hues of night, is owing to reflection, and so also is that beautiful many-colored arch, the rainbow. The varied tints of the clouds, from the gray, pearly, morning dawn, to the brilliant crimson and gold glories of sunset, are produced by a combination of causes, absorption, reflection, and refraction. The deceitful mirage is another effect owing to refraction. It is occasioned by unequal refraction,—that is, when the rays of light enter a medium of different densities,—and is a phenomenon of rare occurrence in temperate climates, occurring chiefly in those subject to the extremes of temperature, whether of heat or cold. In the arid deserts of Africa, the mirage frequently presents the appearance of a delightful tract of country stretching across the wide plain, in which the traveller fancies he may refresh himself and his camels, sheltered by lofty palm-trees, from the scorching rays of the sun; but as the wanderer pursues his onward course, he finds the unsubstantial forms vanish before his eager gaze, making the dreary way still more desolate from the bitterness of disappointment. In the Arctic regions also the mirage presents forms of great interest and beauty, but of a different character from those in the torrid zone, displaying lofty towers and pinnacles, high battlemented walls and aerial palaces, from the refracted forms of the icebergs. There are many pleasing ways of showing the principles of refraction.

EXPERIMENTS ON REFRACTION OF LIGHT.

Put a piece of money at the bottom of an empty basin, and then retire a few steps backwards, till the edge of the basin screens the money from your sight. Keep your head steady, and request some one to fill the basin very gently with water; as the water rises, the coin will come gradually into view, and when the basin is nearly full of water it will be completely visible.

By the assistance of the Duboscq lantern, arranged as already described, with the exception of the diaphragm, which must be removed and a piece of thick cardboard or brass cut in the form of an arrow arranged in its place, and a double convex lens placed in front, a perfect image of the arrow is thrown on the disk, and whilst the picture is visible, if a piece of plate-glass, marked C in the cut, say one inch wide and half an inch thick and six inches long, is held across the shaft of the cardboard arrow, a piece of the shaft is seen to be broken out or refracted, as shown in the picture below.

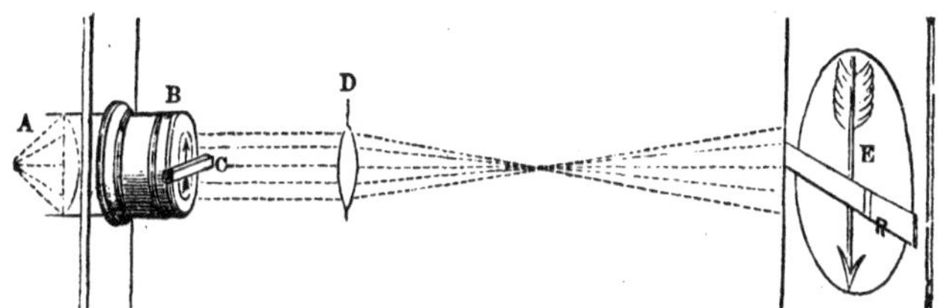

Fig. 46.—A, The electric, or oxy-hydrogen light.
B, The plano-convex lens, or "bull's-eye."
C, The bit of plate-glass, *the refracting medium*, in front of the arrow.
D, The second double convex lens.
E, The image on the screen, showing the arrow-shaft broken, or refracted, at R.

THE MAGIC LANTERN.

The MAGIC LANTERN, one of the most amusing of optical instruments, was invented by Kircher, about the middle of the seventeenth century, and was of the greatest service to the magicians of those times, enabling them to work upon the credulity of the ignorant and superstitious with the utmost facility. As a vehicle of amusement, it contributes in no small degree, in the shape of a galantee show, to the hilarity of a party of merry younkers in a long winter's night; and as a means by which lectures on astronomy can be elucidated, it arrests the attention of the old and wise.

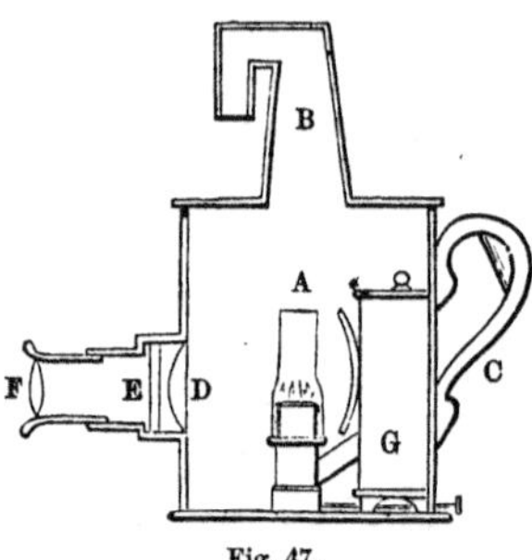

Fig. 47.

The instrument, the construction of which demands our attention first, is represented in the margin. A, is a box made of wood or tin, about eight inches square, having a bent funnel or chimney, B, at the top; a handle, C, renders it a portable instrument, and holes are made near the bottom to feed the flame of the lamp with the air which is requisite for its combustion; in the front of the box there is a tin tube, furnished at the end near the light with a plano-convex lens, D,—which indeed is affixed to the lantern itself,—and at the other, a doubly convex lens, F; this tin tube is fixed to the lantern by a square foot, the sides of which are open, as at E, to admit the sliders, and the end of the tube in which the doubly convex lens is fastened is made to slide in and out for convenience when adjusting the focus; a third lens is occasionally employed when the space is very confined, as a larger field of view can be obtained by its aid than in the ordinary method. The lamp, G, is a common argand burner, furnished with a concave tin reflector, to concentrate the intensity of the light; and if the lamp is made to slide backwards and forwards by means of a wire, it will be so much the more useful.

The Phantasmagorial Lantern varies but slightly from the foregoing, the chief points in which it differs being in the form of the tube containing the doubly convex lens, which is made to project more beyond the lens, F, and in the lens itself being contrived so as to move readily backwards and forwards, either by a rack and pinion, or studs fastened on each side; in a flap to shut off the light abruptly, which may be either a tin slider to run into the groove, or else a piece of tin fastened in the front of all; and in the top of the square chamber, in which the sliders run, being made so as to open on occasion.

PAINTING THE SLIDERS.

The sliders are made of pieces of glass, surrounded by a slight frame, and in dimensions are, of course, regulated by the depth of the aperture intended for them in the lantern. Few hints can be given, beyond naming the colors and the mode of preparing them, toward the painting of the sliders, as taste is the best guide and practice the most impressive instructor in all matters relating to painting. The colors proper are only such as are transparent; and they are the following:—gamboge, scarlet lake, Prussian blue, a green made of distilled verdigris and a quarter of its bulk of gamboge, burnt sienna, burnt umber, and lampblack. A few materials, such as a glass muller, and slab,—which last may be about six inches square,—a palette-knife, and some small bottles to put the colors in after they are ground, are also requisite. The colors should be ground up with Canada balsam and turpentine, equal parts of each, or, if in that proportion they are too thick for grinding freely, rather more turpentine may be added: so mixed they require about a week to dry, and have a very beautiful appearance; but if it is wished to have them harden in less time than that, mastic varnish may be employed instead. When painting, take a very little color at a time out of the bottles, as it soon hardens; and, if too thick, temper it with turpentine. A piece of glass will serve as a palette, and a bit of stick as a means of getting the color out of the bottles. The black pigment used in darkening the surface of the glass round the figures of the Phantasmagorial sliders is composed of lampblack and asphaltum, dissolved in turpentine.

The subjects intended for the sliders must be carefully drawn upon a piece of paper, which should be placed under the glass, and then painted from; and too much attention cannot be paid to the drawing of them; for, when they are thrown upon the wall, all their defects, however minute, are enlarged to an astonishing extent.

Those parts of the subjects which are to appear white must be left entirely destitute of color, as flake and all other whites are opaque pigments. The mixed colors are produced by blending the colors before mentioned: thus, greens are made by means of yellow and blue, orange by yellow and carmine, &c.; this last, although not an exact orange, is near enough for the purpose, for the red which composes the proper tint is opaque, and consequently useless. The shadows may be obtained either by stronger tints of the same colors, or by shades of brown or blue as may be requisite. It is necessary to observe that the sky-tints must be darker than they are intended to appear, for the yellow light of the lamp throwing a yellowish tone upon the colors, they would lose their effect were they not so managed; for the same reason, the green of trees and grass should be painted of a bluish green, the reds be but very slightly used, and never shaded with blue; and purples should also be but sparingly employed, for the yellow tone of the lights, uniting with the blue and lake colors used in the purple, forms a decidedly neutral tint, or blackish purple, much too dark and unintelligible for the purpose. As it is often necessary to remove some parts which do not harmonize even after they have well dried, a penknife will be found of great assistance, and, when bright lines are required upon a dark ground, the effect is easily managed by scratching the color away with a needle or any other pointed instrument; and if the lines are to appear faintly colored, it is only necessary to paint them delicately after the scratching is completed.

The sliders for the common magic lantern are transparent, that is, the figures are painted on a piece of plain glass, whilst

Fig. 48.

on those used in the Phantasmagorial lantern the figures are surrounded by an opaque black tint, as in the illustrations; the figures on the former are usually shown upon a wall, as represented in the headpiece to this chapter, page 495, and invariably have a circle of light around them; whilst those in the latter are thrown upon a semi-transparent screen, which is placed between the spectators and the lantern, and, in consequence of no circle of light accompanying them, have a very beautiful appearance.

Almost magical effects of light, shade, and motion may be produced by means of different glasses; and the sliders so adapted are termed "movable sliders."

Landscape-glasses are glasses on which several views are painted, divided from each other by some slight foreground object, as a tree, or a building, or guidepost. Various effects, from the brightest mid-day to the deepest tints of night, may be produced in these, by means of double sliders; and these contrivances may be thus applied. Cut away the frame of the slider at each end, nearly even with the glass, and fasten two narrow strips of wood along the glass, one at the top and the other at the bottom; the piece of glass which is to be moved should exactly fit the space between the upper and under frames, and act upon the slips, and, to keep it steady in its place, two or three pins may be driven into the slips.

Storm-glasses, which are very ingenious representations of the effects developed by a change from a calm to a thunder-storm, require two glasses, as in the former slider: No. 1 in the annexed illustration shows a common slider painted at one end to represent a calm of sea and sky, and the sun setting in splendor; toward the centre the clouds appear threatening, and a gentle undulation of the water breaks its repose; farther on, a still greater agitation of the clouds and water is shown; and at the other end the lightnings flash, and the sweeping wave tells of the war of elements. The effect is materially heightened by means of the second slider, No. 2, having several ships painted on it; and these, of course, must correspond to the action of the water, from the bark sailing in quiet majesty to the tempest-torn and shattered hulk.

Fig. 49.

The effects of moonlight and sunrise may also be imitated by double sliders, and by a third one figures may be introduced upon the scenes to add to their beauty.

The eyes and mouths of figures and animals may be made to move, and produce a most singular, nay, almost frightful, effect; and by referring to the marginal illustration the modes by which these are managed will be clearly understood. In No. 1 the heads of a crocodile and lion are delineated, and in No. 2 the contrivances for moving the jaw of the one and the eyes of the other. A, represents a piece of talc having

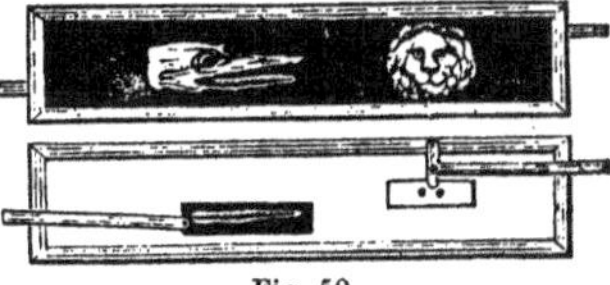
Fig. 50.

the lower jaw painted upon it and surrounded with black, which fills up a space of corresponding size left blank in the perfect slider; a slight lever should be fastened to this piece of talc, act upon a pivot on the frame, and project a little beyond it; and as it moves up and down, so will the crocodile's mouth appear to open and shut. The eyes of the lion must be painted black upon a transparent piece of talc, as at B, from which a side lever should be carried, as in the former case, to a little beyond the frame, and, to prevent the talc from shifting too far either backwards or forwards, a drop or two of sealing-wax, or a little knob of wood fastened to the glass on each side, either of the talc or lever, will be found sufficient.

SCREENS FOR THE LANTERNS.

As we before briefly stated that different media were required on which to shew the effects of the Magic Lantern and Phantasmagoria, we must, in concluding this article, give some directions respecting them. Although any white surface will do very well to receive the objects from the Magic Lantern, yet a clean sheet stretched tightly upon a wall is by far the best, as the chief point is to have a medium of perfect whiteness and quite flat. The screen for the Phantasmagoria may be made of tissue-paper strained upon a frame. Some persons recommend oiled paper as the best medium; but, in our opinion, paper so prepared is too transparent, the plain tissue being thin and translucent enough for any purpose.

Wetted muslin and waxed muslin are also advocated by some persons; but for a screen suited to the pockets of young experimentalists, nothing can be better than the one we recommend.

THE STANHOPE LENS

Is a very simple, portable, and economical species of microscope, invented by the late Earl of Stanhope. It is a cylinder of glass, about half an inch in length and a quarter of an inch in diameter, and is generally mounted in white metal, silver, or gold. Both ends are ground convex, one rather more so than the other, and, as its focus does not exceed its length, it is only necessary to put the object to be viewed either upon or in immediate contact with the end which has the slighter degree of convexity, to hold the instrument up to the light and look through it, when the object will be seen considerably magnified, to the extent, we believe, of 4096 times; its magnifying-power is, therefore, nearly equal

Fig. 51.

to that of many compound microscopes. The animalculæ in stagnant water, the mites in cheese, the farina and delicate leaves of flowers, the beautiful down upon the wings of butterflies and moths, human hair, and hairs of different animals, are among the objects which this lens develops in a lucid manner, as likewise the exquisitely minute crystallization of salts, if a drop of solution of salts be lightly spread over one end of it and viewed instantaneously ere the moisture fully evaporates.

THE CAMERA OBSCURA.

Have a box made about twelve inches in length, four in depth, and six in width; in the middle of one end of it let a hole be bored, as at A, in the annexed diagram, in which put a doubly convex lens; and at the other end, inside the box, place a piece of good looking-glass, as at B, inclining it at an angle of 45°, or, in less technical phrase, in a position midway between the horizontal and perpendicular, so as to reflect objects upwards. Part of the top of the box must be made so as to act the part of a lid, upon hinges, as D, and the space beneath be filled up by a piece of ground glass C, upon which medium the objects are reflected from the looking-glass with the utmost exactness and greatest beauty, so as to appear like an exquisite picture in miniature. Sides are usually added to the lid, as at E, to keep off as much of the circumambient light as possible. In some cameras, instead of a fixed lens, a sliding tube, with a lens at the extremity, is employed. The inside of the box should be painted over with lampblack, or, in default of that, stained with ink.

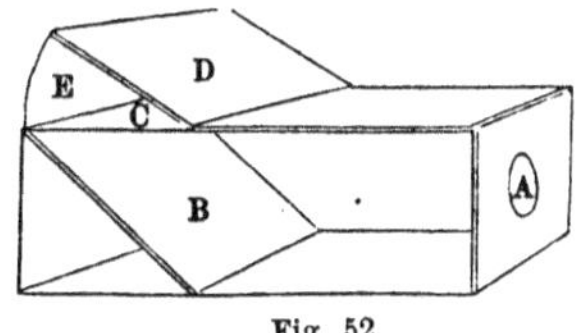

Fig. 52.

SIMPLE MICROSCOPES.

Get a piece of thin platinum wire, and twist it round the point of a pin, so as to make a very small ring with a handle to it. Next break a piece of flint glass into pieces about the size of mustard-seeds, or somewhat larger; put one of the pieces upon the ring of wire, and hold it in the point of the flame of a candle, when the glass melts, it will become of a completely globular form, and serve, when mounted, every purpose to which microscopes can be applied. The simplest mode of mounting these diminutive lenses is either to put one between two pieces of brass, which have holes made in them of just the size to retain the edge of the lens, or they may be fastened to a single piece of brass by the aid of a little gum. It is to be observed that the smaller the drop of glass, the more globular it will remain, and consequently possess greater magnifying powers.

WATER LENSES.

Temporary microscopes of considerable distinctness may be very easily made, by piercing a hole about the size of a pin's head in a piece of brass, and carefully placing a minute drop of water on the hole, where it will assume a globular shape. These lenses, as may be imagined, are very easily rendered useless, being affected by the slightest movements.

THE PRISMATIC COLORS.

Our young readers will find these three experiments upon the colors in a ray of light of great interest and beauty.

Close the shutters of a room into which the sun is shining, and so exchange midnight gloom for meridian brightness; and if there is not an aperture in the shutters, then bore a little one. Hold a prism at a short distance from the aperture, so as to allow the slender stream of sunlight to pass through and be decomposed by it; when, instead of a little round spot on the opposite wall of the room, an oblong image will be displayed, consisting of the seven colors of the rainbow, red, orange, yellow, green, blue, indigo, and violet. This image is called the solar spectrum.

If the hole in the shutter is exceedingly small, and no prism is employed, then only four colors are evident; and these are red, green, yellow, and violet.

The above experiments show, by decomposition, that light is of a compound nature; and to confirm them it is only necessary to re-compose the seven colors, and produce the pure sunlight effect, as follows:—

Take another prism corresponding in every respect with the first, and, placing them both together, so as to form a parallelogram, the seven rays will be reunited, and form a single spot of light.

In concluding this brief sketch of the nature and properties of light, it will be as well to notice the structure of the human eye, the organ by which the glorious works of the all-wise Creator are observed and impressed upon our minds. The human eye is formed, externally, by a hard membrane termed the *sclerotic coat*, or commonly the *white of the eye*; in the fore-part of this coat there is an opening called the *cornea*, from its resemblance in texture to polished horn; the interior of the eye is lined with a fine membrane, the *choroid*, which round the cornea is fringed by the *ciliary processes*, behind the *iris;* through the centre of the latter, or the *pupil*, the rays of light pass into the chamber of the eye. The *crystalline humor* or lens, which is in form like a doubly convex lens, is situated among the ciliary processes, and is the immediate instrument of vision, as it conveys the light from the pupil to a focus at the back of the eye. A delicate membrane called the *retina*, which is an expansion of the optic nerve, lines the back of the eye, and receives the images of every object from the crystalline lens, in most exquisite perfection and most exact proportion. There are two humors for preserving the globular shape of the eye, the *aqueous* and the *vitreous;* the aqueous, as its name implies, is perfectly limpid, and is before the lens, immediately under the cornea; the vitreous fills the large cavity of the eye, to which it gives the globe-like form, and receives its appellation from being enclosed in a transparent spongy structure, so as to resemble, in some degree, molten glass.

The eye is in effect a camera obscura, in which the refracted light gives a very small but brilliant representation of external objects.

OPTICAL AUGMENTATION.

Take a large conical-shaped drinking-glass, and put a shilling into it, and fill it about half full with water. Put a plate upon the top of the glass, and turn it very quickly over, so that the water may not escape, and a piece of silver as large as half a crown will immediately appear in the plate, and some little way up the glass another piece will present itself, about the size of a shilling. This effect is caused by refraction.

THE THAUMATROPE, OR WONDER-TURNER.

The Thaumatrope is an exceedingly amusing toy of very simple construction and pleasing effect. It is made in the following manner. Cut out a circular piece of cardboard, and affix to it six pieces of string, three on each side, as delineated in the margin. Paint on one side of the card a bird, and on the other a cage, being particularly careful to draw them upside-down to each other, otherwise the desired effect will not be produced. When showing the toy, take hold of the centre strings between the forefingers and thumb of each hand, close to the card, and twist or twirl the card rapidly round, and, lo! the bird will appear snugly ensconced in its cage. The principle on which this pleasing toy acts, is, that the image of any object received on the retina or optic nerve, which is at the back of the eye, is retained in the eye for about eight seconds after the object causing the impression is withdrawn; consequently, the impression of the painting on one side of the card is not obliterated ere the painting on the other side is brought before the eye, and it therefore follows that both sides are seen at once. The subjects suited to the Thaumatrope are very varied. Among others, the following are well calculated for display; a juggler throwing up two balls may be drawn on one side of a card, and two balls only on the other, and, according to the pairs of strings employed, he will seem to toss two, three, or four balls; the body and legs of a man on one side, and his head and arms on the other; a candle and its flame; a mouse and a trap; and a horse and his rider: this last is a very good one, as by using the different pairs of strings the relative positions of man and horse may be varied most singularly.

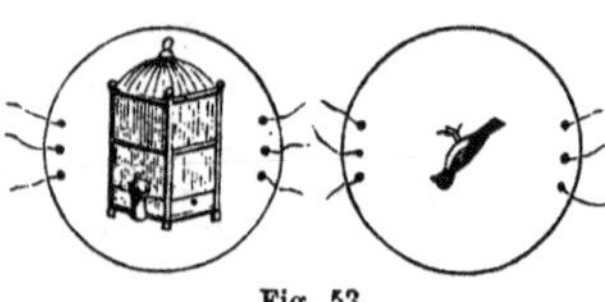

Fig. 53.

THE STROBOSCOPE, OR PHENAKISTISCOPE.

This is a most amusing instrument, and its principle resembles the thaumatrope, its effect depending, like that, upon the continuance of the image of an object upon the retina. It consists of a disk made of stout cardboard, upon which, toward the edge, a series of figures in eight or ten different positions is painted: thus, if it be wished to produce the illusion of a man running, the first position should be quiescent, standing upright, the second advancing forward a little, the third stepping out still more, and so on to the sixth figure, which should be drawn as if running at full speed; the remaining attitudes should show the person gradually returning to the first quiet attitude. Between each figure a slit must be made about three-quarters of an inch in length, and a quarter, or less, in width, running in a parallel direction with the radii of the disk, and extending to an equal

Fig. 54.

distance from the centre, as in the illustration. The disk when completed should be put upon a handle, as in the annexed figure. No. 1 shows a little nut, which must be unscrewed ere the disk can be placed on its axis, and which keeps it in its proper place, so that it cannot lean forward and spoil the experiment; 2 is the disk, and 3 is a nut fixed to the axis by which the rotatory motion is given to the disk. When trying the effect of this instrument, stand before a looking-glass, and hold the painted face of the machine toward the glass; cause it to revolve on its axis, and look through the slits, when, instead of beholding a mass of confusion, as might naturally be expected, and as would undoubtedly be the case were the disk viewed in the ordinary way, the figures will seem to be running as fast as possible, and with very natural movements, their velocity being, of course, proportioned to the rate at which the disk is impelled. The number of subjects adapted for this species of exhibition is considerable, and if they are well drawn they may be made the source of much merriment. Especial care must be taken, when drawing them, to make the figures correspond exactly with each other in shape and depth of tone, as much of the good effect of the display depends upon their accuracy in these particulars.

Fig. 55.

OPTICAL DECEPTIONS.

Faraday has shown that if two equal cog-wheels be cut out of cardboard, placed upon a pin, and turned round with equal velocity in opposite directions, instead of producing a hazy tint, as one wheel would do, or even as the two would if revolving in the same direction, there is presented an extraordinary appearance of a fixed wheel. Again, if one moves somewhat faster than the other, then the spectral wheel appears to move slowly round; if the cogs be cut slantwise on both wheels, the spectral wheel, in like manner, exhibits slant cogs; but if one of the wheels be turned so that the cogs shall point in opposite directions, then the spectral wheel has straight cogs. If wheels with radii or arms be viewed when moving, then similar optical deceptions appear; and though the wheels move ever so fast, yet the magic of a fixed wheel will be presented, provided they move with equal velocities. If they overlap each other in a small degree, then very curious lines will be seen.

Perhaps the most striking deception is the following. A pasteboard wheel has a certain number of teeth or cogs at its edges; a little nearer the centre is a series of apertures resembling the cogs in arrangement, but not the same in number; and still nearer the centre is another series of apertures, different in number, and varying from the former. When this wheel is fixed upon an axle, its face held two or three yards from an illuminated mirror, and spun round, the cogs disappear, and a grayish belt, three inches broad, becomes visible; but, on looking at the glass through the moving wheel, appearances entirely change: one row of cogs appears as fixed as if the wheel were not moving, while the other two give an opposite result: shifting the eye a little, other and new appearances are produced.

With the two wheels mentioned in the first experiment, if only one is turned in the sunlight, a shadow corresponding to its appearance will be produced; but if both are turned in opposite directions, the shadow is no longer uniform, but has light and dark alternately, and resembles the shadow of a fixed wheel.

CURIOUS OPTICAL EXPERIMENT.

Put on a piece of white paper a circular piece of blue silk, of about four inches diameter; next place on the blue silk a circular piece of yellow, of three inches diameter; on that a circle of pink, two inches in diameter; on that a circle of green, one inch in diameter; then one of indigo, half an inch in diameter; and finish by making a small speck of ink in the centre. Place it in the sunshine, look on the central point steadily for a minute or two, and then, closing your eyes, and applying your hand, at about an inch from them, so as to prevent too much light from passing through the eyelids, you will see the most beautiful circles of colors the imagination can conceive, differing widely from the colors of the silks, and also adding to the richness of the experiment by changing in kaleidoscopic variety.

AN OPTICAL GAME.

Give a ring to any person, or put it at a little distance, in such a position that the plane of it shall be turned toward his face, and then desire him to shut one of his eyes and endeavor to push a crooked stick through the ring: to his surprise, he will seldom succeed. The reason is evident: being unaccustomed to use one eye only, he cannot judge of the distance correctly, and, of course, errs; but a person having only one eye would not fail of achieving the trick.

INTERESTING EXPERIMENT WITH RAYS OF LIGHT.

Make a small hole in a stout piece of pasteboard, and set the piece upright on a table in front of two or three candles placed near together; lay a sheet of paper on the table, and the rays from the different candles passing through the hole will form as many spots of light as there are candles,—each spot being perfect and distinct. This experiment proves that the rays of light do not obstruct each other in their progress, although all cross in passing through the hole.

ELECTRICITY, GALVANISM, AND MAGNETISM.

Fig. 56.—The Origin of Galvanism (page 525).

THE primary object of the very elementary scientific articles in this work is to excite *curiosity* in the youthful mind, so as to induce a desire to read and study more extended and complete works on the various subjects to which they relate. The vast increase of knowledge derived from actual experiments with electricity, magnetism, and electro-magnetism precludes the idea of giving a complete description of all the varied phenomena in these branches of the science: brevity and simplicity have therefore been specially studied in the following experiments, which may be very appropriately prefaced with a glance at the historical connections of these imponderable agents.

The exact nature of ELECTRICITY has not been ascertained; but it is considered a highly subtle and elastic fluid. Its name is derived from the Greek word *electron*, signifying amber, on which substance some of its effects were first observed. The name of the person to whom we owe the earliest notice of the property of amber, when rubbed, to attract and repel light bodies, has not been handed down to posterity; but it is said that Thales, a philosopher, born at Miletus in Asia Minor, who flourished 600 years before Christ, and was considered one of the first of the seven sages of Greece, described this remarkable phenomenon. It was also mentioned by another Greek author, 321 years B.C.; but the ancients did not profit by the discovery, and the gleanings of the science were very feeble until the sixteenth century of our era, when Dr. Gilbert of Colchester applied the principles of philosophical investigation to the observations of the ancients.

ELECTRICITY is one of the most active principles in nature. It exists in all bodies, and is exhibited by various means,—one of which, and the most generally employed, is friction. Some substances, such as soot, charcoal, iron, gold, silver, copper, and other metals, water, &c., are called *good conductors*, because they transfer with great facility to other bodies the electric fluid, which glides over their surfaces with the velocity of light; whilst others, such as silk, wool, hair, feathers, dry paper, leather, glass, wax, &c., are called *non-conductors*, because they resist the progress of the fluid, which accumulates all the time the friction continues. It is from these media that the usual phenomena of frictional electricity, as exhibited in the experiments which we shall hereafter describe, are obtained. Its effects are felt in almost every part of nature; the awful lightning is the exhibition of the electric fluid, which accumulates in the clouds, and which is discharged when the heavy lurid masses come in contact with each other; the mysterious sweeping whirlwind, the terrific rising and rolling of the sand in the desert wilds of Africa, the waterspouts, and the beautiful and evanescent aurora borealis of the northern climes, are among a few of the effects attributed to it.

The next branch of the science of electricity is GALVANISM, or, as it is sometimes called, Voltaic Electricity: it is obtained chiefly by chemical action, and is said to have been first discovered at Bologna in the year 1791, by the lady of Louis Galvani, an Italian philosopher of great merit and professor of anatomy, and, indeed, from whom the science received its name. His wife, being possessed of a penetrating understanding and passionately loving him, took a lively interest in the science which so much occupied his attention. At the time the incident we are about to narrate took place, she was in a declining state of health, and using soup made of frogs by way of restorative. Some of these animals, skinned for the purpose, happened to be lying on the table of his laboratory, where also stood an electrical machine: the point of a knife was unintentionally brought into contact with the nerves of one of the frog's legs which lay close to the conductor of the machine, and immediately the muscles of the limb were violently agitated. Madame Galvani, having observed the phenomenon, instantly informed her husband of it, and this incident led to the experiments and interesting discoveries which will transmit his name to the latest posterity. It is proper to state that this somewhat romantic story is denied by some historians of the science.

The uses of galvanic or voltaic electricity for scientific purposes are incalculable, and its phenomena are so various and extraordinary as to render the study of this science exceedingly interesting. By means of a galvanic battery substances are decomposed, colors changed, water is decomposed, and motion is given to lifeless bodies.

The experiments we give on galvanism show the effect of the combination which forms what is called a simple galvanic circle, by means of two metals, zinc and silver, or zinc and copper, and water mixed with sulphuric acid.

Galvanic action is always accompanied by chemical action; and all that is necessary to disturb the galvanic or voltaic electricity is to unite two metals together, and subject them to the action of a fluid which will act chemically upon one of them more powerfully than upon the other.

A galvanic circle may also be formed of one metal and two fluids which have a different action upon the metal employed.

MAGNETISM is probably some modification of electricity: at least there is sufficient evidence that these causes are intimately connected, if not identical; but philosophers are as yet ignorant of its nature. It is equally unknown the exact time when, and the country where, the property of the magnet was first considered. The Greeks of the time of Pythagoras were acquainted with its property of attracting metals. It was also familiar to the Arabs and the Indians, and the Chinese from the earliest ages have known its polarity or directive power, the needle being employed among them one thousand years before Christ to direct travellers by land. In Europe, a Neapolitan, named Flavio Gioia, who lived in the thirteenth century, has been regarded by many as the inventor of the mariner's compass; but it was in use in the eleventh century in Iceland, as is confirmed by the historian Arc Frode, who wrote, about that time, the history of the discovery of his country, and who speaks of the mariner's compass in very definite terms, and thus indirectly shows that it was employed or invented nearly as early as the tenth century.

The property designated by the word "magnetism" is found in an iron-ore of a certain composition, and of a dark-gray color and peculiar lustre. This ore alone is the natural local habitation of magnetism, whilst others are subject to its influence or attracted by it.

This singular property of the loadstone is imparted to iron and steel by rubbing and keeping them close together for some length of time. The steel retains the magnetic principle permanently; but iron loses the power as soon as it is separated from the magnet. The steel thus prepared acquires the same directive and attractive power as the loadstone or natural magnet, and is employed for purposes of the utmost importance.

We proceed to give the youthful amateur the opportunity of exemplifying the principles of electricity, galvanism, and magnetism, by several interesting and simple experiments.

SIMPLE MEANS OF PRODUCING ELECTRICITY.

To show the nature of electrical action, rub a piece of sealing-wax or amber upon the coat-sleeve, and it will be found that while warm by the friction it attracts light bodies, such as straws or small pieces of paper. If a clean glass tube be rubbed several times through a silken or leather cloth, and presented to any small substances, it will immediately attract or repel them· and if a poker suspended by a dry silk string be presented to its upper end, then the lower end of the poker will exhibit the same phenomena as the tube itself,—which shows that the electrical fluid passes through the metal. But if for a metallic body a stick of glass or sealing-wax be substituted, these phenomena will not occur,—which proves that the electrical fluid does not pass through these substances.

Fig. 57.

By this it will be perceived that besides the class of bodies called electrics, there is another which we call conductors. These bodies cannot be excited themselves, but have the power of transmitting the electric fluid through them. These bodies comprise all the metals, some metal and metallic ores; the fluids of animal bodies, water, and other fluids, except oil, ice, snow, earthy substances, smoke, steam; and even a vacuum.

Fig. 58.

When any electrified conductor is wholly surrounded by non-conductors, so that the electric fluid cannot pass from the conductor along conductors to the earth, it is said to be insulated: thus, the human body is a conductor of electricity; but if a person standing on a glass stool (as represented in the drawing) be charged with electricity, the electric fluid cannot pass from him to the earth, and he is said to be *positively electrified*, because he has more than his natural share; he is also *insulated*, and, if he be touched by another person standing on the ground, sparks will be exhibited at the point of contact, where also the person touching will feel a pricking sensation.

ATTRACTION AND REPULSION EXHIBITED.

In order to illustrate certain remarkable facts in this science, of an amusing character, attention must be directed to the figure A B, which is a metal stand; C is a small piece of cork or pith, which is suspended from the hook by a dry silken thread. Having rubbed an electron, as a dry rod of glass, and presented it to C, the ball will be instantaneously attracted to the glass and will adhere to it. After remaining in contact for a few seconds, if the glass be withdrawn without being touched by the fingers, and again presented to the ball, the latter will be *repelled*, instead of attracted, as in the first instance. By being touched with the finger, the ball can be deprived of its electricity, and if after this has been done we present a piece of sealing-wax in place of the glass formerly employed, the very same phenomena will take place. On the first application the ball will be *attracted*, and on the second *repelled*.

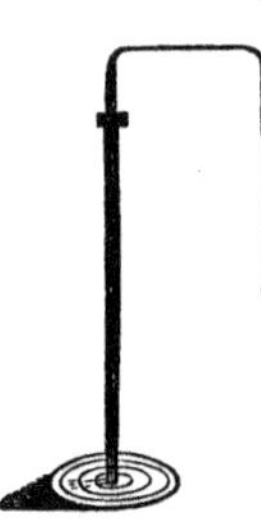

Fig. 59.

Before the young reader can perform any very important experiments with electricity, he must become possessed of an ELECTRICAL MACHINE, which is an instrument contrived for the purpose of rubbing together the surfaces of electrics and non-electrics. They generally consist of a cylinder, or plate of glass, and a piece of silk for it to rub against, covered with an amalgam, the method of preparing which we shall hereafter describe.

HOW TO MAKE AN ELECTRICAL MACHINE.

It is very easy to make a glass machine of the cylindrical form, if the maker cannot afford to buy one. First procure a common wine-bottle of good dimensions and thickish glass. Drill a hole through its bottom, by igniting a piece of worsted tied round it dipped in turpentine, which will do this. Through this hole and the mouth pass a spindle, as represented in the cut. The end of B should be squared to fix a handle on, and the spindle should be fixed firmly in the bottle. The bottle is

Fig. 60.

then to be fixed in a frame in the following manner: the end of the spindle passes through a hole at B; and the other end at C has the handle for turning the machine.

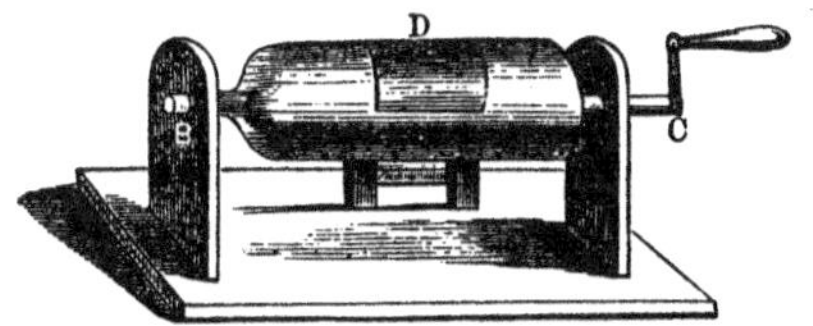

Fig. 61.

Next make a cushion of wash-leather stuffed with wool, and fastened to the top of a frame of the following figure. This frame is to be of such a height that the cushion shall press against the sides of the bottle, and a piece of black silk is sewn on to the top of the cushion, and hangs over the bottle D. The cushion should be smeared with an amalgam, formed by melting together in the bowl of a tobacco-pipe one part of tin with two of zinc, to which, while fluid, should be added six parts of mercury. These should be stirred about till quite cold, and then reduced to a fine powder in a mortar, and mixed with a sufficient quantity of lard to form a thickish paste. When all is done, the machine is complete.

Fig. 62.—Cushion.

THE CONDUCTOR.

The electricity being generated by the friction produced between the rubber and the bottle from the motion imparted by the handle, it is necessary to draw it off for use. This is per formed by what is called a conductor. This is made in the following manner. At right angles to one end of a cylinder of wood about two inches and a half in diameter and six inches long, fix a small wooden cylinder about three-quarters of an inch in diameter and three inches long, rounded at both ends. The other end of the larger cylinder is also to be rounded. Cover the whole with tinfoil, and mount it on a stand on a glass rod. When used, it is to be placed with the even piece in a line even with and about half an inch from the bottle, and it should be of such a height as to come just below the silk apron. When it is wished to charge a Leyden jar, it is to be placed at the round end of the conductor. By these simple means a great variety of pleasing experiments may be performed; but, to show the various phenomena connected with this interesting study, we shall now describe an electrical machine of the newest construction, and perform our experiments with it.

THE PLATE ELECTRICAL MACHINE.

Formerly the electrical machine was made in the form of a cylinder, but now it consists of a plate, A, as seen in the engraving. The plate is turned by the handle F through the rubber B B, which diffuses the excitement over the glass. The points or balls at each side of the plate carry off a constant stream of positive electricity to the prime conductor C. Negative electricity is generated by insulating the conductor to which the cushion is attached, and continuing the prime conductor into the ground, so as to carry off the fluid collected from the plate.

Fig. 63.

HOW TO DRAW SPARKS FROM THE TIP OF THE NOSE.

If the person who works the machine be supported on a stool having glass legs and connected with the conductor by means of a glass rod, the electricity will pass from the conductor to him, and, as it cannot get away, owing to the glass on which he stands being a non-conductor, any person on touching him can draw the electricity from him, which will exhibit itself in small sparks as it passes to the person who touches him. If touched on the nose, sparks of fire will issue from it.

HOW TO GET A JAR FULL OF ELECTRICITY.

A most useful piece of electrical apparatus is called the Leyden jar, here represented. It is employed for the purpose of obtaining a quantity of electricity, which may be applied to any substance. It consists of a glass jar, coated both inside and without, four-fifths of the way up, with tinfoil. A knob rises through a wooden top communicating with the inside of the jar. When it is wished to charge the jar, this knob is applied to the prime conductor of the electrical machine when in action, and, a quantity of electricity being given off, the jar will remain charged with it till a connection is made by some good conductor of electricity between the knob and the outside tinfoil. A piece of brass chain must hang from the stem that carries the knob and connect it with the interior of the jar.

Fig. 64.

THE ELECTRICAL BATTERY.

If several of these jars be united, an enormous quantity of electricity can be collected; but, in arranging them, all the interior coatings must be made to communicate by metallic rods, and a similar union must be effected among the exterior coatings. When thus arranged, the whole series may be charged as if they formed but one jar.

For the purpose of making a direct communication between the inner or outer coatings of a jar or battery by which a dis-

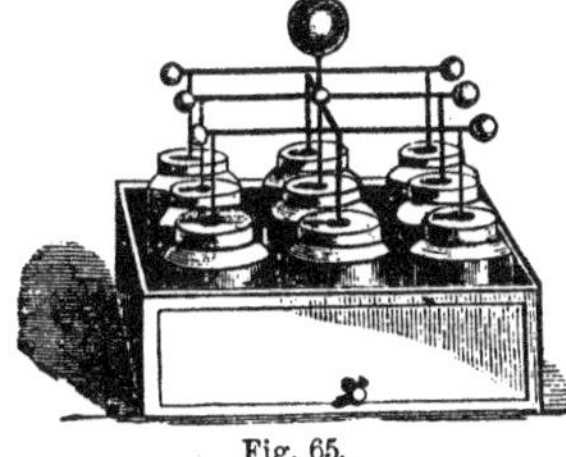

Fig. 65.

Fig. 66.

charge is effected, an instrument called a discharging rod is employed. It consists of two bent metallic rods, terminating at one end by brass balls, and connected at another by a joint which is fixed to the end of a glass handle, and which, acting like a pair of compasses, allows of the balls being separated at certain distances. When opened to the proper degree, one of the balls is made to touch the exterior coating, and the other ball is then brought into contact with the knob of the jar, when a discharge is effected; while the glass handle secures the person holding it from the effects of the shock.

DANCING BALLS AND DOLLS.

Get two round pieces of wood, A B, and coat them with tin-foil; or two pieces of metal plate; attach one of them to the

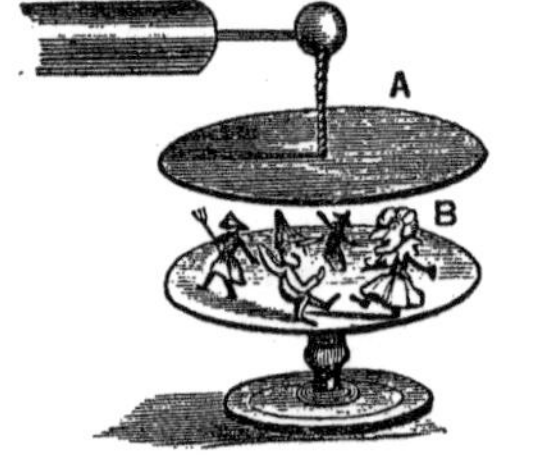

Fig. 67.

Fig. 68.

prime conductor by a chain, and let it hang about two or three inches from the knob. Place some pith-balls upon the bottom piece of wood B, and bring it under the other. Immediately this is done, and the upper piece is charged by electricity from the machine, the pith-balls will jump up and down, and from one to the other, with great rapidity. If some of the pith be formed into little figures, they will also dance and leap about in the most grotesque manner. The same may be made to dance by merely holding the inside of a dry glass tumbler to the prime conductor for a few minutes, while the machine is in action, and then whelm it over them, when they will jump about, to the no small astonishment of the spectators, as the cause of their motions is not quite so apparent.

THE ELECTRICAL KISS.

This amusing experiment is performed by means of the electrical stool. Let any lady challenge a gentleman not acquainted with the experiment to favor her with a salute. The lady thereupon mounts the glass stool, and takes hold of a chain connected with the prime conductor. The machine being then put in motion, the gentleman approaches the lady, and immediately he attempts to imprint the seal of soft affection upon her coral lips, a spark will fly in his face, which generally deters him from his rash and wicked intention.

RINGING BELLS.

Bells may be made to ring by electricity in the following manner. Let three small bells be suspended from a brass wire D D, and supported by a glass pillar A, passing through bell B to the bell E. The electrical apparatus being attached to the knob E, the electricity passes down the wires D D to the bells, which are then positively electrified and attract the clappers C C, that are negatively so, in consequence of being insulated by the silken strings, which are not conductors. The bells therefore attract the clappers till they are charged, when they strike against the centre bell to discharge themselves, and thus a peal is rung on the bells until the electricity is driven off.

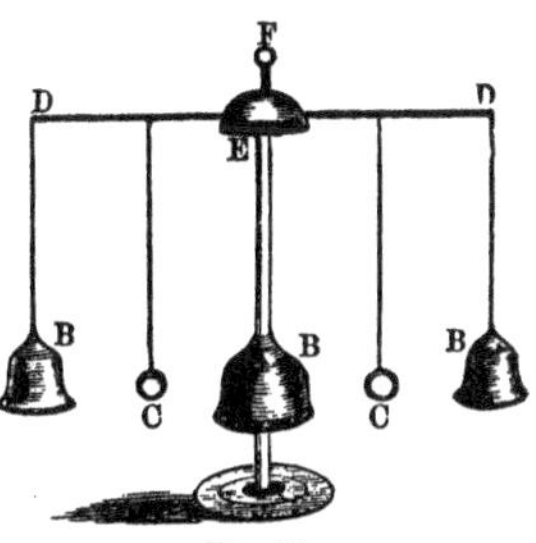

Fig. 69.

WORKING-POWER OF ELECTRICITY.

This may be shown in a variety of ways. The subjoined machine will exhibit the principle upon which many ingenious toys may be made by the young philosopher. In the figure, A is a wooden board or stand, B B B B, four pillars having fine wires, C C, stretched above. On these rest the rotatory wire or wheel F, having its points turned the reverse ways. By means of a chain attached to the conductor, and to the instrument at B, the electricity passes over the pillar B, up the wire C, into the wheel, and off at the points, which causes it to be turned round on an inclined plane till it reaches the top.

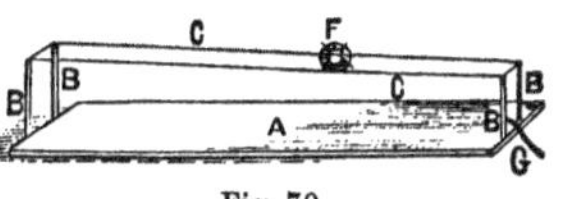

Fig. 70.

THE ELECTRIFIED WIG.

Fig. 71.

While a person is on the electrical stool, if he be charged with much electricity,

> "Each hair will stand on end,
> Like quills upon the fretful porcupine."

A wooden head—not your own, but a real wooden head, with a wig of streaming hair, and a handsome face to correspond—may be made in the following form, with a wire in the neck to support it by, and fixed in the conductor of an electrical machine. When this is put in motion, the hair will rise up as in the figure, to astonish even those who are seldom astonished by or deterred from any thing.

IMITATION THUNDER-CLOUDS.

To show the manner in which thunder-clouds perform their operations in the air. A A is a wooden stand, on which are

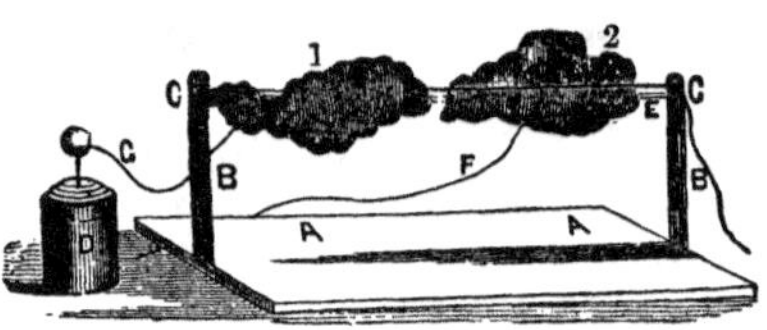

Fig. 72.

erected two uprights, B B; C C are two small pulleys, over which a silken cord can pull easily; E is another silken line stretched across from one upright to another; on these silken cords two pieces of thin cardboard, covered with tinfoil, and cut so as to represent clouds, are to be fixed horizontally, and made to communicate by means of thin wires, *f* and *g*, one with the *inside*, and the other with the outside, of a charged jar, D. Now, by pulling the loop of the silk line, D, the cloud 1 will be brought near the cloud 2; continue this slowly, until the clouds (which are furnished with two small brass balls) are within an inch of each other, when a beautiful flash, strongly resembling lightning in miniature, will pass from one cloud to the other, restoring electrical equilibrium.

THE LIGHTNING-STROKE IMITATED.

If the jar D be put behind the stand, and the cloud 2 removed, a vessel communicating by means of a wire with the

Fig. 73.

outside of the jar may be swum in water under the remaining cloud,—the mast being made of separate pieces, and but slightly joined together. When the cloud is passed over the vessel, the mast will be struck and shattered to pieces.

THE SPORTSMAN.

This apparatus is capable of affording much amusement. A is a stand of wood; B is a common Leyden jar, out of which

Fig. 74.

proceed the wires H H, one terminating in the ball F, the other in the ball D, to which are attached a number of pith birds by silken strings; E is a shelf for the birds to rest upon; C is the sportsman; G his gun.

To put this operation in motion, the Leyden jar is to be charged with electricity by affixing a chain to the bottom part of it, and connecting it with an electrical machine in the usual manner, or by applying it to a prime conductor, when the birds will fly off the knob to which they are fixed, in consequence of their being repelled. If the sportsman and gun be then turned so that the end of his gun shall touch the knob F, an electric spark will pass from one to the other, a report will be heard, and the birds will fall down as if shot, in consequence of the electricity having been taken from the Leyden jar. There should be a communication between the sportsman and the jar, formed of tinfoil, or some metal, as shown by the dotted line on the stand.

MISCELLANEOUS EXPERIMENTS WITH FRICTIONAL ELECTRICITY.

1. Lay a watch down upon a table, and on its face balance a tobacco-pipe very carefully. Next take a wineglass, rub it quickly with a silk handkerchief, and hold it for half a minute before the fire; then apply it near to the end of the pipe, and the latter, attracted by the electricity evolved by the friction and warmth in the former, will immediately follow it; and by carrying the glass around, always in front of the pipe, this will continue its rotatory motion, the watch-glass being the centre or pivot on which it acts.

Fig. 75.

2. Warm a glass tube, rub it with a warm flannel, and then bring a downy feather near it. On the first moment of contact the feather will adhere to the glass, but soon after will fly rapidly from it, and you may drive it about the room by holding the glass between it and the surrounding objects; should it, however, come in contact with any thing not under the influence of electricity, it will instantly fly back to the glass.

3. A stick of sealing-wax rubbed against a warm piece of flannel or cloth acquires the property of attracting light substances, such as small pieces of paper, lint, &c., if instantly applied at the distance of about an inch.

4. Suspend two small pith balls, by fine silken threads of about six inches in length, in such a manner that when at rest they may hang in contact with each other: on applying a piece of sealing-wax excited as in the former experiment, they will repel each other.

5. Take a piece of common brown paper about the size of an octavo book, hold it before the fire till quite dry and hot, then draw it briskly under the arm several times, so as to rub it on both sides at once by the coat. The paper will be found so powerfully electrical that if placed against a wainscotted or papered wall of a room it will remain there for some minutes without falling.

6. And if, while the paper adheres to the wall, a light fleecy feather is placed against it, it will be attracted to the paper in the same way as the paper is attracted to the wall.

7. If the paper be again warmed and drawn under the arm as before, and hung up by a thread attached to one corner of it, it will hold up several feathers on each side; should these fall off from different sides at the same time, they will cling together very strongly, and if after a minute they are all shaken off, they will fly to one another in a very singular manner.

8. Warm and excite the paper as before, lay it on a table, and place upon it a ball made of elder-pith about the size of a pea; the ball will immediately run across the paper, and, if a needle be pointed toward it, it will again run to another part, and so on for a considerable time.

9. Support a pane of glass, previously warmed, upon two books, one at each end, and place some bran underneath; then rub the upper side of the glass with a black silk handkerchief, or a piece of flannel, and the bran will dance up and down under it with much rapidity.

10. Arrange two tumblers (which must be perfectly dry and warm) on a table, in an inverted position; bridge them over with a common pane of window-glass, also clean and dry. If the centre of the pane of glass be rubbed with a stick covered with a silk handkerchief, and some pieces of cut paper are placed on a tin box just under the glass, they will exhibit electrical attraction and repulsion.

ELECTRICAL MACHINES

Are nothing more than extended surfaces of glass provided with simple means of being rubbed when turned by a proper handle; and one of the cheapest and most entertaining instruments for obtaining frictional electricity is the electrophorus, and particularly the instrument as manufactured and described by Mr. Lewis M. Stewart, of the City of London School.

EXCITATION OF THE ELECTROPHORUS.

Beat B, the resinous plate, smartly with a very dry piece of flannel, and hold it closely before a pith ball placed on D; the pith ball will be attracted, or any other light substance.

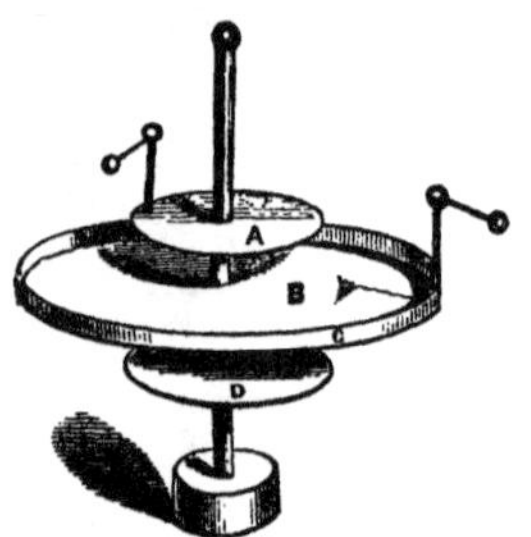

Fig. 76.—Stewart's electrophorus.
A. Brass plate provided with a glass handle, and wire with pith ball attached by a thread.
B. The resinous plate.
C. The brass or tin dish containing the resinous plate, also provided with a pith ball.
D. The lower plate, supported on a glass leg, with a wooden foot, and forming a convenient insulating stand.

ILLUSTRATION OF CONDUCTORS.

After exciting the resinous plate B, place B C upon a table, and A upon B C, and connect the plate A with the table D by means of a fine wire; upon touching A with the finger, and then removing it from B, both A and D will be electrified, provided the fine wire has not touched the table or any other conducting body.

ILLUSTRATION OF NON-CONDUCTORS.

Connect the wire with the glass handle of A, and proceed as before; the plate D will not be electrified, as the glass, representing a part of the connecting chain, is a non-conductor of electricity.

EFFECT OF POINTS.

Electrify A, and the little pith is repelled; if a point, such as a needle, is now brought to A, the pith gradually falls.

EFFECT OF BALLS.

Electrify A, and present a round brass ball to it; the repelled pith ball does not drop, provided the spark does not pass.

With this electrophorus arrangement nearly every fact in frictional electricity shown by more expensive and elaborate apparatus may be displayed; and it is certainly one of the best instruments for class-instruction, as the resinous plate, when once thoroughly excited, will remain in action for many hours.

Fig. 77.

EXPERIMENTS WITH VOLTAIC ELECTRICITY, OR GALVANISM.

1. Place a thin plate of zinc upon the upper surface of the tongue, and a half-crown or a piece of silver on the under surface. Allow the metals to remain for a little time in contact with the tongue before they are made to touch each other, that the taste of the metals themselves may not be confounded with the sensation produced by their contact. When the edges of the metals which project beyond the tongue are then suffered to touch, a galvanic sensation is produced, which it is difficult accurately to describe.

2. Place a silver teaspoon as high as possible between the gums and the upper lip, and a piece of zinc between the gums and the under lip. On bringing the extremities of the metals into contact, a very vivid sensation, and an effect like a flash of light across the eyes, will be perceived. It is singular that this light is equally vivid in the dark and in the strongest light, and whether the eyes be shut or open.

3. Take a piece of copper of about six inches in width, and put upon it a piece of zinc of rather smaller dimensions, inserting a piece of cloth damped with dilute sulphuric acid, of the same size as the zinc, between them; place a leech upon the piece of zinc, and, though there appears nothing to hinder it from crawling away, yet it will hardly pass from the zinc to the copper, because as soon as its damp body touches the copper it receives a galvanic shock, and of course retires to its resting-place, the zinc.

4. Plunge an iron knife into a solution of sulphate of copper (bluestone): by chemical action only it will become covered with metallic copper. Immerse in the same solution a piece of platinum, taking care not to let it touch the iron, and no deposition of copper will take place upon it; but if the upper ends of the metals are brought into contact with each other, a copious deposition of copper will soon settle upon the platinum likewise.

WITH METAL PLATES IN WATER.

If we take two plates of different kinds of metal, platinum or copper, and zinc, for example, and immerse them in pure water, having wires attached to them above, then if the wire of each is brought into contact in another vessel of water, a galvanic circle will be formed, the water will be slowly decomposed, its oxygen will be fixed on the zinc wire, and at the same time a current of electricity will be transmitted through the liquid to the platinum or copper wire, on the end of which the other element of water—namely, the hydrogen—will make its appearance in the form of minute gas-bubbles. The electrical current passes back again into the zinc at the points of its contact with the platinum, and thus a continued current is kept up, and hence it is called a galvanic circle. The moment the circuit is broken by separating the wires, the current ceases, but is again renewed by making them touch either in or out of the water. If a small quantity of sulphuric acid be added to the water, the phenomenon will be more apparent. The end of the wire attached to the piece of platinum or copper is called the positive pole of the battery, and that of the wire attached to the zinc the negative pole.

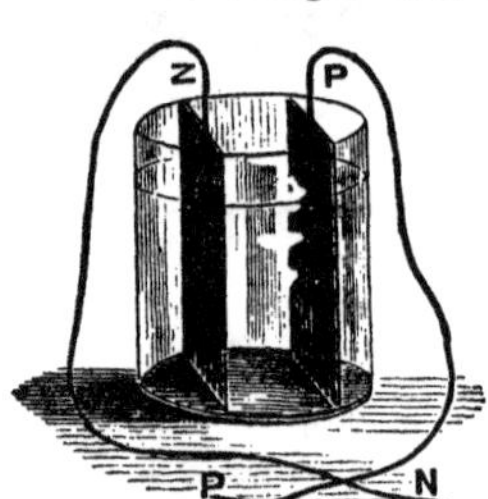

Fig. 78.

The current of electricity here generated will be extremely

feeble; but this can be easily increased by multiplying the glasses and the number of the pieces of metal. If we take six

Fig. 79.

such glasses instead of one, partially fill them with dilute sulphuric acid, and put a piece of zinc and copper into each, connecting them by means of copper wire from glass to glass through the whole series, a stronger current of electricity will be the result. The experimenter must be careful not to let the wire and zinc touch each other at the bottom of the tumblers, and must also remember that the copper of glass 1 is connected with the zinc of glass 2, and so on.

TO MAKE A MAGNET BY GALVANISM.

To effect this, make a connection between the poles of the above or any excited battery with the two ends of a wire formed into a spiral coil, by bending common bonnet-wire closely round a cylinder, or tube, of about an inch in diameter; into this coil introduce a needle, or piece of steel wire, laying it lengthways down the circles of the coil. In a few minutes after the electric fluid has passed through the spiral wire, and consequently round the needle or wire, the latter will be found to be strongly magnetized and to possess all the properties of a magnet.

EFFECTS OF GALVANISM ON A MAGNET.

If a galvanic current, or any electric current, be made to pass along a wire under which and in a line with it a compass is placed, it will be found that the needle will no longer point north and south, but will take a direction nearly across the current, and point almost east and west.

CHANGE OF COLOR BY GALVANISM.

Put a teaspoonful of sulphate of soda into a cup, and dissolve it in hot water; pour a little cabbage blue into the solution, and put a portion into two glasses, connecting them by a piece of linen or cotton cloth previously moistened in the same solution. On putting one of the wires of the galvanic pole into each glass, the acid accumulates in the one, turning the blue to a red, and the alkali in the other, rendering it green. If the wires be now reversed, the acid accumulates eventually in the glass where the alkali appeared, while the alkali passes to the glass where the acid was.

TO TAKE AN ELECTROTYPE COPY OF A WAX SEAL.

Having selected a good and perfect seal, thoroughly black-lead the surface with the ordinary plumbago, laid on and polished with an old and soft tooth-brush. Into the side of the seal, in a portion of the wax seal not covered with the impression, melt in gently a very thin copper wire, so that the surface of the upper side of the wire shall be flush with the seal, and black-lead this juncture carefully; then wind the other end of the thin copper wire round a piece of amalgamated zinc five inches long, one-eighth of an inch thick, and three-quarters of an inch broad, as in this arrangement the seal takes the place of the copper element in the simple voltaic circle.

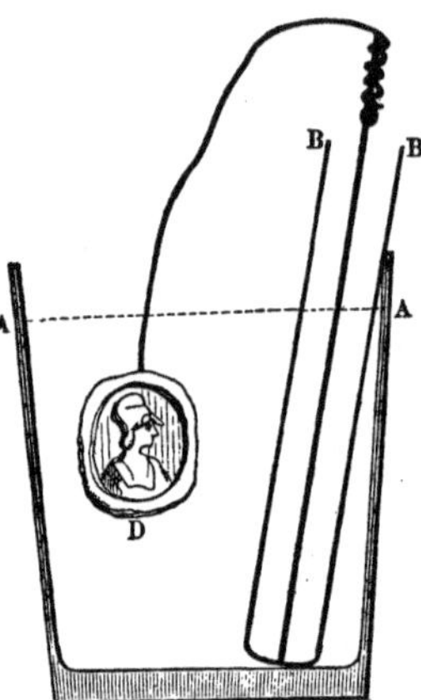

Fig. 80.—Electrotyping. A A. The tumbler containing the solution of sulphate of copper.
B B. The porous cell made of brown paper, holding the dilute acid, and the amalgamated zinc plate.
D. The wax seal black-leaded, attached to zinc plate by the connecting wire.

In half a pint of boiling water dissolve as much powdered sulphate of copper, or bluestone, as the water will take up; place this, when cold, in an ordinary tumbler, and, having rolled a piece of brown paper three or four times round a ruler one inch thick, close the side and bottom with sealing-wax, to make a porous cell. Hold the brown paper tube or cell over the tumbler containing the solution of sulphate of copper, and pour into it a mixture of five parts water and one part oil of vitriol (these latter must be mixed beforehand, and should be quite cold): as the acid is poured into the brown paper cell, let it sink into the sulphate-of-copper solution, and then, finally, having bent the wire that unites the seal to the amalgamated zinc, place the latter in the brown paper vessel, and the former into the solution of copper in the tumbler, and in about twelve hours a beautiful impression of the wax seal will be obtained in copper.

N.B.—Zinc is easily amalgamated by dipping it first into some dilute sulphuric acid, and then, having a little mercury in a plate, it may be rubbed on by means of a flat piece of stick covered with flannel.

EXPERIMENTS WITH MAGNETISM.

1. We have said that the agency of the magnet can be imparted to steel; this may be done in a very easy way. If you pass a magnet (which may be either natural or artificial) over a sewing-needle several times from the eye to the point, the needle will acquire the principle and attract iron filings in the same manner as a natural magnet would do. But the part of the magnet which you apply to the needle must be the north pole, and you must not pass it over the needle backwards and forwards, but lift it always from the point, and again begin from the eye. Suppose you wish to impart the principle to a small bar of tempered steel: tie the piece to be magnetized to a poker with a piece of silk, and hold the part of the poker to which it is attached in the left hand; take hold of the tongs a little below the middle, with the right hand, and rub the steel bar with them, moving the tongs from the bottom to the top, and keeping them steadily in a vertical position all the time. About a dozen strokes on each side will impart quite sufficient magnetical power to the bar to enable the operator to lift up small pieces of iron and steel with it. The lower end of the bar should be marked before it is fastened to the poker, so that the poles may be readily distinguished from each other when it is taken off,—the upper end being the south pole, and the lower the north.

Fig. 81.

2. Scatter some iron filings upon a piece of paper, and hold a magnet underneath it. The instant the contact takes place, the filings will raise themselves upright, and fall down as soon as the magnet is withdrawn. The effect is singular, and, indeed, very amusing,—the diminutive iron particles rising and falling as if by supernatural agency.

MAGNETIC SWAN.

Form a swan of cork, and place within its beak a little bit of steel strongly magnetized, then cover it with a thin coating of white wax, and, to render the image more complete, glass beads may be put in its head to represent the eyes. The swan being thus made, you must provide it with a lake to swim in. A basin of water may supply this, and when your lake is ready and the swan placed in it, the next object is to make it swim about. This you may easily accomplish by holding in your hand a magnetic bar, on which the north and south poles are marked. Show the north pole of the wand to the swan, and the little creature will immediately follow it, moving very gently over the water; you may thus lead it about; and when you wish it to retire, present the south pole of the wand to it, and, like a good, obedient bird, it will readily recede and turn back.

Fig. 82.

If you wish to make a magnetic wand, you may do so by procuring a hollow cane eight or nine inches in length and half an inch thick, and a small steel bar well magnetized. Put this bar in the cane, and close it at both ends by screwing on small ivory tops differing in shape, or having some marks by which you may in an instant recognize the north and south ends of the rod. With this wand you may direct the course of any floating figure you may choose to fashion.

TO SHOW THE EFFECT OF MAGNETISM BY MEANS OF A BALANCE.

Suspend a magnet in one of the scales of a very delicate balance, and carefully adjust it by putting weights into the other scale; when thus counterpoised, hold a piece of iron under the scale to which the magnet is attached, and it will immediately descend. If, instead of the magnet, a piece of iron be attached to the scale, and the magnet held under the iron, the scale will descend as before.

TO SHOW THAT THE POWER OF ATTRACTION RESIDES CHIEFLY AT THE POLES.

Place some iron filings upon a table, and then put among them a magnetic rod or bar. The filings will immediately adhere to the ends of the bar or rod, but not to the middle or centre, where the power of attraction is very little exerted, if at all.

Fig. 83.

TO SHOW THE REPULSION OF THE POLES.

The north poles of two magnets repel each other, and the same happens with the south poles, for the magnetic attraction is exerted only between the contrary poles. Thus, if you fix two magnetized needles in two pieces of cork, and place them in a basin of water, and they are in a parallel position with the same poles together, that is, north to north or south to south, they will mutually repel each other; but if the contrary poles point to one another, then they will be attracted and draw close together.

TO SHOW THE DIRECTIVE POWER OF THE MAGNET.

If you balance a bar of steel or an untouched needle horizontally upon a pivot or centre, it will remain stationary; but magnetize the same, as already indicated, and place it again on its centre, and you will see that it turns round, and does not stop until its north pole is in the direction of the north pole of the earth.

TO MAKE ARTIFICIAL MAGNETS.

This may be done by stroking a piece of hard steel with a natural or artificial magnet. Take a common sewing-needle, and pass the north pole of a magnet from the eye to the point, pressing it gently in so doing. After reaching the end of the needle, the magnet must not be passed back again towards the eye, but must be lifted up and applied again to that end, the friction being always in the same direction. After repeating this for a few times, the needle will become magnetized, and attract iron filings, &c.

HOW TO MAGNETIZE A POKER.

Hold it in the left hand in a position slightly inclined from the perpendicular, the lower end pointing to the north, and then strike it smartly several times with a large iron hammer, and it will be found to possess the powers of a magnet, although but slightly.

THE WATCH MAGNETIZED.

Borrow a watch from the company, and inquire if it will go when laid on the table. Then place it just over the point at which a magnet is fixed underneath the top of the table, and the magnet will attract the balance-wheel of the watch, and cause it to stop.

TO SHOW MAGNETIC REPULSION AND ATTRACTION.

Suspend two short pieces of iron wire, N S, N S, so that they will hang in contact in a vertical position. If the north pole of a magnet N be now brought to a moderate distance between the wires, they will recede from each other as in No. 1.

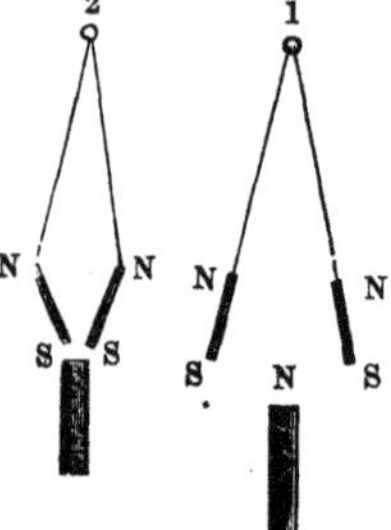

Fig. 84.

The ends S S, being made south poles by induction from the north pole N, will repel each other, and so will the north poles N N. This separation of the wires will increase as the magnet approaches them, but there will be a particular distance at which the attractive force of N overcomes the repulsive force of the poles S S, and causes the wires to converge as in No. 2, the north poles N N still exhibiting their mutual repulsion.

POLARITY OF THE MAGNET.

The best method of proving this is to take a magnet, or a piece of steel rendered magnetic, and to place it on a piece of cork by laying it in a groove cut to receive it. If the cork be placed in the centre of a basin of water, and allowed to swim freely on its surface, so that it is not attracted by the sides of the basin, it will be found to turn its north pole to the north, and its south pole to the south, the same as the mariner's compass. If you fix two magnets in two pieces of cork, and place them also in a basin of water, and they are in a parallel position with the same poles together, that is, north to north and south to south, they will mutually repel each other; but if the contrary poles point to one another, as north to south, they will be attracted.

Fig. 85.

NORTH AND SOUTH POLES OF THE MAGNET.

Each magnet has its poles, north and south: the north and south poles of one magnet repel the north and south poles of another. If a magnet, as in the following figure, be dipped in some iron filings, they will be immediately attracted to one end. Supposing this to be the north pole, each of the ends of the filings not in contact with the magnet will become north poles, while the ends in contact will by induction become south poles. Both will have a tendency to repel each other, and the filings will stand on the magnet as in the figure.

Fig. 86.

THE MAGNETIC FISH.

Fish are to be purchased at the toy-shops, by which the young *magnétique* may perform this experiment: they are made hollow, and will float on the water. In the mouth of each should be inserted a piece of magnetic wire. The angling-rod is like any other rod, and has a silken thread for a line, and an iron hook, also strongly magnetized. To catch the fish, it is only necessary to put the hook in contact with the noses of the fish, and they will be taken without any of the baits mentioned in the "Young Angler."

Fig. 87.

HORSESHOE MAGNETS.

The form of a horseshoe is generally given to magnetized bars when both poles are wanted to act together, which frequently happens in various experiments, such as for lifting weights by the force of magnetic attraction, and for magnetizing steel bars by the process of double touch, for which they are exceedingly convenient. The following is a method of making a powerful magnetic battery of the horseshoe form. Twelve bars or plates of steel are to be taken, and, having been previously bent to the required form,—that is, the horseshoe shape,—they are then bound together by means of rivets at their ends; before being

Fig. 88.

finally fastened, they are each separately magnetized, and afterward finally united.

Horseshoe magnets should have a short bar of soft iron adapted to connect the two poles, and should never be laid by without such a piece of iron adhering to them. Bar magnets should be kept in pairs, with their poles turned in contrary directions, and they should be kept from rust. Both kinds of magnets have their power not only preserved but increased by keeping them surrounded with a mass of dry filings of soft iron, each particle of which will react by its induced magnetism upon the point of the magnet to which it adheres, and maintain in that point its primitive magnetic state.

TO MAKE ARTIFICIAL MAGNETS WITHOUT THE AID EITHER OF NATURAL LOADSTONES OR ARTIFICIAL MAGNETS.

Take an iron poker and tongs, or two bars of iron,—the larger and the older the better,—and, fixing the poker upright, hold to it with the left hand near the top P, by a silk thread, a bar of soft steel about three inches long, one-fourth of an inch broad, and one-twentieth thick; mark one end, and let this end be downwards. Then, grasping the tongs T with the right hand a little below the middle, and keeping them nearly in a vertical line, let the bar B be rubbed with the lower end L of the tongs, from the marked end of the bar to its upper end, about ten times on each side of it. By this means the bar B will receive as much magnetism as will enable it to lift a small key at the marked end; and this end of the bar, being suspended by its middle, or made to rest on a joint, will turn to the north, and is called its north pole, the unmarked end being the south pole. This is the method recommended by Mr. Caxton in his process, which he regarded as superior to those in former use, and of which a more detailed account will be found in his interesting volume.

Fig. 89.

EXPERIMENT TO SHOW THAT SOFT IRON POSSESSES MAGNETIC PROPERTIES WHILE IT REMAINS IN THE VICINITY OF A MAGNET.

Let M be a magnet, and K a key, held horizontally near one of its poles, or near its lower edge. Then, if another piece of iron, such as a small nail, be applied to the other end of the key, the nail will hang from the key, and will continue to do so while the magnet is slowly withdrawn; but when it has been removed beyond a certain distance, the nail will drop from the key, because the magnetism induced in the key becomes at that distance too weak to support the weight of the nail. That this is the real cause of its falling off may be proved by taking a still lighter fragment of iron, such as a piece of very slender wire, and applying it to the key. The magnetism of the key will still be sufficiently strong to support the wire, though it cannot the nail, and it will continue to support it even when the magnet is yet farther removed; at length, however, it drops off.

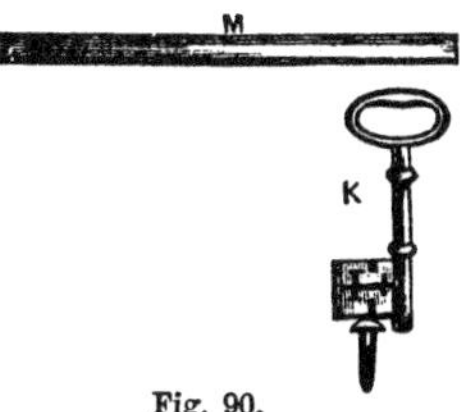

Fig. 90.

TO SUSPEND A NEEDLE IN THE AIR BY MAGNETISM.

Place a magnet on a stand to raise it a little above the table; then bring a small sewing-needle containing a thread within a little of the magnet, keeping hold of the thread to prevent the needle from attaching itself to the magnet. The needle, in endeavoring to fly to the magnet, and being prevented by the thread, will remain curiously suspended in the air, like Mohammed's coffin.

ELECTRO-MAGNETISM.

The identity of magnetism with electricity, alluded to in a former paragraph, has led to the formation of a new science under the above name; and to some of the interesting experiments connected with it we shall briefly allude, for the amusement of the young reader.

POWER OF THE ELECTRO-MAGNET.

The same influence which affects the magnetic needle already described will also communicate magnetism to soft iron. If a bar of that metal, bent as in the drawing, be surrounded with a common bonnet-wire, or a copper wire prevented from touching the iron by a winding of cotton or

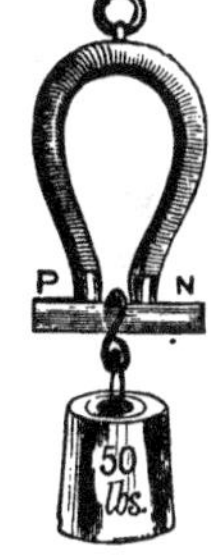

Fig. 91.

thread, and then if a current of voltaic electricity be sent through the wire, the bar becomes a powerful magnet, and will continue so as long as the connection with the battery is preserved. On breaking the contact, the magnetism disappears. This experiment may be easily made by the young reader with a horseshoe magnet surrounded by several coils of wire; P is the positive and N the negative pole.

DIP OF THE NEEDLE.

Another remarkable and evident manifestation of the influence of the magnetism of the earth upon the needle is the inclination or dip of the latter, which is a deviation from its horizontal place in a downward direction in northern regions of its north, and in southern regions of its south, pole. The causes of the dipping of the needle are yet unexplained. In balancing the needle on the card, on account of this dipping, a small weight or movable piece of brass is placed on one end of the needle, by the shifting of which either nearer to or farther from the centre the needle will always be balanced.

VARIATION OF THE NEEDLE.

The magnetic needle does not point exactly north and south, but the north pole of the needle takes a direction considerably to the west of the true north. It is constantly changing, and varies at different parts of the earth and at different times of the day.

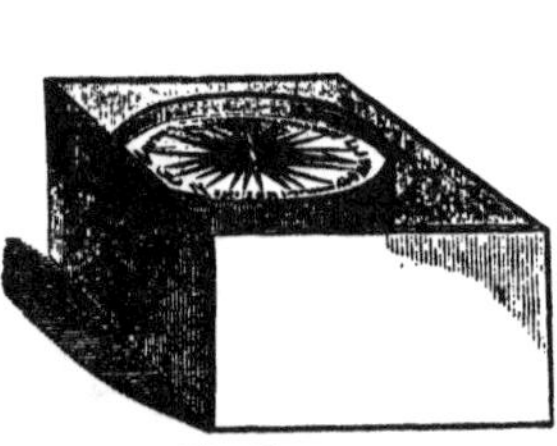

Fig. 92.

Fig. 93.

THE MARINER'S COMPASS, AND EXPERIMENTS WITH A POCKET COMPASS.

The mariner's compass is an artificial magnet fitted in a proper box, and consists of three parts:—1, the box; 2, the card or fly; and 3, the needle. The box is suspended in a square wooden case, by means of two concentric brass circles called gimbals, so fixed by brazen axes to the two boxes that the inner one, or compass-box, retains a horizontal position in all motions of the ship. The card is a circular piece of paper which is fastened upon the needle and moves with it. The outer edge of the card is divided into thirty-two points, as shown in the engraving, called "points of the compass." The needle is a slender bar of hardened steel, having a hollow agate cup in the centre, which moves upon the point of a pivot made of brass.

USEFUL AMUSEMENT WITH THE POCKET COMPASS.

Pocket compasses are to be bought for five or six shillings, and may be used in many ways. In travelling over mountains or a wide-extended moor, they are indispensably necessary; and no one should go a tour into Wales, Scotland, or the lakes without such a companion; and it will be a very useful and amusing exercise for any young person to take the bearings of his own or some particular locality, and make out what may be called a bearing-card. This he may easily do in the following manner. Supposing he wishes, for instance, to take the bearings of his own house: he has nothing to do but set his pocket compass upon a map of the district: a county map will do very well, unless his house stands on the verge of a county; then two county maps will be necessary. He must make the north of the map exactly coincide with the north, as indicated by his compass, and having fixed his map in this situation, he should take a ruler and piece of paper, and dot down the exact bearings of each important town, or place, or village, around him. Let him suppose himself, for instance, in the town of Cambridge, and, laying down his map as indicated by the compass, north to north and south to south, he will find the following places due north,—Wilberton, Wentworth; Little Wilbraham, Teversham, due east; Duxford and Chesterfield, south

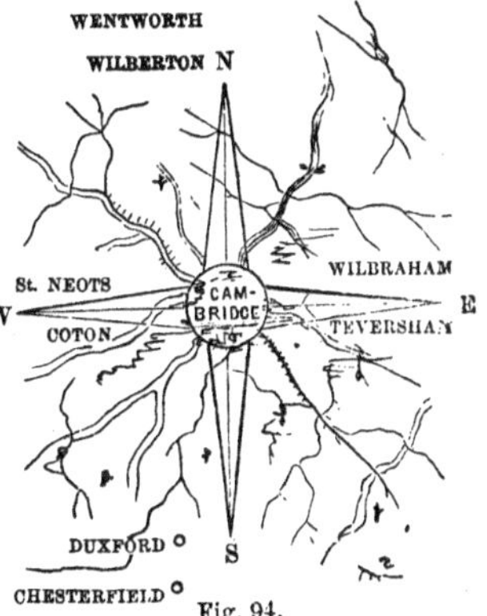

Fig. 94.

Coton and St. Neots in Huntingdonshire, west. The other points of the compass may be filled up in the same manner. Should, therefore, our young friend be upon any elevated situation near his own dwelling, or upon any other elevated spot from which the bearings have been taken, he will be able to inform his young friends that such and such a place lies in such a direction, that this place lies due north, the other northwest, a third southeast, the fourth southwest, &c. &c.; and the information so obtained will be serviceable to himself in many important matters.

INTERESTING PARTICULARS CONCERNING THE MAGNET.

Fire-irons which have rested in one position in a room during the summer months are often highly magnetic.

Iron bars standing erect, such as the gratings of a prison-cell or the iron railings before houses, are often magnetic.

The uppermost of the iron tire round a carriage-wheel attracts the north end of a magnet, and has hence south polarity, while the lower end, attracting the south end of the same, has north polarity.

Magnetism may be made to pass through a deal board; to exhibit which, lay a needle on the smooth part above, and run a magnet along the under side, and the needle will be found to follow the course of the magnet. A magnet dipped into boiling water loses part of its magnetism, which, however, returns upon its cooling.

A sudden blow given to a magnet often destroys its magnetic power.

CONCLUSION.

The preceding experiments in electricity, galvanism, and magnetism we have selected for the simple illustrations which they offer of some of the principles of those branches of philosophy. More elaborate experiments we have refrained from inserting, as although, perhaps, more astonishing and impressive in their effects, the costly apparatus which they require raise them far above the means of most boys, for whose instruction and amusement we cater.

AEROSTATION.

Fig. 95.—Balloon.

FROM the remotest ages of which we have any record, the regions of the air have been a subject of intense curiosity to man. For many centuries fanaticism considered them as the abode of evil spirits and demons; but when knowledge poured her rich stores upon man, he began to consider that air, like water, was a fluid, which he might render subservient to his purposes, and conceived the idea of flying. The first trials of this mode of progression seem to have been achieved by Grecian skill; and the most celebrated imitation of flying on record, of ancient times, is that of the renowned geometrician of Tarento, Archytas,* who constructed a pigeon of wood, which could fly, but which, however, if it fell to the ground, could not raise itself again. In Rome, in the time of Nero, it is said that a man raised himself up by means of wings, but that he lost his life in the attempt. In Scotland, in the reign of James IV. an Italian adventurer made an essay at flying; and the latest endeavor of the kind recorded in history, and which to a certain extent was successful, was that of the Marquis de Bacqueville, who in 1742 rose, by the aid of wings alone, from his residence on the Quai des Théatins, Paris, and directed his flight across the Seine, towards the gardens of the Tuileries;

but, just as he had advanced half-way, he appeared to lose all command of his movements, and, his wings ceasing to act, he fell against one of the floating machines belonging to the Parisian washerwomen, which line the arches of the Pont Royal, and had his leg broken, in addition to other serious injuries.

Flying being found, even in early times, useless, other means of moving in the air were next sought after, and the possibility of rising from the earth, on the same principle that the clouds rise and keep afloat, became the new subject of speculation. In the fourteenth century, an Augustine friar, Father Albert, of Saxony, suggested the first correct notion of rising in the air by means of a balloon. The quiet of the cloisters had furnished this monk, as it had many other inhabitants of those silent mansions of religion, with sufficient leisure to explore the mysteries of science. He had written a commentary upon the physical works of Aristotle, and was probably acquainted with the doctrines of Archimedes, who had established the principle that a body must remain suspended in a fluid denser than itself. However this might be, Father Albert conceived that, "since fire is more attenuated than air, and floats above the region of our atmosphere, a portion of such substance enclosed in a light hollow globe would rise to a certain height." This theory was taken up and agitated by various speculators, but mostly in the cloisters, until Stephen and Joseph Montgolfier, brothers, paper-makers of Ammonay, near Lyons, in France, put it into practice about the latter end of the last century. Though not favored by a liberal education, the Montgolfiers were impelled by natural ingenuity to acquire more knowledge than is generally met with in the class of manufacturers to which they belonged. Stephen was attached to chemistry, Joseph to mathematics; but both of them had directed their attention to the ascent and floating of clouds in the atmosphere. The result of their speculations was the supposition that a factitious cloud, formed of very thin vapor and enclosed in a light bag of great dimensions, would ascend into the higher regions. Their first experiment was made in November, 1782, with a bag of fine silk filled with rarefied air, which answering perfectly, they tried the experiment on a larger scale, and on the 19th of October, 1783, exhibited before the king and court of France, at Versailles, a balloon, having a basket attached to it, in which were a sheep, a cock, and a duck. In about eight minutes the fire which supplied the balloon with rarefied air went out, and the apparatus descended without injuring the aeronauts. This last trial being so completely successful, Monsieur Pilâtre de Rosier offered to ascend in a similar machine; and on the 21st of November, 1783, accompanied by the Marquis d'Arlandes, he made the first aeronautical voyage ever attempted by man.

The balloon used by Monsieur Rosier was highly ornamented, being composed of silk, decorated with gold and spangles and scarlet velvet; the car was a gallery large enough for the voyager to walk round, and the centre of it was hollow, containing an iron grate or brazier. The principle of the machine was that of a fire-balloon, its ascensive power being produced by the rarefaction of atmospheric air, by means of a large fire being kept burning in the grate under the lower part of the balloon, which was open for the purpose of receiving the heated air; and, that the fire and supply of rarefied air might be regulated at pleasure, port-holes were made in the gallery toward the grate. So long as the aeronaut wished to remain in the air, he was obliged to furnish this fire with fuel; and when he purposed descending, he suffered it to decline. This species of balloon is known by the title of the Montgolfière, from the original inventors, the Montgolfiers, and is an exceedingly dangerous one, on account of its liability to take fire from the burning materials in the grate; and indeed the greatest number of accidents which have befallen aeronauts have been through its perilous construction. Monsieur Rosier himself perished, on the 15th of June, 1785, through the conflagration of the machine in which he and a fellow-voyager, Monsieur Romain, were travelling, with the intention of crossing from Boulogne-sur-Mer to England. The apparatus was consumed in the air, and both the luckless gentlemen were dashed to pieces upon the rocks by the sea-shore from Calais to Boulogne.

At the same time that the Montgolfiers were experimenting upon balloons filled with rarefied air, Monsieur Charles, professor of philosophy in Paris, was endeavoring to inflate one with hydrogen gas, and, after enduring much ridicule for attempting to invent another mode of doing that which was already done, achieved his design, and, on the 1st of December, 1783, accompanied by Monsieur Robert, he ascended from the Champ de Mars, and landed in safety, after a completely successful voyage.

To these original discoveries of the science of aerostation many adventurers succeeded in different parts of Europe, and the superiority of the hydrogen gas over the Montgolfière, or heated-air balloon, was fully established; for five persons perished in the space of a few years, through the accidental combustion of their machines, but too appropriately termed *fire-balloons*.

At the present time balloons are filled with carburetted hydrogen gas, the common coal gas, which is considerably cheaper than the hydrogen, and can be procured far more readily, inasmuch as the filling of a balloon, which in former periods cost the labor of two or three days at an enormous expense, can now be done in as many hours. For the discovery of the applicability of this gas to aeronautical purposes we are indebted to Mr. Charles Green, the intrepid voyager of our own days, and who has also invented what he terms a guide-rope, that is, a rope of a thousand feet in length and upwards, which, when the balloon has quitted terra firma, and circumstances render its use advisable, is lowered from the car by means of a windlass. When the specific gravity of the machine is increased, and he begins to descend, the tail of the guide-rope, trailing on the ground, acts like the discharge of a quantity of ballast, and checks her further descent, and she continues progressing on the level so produced, until she attains a reascensive power and quits the earth with all her resources of ballast and gas the same as she had before her course was arrested by the increased weight. This contrivance, simple as it is, is of invaluable benefit to the aeronaut, who, by augmenting or diminishing the quantity of rope he lets out, proportionately increases or lessens the space between himself and the earth, and so does away with the necessity of employing ballast to such an extent as heretofore: indeed, according to the old system of discharging ballast whenever the balloon became so heavy with moisture as to descend, and to release some portion of the gas when, from the diminution of the ballast, she rose too high, it was impossible for an aeronaut to prolong his voyage beyond thirty-six hours: now, however, he may continue it for almost as many days, should it be requisite.

The honor of making the first aerial expedition in England has usually been ascribed to a foreigner, Signor Vincenzo Lunardi; but in reality a Mr. James Tytler claims the merit, he having ascended in a Montgolfière from Comely Gardens, Edinburgh, on the 27th of August, 1784, nineteen days before the signor, who ascended from the Artillery Grounds, Moorfields, on the 15th of the following September. Lunardi repeated his ascents in various parts of England and Scotland, and afterward returned to Italy. Monsieur Blanchard visited England after Lunardi, and made many ascents, and in company with Dr. Jefferies, on a clear frosty day, the 7th of January, 1785, crossed the British Channel from Dover, and landed in safety, after a dangerous voyage of two hours and a half, on the confines of a forest near Calais. This aeronaut made thirty-six voyages through the air, and gained a large sum of money by them. Monsieur Garnerin, another distinguished French aeronaut, who visited England, is celebrated for having been the first person who successfully descended from a balloon in a parachute. This machine consisted of thirty-two gores of white canvas, formed like an umbrella, of twenty-three feet in diameter, at the top of which was a round piece of wood of ten inches in breadth, having a hole in its centre to admit short pieces of tape to fasten it to the gores of the canvas; about four and a half feet below the top was a hoop of eight feet in diameter, affixed by a string from each seam, and below the hoop the car, made of basket-work covered with canvas, was suspended. The parachute is by no means that modern invention which is generally supposed; for Father Loubère, in his account of Siam, published nearly two hundred years since, describes a machine of the same kind as being in use there as a means of descending from great heights. In Europe it certainly was not employed for that purpose till the year 1783, when M. le Normand proved its efficacy by letting himself down from the windows of a lofty house in the city of Lyons. The aeronaut Blanchard was the first who applied it to the balloon, and after trying several experiments by letting down dogs and various animals from different heights, during some of his excursions, he attempted the descent himself at Basle, in 1793; but through some mismanagement the parachute did not expand fully, and the traveller, coming to the ground too rapidly, had the misfortune to have his leg broken. Garnerin's first successful descent was on the 21st of October, 1797, at Paris, and on the 21st of September, 1802, he made his third trial with a parachute, the first time such a machine was ever used in England. Various aeronauts have since endeavored to diminish the inherent perils of parachute descents by different inventions, but without success.

On the 24th of July, 1837, Mr. Cocking made an ascent from Vauxhall Gardens in a parachute appended to Mr. Green's balloon: this parachute was of a shape exactly the reverse of Mr. Garnerin's, that is, it was like an umbrella turned upside down, and so constructed as always to remain expanded. This shape was adopted in order to correct two great defects in the old fashion, viz., its oscillatory motion when descending, and the time which frequently elapsed ere the machine fully expanded to its umbrella-like form; but, so far from remedying these faults, its principles were perfectly erroneous, and when the unfortunate aeronaut detached himself from the balloon, the strings of his parachute gave way, and he was precipitated to the earth and killed upon the spot.

The aerial voyager has sometimes opportunities of observing the grandest effects in the clouds which it is possible for the human mind to contemplate. The rising and setting of the greater and lesser lights of the universe in regions too remote for him to penetrate, the forked lightning flashing its unearthly blaze, and the tempestuous clouds beneath his feet, rolling in mighty masses as far as the eye can reach, are seen by him in all their magnificence; whilst the thousand beauties of the panoramic view stretched below him in all the brilliancy of a noontide sun, or the quiet twilight stealing gently over the face of the earth, receive additional charms from the elevation from which they are viewed. In 1785 Monsieur Charles beheld a most magical spectacle during a voyage he made; for, just as the sun had set, the machine in which he was, shot upwards with such celerity as to rise nearly two miles in ten minutes. At this height he saw the sun again in its full glory, and from his lofty station in the heavens he once more contemplated the parting beams of the fading luminary, until it sunk below the horizon. The evening mists, gradually rising from the ground, collected into clouds, and, hanging in dense masses, screened the earth from his sight; and when the moon rose in silent majesty, and poured forth her mild beams, her rays tinged with various hues the ever-changing forms of the accumulated vapors which floated beneath him. A voyage performed by Monsieur Tester, in 1786, is remarkable for the various events which attended it, and is deserving of a slight notice. After having risen to the height of two thousand eight hundred feet, he descended at half-past five in the afternoon, and alighted in a corn-field in Montmorency, where, being employed in gathering stones for ballast, without leaving his car, he was surrounded by a great number of peasants. The proprietor of the field, seeing his corn thus trampled upon, insisted on being paid for the damage his visitor had occasioned, and, holding fast the balloon by the stay, proceeded, assisted by the peasants, to parade his prisoner through the village. Tester seized the first opportunity to cut the cord, and, taking an unexpected leave of the astonished peasants, rose again to the region of the clouds. At about seven o'clock he heard the blast of a horn, and descried huntsmen below in full chase, to contemplate which scene he opened the valve, and descended between Etuan and Varville. He was again collecting some ballast, when the huntsmen galloped up to him; and for the third time he rose into the air, passing through a dense body of clouds, where thunder and lightning followed each other without intermission. The balloon reached the altitude of three thousand feet, and in this region the intrepid aeronaut sailed until half-past nine o'clock, when he observed the final setting of the sun, and remained enveloped in darkness, amidst a mass of thunder-clouds The lightning flashed on all sides, the loud peals of thunder were incessant, and snow and sleet fell copiously around him for the space of three hours; after which period, to his inexpressible pleasure, the stars showed their pale fires. At a quarter before four o'clock he made his final descent, having seen the first gray dawn of morning and rising of the sun.

The most memorable voyage ever attempted was that performed by Messrs. Holland, Monck Mason, and Charles Green, on the 7th of November, 1836. The balloon, called the Royal Vauxhall Balloon, was of stupendous size, being sixty feet in height and fifty in breadth; and every arrangement was made by the travellers for a long voyage, in the shape of cloaks, carpet-bags, lamps, barometers, wine-jars, spirit-flasks, coffee, and other necessaries. At half-past one in the afternoon the cords were cut, and the mighty vessel rose proudly into the air, and at five minutes past four she neared the city of Canterbury, when the travellers indited a short letter to the mayor of that city, and despatched it by a small parachute, a novel kind of post-conveyance. At forty-eight minutes after four, the waves breaking on the beach gave evidence that they were near the British Channel; and, as they proceeded on their quiet way, the twilight, deepening into murky gloom, hid the English coast from their view, save that, through some scattered lights and the brilliant glare of the lighthouse, they were certain that Dover was yet within their ken. The evening shades had fully set in ere they gained a glimpse of the Calais lights; and, there being no moon to define objects by the soft touches of her silvery rays, the effect was one of great grandeur; and when, still later in the night, when it was perfectly dark, they passed over the city of Liége, the streets and houses marked out by the lights in them, and the numerous fires blazing in the iron-works in the neighborhood, formed a picture of consummate beauty. As the hours rolled on, and midnight passed silently by, the heavens assumed a depth of color rivalling a positive black in intensity of tint, from out of which the stars glittered with additional lustre; earthward no object was to be seen, the weary artisans having long before betaken themselves to their repose. Toward five o'clock in the morning the dawn gradually broke, and disclosed to the travellers the mighty river Rhine, which seemed to lose itself in the vapors which enshrouded the valleys and rested upon the hills; and as the brightness of the light increased, the stars by degrees disappeared, the morning star being the last to make its exit. At a quarter-past six, when at the height of nearly twelve thousand feet above the earth, the first sight of the sun was obtained, and the view at that moment spread before the aeronauts was magnificent beyond description. A rapid descent, which shortly after took place, again brought them into the gloom of night, the bright morning beams not having illumined the lower regions of the air, and again did they rise and see the full glory of the rising luminary. Three times did they thus rise and behold the sun, and twice did they, by descending into the mists and vapors which dimmed the scenery, lose sight of it ere it appeared fully above the horizon. Great was the pleasure of the voyagers when they perceived, as the mists cleared away, every indication of a well-peopled country and industrious population; and they made all possible preparations for descending, when, just as they were hastening their descent in a spot well suited for the purpose, the wind freshened, and, before the grapnel could take a secure hold, the balloon was hurried toward a wooded declivity. To throw out a sufficiency of ballast to carry the machine over that danger was the only remedy; but the sand used as ballast was found to have been frozen during the night into a solid mass, consequently all that could be done was to throw a sack with all its contents out of the car, and fifty-six pounds of sand were instantly dismissed. The balloon immediately sprang up and cleared the declivity, and, to avoid passing by another spot suited to the descent, the valve was again opened, to allow a large quantity of the gas to escape. After various baffling occurrences, on reaching the edge of the wood the valve was opened to its utmost extent, and, the grapnel taking hold almost immediately after, the machine came to the ground in the valley of Elbern, two leagues from Weilburg, in the Duchy of Nassau, at half-past seven in the morning, after a voyage of eighteen hours' duration, in which time it had passed over a great part of five kingdoms, England, France, Belgium, Prussian Germany, and the Duchy of Nassau. The travellers were most hospitably entertained at Weilburg, and the machine was re-christened the Vauxhall Nassau Balloon.

AIR AND FIRE BALLOONS.

The air-balloon should be made of taffeta or lutestring, and in shape similar to a pear,—the best method of making it being by joining many slips together, from end to end: if you take a pear and divide it into twelve or fourteen slices, one of those pieces is the best pattern you can have for the shape of the slips of your balloon.

Having cut them out, each piece must be prepared with drying oil, which you may make yourself, by boiling in every pint of linseed oil two ounces of sugar of lead and three ounces of litharge, for about half an hour. This composition is very drying, and you may then apply it to the slips of your balloon: after which, sew them together, and fell the seams. That the stitching may not have any interstices for the escape of the gas, you must place a piece of brown paper beneath each seam, and another piece above, and then pass a heated poker or flat-iron several times over it, by which means the oil will be softened and the seams rendered perfectly air-tight. When this process is completed, you must give your balloon a coat of varnish. This may be prepared by boiling in a copper or iron gallon saucepan, over a slow charcoal fire, for about half or three-quarters of an hour, a pound of birdlime and half a pint of the drying oil. When the birdlime has ceased to crackle, pour in two pints and a half more of the drying oil, and let the mixture boil an hour longer, often stirring it with an iron or wooden spoon. You must be cautious not to let the varnish boil over, which it is very apt to do when nearly ready, taking the saucepan from the fire as the varnish swells, and replacing it when its bubbling subsides; and, for greater caution, it will be well to have some wet cloths at hand to clap over the vessel in case the contents should happen to boil over and take fire. To ascertain whether your varnish is ready, rub some between two knives; if, on separating them, it forms threads, remove the vessel from the fire, and, when nearly cool, add to it about as much of oil of turpentine as the quantity of the mixture within. The varnish must be lukewarm when applied, and the balloon stretched out, and it will be dry in twenty hours. It should be the aim of the aeronaut to make his miniature balloon as much like a real one as possible: he must make a net to the shape of the machine, so as to come down to about the middle of it, and from thence cords must depend for the purpose of sustaining a light hoop, which should hang a little below the balloon itself; from this hoop other strings must proceed to support the car, which may be made of any light material and elegantly painted.

When the balloon is finished, it may be filled with gas. For this intent, put into a glass bottle, or jar, a pound of iron filings and two quarts of water; to which add gently, and by a little at a time, one pint of sulphuric acid. This done, stop the bottle or jar with a cork; then take a glass tube, introduce one end of it into the bottle, through the cork, and the other end into the neck of the balloon, and the gas resulting from the decomposition of the water will pass through the glass tube into the balloon. When this is full, withdraw the tube, and tie the neck of the balloon very tight. If let free, it will rise very pleasingly.

In making a fire-balloon, you may use India, Bank post, or tissue paper, and omit entirely the drying oil and varnish. If, after having joined and pasted the seams with good strong paste, you perceive any interstice or hole, paste over it a little piece of paper, and let it dry in the open air, or by the fire, but not too near it. A wire must be secured round the neck of the balloon, either by pasting or sewing it, and another put horizontally across it, to the middle of which a piece of sponge dipped in spirit of wine is to be attached. Half a gill of the spirit is sufficient to make the balloon rise. After you have dipped your sponge, set fire to what spirit remains in the cup, holding the neck of the balloon over it, but not so close as to endanger its safety. When you think it is sufficiently filled with heated air, set fire to the sponge, and the machine will briskly ascend, and keep afloat so long as the spirit continues burning.

Very small balloons may be made of goldbeaters' skin, by using gum-arabic to join the seams and any little fissures which may be in the material, filling them with gas from a jar or bottle, as before described, and tying the mouths of the little machines with a piece of cotton, to prevent the escape of the gas: small cars may be also attached to them, and when they are let off in a room they will rise to the ceiling, and remain floating in the air for some time.

At the shops of philosophical-instrument makers, in bazaars, and at toy-shops, a very pretty balloon made of the maw of a turkey can be purchased: when filled with hydrogen gas, in the manner described for air-balloons, it will ascend beautifully, on account of its extreme lightness.

PARACHUTES,

Which are generally the first things a juvenile aeronaut perpetrates, may be made in two ways: the first and simplest is achieved by cutting a piece of tissue paper into a circular form, putting eight or twelve pieces of thread at regular distances and of equal lengths to it, drawing them all up evenly to a centre and knotting them together, and completing the apparatus by affixing a cork or a wisp of paper to the end of the strings: the second mode of parachute-making is more complex, and must be done on a principle similar to that we have described for constructing the air-balloon, but cutting the slips of silk so as to form, when united, the segment of a circle only; the strings must of course be added, and brought to a centre, and a pill-box-shaped car, painted and embellished as tastefully as the genius of the contriver will allow, suspended from the aforesaid centre.

BALLOON SIGNALS.

In the days of the Directory and of the consulate of Napoleon, balloons were much used for taking observations. Bonaparte intended to take some with him to Egypt, but the vessel in which the balloons and materials were stowed away was captured by Nelson's fleet, and the balloons were exhibited to the inhabitants of Cairo for their amusement, and were not employed (as was intended) to the disadvantage of the English.

The Americans have done little in ballooning. One was constructed on quite a different principle to those of the "Old World." It had forty-seven bags for the gas, instead of one. The American *savants* proceeded to try their experiment very cautiously, first letting the balloon up alone, then a man in it, whilst fastened with ropes. At last a carpenter named Wilcox was bribed to ascend. He did so, but soon became frightened, and began to cut the bags nearest to him. Wilcox cut five, and, in consequence of ripping them open all on one side, the balloon turned over and came to the ground very fast, dislocating his wrist only, to the great surprise of the spectators, who fully expected that the carpenter was killed with the concussion.

The object of Napoleon's balloon was partly to examine the surrounding country, and also to communicate to distant parts by signals; and, should war unhappily continue, it is quite possible to suppose that balloon-corps may be attached to the various European armies, although the monstrous range of the Enfield and other rifles might probably make personal ascents for observation somewhat perilous.

One of the most interesting applications proposed for balloons was made in March, 1848, by Mr. J. Wallace, of Leith, to Sir F. Baring, viz.: to make a survey of the icy regions with the help of a captive balloon, which was to have been sent to the greatest possible height the weight of the cord would permit, in order that the person seated in the car might be able, with the help of a telescope, to survey a larger range of country, with the hope of discovering the missing expedition of the unfortunate Sir John Franklin.

For many reasons, this scheme with the captive balloon (*à la Napoléon*) was abandoned. and one substituted for it, which Mr. Shepherd has the credit of having first offered to the Admiralty. The arrangement consisted of a number of printed packets of oiled silk or paper, upon which directions were printed stating the latitude and longitude of the exploring ships, where they were going to, and the localities at which provisions had been left. These were attached at proper intervals to a long slow-match made of rope dipped in nitre; and as the balloon travelled over the country, the match burned gradually away, and when the fire reached the packets they were detached, and would, by the action of the winds, be dispersed over a large space of ground.

About the same time Mr. Darby, the very eminent pyrotechnist of Lambeth, turned his attention to the same subject, and constructed some very ingenious signals, which were attached by a string to a hollow fuse, and as this burnt away the string was detached. By the same means the "petard signals," or explosive shells, giving a report equal to a seven-pounder cannon directly they touched the ground, and dispersing hundreds of little notices in tin-foil, were detached, and used with great success as a means of directing attention, by sound, to the little bills containing the desired information for the missing party of Sir John Franklin. Mr. Darby also constructed a "bill-distributor," attached to his hollow fuse, capable of delivering one hundred thousand bills or notices over a great space of country; likewise a "land and water signal," which remained erect whether dropped on the sea or *terra firma*. The whole of the signals were tried with great success, and three of the "land and water signals" were picked up after

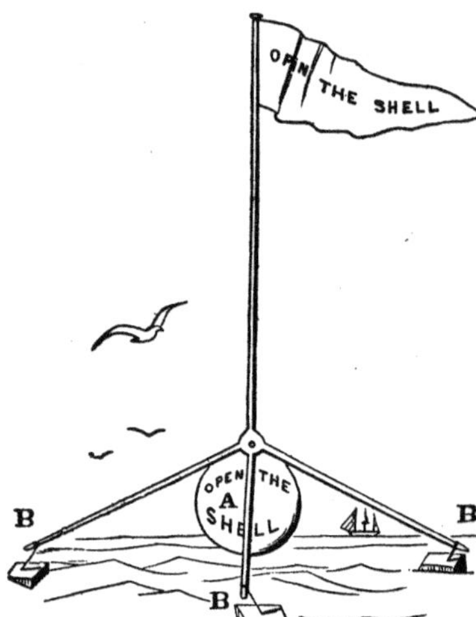

Fig. 96.—Darby's land and water signal. A. The shell, made of gutta-percha, containing the message.
B B B. Four pieces of stout cane, with corks at the extremities.
C. Top cane, with little bunting flag.

being detached from a balloon launched from Vauxhall. One was picked up at Harwich, another at Brighton, and a third near Croydon: the last was discovered by a poor man, who, fearful of something explosive, did not open it; but, calling in a gentleman who resided in the neighborhood, the shell was cut open, and a polite note discovered requesting the finder to state where the signal had fallen, and to address a letter to Mr. Darby, at Vauxhall Gardens.

Fig. 97.—Flying Machine (*theoretical*).

ARITHMETIC.

THE science of ARITHMETIC is supposed to be coeval with the earliest inventions. According to Diogenes Laertius, the Egyptians may lay claim to the merit of being its discoverers; but other authors ascribe it to the Phœnicians. The Phœnician system was perfected by the Grecian astronomers, and transmitted by them to the Romans, who, however, invented a fresh one instead; but both systems merely combined the different divisions of numbers, and went no further. Counters, to assist in reckoning, are, without doubt, as old as the science of Arithmetic itself, as we find that the Egyptians used stones for that purpose, and in calculating by their aid placed them from left to right. The Greeks likewise employed stones, flat, rounded, and polished, and they sometimes signified a large number, and sometimes a small: when counting up, the Greeks ranged their counters the reverse way to that of the Egyptians, putting them from right to left.

The Romans denominated their counters *calculi*, and when luxury taught them to embellish even the smallest articles in use, they then made the counters of bone and ivory, slightly convex, and likewise of porcelain covered with green or blue enamel and ornamented with elegant devices. The Romans also used the *abacus* as an arithmetical assistant: this instrument consisted of a wooden frame divided into small bars, of which there were two compartments, each bar containing beads, which could be moved up and down. The mode of using it was to consider every bead either as a unit or a decimal, adding being performed by uniting, and subtracting by separation, as might be necessary. Besides the counters, and the primitive mode of finger-reckoning, the Romans had a plan of keeping accounts by three different methods, based upon imaginary money; and these methods, styled the *ærrarius*, *sestertiarius*, and *denariarius*, required a particular abacus or table for each.

From the accounts remaining of the Roman method of Arithmetic, their rules were perplexing and incongruous, and the science made but little advancement under their management.

Numeral characters seem to have preceded letters, and the figures we call *Roman characters* are considered specimens of the earliest attempts at a system of notation, a surmise founded on the simplicity of their forms, which are, in fact, only a combination of straight strokes drawn either perpendicularly, horizontally, or transversely; and, indeed, the figures representing a hundred, and five hundred, C, D, which are now circular, were originally composed of three straight lines combined thus, [.]. With these rude symbols the Grecian philosophers performed their arithmetical calculations, and established a system to which Archimedes and other men of most transcendent abilities contributed. Two species of numerical characters seem to have existed from the first: the *decimal*, mentioned by Pliny, Quintilian, &c., which took its origin from the plan of finger-counting, consisted of the numbers counted up to ten;—and the *duodecimal*, or numbers reckoned to twelve. The former was common with the Anglo-Saxons, and the latter with the Northern nations, and from this last also we derive our little hundred, great hundred, dozens, and grosses.

Arithmetic was studied as a science by the Anglo-Saxons; for Aldhelm, Bishop of Sherborne, who flourished in the seventh century, wrote a tract *De Arithmetica*, and at a later period, Hugh, the Lincoln saint, lectured upon it at Oxford. The want of numerals better adapted for complicated accounts than the Roman rendered summing a miserable task, and the use of counters indispensable, until the fourteenth century, when the characters known by the name of the Arabic numerals were introduced into Europe. The Arabs were not inventors of the system, but were indebted for it to the natives of India, though at what period they acquired it is extremely doubtful, neither can we determine whether the Indians themselves invented or received it from some other nation; yet from their own assertions it would seem that the honor is due to them; for, according to Alsephaide, a learned Arabian doctor, they boast of three different inventions,—the composition of Pilpay's fables, the game of chess, and the nine digital characters. The forms of the ciphers were not fully settled till after the year 1531; and perhaps no characters were ever planned more adapted for the various uses to which they are applied than the Arabic numerals, though we doubt not that some few of our readers have frequently wished in their hearts that they never had been invented.

TO FIND THE DIFFERENCE BETWEEN TWO NUMBERS, THE GREATER OF WHICH IS UNKNOWN.

Take as many nines as there are figures in the smaller number, and subtract from them the amount of the number. Request some one to add the difference to the larger number, to take away the first figure of the total, and add it to the last one, and the sum then produced will be the difference between the two numbers.

For example:—John, who is 22, tells George, who is some years older, that he can find out the difference in their ages: he therefore deducts in his mind 22 from 99, and the difference, 77, he tells George to add to his own age; to take away the first figure from the sum so obtained, and to add it to the last figure; the last amount gained being the difference between their respective ages.

Thus, the difference between John's age and 99 is......	77
To which George adding his age..............................	35
produces a total of..........................	112
From which if we take away the first figure 1, and add it to the last figure 2, the product is.................	13
Which if added to John's age..................................	22
exactly gives that of George.............	35

THREE COUNTRYWOMEN AND EGGS.

Three countrywomen went to market with eggs: the first had 50 to dispose of, the second 30, and the third no more than 10. All three sold out at the same rate, and each made the same quantity of money of her eggs. How were they sold? Upon coming to market, they found that eggs were selling at seven a penny, at which rate the first woman sold 49, and received seven-pence; the second sold 28, and of course received four-pence: and the third woman sold only a single penny-worth, so that she had three eggs remaining, whilst her companions had but one and two respectively. In the course of the day, the demand greatly increasing, she advanced her price to three-pence per egg, at which rate she sold the remainder of her stock, and received ninepence for it.

Her companions, following her example, sold off theirs also

at the same price, so that they each realized the sum of tenpence.

1st woman for 49 eggs received	7
and for one egg	3
	10
2d woman for 28 eggs	4
and for 2 eggs	6
	10
3d woman for 7 eggs	1
and for 3 eggs	9
	10

TO MAKE ANY NUMBER DIVISIBLE BY NINE, BY ADDING A FIGURE TO IT.

Suppose, for example, that the number named is 72,857: desire the person naming it to place the number 7 between any two figures of that sum, and it will be divisible by 9; for if any number is multiplied by nine, then the sum of the figures of the product will either be nine, or else the number which is divisible by it.

THE DIGITAL NUMBERS ARRANGED SO AS TO GIVE THE SAME PRODUCT WHETHER COUNTED HORIZONTALLY, DIAGONALLY, OR PERPENDICULARLY.

8	3	4
1	5	9
6	7	2

THE BASKET AND STONES.

It a hundred stones are placed in a straight line, a yard distant from each other, how many yards must a person walk who undertakes to pick them up one by one, and put them into a basket, placed also a yard from the first stone? It is clear that to pick up the first stone and put it into the basket the person must walk two yards, one in going for the stone, and the other in returning with it; that for the second stone he must walk four yards; and so on, increasing by two, as far as the hundredth, when he must, of necessity, walk two hundred yards: so that the sum total will be the product of two hundred and two multiplied by fifty, or 10,100 yards, which amounts to more than five miles and a half.

A MAGIC SQUARE.

A magic square is a square figure formed of a series of numbers in mathematical proportion, so arranged in parallel and equal ranks as that the sums of each row, whether taken perpendicularly, horizontally, or diagonally, are exactly equal.

The several numbers which make any square number (for instance, 1, 2, 3, 4, 5, &c., to 25 inclusive, which compose the square number 25) being arranged one after the other in a square figure of 25 cells, each one in its cell, if you alter the order of these numbers, and put them in such a manner that the five numbers which fill a perpendicular rank of cells being added together shall make the same number with the five numbers in any other rank, whether horizontal or vertical, or with the five in each of the two diagonal rows, then the square so formed is called a magic square, in opposition to the former arrangement, which is called a natural square.

A NATURAL SQUARE.

	A		G		B	
	1	2	3	4	5	
	6	7	8	9	10	
E	11	12	13	14	15	F
	16	17	18	19	20	
	21	22	23	24	25	
	C		H		D	

A MAGIC SQUARE.

A				B
11	24	7	20	3
4	12	25	8	16
17	5	13	21	9
10	18	1	14	22
23	6	19	2	15
C				D

Any five of the sums in the magic square, taken in a right line, will make 65. It will be observed that the five numbers in the diagonals A D and B C of the magical square answer to the ranks E to F and G to H in the natural square, and that 13 is the centre number of both squares.

To form a magic square, first transpose the two ranks in the natural square to the diagonals of the magic square; then put the number 1 under the central number 13, and the number 2 in the next diagonal, downwards. The number 3 should be placed in the same diagonal line; but, as there is no room in the square, you are to place it in that part it would occupy were another square placed under it. For the same reason, the number 4, by following the diagonal direction, falling out of the square, it is to be put into the part it would hold in another square ranged by the side of this. You next proceed to numbers 5 and 6, still descending, but, as the square in which 6 should be put is already filled, you must then go back to the diagonal, and consequently place the 6 in the second place under the 5, so that there may remain an empty square between the two numbers. The same rule is to be observed whenever you find a square already filled.

You proceed in this manner to fill all the empty squares in the angle, where the 15 is put; and as there is no space for the 16 in the same diagonal, descending, you must place it in the part it would hold in another square, and continue the same plan till all the squares are filled. This method will serve for all sorts of arithmetical progressions composed of odd numbers; even numbers being too complicated to afford any amusement.

THE HORSE-DEALER'S BARGAIN.

A horse-dealer, wishing to dispose of a horse at as high a price as he could, induced a gentleman who admired it to become the purchaser, by offering to let him have the animal for the value of the twenty-fourth nail in his shoes, reckoning one farthing for the first nail, two for the second, four for the third, and so on, to the twenty-fourth. The gentleman, thinking it a bargain, gladly accepted the offer; the value of the horse was therefore necessarily great. By calculation, the twenty-fourth term of the progression, 1, 2, 4, 8, &c., will be found to be 8,388,608, equal to the number of farthings the purchaser gave for the horse: the price consequently amounted to £8738 2*s*. 8*d*

A PERSON HAVING AN EVEN NUMBER OF SHILLINGS IN ONE HAND, AND AN UNEVEN NUMBER IN THE OTHER, TO TELL IN WHICH HAND THE EVEN OR ODD NUMBER IS.

Request the person to multiply the number in his right hand by an odd figure, and the number in his left by an even one, and let you know whether, when the products are added together, they produce an odd or even sum. If odd, then the even number is in the left hand, and if even, the even number is in the right. As for instance:

The number in the right hand being *odd*	7
Multiply it by	3
Product	21
Add the product of the left hand	36
and the total is	57

In the left hand, *even*	18
Multiply it by	2
Product	36

The number in the right hand being *even*	18
Multiply it by	3
Product	54
Add the product of the left hand	14
and the total is	68

In the left hand, *odd*	7
Multiply it by	2
Product	14

COUNTRYWOMAN AND EGGS.

A countrywoman carrying eggs to a garrison, where she had three guards to pass, sold to the first guard half the number she had, and half an egg more; to the second, the half of what remained, and half an egg besides; and to the third guard she sold the half of the remainder, and half another egg. When she arrived at the market-place, she had three dozen still to sell. How was this possible without breaking any of the eggs? It would seem at the first view that this is impossible; for how can half an egg be sold without breaking any of the eggs? The possibility of this seeming impossibility will be evident when it is considered that by taking the greater half of an odd number we take the exact half $+ \frac{1}{2}$. When the countrywoman passed the first guard, she had 295 eggs; by selling to that guard 148, which is the half $+ \frac{1}{2}$, she had 147 remaining; to the second guard she disposed of 74, which is the major half of 147; and, of course, after selling 37 but of 73 to the last guard, she had still three dozen remaining.

TO TELL THE NUMBER THOUGHT OF BY A PERSON.

Request a person to think of a number, and, when he has done so, to triple it, and to take the exact half of the triple if it be even, or the greater half if it be odd. Next desire him to triple that half, and ask him how many times it will contain nine, for the number thought of will be the double of the number of nines, and one more, if it be odd. Thus: suppose that 5 is the number thought of, its triple is 15, which cannot be divided by two without a remainder. The greater half of 15 is 8, and if this is multiplied by 3 we shall have 24, which contains two nines: the number thought of will therefore be twice the number of nines, with one added, as before mentioned, for an uneven number, or $4 + 1$, that is, 5.

ANOTHER METHOD.

When the person has thought of a number, tell him to double it, then to add four to it, to multiply the whole by five, and to the product add twelve, and afterward multiply the total by ten. From the sum thus produced, bid him deduct 320, and inform you what is the remainder, which, if you take away the two last figures from it, will give you the number he thought of. Thus:—

Suppose the number selected is................	7
The double of that is	14
Which with the addition of 4 is	18
And that multiplied by 5 is	90
To which 12 added produces..................	102
Which multiplied by 10 is	1020
From which, by deducting 320, there remains	700
And which, by taking away the two ciphers, is reduced to the number thought of.......	7

TO TELL TWO OR MORE NUMBERS WHICH A PERSON HAS THOUGHT OF.

If either of the numbers thought of do not exceed nine, they may be found as follows:—Make the person add 1 to the double of the first number thought of, and then request him to multiply the whole by 5, and then add to the product the second number. Should there be a third number, make him double the first sum, and add 1 to it; request him then to multiply the whole by 5, and to add the third number to it. If there is a fourth number, you, of course, proceed in the same way, requesting him to double the preceding sum, to add 1 to it, then to multiply it by 5, and thereto add the fourth number, and so on. You must next ask the number arising from the addition of the last number thought of, and, if there were two numbers, subtract 5 from it; if three, 55; and if four, 555, and so on; for the remainder will always be composed of figures, of which the first on the left hand is the first number thought of, the next the second, and so on of the rest. Suppose, for instance, the numbers thought of are 3, 4, 6, by adding 1 to 6, which is the double of the first number, we have 7, which being multiplied by 5, gives 35; if 4, the second number thought of, is then added, we shall have 39, which doubled gives 78, and if we add one, and multiply 79 by 5, the result will be 395. Finally, if we add 6, the third number thought of, the sum total will be 401, and if we deduct 55 from it, we shall have for the remainder 346: the figures of which, 3, 4, 6, are the three numbers thought of in their correct order.

A PERSON STRIKING A FIGURE OUT OF THE SUM OF TWO GIVEN NUMBERS, TO TELL WHAT THAT FIGURE WAS.

Peremptorily command such numbers only as are divisible by 9, as, for instance, 36, 63, 117, 126, 162, &c. Then allow a person to choose any two of these numbers; and after adding them together, in his mind, to strike out from the total any one of the figures he pleases. When he has done this, desire him to tell you the sum of the figures, and it follows that the number you are obliged to add to this amount, in order to make it 9 or 18, is the one he struck out. For example, he chooses the numbers 126 and 252, whose aggregate sum is 378. Then, if he strikes out the 7 from this amount, the remaining figures, 3 and 8, will make 11, to which must be added 7 to make 18; but if he strikes out the 3, the sum of the remaining figures, 7 and 8, will be 15, add to which 3, to make 18; and so on, in like manner, for the 8.

TO FIND THE LEAST NUMBER OF WEIGHTS WHICH WILL WEIGH ANY INTERMEDIATE WEIGHT, FROM ONE POUND TO FORTY, EXCLUSIVE OF FRACTIONS.

This problem may be solved through the means of the geometrical progression 1, 3, 9, 27, &c., the peculiar property of which is, that the last number is twice the sum of all the rest, and one more; so that, the number of pounds being 40, which is likewise the amount of 1, 3, 9, 27, these four weights will answer the purpose. For example, if it be necessary to weigh eleven pounds by these weights, the three and the nine pound weights must be put into the one scale, and the one pound weight into the other: therefore, any substance put into this last scale, with the one pound weight, and it remains in equipoise with the other scale, it must consequently weigh eleven pounds. Again, if a weight of fourteen pounds is required, the one, the three, and the nine pounds weights should be put into one of the scales, and the twenty-seven pounds weight into the other, which will then outweigh the first scale by the exact number needed. Any other weights may be made by similar combinations.

THE FIGURES, UP TO 100, ARRANGED SO AS TO MAKE 505 IN EACH COLUMN, WHEN COUNTED IN TEN COLUMNS PERPENDICULARLY, AND THE SAME WHEN COUNTED IN TEN FILES HORIZONTALLY.

10	92	93	7	5	96	4	98	99	1
11	19	18	84	85	86	87	13	12	90
71	29	28	77	76	75	24	23	22	80
70	62	63	37	36	35	34	68	69	31
41	52	53	44	46	45	47	58	59	60
51	42	43	54	56	55	57	48	49	50
40	32	33	67	65	66	64	38	39	61
30	79	78	27	26	25	74	73	72	21
81	89	88	14	15	16	17	83	82	20
100	9	8	94	95	6	97	3	2	91

Each of these files, when added up, makes 505.

Each of these ten columns, when added up, makes 505.

TO FIND HOW MANY SQUARE YARDS IT WOULD REQUIRE TO CONTAIN IN WRITING ALL THE CHANGES OF THE ALPHABET, EACH LETTER WRITTEN SO SMALL AS NOT TO OCCUPY MORE THAN THE HUNDREDTH PART OF A SQUARE INCH.

By multiplying the numbers from 1 to 24 continually into each other, thus—

$$\begin{array}{c} 1 \\ 2 \\ \hline 2 \\ 3 \\ \hline 6 \\ 4 \\ \hline 24 \end{array}$$

the changes of the twenty-four letters will be found to be

62,044,840,175,323,943,936,000.

Now, as there are 1296 inches in a square yard, if we multiply that number by 100, we shall obtain 129,600, which is the number of letters each square yard will contain; if we afterwards divide the above row of figures—the number of changes—by the 129,600, the quotient, which will be 478,741,050,720,-092,160, is the number of yards required to contain the before stated number of changes. But, as all the twenty-four letters are contained in every permutation, the space must necessarily be twenty-four times as large, viz.

11,849,785,210,282,211,840.

As the surface of the whole earth contains but 617,197,435,-008,000 square yards, it would consequently require, to make a space of sufficient dimensions to contain all the changes of which the alphabet is susceptible, a surface 18,620 times larger than that of the globe.

THE NUMBER FORTY-FIVE.

How can the number 45 be divided into four such parts that if you add two to the first part, subtract two from the second part, multiply the third part by two, and divide the fourth part by two, the total of the addition, the remainder of the subtraction, the product of the multiplication, and the quotient of the division, are all equal? The four parts are as follows:

The first is 8, to which 2 being added makes..........10
The second is 12, from which 2 being subtracted leaves 10
The third is 5, which being multiplied by 2 produces 10
The fourth is 20, which, divided by 2, the quotient is.. 10

PROFIT AND LOSS.

A man purchased ninety-six apples at the rate of three a penny, and likewise the same number at two a penny; he sold them again at five for two pence: did he gain or lose? He lost, for as the ninety-six apples at three a penny cost him 2*s.* 8*d.* and the ninety-six at two a penny 4*s.*, the sum he laid out was 6*s.* 8*d.* for the one hundred and ninety-two apples. Now, after he sold thirty-eight two-pennyworths, for which he received 6*s.* 4*d.*, he had but two apples remaining, and therefore he lost a fraction above 3½*d.*

THE PHILOSOPHER'S PUPILS.

Tell me, illustrious Pythagoras, how many pupils receive instruction from thy lips? Nay, said the philosopher, compute the number thyself; one-half of my pupils study mathematics, one-fourth natural philosophy, one-seventh observe silence, and besides those I have three female pupils. The question is to find out a number, the one-half, one-fourth, and one-seventh of which, + 3, shall be equal to that number. The number required is 28.

THE COMPANY OF FOUR MERCHANTS.

Four partners engage to trade in company. Smith's stock is £150; Brown's stock is £320; Collins's stock is £350, and Jenkins's stock is £500; with their money they buy indigo, and gain £730. How much belongs to each, if the profit be divided in proportion to their respective stocks?

	£		£	s.	d.
Smith's stock	150	1320 : 150 :: 730 :	82	19	1*
Brown's "	320	1320 : 320 :: 730 :	176	19	4
Collins's "	350	1320 : 350 :: 730 :	193	11	2
Jenkins's "	500	1320 : 500 :: 730 :	276	10	3
Whole stock........	1320		£730		

Smith...........................	82	19	1
Brown...........................	176	19	4
Collins...........................	193	11	2
Jenkins...........................	276	10	3
	£730		

ROAD-MAKING.

If 100 men make three miles of road in twenty-seven days, in how many days will 150 men make five miles?

Men 150 : 100 :: 27 days.
Miles 3 5

450 500
27

450)13500(30 days.

THE TWO TRAVELLERS.

Two poor boys, Tom and Ned, walk between London and Wolverhampton: Tom leaves the latter at eight o'clock in the

* Fractions omitted.

morning, and walks at the rate of three miles an hour without intermission, and Ned sets out from London at four o'clock the same evening, and walks for Wolverhampton at the rate of four miles an hour constantly. Now, supposing the distance between the two places to be 130 miles, and supposing the boys capable of continuing their journeys, whereabouts on the road will they meet?

Answer—69$\frac{3}{7}$ miles from Wolverhampton.

TO DISCOVER THE BREADTH OF A RIVER BY MEANS OF THE BRIM OF A HAT OR PEAK OF A CAP.

The person seeking to ascertain this fact must place himself at the edge of one bank of the river and lower the brim of his hat, or peak of his cap, till he finds the edge just cuts the other bank; then, after placing the hand under the chin, he must turn round steadily till he faces some level ground on his own side of the river, and observe when the edge of the peak again meets the ground: the measure of this distance will be very nearly the breadth of the river.

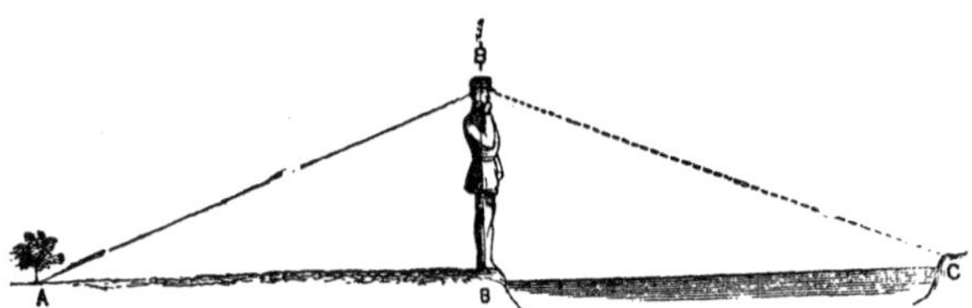

Fig. 98.—Showing that the angles A B B and C B B are equal.

How many dinners would be necessary for a club of seven persons who had agreed to dine with each other as long as they could be differently arranged when they sat down to table?

The number of dinners is 5040, and thirteen years and more than nine months would be the space of time in which the club would eat the dinners.

How much mahogany would be required to produce sixty-four 3-inch cubes?

The quantity is a 12-inch cube.

According to Vitruvius, Hiero's crown weighed 20 lbs., and lost 1$\frac{1}{4}$ lb. (nearly) in water.

Suppose it consisted of gold and silver only, and that 19.64

lbs. gold lost 1 lb. in water and that 10.5 lbs. of silver lose 1 lb.; find the actual quantity of gold in King Hiero's crown, and also the weight of the silver with which it was adulterated.

Answer.—x = the lbs. of gold in crown.
$20 - x$ = the lb. of silver in crown.

Hence we immediately have—

$$\frac{x}{19.64} \times \frac{20 - x}{10.5} = 1\tfrac{1}{4}\text{lbs.}$$

And, solving this equation, we have-

Answer.—$x = 14.77$ lbs. of gold in crown,
and $20 - x = 5.22$ lbs. of silver in do

INDEX.

D.

E.

F.

G.

H.

Q.

R.

S.

T.

THE END

www.ingramcontent.com/pod-product-compliance
Lightning Source LLC
LaVergne TN
LVHW021222110826
845150LV00002B/221

* 9 7 8 1 4 2 5 5 6 4 1 6 2 *